MW01060507

# The Authoritarian International

Stephen Hall argues that democracies can preserve their norms and values from increasing attacks and backsliding by better understanding how authoritarian regimes learn. He focuses on the post-Soviet region, investigating two established authoritarian regimes, Belarus and Russia, and two hybrid regimes, Moldova and Ukraine, with the aim of explaining the concept of authoritarian learning and revealing the practices that are developed and the sources of that learning. Hall finds clear signs of collaboration between countries in developing best survival practices between authoritarian-minded elites, and demonstrates that learning does not just occur between states; rather, it can happen at the intra-state level, with elites learning lessons from previous regimes in their own countries. He highlights the horizontal nature of this learning, with authoritarian-minded elites developing methods from a range of sources to ascertain the best practices for survival. Post-Soviet regional organisations are crucial for the development and sharing of these survival practices as they provide 'learning rooms' and training exercises.

DR STEPHEN G. F. HALL is a lecturer (assistant professor) in Russian and post-Soviet politics in the Department of Politics, Languages, and International Studies at the University of Bath. He earned a PhD at the School of Slavonic and East European Studies (SSEES), University College London (UCL), and completed a Post-Doctoral Fellowship in the Department of Politics and International Studies, University of Cambridge. Both the PhD and Fellowship were funded by the Economic and Social Research Council (ESRC), and he received the SSEES Excellence Scholarship. He has published in various journals including *East European Politics*, *Journal of Eurasian Studies*, *Russian Politics*, *Problems of Post-Communism*, *Post-Communist Economies*, and *Europe-Asia Studies*.

# The Authoritarian International

## Tracing How Authoritarian Regimes Learn in the Post-Soviet Space

STEPHEN G. F. HALL
*University of Bath*

# CAMBRIDGE
## UNIVERSITY PRESS

Shaftesbury Road, Cambridge CB2 8EA, United Kingdom

One Liberty Plaza, 20th Floor, New York, NY 10006, USA

477 Williamstown Road, Port Melbourne, VIC 3207, Australia

314–321, 3rd Floor, Plot 3, Splendor Forum, Jasola District Centre, New Delhi – 110025, India

103 Penang Road, #05–06/07, Visioncrest Commercial, Singapore 238467

Cambridge University Press is part of Cambridge University Press & Assessment, a department of the University of Cambridge.

We share the University's mission to contribute to society through the pursuit of education, learning and research at the highest international levels of excellence.

www.cambridge.org
Information on this title: www.cambridge.org/9781009098540

DOI: 10.1017/9781009089630

First published 2023

*A catalogue record for this publication is available from the British Library.*

*Library of Congress Cataloging-in-Publication Data*
Names: Hall, Stephen G. F., author.
Title: The authoritarian international : tracing how authoritarian regimes learn in the post-Soviet space / by Stephen G. F. Hall.
Description: [New York] : Cambridge University Press, [2023] | Includes bibliographical references and index.
Identifiers: LCCN 2022056968 | ISBN 9781009098540 (hardback) | ISBN 9781009096324 (paperback) | ISBN 9781009089630 (ebook)
Subjects: LCSH: Europe, Eastern – Politics and government – 1989– | Russia (Federation) – Politics and government – 1991– | Former communist countries – Politics and government. | Authoritarianism – Europe, Eastern. | Authoritarianism – Russia (Federation)
Classification: LCC DJK51 .H35 2023 | DDC 320.530947–dc23/eng/20230113
LC record available at https://lccn.loc.gov/2022056968

ISBN 978-1-009-09854-0 Hardback

# Contents

# Figures

vi

# Tables

# *Preface*

On a cold day in 2015, protesters congregated near Hermitage Park in Moscow's Tverskoy District. They were not opposition demonstrators, but came from pro-Kremlin[1] groups, such as the All-Russian International Youth Union, Cossack units, and pro-Kremlin parties like the (il)Liberal Democrats. In a show of strength, they marched through central Moscow. These factions united under the anti-Maidan banner. Established by the Kremlin, anti-Maidan incorporates many pro-Kremlin organisations, and its very name provides its raison d'être, to counter a potential Euromaidan on Moscow's streets. Anti-Maidan highlights a clear example of Kremlin learning. The anti-Maidan case emphasises the aim here to investigate authoritarian learning, and how leaders and political elites look to others both externally and internally to gauge what has worked previously and determine which practices are best for consolidating power. By investigating why and how authoritarian learning occurs and explaining what and when leaders attempt to develop best practices, we provide understanding to how – and when – authoritarian learning happens, and the practices developed. The four case studies chosen are Belarus, Moldova, Russia, and Ukraine. These choices will be justified fully later but for now a brief explanation serves to help frame how authoritarianism is defined in this book.

When Alyaksandr Lukashenka and Vladimir Putin came to power in 1994 in Belarus and 2000 in Russia, both had authoritarian ambitions and tendencies. Before Lukashenka and Putin obtained power, both countries were weak democracies with different elite factions competing for power. Once Lukashenka and Putin took over, they

---

[1] While the term 'the Kremlin' is quite general and does not detail the nuances of a regime consisting of many different – and fluid – factions, we feel that such terms as the Kremlin and Bankova – in the Ukrainian context – provide a useful shorthand. This is not to say that we are unaware of the nuances and complexity, but for clarity's sake we use such terms when necessary.

began creating more authoritarian political systems, which took time to fully consolidate. Both had authoritarian tendencies and ambitions and were able to re-shape the political system to create a more hierarchical power system. Power was consolidated – partially at least – by learning from other examples. For instance, Lukashenka spent much time in the early 1990s in Uzbekistan discussing the practices Uzbek president Islom Karimov had used to consolidate power.[2]

Before continuing, it is necessary to explain why Moldova and Ukraine are included as cases in understanding authoritarian learning. Both states have had leaders who have attempted to consolidate power in their own hands. Examples of this are Vladimir Voronin in Moldova and Viktor Yanukovych in Ukraine, who upon coming to power attempted to create political systems that gave them and their allies as much power as possible. To best consolidate power, it is likely that Voronin and Yanukovych looked to established authoritarian regimes – Belarus and Russia among others – to ascertain which practices worked best. Moldova and Ukraine are case studies because elites in each state demonstrated mimetic behaviour, where they look to others for how to act. The term 'mimetic' refers to imitation and mimicry and both cases are examples of the mimicry of others. This is a crucial part of authoritarian learning and is represented well by Moldova and Ukraine. Yet authoritarian learning is more than imitation. It involves transmissive copying, where ideas are directly discussed between authoritarian-minded elites. Consequently, authoritarian learning is a mixture of diffusion, copying, and imitation.

There has been a gap in the literature on learning for a while, on *authoritarian* learning specifically. Much of the literature on political learning has concentrated on democratic learning and has only given a perfunctory analysis as to how authoritarian regimes and leaders with autocratic tendencies learn. Both established autocracies and individual leaders look to internal and external examples to develop best practices to establish their control. With only 10 per cent of the world's population living in fully established democracies and the other 90 per cent living in weak democracies, semi-authoritarian, or fully autocratic regimes, understanding this process is crucial. Established

[2]  Personal Interview: IR39203

autocracies need to continue to learn to react to an ever-changing political and economic environment. Similarly, in weak democracies leaders come to power looking at neighbouring autocracies as examples of how to consolidate power. Understanding how these processes operate and determining the practices used to retain power offers ways for Western governments and regional organisations to develop best practices to frustrate the growth of pseudo-democracies. Establishing these practices will help counteract democratic backsliders and reduce opportunities for leaders with authoritarian ambitions to consolidate power. By knowing that authoritarian regimes learn and developing methods to counteract this, Western democracies and international organisations can begin to develop practices to weaken the capacity of authoritarian-minded elites to establish this regime type.

For authoritarian regimes and leaders with authoritarian tendencies, learning and adaptation are important for survival. By investigating four post-Soviet[3] case studies – or other cases from the same region as each other – it can be asserted that we are only investigating learning, rather than *authoritarian* learning. It is natural that regimes in a region cooperate with one another. In the post-Soviet context, because networks and connections have existed since the Soviet Union, and regional organisations have been established, this is learning, rather than authoritarian learning. This is one interpretation that is a viable explanation for what is happening in the post-Soviet space. However, there is an alternative explanation. As will be shown, there are specific lessons being learnt. These are practices to better consolidate power and, in established autocracies, to restrict alternatives that could – if left alone – result in power loss. Consequently, what is being learnt are survival strategies for authoritarian leaders to retain power.

---

[3] It is with reticence that this category is used. Especially after the most recent events with Russia's annexation of Ukraine – but even before – the post-Soviet label was an oxymoron. These states have been independent for over 30 years and have become their own entities. The perception of the term post-Soviet implies that the only thing that binds them is the fact that they are successors to the Soviet Union, an event that occurred at the end of 1991. However, for the sake of simplicity the term 'post-Soviet' is used here. After all, there is still not better categorisation in existence to combine the cases of Belarus, Moldova, Russia, and Ukraine other than to use the tired label of post-Soviet.

This learning encompasses external and internal examples and takes in cases of failure and success. Authoritarian leaders are concerned with ensuring their survival and look to others for examples of what to do and what not to do. Although the leaderships in Belarus and Russia portrayed the 1990s as a time of internal disunity, they learnt from these failures what not to do. Leaders with authoritarian tendencies will also be concerned by revolutions that either see the demise of established autocracies – the Arab Spring – or happen in the neighbourhood – the 2013–14 Euromaidan in Ukraine – that could become a beacon for opposition to unify around. Similarly, examples of successful authoritarian consolidation will be copied. One example of this is Belarus's preventive counter-revolution, which began in 2000 and partially served as an example to Russia. Authoritarian leaders will also learn from internal examples. This is especially the case in Moldova and Ukraine. Since independence in 1991, both states have had leaders with authoritarian ambitions, but due to the vagaries of the political system of both no leader has been able to consolidate power for long enough to establish an autocracy. Consequently, leaders with authoritarian ambitions in Moldova and Ukraine will likely look to established autocracies to learn. They will also learn from previous domestic leaders with authoritarian tendencies to ascertain what lessons can be drawn from previous internal failures or successes.

Although Belarus is somewhat of an outlier, the other three cases at the very least claim that they are democracies. All four look to what is happening in Western democratic states and learn from these polities. For instance, the Russian government claimed that the 2012 legislation that required non-governmental organisations in receipt of funding from external sources to register as foreign agents was a direct cognate of the American Foreign Agents Registration Act. Leaders in Moldova and Ukraine have tried to keep equidistance between the EU and Russia, with most elites wanting closer integration with the EU. While reforms and legislation may be taken from the EU playbook, their spirit can be re-interpreted to ensure regime survival. Authoritarian learning is not about learning 'among' autocracies, but how leaders with authoritarian ambitions develop best survival practices – and these can even come from democratic examples. Therefore, to understand authoritarian learning we need to concentrate on learning 'by' leaders with these tendencies. Learning can be from established authoritarian regimes, democracies, and internal examples.

Here we analyse learning rather than other issues like mimicry. While imitation of legislation and political structures, such as Russia making Sevastopol a federal city as it was in the Soviet Union, is relevant, this book concentrates on learning processes. To an extent imitation is a part of learning, but there are other areas that need to be addressed to best understand authoritarian learning. As shown later, authoritarian learning includes diffusion, emulation, adaptation, policy transfer, and learning and linkage. Authoritarian leaders, whether in established autocracies or wanting to preserve their power, are concerned with survival and use a mixture of diffusion, emulation, adaptation, policy transfer and learning, and linkage to increase their survival chances. While mimicry across the post-Soviet space has occurred regarding legislation and political structures, authoritarian regimes directly learn from one another to aid survival. Direct interaction is not required to induce learning as diffusion, emulation, and adaptation are all crucial authoritarian learning methods. However, as will be shown, there is plenty of evidence of direct interaction, which remains the most important tool for authoritarian learning. Regimes do not just learn from each other but also from domestic examples. The failure of authoritarian regimes can be traced as it often results in revolution and violence, which is easier to see. However, this only tells half the story of authoritarian learning. To truly understand authoritarian learning, learning from success is important too.

Retrieving information from authoritarian regimes is difficult, as when evidence does percolate out, it tends to be old. Personnel who were regime members tend to be tight-lipped about the intricacies of the system and few current regime personnel are willing to discuss how the regime increases its survival chances. The authoritarian black box remains shut and the information hidden behind access codes. This makes gathering information a convoluted task. Researchers have difficulty understanding the inner workings of these types of regimes and their learning capacity. Gathering evidence of authoritarian learning remains an inestimable challenge and one that involves the researcher becoming a poor man's Sherlock Holmes to get data. It is possible that there are other explanations for what is occurring. But as the evidence shows here, authoritarian learning, where elites with authoritarian tendencies develop best practices through learning to strengthen their survival chances, is something that occurs in the post-Soviet region and is very real.

When starting research on this subject thirteen years ago, I naïvely imagined that authoritarian learning followed the model of a school, at which Nursultan Nazarbaev, Putin, and Lukashenka were either star pupils or teachers telling other autocrats how to establish best survival practices. It turned out the school analogy was incorrect. Rather, it is one of mad scientists who run solitary experiments in their laboratories and then share notes at a monthly – or sometimes annual – conference. This is an apt analogy as not all learning is successful and sometimes leads to regime failure; two test tubes when mixed can cause an explosion. As shown in Chapter 1, there is direct interaction in authoritarian learning, and the role of networks is important. However, diffusion, adaptation, emulation, and experimentation are also crucial.

Further naivety surfaced again during my first research field trip to these four countries in 2016 where I assumed it would be *Belarus* where interviewees would require anonymity, as it is often considered the last European dictatorship. I felt people would be wary of speaking to an outside researcher who would be followed by the security services and might put interviewees – and himself – in danger. But many Belarusian interviewees did not require anonymity, and nor – disappointingly – did the security services appear to be interested in the research or researcher, at least not openly. Rather, it was in Moldova where interviewees were cautious. As one friend explained at the time, 'He has ears everywhere.' This was a reference to oligarch Vladimir Plahotniuc, who until 2019 controlled Moldova from behind the scenes. This explanation clarified why there were more requests for anonymity among Moldovan interviewees than in the other three cases.

Authoritarian learning is a fact. As the examples of Belarus, Moldova, Russia, and Ukraine emphasise, it is different to its democratic counterpart. For instance, leaders with authoritarian tendencies and established authoritarian regimes revert to repression more easily; rely on networks to a far greater extent with only limited central control; and learn from success and failure as well as internal and external examples. While failure compels other authoritarian regimes to learn – as they are concerned with their survival and authoritarian breakdown forces others to quickly adapt – success is relevant, as other regimes want to emulate a winning model. There are several reasons why this monograph is relevant and timely. The literature on authoritarianism lags that of democratisation. Through tracing learning in four post-Soviet cases, learning processes and convergence can be investigated. Convergence is defined as the merging of distinct attributes. The post-Soviet region has many authoritarian regimes and authoritarian-minded elites. This gives researchers an opportunity to enhance their understanding of authoritarian learning and corroborate the assumption that learning is important for authoritarian survival.

As the number of authoritarian and semi-authoritarian regimes and weak democracies increases globally, understanding how they learn to keep control is important to better understanding how autocrats and proto-authoritarians are surviving and increasing in number. If leaders with authoritarian ambitions share ideas, it helps them consolidate power quickly, making democratisation harder as they become impervious to these efforts. The growing authoritarian challenge could affect processes such as globalisation or democratisation as the only-game-in-town, threatening, reinterpreting, or even reversing these trends. The authoritarian challenge may shape the world and lead to a less harmonious global order.

Through investigating learning and consolidation practices the authoritarian learning literature is expanded. Currently, this literature is vague in what constitutes authoritarian learning and has a limited basis in wider learning theory. By establishing a theory of authoritarian learning – even if like democratic learning – the authoritarian learning literature will be significantly improved.[4] Existing literature has largely focused on interactions between autocracies and their mutual support for one another. There has been little literature specifically on how autocracies have learnt from the failure of other authoritarian regimes. Existing literature has largely focused on the 'between', rather than the 'by', which encompasses a range of tactics to improve survival chances. By contrast, analysis of the 'between' does not provide all the nuances of how authoritarian learning operates. Through in-depth investigation of the factors behind learning 'by', we significantly contribute to the existing

---

[4] Conversation with Thomas Ambrosio and Andrew Wilson at Aarhus University, 02/12/2016 and many conversations with both afterwards.

authoritarianism and learning literature and increase understanding of authoritarian learning.

The four case studies of Belarus, Moldova, Russia, and Ukraine provide excellent examples for understanding authoritarian learning. The investigation of authoritarian learning in the four cases starts in 2000 and ends in early 2021. The year 2000 was chosen as it is the start of Putin's first presidency and was a period when the authoritarian tendencies of President Leonid Kuchma of Ukraine came out into the open. In 2001, the Communist Party of Moldova (PCRM), under President Voronin, came to power, and Voronin began to consolidate power. Lukashenka in Belarus had also fully consolidated power by the early 2000s. Therefore, 2000 seemed the most appropriate year to begin analysis. Early 2021 was chosen as the cut-off date as it allows for the 2020 Moldovan presidential elections to be analysed for learning examples. Having briefly explained authoritarian learning and framed how the case studies fit into investigating the concept, analysis of necessary literatures and providing greater explanation of fit will be addressed in the next chapter.

Although the analysis ends in 2021, there are a few points that need to be addressed. While it is likely that neither British or Australian prime ministers Harold Wilson and Gough Whitman ever said 'A week is a long time in politics,' this misquote attributed to both is relevant to recent events in the post-Soviet space and the four case studies. In August 2020, Lukashenka was re-elected for a sixth term. His victory at 80.1 per cent is of course likely pure fiction, as his challenger Svitlana Tsikhanouskaya galvanised a populace against the authorities' poor handling of the economy and the COVID-19 pandemic. Having experienced state-wide protests, the Belarusian government failed to react and resorted to electoral practices used previously to get Lukashenka re-elected. Relying on repression, the regime appears to have won for now, but increasingly Lukashenka is an emperor with no clothes.

Another major event was the Russian invasion of Ukraine in February 2022. Initially planned by the Kremlin as a short war – reminiscent of the annexation of Crimea in 2014 – the war seems to have been underpinned by faulty intelligence coupled with a tenacious defence by the Ukrainian armed forces. At the time of writing, this has left Russia in a dire predicament. The Russian army has been ineffective, and factions appear to be fighting their own individual wars. The Kremlin did not expect the collective West to unite in support of Ukraine and issue withering sanctions against Russia. After 2014, Putin began reforming the Russian army into a more effective fighting force, while also reducing economic reliance on the West. However, the invasion of Ukraine has highlighted that fortress Russia was built on sand. Russia may emerge victorious in Ukraine, but if that happens it is likely to be in control of a destroyed country with a populace perceiving Russia as an occupier, as well as a domestic economy in tatters. Having started a war it is unlikely to win, Russia is left in an impossible situation. It cannot afford to withdraw from Ukraine as this would be cataclysmic for Putin's domestic image, but nor can it win and turn Ukraine into a supportive ally. Consequently, Russia is in a trap of its own making and the regime will continue to fall back on repression. With Russia's rapidly declining economy, it is likely what little money the regime has will go into repression and propaganda. Putin has always had at least one blind spot regarding Ukraine, having consistently failed to understand that Ukraine is different to Russia. As will be seen, the Kremlin has tried to impose what works in Russia on Ukraine and has been unsuccessful every time.

This raises an interesting point for authoritarian learning. Although out of the remit of this book, it is likely that authoritarian-minded elites learn when they feel threatened and that there are many possible threats. Learning is a crucial part of developing best survival practices for authoritarian-minded elites, and, because there are multiple threats at any given time it is like these elites are constantly learning. Consequently, by playing the percentage game, it is likely that authoritarian-minded elites make mistakes and learn the wrong lessons. This can be fatal, but established authoritarian regimes can mostly turn these mistakes around. As will be shown later, social learning is a crucial aspect of learning. According to this theory, people learn from previous experiences and how they were socialised. Russians of Putin's generation appear to really believe that Russians and Ukrainians are the same people, and this is a holdover from the Soviet period. Therefore, Putin is likely to continue to make the same mistake over Ukraine because he honestly believes that both countries are the same people. Hopefully the violence and death of about 12,000 Russian soldiers in eighteen days will end Putin's erroneous belief.

Another interesting point in the events in Belarus and Russia is that authoritarian learning may have a time limit. Both regimes have been effective at learning best survival practices over the past two decades. Yet, as the Belarusian example highlights, authoritarian regimes with a long tenure may eventually stop learning. Authoritarian leaders surround themselves with allies and sycophants and so information flows may get stifled, resulting in the top echelons of the regime being unable to react to events or understand changes in society. The Belarusian regime appears not to have reacted to events in 2017 and sleepwalked into the 2020 protests. Similarly, the inner circle around Putin appear to share the same views, and information that does not fit existing perceptions is not passed up the channels of government. The war in Ukraine was allegedly based on intelligence from the security services that stated that Ukrainians were angered at their government and would welcome the Russian army. The first part may have been true, but once the Russians appeared and began shelling Ukrainian cities, any dislike of the government in Kyiv quickly dissipated, and Ukraine united against the Russian invasion.

Although the Belarusian and Russian regimes have been effective at learning to develop the best survival practices in the past, it is possible that both regimes are experiencing what we term 'ivory tower syndrome'. For highly personalised regimes, this is a serious problem, as if the leaders do not have all information, they are likely to make mistakes. However, both leaders – especially Lukashenka – are survivors, and Putin has been a planner in the past. Although both regimes were reactive – rather than proactive – they were effective learners. Time will tell whether both regimes can re-develop their learning capacity, but it increasingly appears that both are suffering from ivory tower syndrome and increasingly reliant on repression. There are pointers towards re-invigorated learning – at least on the part of Russia – with the Russian authorities developing repressive tactics for anti-war protests like those used by the Belarusian regime during the 2020–21 protests. While outside the scope of this book, it may point to a return to learning in Russia.

It is unlikely that there will be much discussion between Russian and Ukrainian elites – other than negotiating an end to the conflict – for the next few years. As will be shown, much learning among authoritarian-minded elites is conducted through dialogue. Consequently, a direct conversation appears unlikely for now. Of course, it all depends on the outcome of the invasion. On the one hand, if Russia manages to win, then a quisling imposed on Kyiv by Moscow is unlikely to do much learning. Rather, they will simply implement diktats from the Kremlin. On the other hand, if Russia is defeated or an independent Ukrainian government exists, then direct dialogue will be unlikely.

However, this does not mean that learning will not occur, and that Russia will not be a model for future Ukrainian authoritarian-minded elites to copy. Presently, there are Ukrainian elites who view close association with Russia as the endgame for Ukraine's foreign policy. Although these factions are keeping a low profile now, they are unlikely not to be involved in politics in the future – unless groups like the Opposition Bloc – For Life are banned. These elites will remain close to the Russian regime and will try to lead Ukraine on a path closer to Russia. Even if these factions are unsuccessful – due to the Russian invasion – Russia can still be a model of how best to consolidate power. Ukrainian elites from all sides of the political spectrum will still emulate and copy what Putin has done in Russia and try to implement some of these lessons in Ukraine.

Volodymyr Zelensky came to power in 2019, promising to only be president for one presidential term, but by late 2021 was already making statements about standing for a second term. While efforts to tackle corruption have been made on paper, organisations like the National Anti-Corruption Bureau (NABU) have faced pressure, as have journalists and investigative newspapers. Zelensky's party – Servant of the People – holds a majority in parliament and allies have been put in positions of power. It is possible that by late 2021, Zelensky and his team were looking to the 2024 presidential election and a re-election bid. There was also growing dissatisfaction among Ukrainians. This was due to the perception that Zelensky – who was seen as an outsider – seemed either ineffectual or part of the political elite. The recent moves towards consolidation were likely a preventative response to potential protests. Russia would be an appropriate model to copy and emulate for consolidation.

Of course, Zelensky is leader during a time of war and so will consolidate power, due to the external existential threat. The same could be said of his predecessor Petro Poroshenko as well. However, this does not detract from the fact that they must learn best practices from somewhere. This can be done from domestic sources – what worked for other Ukrainian presidents before – or from an external source. It is unlikely that Ukraine is a Petri dish for developing ideas to control power. Rather these are taken – and learnt – from somewhere else, either internal or external. Should Ukraine repel the Russian invasion, Zelensky is likely to emerge with immense power and support externally and internally. This will provide Zelensky with an opportunity no other Ukrainian leader has had, the chance to consolidate power. Ukraine, which was once the quintessential 'pluralist by default' state, may have become a whole lot less pluralist. With North Atlantic Treaty Organization (NATO) membership off the table – at least for now – and the fear that the EU may decide in June 2022 to kick the can of Ukrainian membership further down the road, the West will stop being attractive and there will be little incentive to reform and democratise. Time will tell if this scenario happens, but what can be said is that authoritarian-minded elites in Ukraine will continue to look to external and internal sources for developing the best practices for power consolidation.

By contrast to the other three case studies, Moldova has not been greatly affected by recent events, although it remains to be seen whether the de facto break-away territory of Transnistria will manage to break away formally. For now, this scenario appears less and less likely as the Russian army becomes further bogged down in Ukraine. In 2019, Vladimir Plahotniuc over-played his hand and tried to blackmail Igor Dodon into staying in the cartel Plahotniuc had created to run Moldova. Plahotniuc's Party of Democracy (PDM) had close ties with Dodon's Party of Socialists (PSRM), and both had been negotiating a coalition. But by trying to blackmail Dodon, Plahotniuc had the opposite effect and the PSRM joined the ACUM (Now) Bloc in an anti-PDM and anti-Plahotniuc coalition.

Yet, the PSRM – which is pro-Russian – and the ACUM Bloc – which was pro-European – were ideologically opposed, and the coalition of convenience to remove Plahotniuc from controlling the state behind-the-scenes fell apart five months later. The PSRM pulled the plug on the coalition and formed a new government with the PDM. For a moment, it appeared the cartel was back. However, the coalition lasted less than a year with the PDM withdrawing their support. The PSRM stumbled on as a minority government until the parliamentary election in July 2021. In November 2020, Dodon lost the presidency to the pro-European Maia Sandu, and in July 2021 the pro-European Party of

Action and Solidarity won the parliamentary elections. This gave the pro-European elites control of parliament and the presidency.

For the most part, out of the four cases, Moldova has recently been the success story: staying out of geopolitics, not experiencing state-wide protests, and slowly making progress on democracy. However, there are still questions of how far judicial reform will go, and the current reform proposal does allow for a future government to implement judicial controls. The run-up to the 2024–5 electoral cycle may see the current government attempt to increase their control, and the opposition Bloc of Communists and Socialists still retain authoritarian tendencies. If they survive to parliamentary elections in 2025, they will offer staunch opposition and could win. This would weaken democratic reforms and bring authoritarian-minded elites back to power.

The next few years will be an interesting time for authoritarian learning. Authoritarian-minded elites learnt in the past and it is unlikely this has changed. The Belarusian and Russian regimes are likely to re-engage in learning, as this helps with survival. If not, then the results will be cataclysmic for current Belarusian and Russian elites. While both regimes may have reached that ivory tower moment – which is itself interesting for authoritarian learning – this seems unlikely. Similarly, there remain authoritarian-minded elites in both Moldova and Ukraine, and the trend in both countries has been that as time has gone on, incumbent governments have sought to protect themselves from losing elections by developing a palette of best tactics. It is unlikely that this trend will be broken anytime soon. For all the tribulations that have befallen the four case studies in the past three years, authoritarian learning remains relevant, and its investigation has never been more pertinent to better understanding authoritarian survival and consolidation.

# Acknowledgements

While readers will ultimately be the judge of its quality, this book is far better than it otherwise would have been thanks to many others who devoted a great amount of time and effort in helping me over the years. There are many other people I want to thank. I am grateful to David McDowell and Theresa Callan, whose passion and stark views – having grown up on opposite sides of the Belfast divide – gave me my first experiences of political science and a passion that never left. Vitali Silitski inspired this work, but his untimely death meant there was never a chance to meet him. Thomas Ambrosio wrote what effectively became the Bible for this research, *Authoritarian Backlash*, and there were many meetings and discussions with Tom that helped bring this work to fruition. Tom read earlier drafts and always made time for discussion, and a great amount of thanks goes out to the time he devoted to the book.

Similarly, further thanks must go out to various members at the School of Slavonic and East European Studies at University College London. Andrew Wilson and Peter Duncan were incredibly helpful and generous with their time and ideas. Both dealt with numerous questions and read many drafts – not all of them relevant – but still had the patience to recommend new avenues to follow. Andrew helped open doors to interviewees and the wider academic world, with one interviewee starting the interview with 'I am only meeting you because you are Andrew's student.' Ben Noble helped form the arguments and Felix Ciută took the argument apart, which resulted in better framing. Special thanks must go to Sherril Stroschein, who set the ball in motion in 2009 by advising investigation of the then new concept of authoritarian learning. University College London provided an excellent and stimulating intellectual environment to undertake the bulk of this book's research. A special mention must also be made to my fellow PhD candidates Paris Chen, Andrea Peinhopf, Rasa

Kamarauskaitė, Bohdana Kurylo, and Peter Braga, who helped keep me sane.

Others that deserve thanks are Roberto Stefan Foa, Oisín Tansey, and Sarah Whitmore, who read earlier drafts of this book and contributed many thoughts throughout its writing and in the earlier PhD. Roberto acted as mentor while at the Department of Politics and International Studies at the University of Cambridge. His support and enthusiasm made writing the first monograph draft a joy and he helped frame the ideas. Elena Korosteleva deserves thanks for offering contacts in Belarus. Similarly, Mychailo Wynnyckyj, Anaïs Marin, and Ekaterina Schulman offered thoughts on framing and how to improve the arguments. All interviewees who contributed to this research deserve thanks for the time they gave. I am grateful to Chris Sampson and Lucia Noor Melita, who over tea late at night took apart the methodology and forced a re-think on how to shape and show learning. Further thanks go to Liza Navoshchik, Anna Shapovalova, Mihaela Stariş, Lana Zhukovskaya, Bohdana Kurylo, Iryna and Sasha Syanchuk, and Volha Stasevich for being guides, language teachers, translators, and support during the field work.

Without the Economic and Social Research Council's funding for my field work and research during my PhD at University College London and postdoctoral fellowship at the University of Cambridge, this book simply would not have been completed. Cambridge University Press and John Haslam deserve special thanks. John agreed to publish a book from an unknown doctoral candidate, for which I am very grateful. He and the rest of the Cambridge University Press editorial staff have devoted much time to getting this book over the line. Thanks as well to the two anonymous reviewers, who provided feedback on the original draft and helped improve the focus and argument of the book. The research was completed at the Department of Politics, Languages, and International Studies at the University of Bath, and it has been an honour to work in the department with amazing colleagues. An enclosed environment set in beautiful downland above a stunning city, Bath is a perfect place to conduct research.

There are three other people who deserve special thanks. Sasha has been incredible throughout this process, and has devoted much time and energy to keeping me sane. While I'm not sure just how interested she is in the topic, she has at least been very good at feigning curiosity while hearing about the research on an almost daily basis. Most of all,

I thank my parents, Jane and Jeremy. I cannot really express how grateful I am to you. I know you have not always understood what I am interested in or trying to achieve. However, you have shown nothing but support and encouragement, giving me your time and energy. You have always been there. I hope this dedication goes some way to thanking you for everything.

# Notes on Transliteration

Cyrillic (in this volume, Belarusian, Russian, and Ukrainian) source material is transliterated here using the Library of Congress system, with the following exceptions:

*General Exceptions*
- Y is used at the beginning of soft vowels (ya, ye, yu) that are the first letter in words.
- Soft signs are omitted at the end of proper names (for example Luhansk, not Luhans'k).
- Common spellings are employed for words or names that widely appear in English-language media (e.g., Alexey Navalny, not Aleksei Naval'ny).
- When transliterating the unique Ў from Belarusian, we use the English letter u. This is a closer representation of Ў than w or v.

*Exceptions Made for People's Names*
- Soft signs are omitted from people's names (e.g., Navalny, not Naval'ny).
- The letter y is used at the end of names that would otherwise end in ii, yi, yy or iy (e.g., Zelensky and Kolomoisky, not Zelens'kyy and Kolomois'kyy; Sergey Lavrov, not Sergei Lavrov; Yury Boyko, not Yuriy Boyko).
- The letters ie are substituted for 'e (e.g., Glaziev, not Glaz'ev or Glazev).
- The spellings people themselves use as authors of English-language publications are generally used here regardless of this system (e.g., Vladimir Gel'man, Serhiy Kudelia, and Mychailo Wynnyckyj).
- However, we do refer to the names of individuals in the local language (e.g., Vlodymyr Zelensky, not Vladimir Zelensky; Alesksandr Lukashenka, not Aleksandr Lukashenko or Alexander Lukashenko; Islom Karimovand, not Islam Karimov).

*Exceptions Made for Place Names*

- When referring to a place, we use the local language (e.g., Kyiv, Luhansk, and Toshkent, not Kiev, Lugansk, and Tashkent).
- We remove soft signs in place names (e.g., Sevastopol, Luhansk, and Dontesk and not Sevastopol', Donets'k, and Luhans'k).
- The exception to this is Minsk, which could be spelt as Mensk. However, most local people and academics use Minsk, so we stick with this spelling.

# Abbreviations

| | |
|---|---|
| AEI | Alliance for European Integration (Moldova) |
| BRSM | *Belaruski Respublikansky Sayuz Moladzi* (Belarusian Republican Youth Union) |
| CCECC | Centre for Combating Economic Crimes and Corruption (Moldova) |
| CIS | Commonwealth of Independent States |
| CIS-IPA | Commonwealth of Independent States Inter-Parliamentary Assembly |
| CSASS | Council of Security Authorities and Special Services (of the CIS) |
| CSS | Supreme Security Council (Moldova) |
| CSTO | Collective Security Treaty Organisation |
| CSTO-PA | Collective Security Treaty Organisation Parliamentary Assembly |
| EAEU | Eurasian Economic Union |
| EU | European Union |
| FSB | *Federalnaya Sluzhba Bezopasnosti* (Russian Security Service) |
| IAC | Information Analytical Centre (Belarus) |
| KDB | *Kamitet Dzyarzhaunay Byaspieki* (Belarusian State Security Agency) |
| KGB | Komitet Gosudarstvennoi Bezopasnosti (State Security Committee (Soviet Union)) |
| KPRF | Communist Party of the Russian Federation |
| NATO | North Atlantic Treaty Organization |
| OCCRP | Organized Crime and Corruption Reporting Project |
| OMON | *Otryad Mobilny Osobogo Naznacheniya* (Russia) |
| PCRM | Party of Communists of the Republic of Moldova |
| PDM | Democratic Party of Moldova |
| RISI | *Rossysky Institut Strategicheskikh Issledovany* (Russian Institute for Strategic Studies) |

| SBU | Sluzhba Bezpeki Ukraini (Ukrainian Security Service) |
| SCO | Shanghai Cooperation Organisation |
| SCO-RATS | Shanghai Cooperation Organisation Regional Antiterrorist Structure |
| SCPTA | Singaporean Cooperation Programme Training Award |
| SIS | Information and Security Service of the Republic of Moldova |
| SOBR | *Spetsialny otryad bystrogo reagirovaniya* (Special Rapid Response Unit, Russia) |
| VTsIOM | Russian Public Opinion Research Centre |
| ZPB | *Związek Polaków na Białorusi* (Union of Poles in Belarus) |

# 1 | *Introduction*
## *A Contextual Overview*

So far ... democracies have not taken seriously the authoritarian challenge.[1]

## 1.1 Introduction

The merger of an array of pro-Kremlin groups into the anti-Maidan represented a lesson drawn directly by the Russian authorities from the Euromaidan in Kyiv in winter 2013–14. The emergence of the anti-Maidan highlights a phenomenon that we seek to address, understanding how, why, what, and when authoritarian regimes learn. Authoritarian learning in the post-Soviet region began with the Colour Revolutions in Georgia (2003), Ukraine (2004), and Kyrgyzstan (2005), which rocked the region and alarmed other authoritarian regimes. While the first successful effort at countering Colour Revolutions was the May 2005 Andijon massacre – which made Uzbek president Islom Karimov 'a hero' to other post-Soviet leaders, such as Russian president Vladimir Putin (Zygar, 2016: 107) – a subtler approach was needed for other post-Soviet regimes who did not have the same coercive capacity as the Uzbek regime or could not afford the repercussions if any news of a massacre seeped out (Levitsky and Way, 2010: 45).

One regime had been developing subtler methods for keeping the authoritarian regime in power: Belarus. Since an earlier revolution in 2000 in Serbia, the Belarusian authorities had developed tactics to limit such an event occurring in central Minsk (Hall, 2017b). Former Serbian president Slobodan Milošević and incumbent Belarusian president Alyaksandr Lukashenka had regularly visited one another until Milošević's fall from power.[2] The demise of Milošević worried Lukashenka, especially when protesters in Belgrade shouted, 'Today

---

[1] Diamond et al., 2016: 17.   [2] Personal interview: IR39203.

Milošević, tomorrow Lukashenko.' Throughout the 2000s, the Belarusian authorities faced protests due to Lukashenka's fraudulent electoral victories. In response, best practices were developed and adapted throughout the decade, whether that was by infiltrating the opposition, using media to galvanise support for Lukashenka (Wilson, 2021a: 194–6), or using regime-controlled candidates at elections to give the façade of competitive elections (Shraibman, 2018) and keep the regime in power.

At this time, Belarus became something of a testing ground for devising authoritarian practices and stopping Colour Revolutions (Wilson, 2021a: 209). Throughout the decade, the regime continued to learn and devise best counter-revolutionary practices (Hall, 2017b). State structures such as the *Kamitet Dzyarzhaunay Bezopasnosti* (KDB)[3] have been at the forefront of this learning, highlighted by the dossier the KDB compiled in 2005 on previous Colour Revolutions and Belarusian protests, allowing the regime to devise anti-protest tactics (Korosteleva, 2012: 45). The document's focus was on the 2004 Orange Revolution, with information compiled by Belarusian embassy staff in Kyiv.[4] The Belarusian authorities' learning has been a constant process, as they adapt to both domestic failures and those of other regimes.

After all, authoritarian regimes must continuously learn, as failure is not an option. However, this process of constant adaption is not always successful. For example, during protests in 2006, the Belarusian authorities allowed protesters to set up a tent city with 10,000 demonstrators congregating in central Minsk (Korosteleva, 2012: 39), forcing the government to use extensive force to clear protesters, resulting in increased sanctions from Western states.[5] Therefore, during protests in 2010 the regime did not allow protesters to congregate in central Minsk,[6] with security forces quick to arrest protesters. The speed and force of the crackdown was a direct lesson from the 2006 failure.[7]

The Belarusian example emphasises how authoritarian regimes adapt and learn from previous events, and that learning encompasses success

---

[3] To differentiate the Belarusian security services from its Soviet namesake, we use the Belarusian transliteration.

[4] Personal interviews: TK02846, HT69204, and KR48280 all argued that staff from most embassies in Kyiv would be at the Maidan ascertaining what was occurring, and that it is certain Belarusian embassy staff were there.

[5] Personal interview: MU19837.   [6] Personal interview: MU19837.

[7] Personal interviews: MU19837 and NJ08269.

and failure. Learning is not just a Belarusian phenomenon. As Gel'man (2015b: 6) argues, during the 2011–2012 protests, the Kremlin copied Belarusian practices from demonstrations in 2010. A similar point is made by Hall (2017b), who contends that the Kremlin learnt from Belarus's preventive counter-revolution. There is evidence that authoritarian elites learn. In this book, we draw out questions like what, how, and why they learn, what constitutes authoritarian learning, and when it takes place. This will be analysed in due course, but first it will be necessary to define a few of the book's key concepts.

## 1.2 Some Definitions

To better tackle this book's subject, definitions of authoritarianism, learning, and authoritarian learning need to be made. While we will define authoritarianism, the wider literature on authoritarianism will not be analysed in this chapter. Rather, the focus is on authoritarian tendencies, as it is the leaders and personnel, rather than the regimes and institutions, that are of concern here. It is why we analyse patronal politics here to explain why authoritarianism has not consolidated in Moldova and Ukraine but there are periods of attempted consolidation. After defining authoritarianism and authoritarian tendencies, definitions of learning and authoritarian learning follow.

### 1.2.1 Defining Authoritarianism

Although the focus here is on authoritarian learning, which does not necessarily mean that only authoritarian regimes learn, it is necessary to explain what is meant by authoritarianism. We define 'authoritarianism' as the political system of polities that regularly hold elections but violate these to such an extent that they become mere box-ticking exercises, and in which freedom of association, information access, and freedom of expression are highly circumscribed. This definition accounts for the two case studies of Belarus and Russia. However, to understand authoritarian learning fully, it is necessary to analyse authoritarian-minded leaders and not just fully-fledged authoritarian regimes. Not all post-Soviet states can be classified as authoritarian, but there have been attempts by previous and (current) leaders to consolidate power. This is done through learning and copying established authoritarian regimes. Consequently, we need to address the concept of authoritarian tendencies. This is seen in the example of former Ukrainian president Viktor Yanukovych, who, in the first 100 days of his presidency after 2010, set about weakening parliament, bringing the judiciary closer to him personally, and bringing in his clan – or family[8] – to positions of power in the state. This allowed Yanukovych to begin to consolidate power, and the regime focused on examples of what Russia had done previously in similar situations, with Yanukovych often saying – when given examples of practices from European states – 'That's great, but what about Russia.'[9] Glasius (2018: 517) defines authoritarian practices as 'patterns of action that sabotage accountability to people over whom a political actor exerts control, or their representatives, by means of secrecy, disinformation and disabling voice'. However, the definition of authoritarian tendencies used throughout this book is one where leaders try to quickly consolidate power. This explains the situation in Belarus and Russia, as well as periods of attempted authoritarian consolidation by leaders in Moldova and Ukraine.

Patronal politics explains how the four case studies operate and function. Hale (2015: 9–10) explained patronal politics as how 'individuals organize their political and economic pursuits primarily around the personalized exchange of concrete rewards and punishment through chains of actual acquaintance'. Power resides with persons who can enforce it, and these people act as patrons to 'a large and dependent base of *clients*' (Hale, 2015: 10). Within patronal societies, politics 'revolves chiefly around personalized relationships joining extended networks of patrons and clients, and political struggle tends to take the form of competition among different patron–client networks' (Hale, 2015: 21). Analysing state structures through the prism of patronal politics explains the four political systems studied in this book, and patronal politics accounts for why regimes in Belarus and Russia have held power longer than regimes in Moldova and Ukraine. Hale (2015: 64) differentiates between states with single and multiple pyramids of power. If there is a single pyramid of power, then there is one leader who acts as patron and all patron–client ties are hierarchical. This makes authoritarian consolidation relatively easy, and accounts for how politics operates in Belarus and Russia. By contrast, multiple pyramids of

---

[8] Not blood relatives – although also true – but people close to him personally.
[9] Personal interview: ZD49618.

power mean that there is more than one patron able to establish patron–client ties. This makes it much harder for any one person to gain ascendancy and consolidate power, due to competition. Such a system operates in Moldova and Ukraine, and explains why there are periods of attempted authoritarian consolidation but little success.

Authoritarians have found ways to protect themselves (Carothers, 2006; Gershman and Allen, 2006; Krastev, 2006; Schedler, 2002), often acting with confidence and challenging the West (Diamond, 2008; Gat, 2008). One should not just study these regimes but try to understand why they are surviving. Much authoritarian endurance is due to dialogue, emulation, copying, and learning. If democracy is no longer resurgent and authoritarian regimes collaborate to counter democratic norms (Cooley, 2013; 2015; Diamond, Plattner, and Walker, 2016: 4; Koehler, Schmotz, and Tansey 2016) and develop best survival practices, then it is crucial to understand how authoritarian regimes do so – through learning. So, it is essential to better understand authoritarian learning: what it is, how it occurs, why it occurs, and when it occurs.

## 1.2.2 *Defining Learning*

Learning is a process that weighs the costs and benefits of a particular decision (Breslauer and Tetlock, 1991: 5). Regime learning involves individual and collective learning, making it hard to differentiate what learning is and what it is not (Levy, 1994: 280). A restrictive definition of learning would show little, but a broad definition would show too much (Breslauer and Tetlock, 1991: 17). For Braun and Gilardi (2006: 299), learning combines the effect A has on B and analysis of the actions of others. This sequence of processes allows learning to be gauged. Simmons and Elkins (2004) agree that learning happens because people learn from external actors and historical examples; however, both explanations do not cover personal learning. Levy (1994: 296) defined learning as a 'change of beliefs, skills, or procedures based on the observation and interpretation of experience'. But this is the result of learning. Learning is the *process* of engagement, leading to the development of beliefs, skills, ideas, and discernment. This definition explains learning without being too broad or narrow. It is individual- and state-focused, accounts for success and failure, explains knowledge from foreign and domestic experiences, and incorporates new knowledge. Therefore, the definition of learning used here refers to changes of beliefs, skills, or procedures. As shown later, ascertaining a change in beliefs – at least in the case studies – will be hard to investigate. But changes in skills – in how tactics change – and procedures – legislative changes and institution structures – can be shown. This will point to learning and highlight instances of authoritarian learning.

### 1.2.3 Defining Authoritarian Learning

In the 1990s, much research assumed that democratisation would become the political system of most – if not all – states. But the Afghan and Iraq wars – coupled with the resurgence of international terrorism – contributed to a decrease in the promotion of democracy. With events like the Colour Revolutions in the post-Soviet space, which saw the collapse of some authoritarian regimes, other neighbouring autocracies – or as Tolstrup (2014: 2) labels them 'democracy-inhibiting powers' – initiated preventive counter-revolution measures to limit the capacity of external democratisation pressures. Learning best survival practices is the best way to limit these stresses. To perform best, autocrats and like-minded leaders must develop appropriate practices for retaining control. Solnick (1998) explained the collapse of the Soviet Union using an analogy of a bank run. As the regime became increasingly weak, state personnel stopped following orders, which precipitated further collapse. In this way, authoritarian-minded leaders must stop all opposition to ensure the bank survives. Ultimately, they must be right all the time, as the opposition only has to be right once. Learning helps this survival by developing methods to stop future bank runs.

Using the definition of authoritarian learning provided by Hall and Ambrosio (2017: 143) – 'a process in which authoritarian regimes adopt survival strategies based upon prior successes and failures of other governments' – as a starting point, we add a new dimension to this definition. Hall and Ambrosio (2017) focus on learning between states, but we see authoritarian learning as incorporating internal learning from examples of success and failure. For instance, Hall (2017a) showed how Yanukovych had learnt from his own failures during the 2004 Orange Revolution when he became president in 2010 – even though he went on to make other mistakes that precipitated the Euromaidan in 2013. Authoritarian learning is a process of engagement leading to development, and in many circumstances resulting in a change of beliefs, adaptation of skills, and ideas.

## 1.3 Research Findings

There are several key findings from our analysis of authoritarian learning in the four case studies. Firstly, authoritarian learning had been an under-theorised topic with only a few attempts, principally by Hall and Ambrosio (2017) and Bank and Edel (2015), to conceptualise and explain it. Existing literature stuck with the mantra that because authoritarian states B, C, and D do something like authoritarian state A in a short space of time, there must have been learning. Through an in-depth analysis of authoritarian learning from various perspectives, we have expanded current thinking. We provide a theoretical basis for authoritarian learning that combines experiential and social learning theories and policy transfer, diffusion, linkage and leverage, and lesson-drawing to provide a theoretical basis for authoritarian learning. Authoritarian leaders constantly learn and adapt to stay in power, and they regularly collaborate to develop best practices to remain in power.

Second, authoritarian learning is less hierarchical than widely considered by the existing literature. For example, Hall (2017b) found that Belarus was a testing ground for the Kremlin to learn methods developed in Belarus to counter democratisation pressures, thereby stopping a Colour Revolution in Moscow. However, existing literature has concentrated on the notion that Russia dominates the post-Soviet region and dispenses diktats that other post-Soviet regimes follow. This notion of Russian dominance results in concepts like 'authoritarian promotion' and 'authoritarian gravity centres'. For advocates of authoritarian promotion, the Kremlin promotes authoritarianism in other post-Soviet states. Even if true – which is by no means certain – there appears little account for the Kremlin's seeming lack of interest in promotion, and little to explain how Russia can promote authoritarianism to established authoritarian regimes that have been around longer than Putin has been in the Kremlin. Similarly, for advocates of the concept of authoritarian gravity centres, some authoritarian regimes are magnets for others to learn from. Yet, we show that the hierarchy is far flatter than widely considered, and authoritarian learning is a cooperative process in which best practices are shared. In the post-Soviet region, Russia is the regional hegemon. However, it does not dominate learning, and learns itself from best practices developed by others. Of course, once the Russian author-ities instigate policy, other post-Soviet regimes follow, with the foreign agents law being a good example of this.[10] However, the notion that other post-Soviet regimes learn solely from Russia does not truly repre-sent the nuances of authoritarian learning.

Third, both external and internal networks of authoritarian learning are extensive, with both network types offering opportunities for dia-logue, sharing of best practices, and learning. Existing literature on authoritarian learning has not delved deeply into the regional institu-tions, state structures, or elite networks to determine which are engaged in learning. Rather, current literature often focuses on the presidential level. But as shown here, much learning occurs in *siloviki* structures, such as the presidential administration, security service, interior ministry, and security council. Although there is a lack of evidence – due to information being simply unavailable – it is likely that regular meetings are held by junior personnel. Consequently, learning occurs at many levels. For now, this is supposition, and future research can address this, but there is information from higher echelons that these are the key learning networks.

Fourth, existing literature investigated the inter-state level, analysing interactions between authoritarian elites. However, this misses a key aspect of authoritarian learning: the intra-state level. By analysing intra-state-level learning in the four case studies, we show that there is significant inter-linkage between factions and clear opportunities for dialogue, sharing of best practices, and learning. Elite inter-linkage in the four case studies means the elites all know each other, learn from each other, and are concerned with protecting their own power and that of their allies. Regarding Moldova and Ukraine, this has been detrimental to the full democratisation of both states, and it is one reason why the Belarusian and Russian regimes are consolidated authoritarian regimes.

---

[10] The foreign agents law was passed in July 2012 and requires any organisation – and in later renditions of the law individuals – in receipt of 'support' or under the 'influence' of a foreign government to register as a foreign agent. The term 'foreign agents' was used in the 1930s under Stalin to jail and torture people accused of being enemy agents.

Fifth, analysing regional organisations provides a clear understanding of authoritarian learning. The Commonwealth of Independent States (CIS), the Collective Security Treaty Organisation (CSTO), the Shanghai Cooperation Organisation (SCO), and the Union State between Belarus and Russia all provide a perfect opportunity for dialogue, information sharing, and learning. The CIS, the CSTO, and the SCO bring members together in training exercises to develop best practices to ascertain which tactics are effective at keeping incumbent leaders in power. In particular, the CIS and the CSTO regularly hold training exercises for members to gauge which methods work best in each scenario. This notion of learning through training is one that is represented by the CIS's anti-terrorist centre, which regularly holds training exercises to develop tactics to deal with protesters. Although evidence is scant, it is likely that the SCO's anti-terrorist centre develops similar methods against protesters too. Consequently, regional organisations provide learning through training. These regional organisations hold regular meetings of different committees, thereby increasing networks that exist between post-Soviet states. There are recurring CIS inter-departmental meetings. These become venues for dialogue, as well as opportunities to share best practices and engage in learning. The Union State is crucial for dialogue and learning, as it allows personnel to regularly meet and harmonise legislation, which helps learning. Membership or having observer status of most of these organisations helps the Belarusian and Russian authorities learn and consolidate power. By contrast, Moldova and Ukraine are not members of many of these organisations, which likely affects an authoritarian leader's capacity to consolidate authoritarianism in both states, as there is less opportunity to learn. It is likely that the role of regional organisations in authoritarian learning is not a post-Soviet phenomenon, but this needs to be investigated in future studies.

Sixth, while diffusion certainly plays a role in authoritarian learning, epitomised by the joke that '90 per cent of what to do can be found on Google',[11] there is something stronger than diffusion occurring. On the one hand, there is emulation and diffusion, where authoritarian elites decide what to implement and imitate one another by looking at what each other are doing. On the other hand, there is actual dialogue and the sharing of best practices. Elites in Belarus, Moldova, Russia, and

---

[11] Personal interview: HW29578.

Ukraine collude and there are strong pointers towards direct dialogue and cooperation on techniques, a much stronger concept than looking at what is occurring elsewhere and implementing accordingly. Of course, this does not detract from the relevance of diffusion, policy transfer, and emulation, which are integral aspects of authoritarian learning. However, there appears to be a concerted effort by authoritarian elites to talk with one another, share best practices, and learn. This is something far stronger than merely looking at what other authoritarian elites do and copying them.

Seventh, learning from failure has received much analysis in the literature partly because it is easier to see failure. As authoritarian leaders try not to provide many opportunities for the public to replace them non-violently, their demise is often violent, with mass protests and previous elites imprisoned or dead. Naturally, other authoritarian leaders do not want to share that fate, so they ascertain the causes of failure and develop practices to counter such possibilities occurring domestically. Learning from success is harder to measure for researchers, but it is no less relevant to authoritarian learning. Internal sources of learning are the main sources of learning from success. For example, Vladimir Plahotniuc and Petro Poroshenko – in Moldova and Ukraine respectively – learnt from the success of previous domestic regimes to control power. While success is hard to measure, it is as relevant to authoritarian learning as failure.

Eighth, the existing literature has concentrated on the inter-state level. However, to fully understand authoritarian learning, it is necessary to bring in the internal dimension as well. Authoritarian leaders and elites are as likely to learn from internal examples as from external examples. The internal dimension is crucial for understanding authoritarian learning. This is particularly so for Moldova and Ukraine, as current elites in both countries have worked in past regimes and so retain knowledge of past mistakes and successes that can be used for learning in the present.

## 1.4 What Is Authoritarian Learning?

Having briefly defined authoritarian learning in Section 1.2.3 and explained that it is more than 'a process in which authoritarian regimes adopt survival strategies based upon prior successes and failures of other governments' (Hall and Ambrosio, 2017: 143) including learning from internal examples, this section analyses the concept in more detail. We will first investigate some of the literature on diffusion, policy transfer, linkage, and lesson-drawing. Then, the different elite networks involved in authoritarian learning will be analysed, which will be shown to be extensive.

Treisman (2020) shows that historically most authoritarian regimes begin a democratic transition not because the elite initiates such a process, but because they make a mistake that they cannot control and consequently lose power. Therefore, learning from external and internal examples is a way for authoritarian leaders, or those similarly minded, to reduce the potential for making a mistake that leads to either democratisation or a more open system. However, there is nothing to stop autocratic-minded leaders from learning the wrong lessons. For example, Viktor Yanukovych learnt some lessons from his failure to become Ukrainian president in 2004, which he implemented when he finally became president in 2010. Leonid Kuchma had not had a party of power or attempted to dominate state institutions. Kuchma had allowed too many competing regime clans. Yanukovych perceived these as mistakes on the part of Kuchma and so strengthened control over state institutions and restricted access to resources for other clans. However, the attempted power grab and ostracising of important factions led to regime disunity and increased support for the opposition. Once the Euromaidan began, elites who were alienated by Yanukovych had their excuse to help depose him (Hall, 2017a). While learning often helps authoritarian-minded elites, it can also result in failure and precipitate collapse. This makes learning a quandary for autocratic-minded elites.

Authoritarian learning occurs by combining policy transfer, diffusion, linkage and leverage, and lesson-drawing. Authoritarian-minded elites regularly collaborate with one another on best practices to remain in power. Authoritarian learning is less hierarchical than widely considered by existing literature. Unlike the literature on authoritarian gravity centres – which perceives learning as coming from authoritarian regimes that act as models to lesser regimes (Kneuer and Demmelhuber, 2016; Kneuer et al., 2019), we show that authoritarian learning is more horizontal, with the authorities in Minsk and likely Nur-Sultan, Baku, and Toshkent bringing best practices to the table.

Both external and internal networks of authoritarian learning are extensive and offer dialogue opportunities, sharing of best practices, and learning. Existing literature has not delved deeply into regional institutions or state structures to determine which are engaged in learning. Analysis here shows that presidential administrations, security councils, interior ministries, parliaments, and even ambassadors are involved in learning. In the presidential administrations and interior ministries, there are regular meetings held at senior and junior levels. This provides one venue for learning, and with regular meetings at all government levels, there are many opportunities for learning. Within the four case studies, elites have – mostly – long known one another, learn from each other, and are concerned with protecting their own and allies' power. Such practices in Moldova and Ukraine have been detrimental to democratisation, and this is one reason why the Belarusian and Russian regimes are consolidated authoritarian regimes.

For the case studies, post-Soviet regional organisations are central to understanding authoritarian learning. These institutions provide opportunities for dialogue, sharing information, and learning by bringing member states together in training exercises to ascertain which tactics are most effective to retain power. Regional organisations hold regular meetings, thus increasing the learning networks between post-Soviet states. The Belarusian and Russian regimes are members or observers of most of these regional organisations. These institutions provide learning opportunities and share best practices, thereby helping both regimes with learning and power consolidation. By contrast, Moldova and Ukraine are not members of many post-Soviet regional organisations, which could go some way to explaining why there has been no successful authoritarian regime in either.

Diffusion is crucial to authoritarian learning – epitomised by the joke[12] that '90% of what to do can be found on Google'. There is emulation and diffusion, where authoritarian regimes decide what to do based on what others do, and imitate one another. Then there is actual dialogue and the sharing of best practices. There are strong pointers to direct dialogue and cooperation on strategies and techniques, where regimes go beyond simply imitating what is occurring in another authoritarian state. While learning from success is harder to demonstrate, it is as crucial to understanding authoritarian learning as learning from failure. Similarly, internal examples are as important as external examples for authoritarian-minded elites to learn from.

---

[12]  Personal interview: HW29578.

There is a debate within the literature on authoritarian diffusion as to quite what is happening, with different conceptualisations of diffusion put forward. Silitski (2010) labelled collaboration between the Belarusian and Russian regimes an 'authoritarian international'. While we will show that there is direct dialogue and far more than just governments looking at what other governments do, the idea of an authoritarian international, where authoritarian leaders and elites try to make the world safe for authoritarianism, is too much of a stretch. There has been a wealth of literature on this idea, centred around authoritarian promotion (Brady, 2016: 190; Burnell, 2010; Kurlantzick, 2013; Lankina, Libman, and Obydenkova, 2016: 1603; Melnykovska, Plamper, and Schweickert, 2012; Vanderhill, 2013; 2014; Yakouchyk, 2016). This literature contends that at least some authoritarian regimes – such as China, Iran, and Russia – are promoting authoritarianism to other regimes.

While authoritarian promotion is a type of diffusion, with one regime providing lessons for others, it is a very vertical perception of authoritarian learning. As argued here, authoritarian learning is more horizontal than vertical. Similarly, if the notion of authoritarian promotion exists, it is 'more opportunistic than strategic' (von Soest, 2015: 624). Yakouchyk (2016) writes about active and passive autocracy promotion, although passive promotion is something of an oxymoron in terms (Tansey, 2016: 147–8). Melnykovska, Plamper, and Schweickert (2012: 750) argue that the Central Asian states are susceptible to Russian and Chinese autocracy promotion, and Vanderhill (2013: 76) contends that Putin helped Lukashenka consolidate power. Examples like these highlight potential failings of authoritarian promotion. Melnykovska and colleagues (2012) fail to explain how the fully consolidated authoritarian regimes of Central Asia required Russian authoritarian promotion. This is also true for Vanderhill's (2013) analysis of Russia and Belarus. Rather, authoritarian learning is less vertical than authoritarian promotion accounts for.

This is also the case for the literature on authoritarian gravity centres. This concept sees authoritarian regimes coalescing around authoritarian models – such as China, Russia, and possibly Singapore – with these models providing learning opportunities for their satellite states. Kneuer and Demmelhuber (2016) and Kneuer and colleagues (2019) are correct to highlight the importance of learning among authoritarian regimes. Similarly, this literature is right to mention that there are some authoritarian regimes that likely serve as models for other authoritarian leaders. However, too much emphasis is placed on these authoritarian models, making other states mere satellites with limited independence – unable even to leave the sphere of influence – other than to learn from the centre. As shown in this book, authoritarian learning is more horizontal than widely perceived in current literature.

Certainly, there are authoritarian models that other authoritarian leaders copy, but as Hall (2017b) showed, authoritarian gravity centres also learn from so-called satellites. We follow the notion of diffusion laid out by Ambrosio (2010), where diffusion is a mix of learning from applicable models from across the political spectrum rather than copying everything from a single model regardless of local applicability. While diffusion relies on 'simple demonstration effects' (Ambrosio and Tolstrup, 2019: 2746), we show that it not just about analysing what others do and implementing accordingly. Rather, there is regular dialogue and authoritarian learning is heavily networked and horizontal. This will be explained later in the chapter and in more detail in later chapters.

As authoritarian-minded elites are concerned with losing power, they will learn from all sources, both internal and external. But they do not just learn from other authoritarian regimes. Rather, it is more nuanced. Concerned with survival at all costs, authoritarians learn from any pertinent examples. Consequently, learning from successes and failures of democracies are also taken into consideration. Political systems and policies developed in democracies have been copied and re-interpreted to help consolidation.[13] To better ensure survival, authoritarian leaders will copy successful policies from democracies to placate citizens, highlight that the governments are democratic – or at least modernising – and offer increased legitimacy. Therefore, authoritarian learning is not learning between authoritarians but learning from all sources to better ensure survival.

Authoritarian learning occurs through dialogue, emulation, and copying. Regimes learn by analysing internal and external examples of what worked and what failed. Authoritarian learning is continual, as authoritarian regimes must constantly learn to halt anything that could precipitate regime collapse. Therefore, authoritarian learning is about constant

---

[13] Personal interview: LD03148, who showed how the Russian authorities have consistently changed the electoral system – originally copied from Germany – to ensure electoral victory. Similarly, the 2012 foreign agents law was copied from the American Foreign Agents Registration Act but made more restrictive.

adaptation, although this adaptation is not always successful. Authoritarian learning is a collaborative process with some regimes acting as testing grounds for others and all authoritarian regimes trying to develop best practices that other authoritarian regimes can use. Consequently, authoritarian learning is highly networked and less hierarchical, with all regimes able to bring ideas and practices to the table for consideration. Regional organisations play a significant role in providing dialogue venues, opportunities to share best practices, and ascertain through training exercises what works directly. Therefore, learning is crucial to increasing understanding on why authoritarian regimes persist.

## 1.4.1 Theoretical Framework

The theoretical framework designed for explaining authoritarian learning is explored here and is tabulated to provide clarity on the terminological mess that is the literature on political learning. When studying this literature, researchers use different idioms to mean the same thing. Within this framework we analyse different learning theories that help explain authoritarian learning, assessing experiential and social learning in Table 1.1. Table 1.2 investigates the literature on political learning and shows how parts of this literature help explain authoritarian learning. After investigating theory and political learning, we turn to analysing diffusion and linkage and leverage, as both are crucial to authoritarian learning.

Experiential and social learning help explain authoritarian learning as they account for both success and failure. Social learning is relevant as it includes habitus and communities of practice, which are relevant to authoritarian learning, as authoritarian elites rely on their past and networks for learning examples. Diffusion – which is a crucial part of authoritarian learning – fits into social learning theory. Before addressing diffusion, we investigate how authoritarian learning fits into the literature on political learning. We define political learning as 'any change in behaviour due to a change in perception about how to solve a problem' (Haas, 1991: 63). In this literature there is policy transfer, adaptation, and learning. The differences between them are small and we use policy transfer as an umbrella term as it includes both learning and adaptation. Three other literatures of relevance are diffusion, emulation, and lesson-drawing. Each is briefly explained in Table 1.2.

Table 1.1 *Theoretical framework of authoritarian learning*

| Theory | Explanation | Example(s) |
|---|---|---|
| Experiential learning | In experiential learning, the learner acquires knowledge by devising questions and investigating those questions to construct meaning (Marin, 2015: 855), combining concrete experience, reflective observation, abstract conceptualisation, and active experimentation (Brookes, 1995: 66). It incorporates examples of failure and success (Marin, 2015: 855). | Governments improving capabilities by learning from external and internal successes and failures. |
| Social learning (includes habitus and communities of practice) | Social learning is how a person learns from their social environment. People observe others and learn what to do (success) and what not to do (failure) (Bandura, 1963, 1971: 3). | Learning from others' successes and failures and learning from domestic experiences, which shapes how individuals learn. |
| Habitus | How people use past experiences to adapt to present situations (Bourdieu, 1972, 1992, 2000). | Many elites in the four case studies lived during the Soviet Union, so they internalise Soviet experiences for use now. |
| Communities of practice | Everyday networks that allow people to share best practices and learn from what worked or | There is evidence that bodies of the CIS, such as the Council of Heads of State, hold informal |

Table 1.1 (*cont.*)

| Theory | Explanation | Example(s) |
| --- | --- | --- |
|  | did not (Lave and Wenger, 1991: 29; Wenger, 1998: 7; Wenger, McDermott, and Snyder, 2002). | meetings, making this council and the CIS networks of sharing best practices and learning. |

Diffusion, emulation, lesson-drawing, linkage and leverage, and policy transfer are crucial to understanding authoritarian learning. Each is referred to throughout the book to explain examples used to highlight authoritarian learning in the four case studies. Each is relevant to authoritarian learning, but policy transfer and diffusion are crucial. Authoritarian leaders and elites diffuse information between one another. According to Ambrosio and Tolstrup (2019: 2746), diffusion involves 'any intentionality on the part of the policy innovator and can occur through simple demonstration effects'. However, as will be shown here, authoritarian learning involves direct meetings and sharing of experiences, rather than simply demonstration effects. While the statement '90% of what to do can be found on Google'[14] is true, what will be shown is that there is something more happening than the spread of ideas. Lemon and Antonov (2020) correctly highlighted policy transfer in the CIS Inter-Parliamentary Assembly, but we feel that rather than being distinct, policy transfer is a part of authoritarian learning. Emulation is crucial to understanding authoritarian learning, allowing other authoritarian leaders and elites to ascertain what worked elsewhere and act accordingly (Beissinger, 2007: 259). Demonstration effects are important. If it can be demonstrated that something works, it is likely to be copied.

Similarly, we show that authoritarian learning is far more horizontal than the literature considers. Kneuer and Demmelhuber (2016) and Kneuer and colleagues (2019) have postulated the concept of authoritarian gravity centres, where some authoritarian regimes – for example China and Russia – are models for other authoritarian regimes. This is indeed the case with economic and political models – especially

[14] Personal interview: HW29578.

Table 1.2 *Learning-related topics and authoritarian learning*

| Types of political learning | Explanation | Example(s) |
|---|---|---|
| Diffusion | Strang (1991: 325) defined diffusion as 'any process where prior adoption or practice in a population alters the probability of adoption for remaining non-adopters'. | • It is likely that the 2012 Russian foreign agents law was diffused, as restrictive NGO legislation occurred later in Azerbaijan (2013), Tajikistan (2014), Kazakhstan (2016), Ukraine (2017), and China (2017).<br><br>• Many post-Soviet states copied Russian legislation, although there is no direct policy transfer (Bader, M, 2014). This points to diffusion, where elites look at examples rather than learning directly. |
| Emulation | Effort to match – or even surpass – a policy or practice through imitation. | • During the mid-2000s various post-Soviet authoritarian regimes tried to out-do one another in developing best practices to stop Colour Revolutions, which had led to authoritarian collapse in Georgia (2003), Ukraine (2004), and Kyrgyzstan (2005). |
| Lesson-drawing | Policy-makers draw lessons to achieve best results and learn from others about what to do and what not to do (James and Lodge, 2003: 180; Tosun, 2013: 19). | • Governments draw lessons from other policies to 'apply to their own political system' (Dolowitz and Marsh, 1996: 344). |

| Linkage and leverage | Linkage refers to political, economic, and cultural ties between states and generally allows richer states to exert leverage over weaker states. The literature mostly addresses how Western democracies use economic links with authoritarian neighbouring states to exert leverage over them and initiate democratisation (Levitsky and Way, 2005: 23, 26, 2006: 379). | • In the post-Soviet space Russia, as the hegemon, uses cultural, economic, and political ties to link with other post-Soviet states (Cameron and Ornstein, 2012; Strzelecki, 2016).<br><br>• However, as people with authoritarian tendencies are averse to losing power, Russia has been unable – at least to an extent – to exert leverage on other post-Soviet states (Way, 2015) but maintains linkage. Linkage is more important than leverage. Linkages between states help reinforce authoritarianism while precipitating diffusion, copying, and sharing. Brownlee (2017: 1335) contends that the greater linkages authoritarian regimes have, the greater chance ideas will spread, helping authoritarian leaders better consolidate power and deter external democratisation pressures. Authoritarian regimes have increased trade with one another in 'an intentional move to close ranks internationally' (Tansey, Koehler, and Schmotz,. 2017: 1231), thereby improving linkages. |
| Policy transfer | How policy transmission between states occurs with policy originating in state A being transferred to state B, which | • During the 2013–14 Euromaidan, the Yanukovych regime passed the dictatorship laws, which were copied from previous Belarusian and Russian legislation. |

Table 1.2 (*cont.*)

| Types of political learning | Explanation | Example(s) |
|---|---|---|
| | perceives the policy as successful (Zito and Schout, 2009: 1114). | • Lemon and Antonov (2020) demonstrated that legislation on right to assembly, civil society, and political participation in Kazakhstan, Kyrgyzstan, Russia, Tajikistan, and Uzbekistan has the same wording. While all five regimes could have collaborated directly, it is likely that the CIS's Inter–Parliamentary Assembly – which harmonises member state legislation – was crucial in these legislative carbon copies. |

regarding China. Bader, Grävingholt, and Kästner (2010: 84) argued that authoritarian regimes have inspired others. However, while these regimes may be models for others, it does not necessarily mean that learning is unidirectional from Beijing and Moscow to other capitals. Rather, we show that authoritarian learning is more networked and horizontal than widely considered. We turn to analysing networks and the actors involved in authoritarian learning.

## *1.4.2 Networks of Authoritarian Learning*

Although networks are investigated in more detail later, it is crucial to explain what a network is, and which regional and state institutions are relevant for authoritarian learning. Using Solnick's (1998) bank run analogy, authoritarian leaders want to restrict any possible regime change. To do so requires that they learn from successful and failed examples to better retain power. As the leader and elites do not want to lose power, they develop best survival practices and have a direct stake in regime preservation and power retention. Consequently, there are extensive networks involved in authoritarian learning. We argue that authoritarian learning is not just learning from external sources, but involves internal examples too. Table 1.3 shows which regional and state institutions, and elite groups are involved in learning in the four case studies at both levels.

These networks are crucial to authoritarian survival. Such networks are extensive – especially external networks – with diverse groups involved in learning. Authoritarian-minded leaders and elites, whether in consolidated or unconsolidated regimes, are concerned with remaining in power and so they learn from external and internal examples of success and failure. Learning is constant although not always successful. It is crucial to understand that authoritarian learning is constant, as elites look to preserve power, although it is not always effective.

As authoritarian leaders and elites are constantly learning to preserve power and reduce chances of regime collapse, learning networks are extensive. Although we list these networks by state institution or regional organisations, they are likely to cross structures and be less centralised than we represent here. Similarly, many networks overlay themselves on formal government structures that do not necessarily represent these actual institutions. This creates a dichotomy, where networks are both centralised and decentralised at the same time.

Table 1.3 *Regional and state institutions and personnel involved in learning*

| Institution | Involvement in external learning | Involvement in internal learning |
| --- | --- | --- |
| Ambassadors | Heavily involved in providing information on what is happening in their own country to the elites in the country of their ambassadorship and vice versa. Many ambassadors – particularly for Russia – had close ties with the elites in the countries they are ambassadors to. This allowed them to give information on what was happening in their own country. During protests between 2015 and 2016, the Ukrainian ambassador to Moldova met interior ministry personnel to discuss the Euromaidan in Ukraine between 2013 and 2014. Embassies play a role with Belarusian and Russian embassy staff allegedly on Kyiv's streets during the Orange Revolution (2003–4) and Euromaidan (2013–14) taking notes and sending these back to higher-ups in Minsk and Moscow. | As an external network, ambassadors have little role in internal learning. |
| Foreign ministries | Personnel in these institutions regularly meet one another in regional organisations and inter-foreign ministry commissions, allowing for discussion and learning. There are regular meetings between foreign ministries due to state visits too. Agreements to share information are crucial to learning opportunities provided by this institution. | Limited involvement in internal learning. |

| | | |
|---|---|---|
| Internal affairs ministries | There are regular meetings in regional organisations and there are inter-state commissions too. There are agreements between internal affairs ministries to collaborate and share information. | Plays a significant role in internal learning through regular meetings of personnel. These institutions incorporate many branches that share information and regularly meet. In a country as large as Russia, regional personnel share information to determine whether tactics to disperse protests in Moscow can be used in Saransk. The Kremlin learnt that protest-dispersal practices used in the regions resulted in more protests in Moscow due to the heavy-handedness of regional personnel. Consequently, tactics have changed in how interior ministry personnel deal with protests in Moscow and St Petersburg for fear of creating a spiral. |
| Parliaments | There are inter-parliamentary commissions, allowing for legislative and best practice sharing. Parliaments also have committees on foreign relations. For example, the upper house of the Russian parliament – the Federation Council – has a committee on the post-Soviet states. Consequently, Russian parliamentarians regularly visit | There are parliamentary committees dealing with domestic affairs, which is one way for learning to happen. Many parliamentarians in the case studies have been in parliament for a long time. This |

Table 1.3 (*cont.*)

| Institution | Involvement in external learning | Involvement in internal learning |
|---|---|---|
| | other post-Soviet states, allowing for discussions that help both sides learn. | makes sharing best practices from the past domestically easier. |
| Political parties | Political parties across the post-Soviet space work closely together. For instance, United Russia has a collaboration agreement with the Party of Socialists of the Republic of Moldova and with Party of Regions in Ukraine, when the latter was in power under Viktor Yanukovych. This allows elites to share past experiences externally. | As with parliaments, many party members have been in politics for a long time. Consequently, these personnel impart information on previous events to help learning in the present. |
| Prime ministers | There are meetings in regional organisations for prime ministers allowing experience to be shared. They meet regularly in inter-state meetings, thereby providing other learning opportunities. | As many prime ministers have been members of various governments – regarding Moldova and Ukraine – and part of existing regimes in Belarus and Russia, they have experience to share. |
| Presidential administrations | Regular meetings occur among structures of the presidential administration at the external level. For instance, a week after the head of the Belarusian presidential administration, Viktar Sheiman, visited China and liaised with the Chinese Communist Party, legislation tightened Internet access. | Various presidential administration structures are involved in internal learning. For instance, the Russian presidential administration experiments with different ideas to ensure regime electoral victory. |

| | | |
|---|---|---|
| Regional organisations | Various post-Soviet regional organisations provide opportunities for best practice sharing and learning. There is some information about how these organisations help members counteract protesters under the façade of anti-terrorist operations. | Plays a very limited role – if any – in internal learning. |
| Security councils | Regular meetings between security councils provide learning opportunities used externally. For example, after the Arab Spring, the secretary of the Russian Security Council, Nikolai Patrushev, visited Algeria, Egypt, and Morocco to discuss successes and failures from these protests. | As these institutions consist of personnel from across other state structures, there is much that can be learnt. |
| Security services | Regular contact between post-Soviet security services, with opportunities for learning and sharing of best practices. Personnel from the Belarusian and Russia security services regularly meet and share ideas. | These structures play a key role in internal learning by developing best practices. One example is the training of Russian security forces outside Lyubertsy in the Moscow region against protesters while protests happened in Moscow in 2016. Similarly, state security services are split into various branches – fourteen in the case of Belarus – and so it is likely these branches consult one another, thereby helping with internal learning. |

However, due to the lack of information on these networks and the fluidity of personnel in these structures,[15] it remains challenging to really represent these structures. One example is all the models put forward representing relations between Putin and other elites.[16] So, understanding learning networks involves guesswork and we can only offer a limited analysis of the learning network that exist. But by analysing various institutions we have located ten places learning networks exist. These are a mixture of centralised and decentralised entities overlaid on existing institutions. Consequently, these networks are opaque, and it is likely that most learning takes place where no information can be found.[17] Although the limited available evidence points to networks being hierarchical, with top institutional elites involved in learning, it is likely that more junior members also engage in dialogue.[18] As leaders and elites do not want to tarnish their image as aspiring democrats by letting information about these networks seep out and highlight, for example, that there were discussions restricting foreign funding for NGOs, such networks are well hidden. However, these remain integral to explaining authoritarian learning and highlight that learning is constant, includes many personnel, and is more horizontal than widely considered.

Figure 1.1 shows the different networks involved in external learning. These networks engage in extensive learning, although this does not occur solely from one network to another. Most networks engage in diffusion, linkage, lesson-drawing, and policy transfer. As Figure 1.1 shows, the ten networks are engaged intensively in learning from external success and failure. Due to inter-linkage between elites in the four case studies, diffusion, linkage, and lesson-drawing are crucial to external learning. If we perceive that policy transfer includes any course

---

[15] Personal interview: AM01079, who explained that many Russian elites show little loyalty to one another and coalesce around a resource. However, when interests change, they unite with other elites. It is likely this is so for the other case studies.

[16] Different models have seen these relations as planets (Ledeneva, 2013: 60), a politburo 2.0 (Michenko Consulting, 2017), or a royal court (Haase, 2012).

[17] Personal interview: YR52870, who explained how much discussion occurs in state sanatoria. This is a likely source of learning. For example, former director of the *Federalnaya Sluzhba Bezopasnosti* (FSB) Nikolai Patrushev regularly conducted meetings while watching Dynamo Moscow's ice hockey team (Soldatov and Borogan, 2010: 88–9).

[18] Personal interviews: YR52870, ND30192.

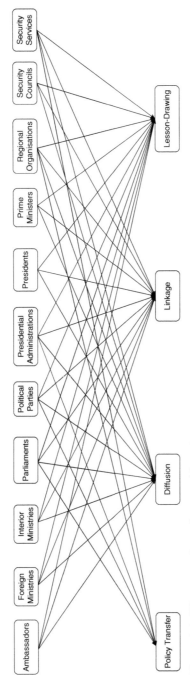

**Figure 1.1** Elite networks and external learning

of action, then all structures are involved in this learning type. However, we contend that policy transfer is specific to legislative development and the spread of laws from one state to another. Learning through action is explained by diffusion, lesson-drawing, and linkage. While all nine external learning networks investigated here are involved in these three learning types, only a few are engaged in policy transfer. Having addressed these external learning networks, we turn to internal learning networks.

Figure 1.2 presents how internal networks are involved in authoritarian learning and the learning types used. As diffusion is a learning type occurring at the inter-state level, we do not include it as part of learning happening among internal networks. Similarly, as linkage implies links between states, we do not include it here when analysing internal learning networks. There are fewer networks playing a role in internal learning networks, but they are significant in their operation and in understanding authoritarian learning. Figure 1.2 clearly sets out which networks are involved in which learning type. We argue that with internal learning, authoritarian-minded leaders are more likely to draw lessons from previous examples than use policy transfer. As authoritarian leaders are concerned with survival, they are more likely to draw lessons from past internal failures than successes – although learning from successes is also possible. It is also unlikely that an authoritarian leader will publicly admit to integrating a previous successful policy – and certainly would not use one that failed. Therefore, it is likely that lesson-drawing has more pertinence to internal learning than policy transfer, although the latter remains relevant.

Internal learning is crucial to authoritarian learning, as people use experiences from childhood in the present. Politicians in the four case studies grew up in the Soviet Union and not only survived the 1990s but

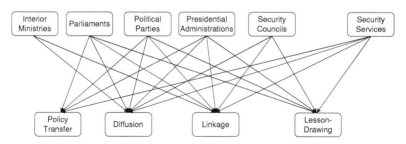

**Figure 1.2** Elite networks and internal learning

wrote the rulebook on how to survive it.[19] Therefore, they are likely to resort to authoritarian practices and draw on Soviet experiences and the 1990s. Many elites have been in or around for power years and so to better understand authoritarian learning, one must investigate internal learning. Another aspect of how networks contribute to internal learning in the cases studied is through patronal politics. Moldovan and Ukrainian elites have simply changed position when a new regime takes power, giving these factions opportunities to learn from previous governments. There is likely even learning from the Soviet Union. One example is the failed social parasite law in Belarus, which the Belarusian authorities took from Soviet legislation. The only difference was that the Soviet Union internally exiled the unemployed, whereas the Belarusian regime taxed them (Loushnikova, 2015). Whereas there is some turnover in Belarus and Russia, elites in both states have been in power – overall – longer than personnel in Moldova and Ukraine. This allows Belarusian and Russian elites to learn from past successes or mistakes and draw lessons from the Soviet period. Although both regimes have elite renewal, younger elites learn from those who came before.[20] In Moldova and Ukraine, regimes come and go, but elites remain, with changed power remits in existing structures. Therefore, the elites have been members of previous regimes and so use lesson-drawing and policy transfer to effectively learn from internal experiences. Having analysed authoritarian learning and the networks involved we turn to setting out the plan for the rest of the book.

## 1.5 Organisation of This Book

A comprehensive analysis of authoritarian learning is necessary to better understand how authoritarian regimes and authoritarian-minded elites attempt to survive. Within authoritarian learning, emulation and linkage play a role, but most significant is a strong diffusive practice of direct dialogue, collaboration, sharing of best practices, and cooperation on training exercises to ascertain what works in practice. The rest of the book investigates why authoritarian regimes learn, how they learn, and what they learn. Chapter 2 provides the methodology that will be used throughout the book. This incorporates a comparative research design, using case studies, and a research methodology of

---

[19] Personal interview: DP24850.    [20] Personal interviews: KG84027, ND30192.

interviews and process-tracing. The chapter then goes on to analyse the authoritarian tendency trajectories of the four case studies before investigating the research questions that will lead the rest of the book chapters.

From there, we address learning from external failure in Chapter 3. Defining what we mean by failure allows the chapter to analyse examples of authoritarian-minded elites learning from failure. We investigate a range of examples, with China learning from the failure of the Soviet Union, which saw the creation of a mixture of a state-controlled market economy, political reforms, and the promotion of a nationalist identity. This has helped the Chinese regime gain increased popular legitimacy. We then investigate case learning from the Orange Revolution, Arab Spring, and Euromaidan. In particular, the Belarusian and Russian authorities have particularly focused on these events to learn from these failures.

Having analysed external failure in Chapter 3, we turn to learning from internal failure in Chapter 4. Lessons from the Soviet Union and 1990s taken from Belarus and Russia are addressed in the chapter, before it investigates the lessons Putin took from his initial image failure of the Kursk submarine sinking to become the macho-man depicted in many memes today. A further example of learning from internal failure is the 2009 Moldovan Twitter Revolution and the lessons that Plahotniuc took from Voronin's failure to retain power during these protests. We then assess various Ukrainian governments' learning from the 2004 Orange Revolution and the 2013–14 Euromaidan, with Yanukovych drawing lessons from Kuchma's failures in 2004 and Poroshenko doing the same with Yanukovych's mistakes during the Euromaidan. A final section of the chapter addresses Russian failure to learn from pension protests in 2005 when implementing a new pension policy in 2018, which led to protests. The other example in the section is the social parasite law in Belarus. This saw the Belarusian authorities' tax the unemployed and led to the first state-wide protests under Lukashenka. Yet the government failed to learn from these events and continued similar policies that in part precipitated protests in 2020.

Chapters 3 and 4 investigated learning from failure. By contrast, Chapter 5 analyses learning from external and internal success. To begin with, the chapter looks at whether China, Singapore, and possibly Kazakhstan are models that the four case studies look to copy.

China is a clear model for the four case studies. Yet, Kazakhstan and Singapore are relevant as well. The chapter then investigates the copying of NGO legislation and how the other case studies have tried to incorporate the 2012 Russian foreign agents law. A final section of the chapter investigates learning from domestic success. One example is how Lukashenka has taken successes from the Soviet Union and implemented these in Belarus. Another example is the successes of previous domestic regimes learnt from by Moldovan and Ukrainian governments.

The next three chapters address different aspects of networks that are crucial for learning by authoritarian-minded elites. Chapter 6 analyses the role that post-Soviet regional organisations play in authoritarian learning. These institutions provide many opportunities for meeting, dialogue, legislative sharing, the sharing of best practices to consolidate power, and engagement in training exercises. Analysis of the CIS, the CSTO, the SCO, and the Union State between Belarus and Russia highlights that these four organisations provide many opportunities for learning. As Moldova and Ukraine are not members of many – or any – of these organisations, this may explain why authoritarian-minded elites in these two case studies have failed to consolidate power.

After this, Chapter 7 investigates the external and internal formal networks that exist in the four case studies. These networks exist in formal state structures and there are ten institutions involved in these learning networks. All these networks engage in external learning and the majority participate in diffusion, linkage, and lesson-drawing. Fewer institutions are involved in policy transfer. We define policy transfer as actions that specifically are focused on legislative development. This explains why fewer institutions are involved in this aspect of learning. Similarly, fewer structures are involved in internal formal networks – with only six institutions engaging in internal networks. Only half of these structures use policy transfer as an aspect of learning.

Chapter 8 investigates external and internal informal networks. Due to the difficulties of locating these types of networks, we concentrate on a couple of examples. As the book is focused on learning and how learning percolates between authoritarian-minded elites, we start the chapter by analysing Russian links to authoritarian-minded elites in Moldova and Ukraine. These are extensive, and while the current governments in Moldova and Ukraine are – for now at least – pro-European, by maintaining ties to other elite factions in both states, the

Russian authorities are playing a waiting game in the hope that public opinion swings to a more pro-Russian attitude. Due to the war in Ukraine, it is unlikely this will occur anytime soon in Ukraine, but it is always best to be prepared. The chapter then investigates the extensive internal informal networks in the case studies, with these structures helping authoritarian-minded elites learn.

In conclusion, Chapter 9 reiterates the book's findings, providing a comprehensive picture of authoritarian learning. It addresses areas for future research, with particular emphasis placed on the need to ascertain if the findings here can be extrapolated to cases in other regions like Africa, the Middle East, and East Asia. The chapter concludes by providing some policy recommendations, providing measures and suggestions to cope with and react to the continued growth of authoritarian regimes worldwide.

# 2 Measuring Authoritarian Tendencies in Belarus, Moldova, Russia, and Ukraine

Recent decades have seen the spread of regimes that claim the mantle of democracy even as their true democratic status remains uncertain ... They resist easy comparisons, both to each other and across different measures – which has made reliable indicators of their democratic quality all the more important for both academics and policymakers.[1]

## 2.1 Introduction

In the 1990s democracy became the only game in town with international organisations and Western states – principally concerned with making the world democratic – and authoritarian regimes had to cloak themselves in the vestments of a democracy. These regimes created parliaments and political parties, and ran elections. While these structures were controlled, it was hoped that their formation would hide the undemocratic reality. Although such events as the American intervention into Afghanistan and Iraq tarnished external democratic promotion, copying the trappings of democracy remains a key survival strategy of authoritarian leaders and those wanting to consolidate power. This chapter will provide a methodology for gathering evidence of authoritarian learning in the four case studies and assess the extent of authoritarian tendencies in the four case studies.

Having investigated in the previous chapter what is meant by authoritarian learning and the different networks involved, we turn to a brief chapter on providing a methodology of authoritarian learning and highlighting authoritarian tendencies in the four case studies. First, there is the so-called black box problem when analysing authoritarian regimes and those governments that do not publish much information on actions. The governments of Belarus and (especially) Russia claim that they are democracies and so do not want to publish information

---

[1] Gunitsky, 2015b.

that diminishes this perception. Similarly, leaders with authoritarian tendencies in Moldova and Ukraine who want to retain ties to regional organisations like the EU and the North Atlantic Treaty Organization (NATO) are unlikely to publish information that could reduce those ties. Therefore, it is essential to provide a comprehensive methodology that gathers sufficient information to show that authoritarian learning does exist and is happening. The first section of this chapter addresses this.

Second, the chapter analyses trajectories of authoritarian tendencies in the four case studies. we use V-Dem to highlight to highlight different periods of attempted authoritarian consolidation. Third, the chapter analyses several research questions to be addressed in subsequent chapters. Analysis of an appropriate methodology, investigation of periods of authoritarian tendencies, and exploration of research questions will provide clarity on the authoritarian learning analysed in the next few chapters.

## 2.2 The Black Box Problem: A Methodology for Authoritarian Learning

Tracing authoritarian learning remains difficult, as authoritarian regimes are opaque and information, when it does permeate out, is nearly always out of date. The difficulty of finding evidence is complicated by the fact that little is written down, as decisions are often given orally or left to others to implement. For instance, in Belarus, Lukashenka does not write down orders but vocalises them, giving him deniability should the order go too far, or not be executed appropriately.[2] Similarly, the Kremlin uses *otmashka*,[3] which gives the implementer leeway and Putin deniability should the person carrying out the order go too far, or not far enough (Pavlovsky, 2016). Putin signs 'I agree' to documents, failing to state what it is that Putin agrees with, thereby leaving it to other personnel to implement these plans.[4] Therefore, with no direct evidence of learning emanating from the four case studies, the researcher must take a circuitous route to locate examples of authoritarian learning.

---

[2] Personal interview: TK02846.    [3] Meaning 'Go ahead'.
[4] Personal interview: RW39802.

This indirect path forces the researcher to rely extensively on inference, although there are ways to make these more concrete, and show that through the available evidence it is highly likely that learning happens. One way to do this is to analyse legislation say on NGOs and trace similarities in legislation back to their source. As mentioned, Azerbaijan (2013), Tajikistan (2014), Kazakhstan (2016), Ukraine (2017), and China (2018) passed legislation which either directly limited foreign funding for NGOs or increased their bureaucratic workload. This trend of five restrictive laws over a five-year period, points to learning from a common source, and except for Ukrainian and Chinese legislation, legislation in Azerbaijan, Kazakhstan, and Tajikistan appears 'to be largely copied; the legislation is almost identical in its language and effect' to the 2012 Russian legislation (Van de Velde, 2017). Although not copying Russian legislation word-for-word, the Chinese NGO law shares characteristics to the 2012 Russian foreign agents law, as it restricts foreign funding for NGOs, so it is likely that the Chinese regime learnt from earlier Russian legislation (Plantan, 2017). Similarly, the Russian 2012 foreign agents law served as inspiration for Bankova to pass restrictive NGO legislation, and much of the Ukrainian law comes from earlier 2006 Russian legislation that bureaucratised the work of NGOs.[5]

Following legislative trajectory is one way to determine that authoritarian learning occurs. If several states, particularly those from the same region, pass similar legislation, there is likely a common denominator and they are learning from each other. This is the approach taken by scholars such as Max Bader (2014), and Lemon and Antonov (2020). Investigating policy transfer emphasises that autocracies share legislation and likely are engaged with one another to discuss said laws. Analysing the legislative trail is itself part of authoritarian learning, as elites look at neighbouring laws and likely engage in dialogue with one another on the issue. While a crucial part of authoritarian learning, policy transfer does not explain why authoritarian elites learn, how they learn, and what they learn.

---

[5] Personal interview: JH58291.

Policy transfer is one method to open the black box of authoritarian regimes and show that learning occurs, but there are other techniques that can be used to locate evidence of authoritarian learning. One approach is to analyse known meetings and see what was said through document analysis, or the websites of governments or organisations, which act as pointers to learning.[6] It is difficult to show the smoking gun, but deductions can be made which highlight learning. However, for the most part determining what was said at meetings remains difficult, due to the informality of most meetings, resulting in only vague details leaking out. Another option is to trace the comings and goings of people in each regime and locate who they meet with and how often. Determining familial or business ties is another way of finding out who an individual is close to. Tracing the location of people in each regime is a way to infer learning. This is made easier when regimes share people, which is a particular characteristic of the Kremlin. For instance, Surkov, a former deputy head of the Russian presidential administration, was until 2020 the Kremlin's man in Ukraine. When former Ukrainian president Viktor Yanukovych fled in 2014, Surkov became the Kremlin's man in the Donetsk People's Republic and the Luhansk People's Republic (Peshkov, 2016). Viktor Zubrytsky, who ran the Titushki and Anti-Maidan militias during the Euromaidan, worked closely with Surkov after he fled to Russia, exchanging information on the Euromaidan (LB. ua, 2017a). In 2004, during the Ukrainian presidential election, President Kuchma hired Russian political technologists such as Gleb Pavlovsky, who was the Kremlin's master political tactician, to win Yanukovych the presidency (Trenin, 2011: 89). As well as Russian influence in the other three case studies, many personnel in these case studies were born, lived, or worked in Russia, and this is particularly the case for personnel in the Belarusian, regime who retain close ties to the Kremlin.[7]

Getting inside the black box of regimes that do not provide much information on their activities is difficult and the researcher is likely to have to take a convoluted path to uncover evidence. Authoritarian learning can only ever be inductive, as it is nearly impossible to access intricate details of a regime and attend top security meetings. Therefore, one is left with inference, using the strongest evidence to state that X, or Xs, cause Y, or Ys. The task of locating viable data is

---

[6] Personal interview: UR24751.     [7] Personal interview: YR52870.

made easier using an appropriate methodology that opens the black box to gather sufficient evidence that this process does indeed occur.

While one option was to analyse a single case study to determine whether authoritarian learning occurs; we wanted to understand how authoritarian regimes learn, why they learn, and what they learn. Therefore, to explain authoritarian learning, we concentrated on states from a single region, specifically the post-Soviet space. It is difficult to investigate phenomena in the post-Soviet region without including Russia, so Russia as the regional hegemon became one case study. However, we felt that at least one other case study was needed. We considered countries like Azerbaijan, Kazakhstan, and Uzbekistan. While Kazakhstan has close cultural, economic, historical, and political ties with Russia, we felt that a more appropriate case study of an established authoritarian regime with such links to Russia was Belarus. But analysis of two established authoritarian regimes is insufficient to understand authoritarian learning. As we are interested in authoritarian tendencies in understanding authoritarian learning there needs to be analysis of case studies that are not established authoritarian regimes but have periods where leaders with authoritarian tendencies look to try to consolidate power. Therefore, to best understand authoritarian learning, we needed to have case studies on these regime-types as well.

Consequently, we needed to analyse one post-Soviet state where leaders and elites have had authoritarian tendencies and periods of attempted consolidation. As a comparison with Belarus and Russia, we chose to study two cases that had periods of attempted authoritarian consolidation. In the post-Soviet space, there are not many examples of this regime-type. While we could have chosen Armenia and Kyrgyzstan, the feeling was that at least one of the case studies needed to have strong links to Belarus and Russia. Therefore, Ukraine was considered the most relevant case, with strong ties to the first two case studies while not being an established authoritarian regime. The choice of the final case study followed similar selection criteria, with the necessity that the chosen case required links with the other three. Although harder to justify, Moldova was chosen due to cultural, political, economic, and especially geographical ties.

Pinpointing a viable time frame is relatively arbitrary, as the time frames of the individual regimes are distinct from one another. Including every learning event from the demise of the Soviet Union

in 1991 to the present (2021) would make any investigation convoluted and could detract from explaining learning. Therefore, 2000
was chosen as the start date of the analysis the year 2000 was chosen
as the start of the analysis because it is when Putin took power in
Russia. This was considered the most appropriate starting point. As
the regional hegemon in the post-Soviet space, Russia dominates,
and Putin has dominated Russia. Although Lukashenka does control
Belarus, Belarus does not have the same pulling power as Russia and
having rejected analysis starting in 1991 due to the long time frame it
would seem strange to begin the investigation three years later in
1994 when Lukashenka came to power. Choosing a time-period
based on Moldova and Ukraine would present other challenges as
there has not been one dominant leader – with the partial exception
of Leonid Kuchma and Vladimir Voronin. Moldovan and Ukrainian
regimes do not historically have long tenure, with few regimes having more than one term in power.[8] The year 2000 was the most
appropriate date. In 2000, Putin became Russian president and
Kuchma moved Ukraine towards semi-authoritarianism. In 2001,
Voronin – who had been interior minister of the Moldavian Soviet
Socialist Republic – came to power and began consolidation. The
disappearance of opposition activists in Belarus began in 1999 and
by 2004 Lukashenka had fully consolidated power. Therefore, 2000
is the most appropriate year to begin analysis. The end point of the
investigation is early 2021 because (1) the analysis needs to stop
somewhere and (2) the Moldovan presidential elections in
November 2020 are a good cut-off date as there are no other elections in the case studies until at least 2023, unless something dramatic occurs. Early 2021 is a good date as a cut-off as it allows for
the Moldovan 2020 elections to be analysed to ascertain possible
learning. Any cut-off point is always arbitrary, and a day is a long
time in politics, with information only coming out later. Therefore,
2021 is as good a time as any to end the analysis.

As much evidence for authoritarian learning is inferred by analysing
how X, or Xs, cause Y, it is crucial to choose research methods that turn

---

[8] The exceptions are Kuchma in Ukraine and Voronin in Moldova. However,
Kuchma's first term began in 1994, which like Lukashenka, would result in too
long period of analysis.

the *inference* that learning happens into *concrete evidence* that it does. We use process-tracing and interviews, as these methods will support the evidence that X does cause Y and complements the comparativist research design used here. Process-tracing acts as 'a procedure for identifying steps in a causal process leading to the outcome of a given dependent variable of a particular case in a historical context' (George and Bennett, 2005: 176). Process-tracing breaks down causal processes into smaller pieces to better understand social phenomena, thereby connecting one procedure to another to allow researchers to assess how decisions are made and the reasons for those choices. Process-tracing attempts to 'validate a causal relationship between independent and dependent variables' (Anbrosio and Tolstrup, 2019) and 'is a method for unpacking causality, that aims at studying what happens between X and Y and beyond' (Trampusch and Palier, 2016: 438). With process-tracing, a researcher can trace engagement and dialogue, and analyse where a policy originated. Solid inferences can be made by in-depth analysis that authoritarian regimes share policies and practices.

There is one important issue regarding process-tracing and authoritarianism, which is the problem that Gonzalez-Ocantos and LaPorte (2021) term 'missingness', where the causal chain has missing links, making process-tracing, with its reliance on causal links, difficult to implement. This can be because of denial of access to state archives or regime members refusing to speak. The Kremlin provides more data than the other case studies, especially Belarus and Moldova, as unlike the other three case studies, the Russian authorities provide websites and documentary evidence. By contrast, the Belarusian presidential administration and various security services remain 'hidden' and do not publish information,[9] making gathering data hard. Gonzalez-Ocantos and LaPorte (2021) address how to deal with gaps in 'the evidentiary record', focusing on how to 'contextualize the data generation process', which considers what an actor's actions would be, and accounts for data loss. Gonzalez-Ocantos and LaPorte (2021) contend that data loss can be rectified through in-depth understanding of the subject and the use of second-hand sources if primary sources such as interviews are unavailable. This is the process that I rely on to provide evidence that the four case studies engage in authoritarian learning.

---

[9] Personal interview: KW37410.

An example of how process-tracing will be used in the four case studies is the 2014 Ukrainian dictatorship laws passed during the Euromaidan to help Bankova justify clearing central Kyiv. This package of fourteen laws was copied from earlier Russian and Belarusian NGO and judicial legislation, often being copied word-for-word from previous Belarusian and Russian laws (Coynash, 2014; Wilson, 2014a; Snyder, 2014; Koshkina, 2015: 173). The legislation was forced through parliament, eight days after Yanukovych met Putin secretly in Russia (Wilson, 2014c: 81; Leshchenko, 2014b). By analysing meetings, legislation, and practices, learning can be shown to occur, and an appropriate methodology of case studies, process-tracing, and interviews provides information on elite movements and meetings, thereby giving conclusive evidence of learning.

Interviews are a process of trial and error with the researcher engaging in self-learning when conducting interviews, as in my experience every interview is different and is therefore a learning opportunity. We use semi-structured interviews as these personalise interviewee experiences and responses and allow open-ended questions where the respondent can expand on an issue and give further information. Semi-structured interviews help interviewees relax, as they are a conversation, and they provide information that a structured interview would simply not return due to its specificity and rigidity. By using semi-structured interviews follow-up questions can be asked as can personal and theoretical questions to increase understanding of a topic. Interviews were conducted with researchers, academics, journalists, current and former government officials, and people working in civil society organisations. Interviews were conducted between 2016 and 2022 with initial and follow-up interviews occurring during this six-year period. In total, ninety people from across the four case studies – and outside – were interviewed for this monograph. Due to the research focus of investigating authoritarian regimes we decided to anonymise all interviews giving each interviewee a distinctive code – using numbers and letters – that protects their identity and makes it harder for them to be located and face any repercussions.

Triangulation allows researchers to overcome intrinsic weaknesses and biases that may exist in the data. By combining research methods, triangulation reduces such eventualities, while increasing the validity of the research. By using more than one research method I use what is termed multiple methodologies, using different qualitative research methods to find applicable data. When conducting elite interviews, triangulation is useful as it allows data to be collected from different sources, such as documentary sources and background work, before conducting the said interview. Triangulation allows researchers to use different research methods to complement one another and locate specific areas that increase evidence gathering. Triangulation is useful in interviews, as interviewees may not remember key events, or may look at events with rose-tinted spectacles, or even lie. Use of other research methods to triangulate evidence reduces the chances of incorrect information making it into the analysis and increases validity.

## 2.3 Representation and Analysis of Authoritarian Tendencies

To analyse authoritarian learning and argue that there are periods of attempted authoritarian consolidation in the cases studied, we investigate the democracy scores of each state. Gunitsky (2015a) correctly argues that measuring democracy is difficult due to the different democracy-measuring datasets having distinctive definitions of what democracy is. This has affected scores have seen considerable divergence in democratic datasets when analysing the same country. (Gunitsky, 2015b: 113). On the whole, scores provided by these datasets have been effective at finding highly authoritarian states such as Turkmenistan – and Belarus in the case of this analysis – but have seen highly skewed results for states like Moldova, Ukraine, and even Russia (Gunitsky, 2015b: 139). Although Freedom House is by no means the only offender, it is seemingly the most popular measure. We are not concerned here with the potential ideological biases of an organisation with close ties to the American government (Giannone, 2010; 2014), but rather with the methodological problems that lead to us rejecting the use of Freedom House data.

There has been a wealth of literature on the difficulty of Freedom House turning largely qualitative data into a quantitative score (Armstrong, 2011: 661–2; Bollen and Paxton, 2000: 79; Cheibub, Grävingholt, and Kästner, 2010; Coppedge and Gerring, 2011: 250–1; Denk, 2013: 3462–3; Munck and Verkuilen, 2002: 21). Freedom House uses an array of scores but provides little justification in how these individual scores are weighted (Gunitsky, 2015b: 117) and the range of these scores results in a skew for those countries that are neither fully democratic nor authoritarian. This skews results, so that states closer to the authoritarian end of the spectrum look worse than they should (Gunitsky, 2015b: 125).

However, this leads to a quandary. Gunitsky rejects a range of datasets for providing skewed results but leaves it up to researchers to decide by acknowledging that scholars must accept certain trade-offs when using a particular dataset (Gunitsky, 2015b: 121). However, there is one measure that does not receive analysis, and this is the Varieties of Democracy (V-Dem) dataset. Unlike other measures, which start with a definition of democracy, V-Dem takes a multi-dimensional approach, negating a definition and allowing researchers to use the categories that fit their own understanding of democracy. The use of highly disaggregated indicators allows for investigation of what constitutes democracy in the minds of individual researchers (Lindberg et al. 2014: 159–60). The dataset stretches back – in many cases to 1789 – thereby providing a comprehensive analysis over time. While historical data gathering can be seen as subjective depending on the views of individual researchers, this is less of an issue here, as the period of analysis runs from 2000 to 2021.

V-Dem offers five principles of democracy: deliberative, egalitarian, electoral, liberal, and participatory. Although there are always questions about data reliability collected by coders through a questionnaire that may be tainted by bias, V-Dem provides comprehensive data 'that was previously understood to be too expensive to collect' (Bernhard et al., 2017: 344). The V-Dem dataset uses over 350 variables to measure democracy and goes as far back as 1789. Therefore, it offers a comprehensive picture of democratisation in 202 countries over a long time period, considering nuances in each country and providing a level of data that other democracy datasets miss (Coppedge et al., 2016: 581; Lindberg et al., 2014: 161). Therefore, on V-Dem if a state scores between 0 and 0.5 it is some form of autocracy. Scores of 0.5 to 1 denote a democracy. This is somewhat arbitrary, but, as we argue, autocracies and democracies are opposite ends of the same spectrum so there will be strong and weak autocracies and democracies. We took the yearly scores for the two main democracy variables of electoral (polyarchy) and liberal democracy. It was felt that these two variables were the most appropriate when defining democracy – or autocracy when it comes to the cases studied. These two variables were the most representative for highlighting that Belarus and Russia can be classified as established authoritarian regimes and that Moldova and Ukraine have periods – at least – of weak democracy Using Python, we ran a regression analysis of the two variables, took the score for both, and developed an average for our democracy score. We gave each a weighting in terms of importance to our understanding of democracy. This provides a single yearly score and highlights a trend of authoritarian consolidation in Belarus and Russia, or periods of attempted consolidation in Moldova and Ukraine.

The purpose of this section of the chapter is to highlight that there are periods of attempted authoritarian tendencies in the four case studies, although consolidation is further along in some than others. However, authoritarian consolidation is but one practice that authoritarian-minded elites would use. A controlled liberalisation may also be a tactic used to increase popular legitimacy and reduce the potential of protest pressure. The V-Dem data cannot show that learning is happening, but it can show that – at the very least – there are periods of attempted authoritarian consolidation. By showing the V-Dem scores for each case we can highlight the trends of authoritarianism in the four case studies, emphasising that Belarusian and Russian elites have created established authoritarian polities, whereas periods of authoritarian consolidation are more fluid and shorter in Moldova and Ukraine. We are not concerned here with providing a historical analysis of the political trends in the four case studies between 2000 and 2021.

As mentioned, we are using the graph below to show trajectories of authoritarian tendencies in the four case studies. Gunitsky (2015b) was correct to state that all the datasets used to measure democracy had methodological issues. The two most popular measures – Freedom House and Polity IV – had significant methodological shortcomings. This is especially so for Freedom House, which has changed its methodology and scoring system at times but has not changed previous scores to fit the new methodology or scoring systems (Gunitsky, 2015b: 123). This makes highlighting a trend using Freedom House data difficult as scores before changes do not correlate with scores after. For instance, Freedom House changed its scoring system from 1 to 7 to 1 to 100 after 2018, which has heavily skewed

Of course, there are likely methodological issues with using the V-Dem measure, but allowing researchers to use the variables that represent their interpretation of democracy is more an issue of the researcher's understanding of democracy than the data being at fault.

By using all the labelled democracy variables, we provide a clear representation of the nuances of democracy. While our weighting system
could be re-interpreted, we feel that this is a good representation of the
meaning of democracy. Unlike the skewed data that befalls Freedom
House and Polity IV measures (Gunitsky, 2015b: 137), V-Dem measures are left to the interpretation of the researcher. Therefore, any
criticisms are left at our door rather than with the dataset.

Figure 2.1 shows the V-Dem scores of the four case studies between
2000 and 2021. Although these scores are somewhat arbitrary, we argue
that states that score between 0.5 and 1.0 are closer to the democratic
end of the spectrum and that those that score between 0.0 and 0.5 are
nearer the authoritarian end of the scale. As the graph clearly shows,
elites in Belarus and Russia have established authoritarian regimes. By
contrast, Moldova and Ukraine have scores that fluctuate significantly
with periods of weak democracy and weak autocracy, although it is the
periods of weak autocracy that are in the majority.

The measures cannot show learning, but they do emphasise periods
of attempted power consolidation or reductions in this trajectory.
Although further consolidation – or attempts to initiate it – points
to learning, periods of liberalisation can point to learning as the
regime relaxes control to increase popular legitimacy. The data cannot show learning, but it can highlight trends, and it is up to the next
chapters to really bring the evidence about authoritarian learning to
light. Treisman (2020) showed that authoritarian elites often lose
power because they made mistakes, rather than because of popular

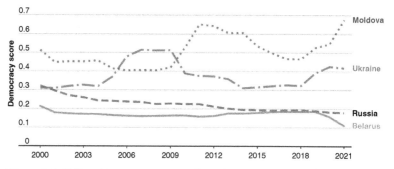

**Figure 2.1** V-Dem Democracy scores from 2000 to 2021 in Belarus, Moldova,
Russia, and Ukraine
Source: V-Dem

mobilisation. Consequently, elites fearing a possible Muammar al-Gaddafi scenario of having their bodies dragged through the streets of the capital or being tried and executed like Saddam Hussein learn methods to ensure survival. Often, they get these wrong, but it is a process of constant adaptation. Through a combination of diffusion, lesson-drawing, policy transfer, and linkage, authoritarian-minded elites – particularly those in a neighbouring vicinity – are likely to draw lessons from one another in the quest for retaining power.

Although the V-Dem data cannot show learning, it highlights the different nuances of authoritarianism in the four case studies. The measures show consolidation in Belarus and Russia, with Belarus showing a slight liberalisation between 2010 and 2020, perhaps pointing to the fear that the economic recessions that befell Belarus after the global recession in 2008 and sanctions against Russia would lead to protests if the authorities retained the level of control in the 2000s. Moldova and Ukraine paint a different picture of fluctuations over time with greater attempts by elites at power consolidation or less. The V-Dem data offers a representation pointing to the likelihood of learning being of crucial importance in how elites in the four case studies operate. Having investigated the methodology and use of V-Dem in this section and the previous one, we turn to addressing the research questions before concluding the chapter.

## 2.4 Analysis of Research Questions

To provide a base for the next chapters, we provide research questions and explain how these fit with the research. The seven research questions form the basis for the investigation of authoritarian learning, using the four case studies throughout the rest of the book. Each is tabulated below, complete with explanations about how we intend to analyse them:

---

1 **Do authoritarian regimes collaborate, support, engage in dialogue, and learn from each other?**
   A key point is to ascertain whether authoritarian regimes support and engage in dialogue with one another, the extent of that dialogue, and which state institutions are involved. This helps determine the extent of learning in the four case studies.

---

2  What specific circumstances exist for an authoritarian regime to support others?

   We establish the circumstances for regime support. Does it occur during protests, or do regimes engage in developing tactics during peaceful periods to counter future protests? Are secure regimes or regional hegemons the ones who engage in supporting other authoritarian regimes? Understanding these questions determines when learning occurs.

3  Did the other case regimes react to democratic revolutions (such as the Colour Revolutions, Arab Spring, and Euromaidan) like Russia did? Why and when do these regimes collaborate, support, talk, and learn from one another?

   It is often advocated that the Kremlin reacts to these events, but do other authoritarian regimes respond similarly? If so, it points to possible authoritarian collaboration to prevent such events and emphasises that Russia is not only doing this. It is pertinent to understand why authoritarian regimes learn. It could be for survival, or to counter democratic principles. The when is also imperative, for when do regimes offer support and determine when it is necessary?

4  Does the regional hegemon diffuse learning to others, or can other regimes diffuse methods to the hegemon?

   Within the post-Soviet space, does Russia, as the regional hegemon, bolster or promote authoritarianism, and is the learning strictly hierarchical with the regional hegemon on the top, or can Russia learn from other regimes in the post-Soviet region?

5  How can deliberate support for democracy prevention be distinguished from general authoritarian collaboration?

   Determining general authoritarian collaboration and democratisation prevention are difficult to measure. But it can be determined that dialogue, tactics, and meetings between regimes to counter democratisation points to a distinction between authoritarian collaboration and say economic cooperation.

6  What tactics or methods do these regimes copy from each other?

   Do regimes copy tactics from each other? Do they, for instance, copy ideas on preventing NGOs, the media, and the opposition, or do they also improve the economy, thereby improving their legitimacy and reducing the potential for protests?

7 **Why do authoritarian regimes copy each other?**
This can be summed up in one word: survival! But is this the only reason or do authoritarian regimes club together to undermine democratisation? Do they prefer having other authoritarian regimes in the region?

## 2.5 Conclusion

The chapter set out to provide a methodology that will underpin the rest of the book. We use a research design of case studies, analysing Belarus, Moldova, Russia, and Ukraine, and a methodology of process-tracing and interviews. Having discussed the methodology, we moved to analysis of authoritarian tendency trends in the four case studies over the 2000 to 2021 period of analysis. Using V-Dem measures we showed that there are fluctuations in the cases studied and that it is possible that these points are – in part at least – due to learning. We then drew up some research questions that will form the basis for understanding authoritarian learning in the preceding chapters.

# 3 | *Learning from External Failure*

We only remember Gorbachev not because he succeeded but because he failed![1]

## 3.1 Introduction

The quote above emphasises the issue of failure and that one remembers failure far more than success as failure tends to lead to significant change. While Mikhail Gorbachev is lauded in Western states for significantly contributing to the end of the Cold War and communism in Eastern Europe and the Soviet Union, he had not set out to achieve these outcomes when he became Soviet leader. Therefore, he is remembered for failure globally.[2] In Russia, Gorbachev is reviled as the villain who single-handedly ended the Soviet Union (Monaghan, 2016: 7; Yablokov, 2018: 59). As with many Russians and peoples in other post-Soviet States, Putin retains a poor view of Gorbachev's attempted reforms, as Putin was in Dresden during most of the Gorbachev period and so was 'an outsider to perestroika', which left Putin upon his return to St Petersburg in 1990 isolated, with Gorbachev's policies a ready source of blame for the Soviet collapse (Hill and Gaddy, 2015: 118). Gorbachev's reneging on the Brezhnev Doctrine and proclamation of the Sinatra Doctrine[3] precipitated the collapse of the East European satellite states, which in turn contributed to the weakening of the Soviet Union. Putin, who witnessed first-hand the collapse of the East German regime, retains a fear that events such as the collapse of the East European satellite states and the Soviet Union could happen again (Hill and Gaddy, 2015: 113). As many current Kremlin elites were officials of the Soviet *Komitet Gosudarstvennoi Bezopasnosti* (KGB)

---

[1] Personal Interview: VB18259.    [2] Personal Interview: VB18259.
[3] The alternative name for Gorbachev's allowing East European satellite states to control their own affairs.

and other Soviet institutions, even in 2019, the Russian security services have drawn lessons from the 1980s, expressly from the Solidarność[4] movement and the economic protests in Gdańsk, which spread across Poland and eventually into Eastern Europe, culminating in the demise of the Eastern European communist satellite states. The Kremlin is averse to any reforms, radical or otherwise, for fear that they may lose control as Gorbachev did (Galeotti, 2019c).

The run on the bank that Solnick (1998) uses to describe the collapse of the Soviet Union is apt when describing how authoritarian leaders react to crises. They need to stop all bank runs for fear that one will result in their loss of power. Putin is likely not the only post-Soviet leader who fears a bank run as extensive as the one that led to the Soviet collapse. It is likely that other post-Soviet leaders such as Lukashenka also fear such an event and are, therefore, constantly adapting and learning. While many Moldovan and Ukrainian elites are less likely to have the same power longevity as in Belarus and Russia, many elites in Moldova and Ukraine lived through the Soviet period. Many were former Soviet officials. For example, Vladimir Voronin was minister of internal affairs of the Moldavian Soviet Socialist Republic between 1988 and 1990, and Leonid Kuchma was a member of the Central Committee of the Ukrainian Communist Party from 1976 until 1989. Both Voronin and Kuchma managed to gauge the political winds and left their posts before the Soviet collapse. But the Soviet period and collapse likely resonated for both – and other post-Soviet leaders – and for Voronin, who created the Party of Communists of the Republic of Moldova (PCRM) in 1993, he never really left. Consequently, it is likely the Soviet collapse coloured the thinking of many post-Soviet elites and is an example of learning from internal failure.

External failure has been a core argument of the authoritarian learning literature to explain why other authoritarian regimes learn. The scenes of an authoritarian leader being dragged through the streets and then beaten to death, as with Muammar al-Gaddafi in Misrata, Libya, fleeing the presidential palace as crowds pour through the entrance, as with Nicolae Ceaușescu in Romania, or escaping at night after protesters won the streets, as Viktor Yanukovych did in Kyiv, not only

---

[4] Solidarity (Solidarność in Polish) was formed in 1980 at the Lenin Shipyard in Gdańsk. Led by Lech Wałęsa, it became the largest non-communist trade union in Poland and by 1989 had negotiated semi-free elections, resulting in the defeat of the communist regime and the emergence of a Solidarność-led government.

make for great media footage but worry other authoritarian regimes. The demise of authoritarian regimes across the Middle East and North Africa with longevity of over thirty years would have alarmed post-Soviet regimes, and as will be seen in this chapter, the Kremlin especially was worried. Similarly, the demise of an authoritarian leader in a neighbouring state brings possible copycat implications and the diffusion of protests from one state to bordering polities. The end of the Euromaidan in Kyiv has alarmed other post-Soviet authoritarian regimes. External failure has understandably received much attention in the authoritarian learning literature. However, as seen in this chapter and Chapter 4, internal and external failure and success are crucial to better understanding authoritarian learning.

To investigate failure and its relevance to authoritarian learning, it is necessary to briefly define what is meant by failure. Leaders with authoritarian tendencies want to maintain control at all costs. Therefore, anything contributing to loss of control is a failure. Clearly if the leader is forced to flee – Yanukovych in 2014 – or is deposed – Muammar al-Gaddafi in Libya – this is failure. Taking Solnick's (1998) bank-run analogy, where the bank does not want investors to know it lacks cash, authoritarian elites do not want people to believe they cannot maintain power. A bank is only viable if people believe it has money. If there are stories that the bank lacks liquidity, then there is a run as people withdraw their savings potentially causing a collapse. This is similar for authoritarians, who must show that they can keep power. If they cannot, it will likely lead to a bank run that becomes increasingly harder to stop. Similarly, authoritarians must continually adapt, fearing any potential threat as the one that could spiral, resulting in protests and possible loss of power. Authoritarian leaders cannot be seen to fail and so they develop the best palette for survival.

However, what constitutes a failure for authoritarians? The most recent example of collapse in the post-Soviet space is Yanukovych fleeing after the Euromaidan protests in February 2014. Although protests often occur in the four case studies, authoritarians nearly always survive – particularly so in Belarus and Russia. While there were protests in Russia in 2005, 2011–12, 2016, 2017, 2018, and 2019, with the 2011–12 protests being particularly significant, the Kremlin has survived them all. Similarly, protests in 2006, 2010, 2017, and 2020 did not result in regime change in Belarus, and in the case of the current protests have not led to Lukashenka's downfall.

The ongoing protests may eventually be the start of the end of Lukashenka, but at the time of writing he remains firmly in power. Therefore, protests, if survived, are not a failure, as the leader did not lose power. Rather, previous protests are learnt from to better enhance survival chances in the future. Regime collapse such as the downfall of the Yanukovych government in 2014 is one instance of authoritarian failure. This chapter and the one following analyse learning from failure. Here we investigate learning examples from external failure, looking at reaction to the 2004 Orange Revolution, the Arab Spring, and the Euromaidan in the four case studies. While some evidence of learning is missing, particularly for Moldova, available data raises interesting questions and shows learning. We start with another regime's reaction to the collapse of the Soviet Union, China.

## 3.2 Learning from External Failure

Learning from external failure is when authoritarian regimes learn from the failures of other authoritarian regimes, with the collapse of one authoritarian regime, or in some cases several regimes, creating fear in neighbouring authoritarian regimes, which induces learning to reduce the chance that the neighbours' failure will occur domestically. The failure of authoritarian regimes can live long in the memory for other authoritarian leaders. This longevity of failure is highlighted by the Kremlin developing lessons from the 1989 revolutions in Eastern Europe and the resulting collapse of the Soviet Union in 1991. In 2019, the Russian security service trained against a potential Solidarność movement, developing methods to cope with protests precipitated by economic failure (Galeotti, 2019c). This points to a realisation in the Kremlin that economic-induced protests are likely in this current period of sanctions and low natural resource prices and so they are learning how to cope with future protests. Many personnel in the top echelons of the Kremlin, including Putin himself, were former KGB agents or worked in Soviet state institutions, and so have first-hand experience of events that started in the docks of Gdańsk and culminated in the collapse of the communist satellite states in Eastern Europe. During the last days of the East German regime, Putin faced down a crowd in Dresden outside the KGB building, and when Putin asked for support from the local Soviet military, the message that 'Moscow is silent' resonated with him, seeing this as the increasing failure of the

Soviet Union (Hill and Gaddy, 2015: 181). Witnessing one of the 1989 revolutions first-hand was a life experience for Putin and has affected his thinking in trying to stop such a situation in Russia. Therefore, Putin and others in the Kremlin have been so averse to large protests (Hill and Gaddy, 2015: 115, 181–2) for fear that an East European situation or a Colour Revolution may occur. It is likely that external failure, especially of neighbours, resonates with authoritarian regimes as this failure may diffuse from the neighbours, and so authoritarian elites pay attention to external failure. Even failure from thirty years later still resonates for authoritarian leaders who learn from such examples.

### 3.2.1 Chinese Learning from the Soviet Collapse

A cataclysm such as the Soviet collapse likely induced and continued prompt learning from other authoritarian regimes, and China is an example of authoritarian learning from the Soviet collapse. This is highlighted by the reaction to the collapse of communist regimes in Eastern Europe epitomised by the 1989 massacre on Tiananmen Square. While the regime was prepared to use repression, when necessary, the Chinese authorities undertook a detailed analysis of the Soviet collapse, deciding that top-down reforms would weaken the structure of the state. Being seen to react to bottom-up demands early on would give the regime legitimacy. The Soviet Union had tried to impose reforms that state structures were unable – or unwilling – to adhere to. Adaptation and fluidity were seen by the Chinese government as an effective means to alleviate a collapse like in the Soviet Union (Gregory and Zhou, 2009). For the Chinese authorities, Gorbachev had retreated from Stalinism and this weakened Soviet ideology, which for the Chinese government had been the basis of Soviet legitimacy. By damaging the main source of regime legitimacy Gorbachev made his reforms unpopular among the Soviet bureaucracy and wider populace, thereby creating a large anti-regime support base (Greer Meisels, 2013). For the Chinese authorities, Gorbachev was viewed 'not as a far-sighted reformer but as a disastrous failure, a man who led his country, and his party, to national calamity' (Palmer, 2016). Gorbachev's reforms of *Perestroika* and *Glasnost* opened the system to criticism, which weakened Soviet legitimacy (Dimitrov, 2013: 37). By retracting the Brezhnev Doctrine – allowing the Soviet Union to intervene in the

East European communist satellite states – Gorbachev emphasised Soviet weakness and left allies to fend for themselves. The collapse of these regimes served as an example of how to change the Soviet Union, and these ideas diffused back to the Soviet Union and undermined support in the bureaucracy and security services to maintain the Soviet experiment. Soviet failure to make its citizenry richer left the regime lacking legitimacy. Although the Chinese regime had started economic reforms in the mid-1980s, these were continued after the Soviet collapse to create wealth among Chinese, thereby improving government legitimacy (Dimitrov, 2013: 25; Guihai, 2010: 512).

Since the collapse of the Soviet Union, the Chinese regime has developed highly effective opinion polling capabilities with the purpose being to gauge public opinion to make minimal reforms when necessary (Dimitrov, 2013: 7). While this is not a direct consequence of learning from the Soviet collapse, the operation of efficient opinion polling capacity allows the government to know what is likely to lead to protests. This allows the authorities to stay one step ahead of what could lead to a spiral in demonstrations. The Soviet collapse was one of the pivotal moments of the twentieth century, and for China, a regime ideologically aligned, the collapse of the model would have had a significant effect on thinking among its elite (Greer Meisels, 2012). Consequently, developing effective opinion polling capabilities was likely influenced by the collapse of the Soviet Union and the inability of the Soviet elite to adapt quickly. The Chinese regime uses polls to gain feedback on legislation and new policy, while allowing citizens to voice opinions (Truex, 2017: 330, 353). Keane (2018) had labelled the Chinese Communist Party – and by association the elite – as the 'listening party', using polls to ascertain the public mood towards controversial policy changes and to offer an early warning system for growing dissatisfaction (Keane, 2018).

Although more research needs to be done to ascertain whether there has been copying, public opinion polling is run in Belarus and Russia, with the Belarusian regime using several polling firms to return opinion that the regime may not like,[5] likely acting as an early warning system against future demonstrations. Future research needs to determine whether this effective public opinion polling was a direct lesson learned by the Belarusian regime from the Soviet collapse or whether it was

---

[5] Personal interview: KW37410.

copied from China. The Russian authorities also have efficient public opinion polling capacity, although it is used to gauge public opinion and then use state television to re-cast views into a positive regime view (Rogov and Ananyev, 2018: 204–5). While this has created twisted feedback which distorts what is really occurring,[6] many in the Russian elite look at China as an example of what the Soviet Union would look like had it existed.[7] Therefore, China has become a model for the Russian authorities to copy and it is likely that the effective Chinese public opinion polling system has been copied by Russia, although it is also likely that the Russian authorities learnt from the Soviet collapse.

Although the Chinese authorities had begun policy experimentation using regions as testing grounds before the Soviet collapse, these experiments grew in number in the 1990s and 2000s. For the regions, knowing that their experimentation could go country-wide leads to efficiency and competitiveness (Perry and Heilmann, 2011: 20). A dialogue between the regions and the Beijing bureaucracy means the regime knows what is happening in the provinces. Experimentation corrects for mistakes, allowing the regime to create an adaptive authoritarianism to alleviate potential crises (Heilmann, 2008: 2–3, 23). Representatives in parliament have increasingly become more representative of the interests of their constituents, reporting back to the central government about what may lead to protest at the regional level (Truex, 2016). The authorities allow the public to make petitions to the central government, allowing the government to know what issues are affecting public opinion (Dmitriov, 2015). Although likely to be the evolution of an authoritarian system, it is likely that the Soviet collapse was the catalyst for the change. More research needs to be undertaken to ascertain whether this is indeed the case.

### 3.2.2  Learning from an Orange Protest, the Arab Spring, and Euromaidan

The 2004 Orange Revolution was an event that had ramifications in the post-Soviet space and for two of the cases studied in this book in particular. Table 3.1 summarises the event and provides an explanation of what happened. We then analyse the reactions of the Belarusian, Moldovan, and Russian authorities to the Orange

---

[6]  Personal interview: AM01079.    [7]  Personal interview: AM01079.

Table 3.1 *Impact of the Orange Revolution, Arab Spring, and Euromaidan on authoritarian learning in Belarus, Moldova, Russia, and Ukraine*

| Event | Brief analysis | Impact |
|---|---|---|
| Orange Revolution (2004–5) | There had been previous protests about fraudulent elections that had toppled authoritarian leaders in 2000 in Serbia and 2003 in Georgia. However, Ukraine was far less peripheral to two key authoritarian leaders in the post-Soviet space. While Lukashenka was close to Serbia's Slobodan Milošević, Serbia was far enough away to be of little direct concern. Similarly, Eduard Shevardnadze had never been a close ally to either Lukashenka or Putin. | • Loss of power for authoritarian leader. <br>• Spill-over effects: there could be a Maidan in Chişinău, Minsk, or Moscow. Serves as an example to Belarusian, Moldovan, and Russian opposition groups. <br>• Perception that events were led by Western groups and moved Ukraine into Western sphere of influence. |
| | By contrast, Leonid Kuchma had become increasingly aligned – particularly to Moscow – and Ukraine was a neighbouring country. Kuchma tried to run for a third term as president but was dissuaded of this by both Russian and Ukrainian elites. Therefore, Kuchma tried to get his chosen successor, Viktor Yanukovych, elected president – although in truth it was half-hearted as Yanukovych had been forced on Kuchma by the increasingly powerful Donetsk clan. | |
| | The 2004 presidential election pitted Yanukovych against opposition leader Viktor Yushchenko. Unlike Yanukovych, who had criminal conviction, Yushchenko was widely seen as non-corrupt and became a threat to the existing elite's hold on power. Yushchenko was poisoned – but survived – and the elections were stolen. | |

**Table 3.1** (*cont.*)

| Event | Brief analysis | Impact |
|---|---|---|
| | Getting Yanukovych elected required significant electoral fraud and vote-rigging. Ukrainians went to bed believing Yushchenko was president only to wake up to the news that Yanukovych was. Protests erupted on the streets of Kyiv, with about 500,000 protesters regularly camping out on Kyiv's central square – the Maidan.<br><br>Eventually, on 3 December 2004, the Supreme Court stated that there had been such high levels of fraud that the election was null and void. The Supreme Court called for a new election on 26 December 2004. Unable to rely on the vote-rigging that had won him the initial fraudulent election, Yanukovych was defeated and Yushchenko became president. | |
| Arab Spring (2010–15) | The Arab Spring began in Tunisia in December 2010 when Mohammed Bouazizi – a fruit seller – set himself on fire at being asked to pay yet another bribe he could not afford and having his wares confiscated. This resulted in mass riots in his hometown of Sidi Bouzid, which grew into protest across Tunisia. Within two weeks Zine El Abidine Ben Ali, who had ruled Tunisia for 23 years, fled to Saudi Arabia after the army refused to support him. The death of Mohamed Bouazizi resonated across the region, as people were able to draw on local stories of corruption to link to events in Tunisia. Some governments, such as in Egypt and Syria, also ran news stories of events in Tunisia, thereby giving people | • Collapse of authoritarian governments with long tenure.<br>• Social media played a crucial role in spreading information and organising protests.<br>• Perception that the West organised the Arab Spring and this could be used in the post-Soviet region. |

first-hand experience of what was happening. Social media was also the main source of information spreading news across the region, resulting in mass protests and information sharing. Protests erupted across the region, leading to the loss of power for authoritarians in Egypt, Libya, and Yemen. While some governments survived in Algeria, Bahrain, and Morocco, no state in the region was unaffected. This is epitomised by the violence that occurred in Libya and Syria – both of whom currently have a civil war.

Euromaidan (2013–14)

The protests that became the Euromaidan were caused by Yanukovych refusing to sign an association agreement with the EU. However, protests were small and appeared to be breaking up. This led to Yanukovych making the first of many mistakes by getting the security services to remove the protesters. Since they were mostly students and children, the violence meted out to them brought more people onto the streets.

The violence of the authorities became a hallmark and created a zero-sum game between the government and the protesters. Neither side was prepared to give ground, and the authorities in particular used repression but it was never enough to defeat the protesters. Unlike in 2004, where Kuchma had largely refused to

- Spill-over effects: there could be a Maidan in Chişinău, Minsk, or Moscow as it could serve as an example to **Belarusian, Moldovan, and Russian** opposition groups.
- Role of social media in organising the initial protests. Although the idea that the Euromaidan was caused by a single Facebook post is a romanticised version of events, it resonated and

Table 3.1 (*cont.*)

| Event | Brief analysis | Impact |
|---|---|---|
| | use violence, Yanukovych was prepared to do so but could not finish clearing the streets. | highlighted further the threat of social media. |
| | The protesters erected barricades and set up various siege weapons to protect against the violence of the authorities. However, for the most part the protests were peaceful. On 16 January 2014, the government passed the Dictatorship Laws, which made protests illegal. This ratcheted up the winner-takes-all scenario that the protests had become and led to the demonstrators hunkering down on the Maidan. | |
| | Yanukovych used tactics of repression and conciliation but did not do either well, which further antagonised the protesters. It was difficult to trust a government that called for negotiation while also spilling blood. The Euromaidan effectively became a siege, a situation the government tried to end by clearing the streets, opening fire on protesters. The failure to clear the Maidan precipitated government collapse and led to Yanukovych fleeing Kyiv to Russia on 22 February 2014. | |

Revolution. Although the Belarusian authorities had already begun a preventive counter-revolution, the Orange Revolution gave this new impetus and increased its pace. Similarly, the Russian government also began a preventive counter-revolution, directly caused by the Orange Revolution. Reaction to the Orange Revolution is for the case studies a combination of diffusion, lesson-drawing, and to an extent linkage as well – due to the proximity culturally, geographically, and politically between Belarus, Russia, and Ukraine.

The Orange Revolution led to the Kremlin instigating many practices to stop such an event from occurring in Moscow. There have been several analyses of the key aspects that the Kremlin initiated after 2004 to stop the possibility of a Moscow Orange Revolution (Finkel and Brudny, 2012; Horvath, 2013). Almost immediately after the Orange Revolution, the Kremlin developed a preventive counter-revolution, which appropriated 'the revolutionary methods' of the Kremlin's opponents, and the tactics used by protesters in the Orange Revolution (Horvath, 2013: 6). The Kremlin's preventive counter-revolution established the 'ideology' of sovereign democracy to unite regime factions and a majority of the populace. Sovereign democracy relegated democracy to the 'necessity' of sovereignty and regime dominance. Patriotic cliques were mobilised from regime-funded NGOs to Nashi, a pro-Kremlin youth group, which was created to stop anti-regime protesters taking control of squares and streets. Nashi was opposed to 'the unnatural alliance of liberals, fascists, sympathizers of the West and ultranationalists, international foundations, and international terror, united by one and only thing – the hatred for Putin' (Finkel and Brudny, 2012: 19). Nashi united with Spartak and CSKA football hooligans to provide muscle should a Colour Revolution occur in Moscow, and they trained regularly in the Moscow satellite town of Lyubertsy (Horvath, 2013: 117). The preventive counter-revolution saw the Kremlin instigate further repressive legislation to target parties, NGOs, and public demonstrations, which could form the basis of a Moscow Colour Revolution and mobilise protesters.

The 2004 Orange Revolution in Kyiv still resonate for Kremlin personnel, as the Russian authorities are constantly trying to counter an Orange scenario in Moscow, and often refer to potential new Colour Revolutions occurring in Russia and the post-Soviet space. The secretary of the Russian Security Council, Nikolai Patrushev (Security Council of the Russian Federation, 2012a), stated that

'Russia was a "training ground" for using informational, organizational and other external levers of interference in internal affairs'. The idiom of Colour Revolution has become synonymous for the Kremlin as a label to mark all protests, with Putin (2016a) claiming that the Syrian conflict was the final Middle Eastern Colour Revolution, and deputy secretary of the Security Council Rashid Nurgaliev (Security Council of the Russian Federation, 2019) claiming that Western states will continue to promote Colour Revolutions in the post-Soviet space.

The Belarusian regime reacted in a similar way to the kremlin in countering the Orange Revolution and the wider phenomenon of Colour Revolutions in general. Although Hall (2017b) detailed how the Belarusian regime began its own preventive counter-revolution after the fall of Slobodan Milošević in the 2000 Bulldozer Revolution, which preceded the Kremlin's preventive counter-revolution and provided lessons for the Russian authorities, the Belarusian regime 'learnt the apparent lessons of Ukraine's Orange Revolution better than the opposition'. This was, in part, because Belarusian embassy staff had been on the streets of Kyiv taking notes and photos of the protests, which were then sent to the KDB in Minsk.[8] The Orange Revolution was closely watched in Minsk, with prominent protesters monitored in case they came to Belarus and tactics devised to counter an Orange Revolution in Minsk (Korosteleva, 2012: 45).

The Belarusian authorities learnt several other lessons from the Orange Revolution. One was that Yanukovych's claim that the Orange protesters were paid by the American government had not resonated with Ukrainians (Wilson, 2021a: 213–14). Therefore, the Belarusian regime looked for an alternative 'enemy' to America to galvanise public support. To this end the authorities emphasised that the 2006 presidential opposition candidate, Alyaksandr Milinkievich, spoke fluent Polish, which allowed the regime to claim he was pro-Polish (Wilson, 2021a: 214). For good measure and to really emphasise the apparent nefarious activities of the Polish government, the *Związek Polaków na Białorusi* (ZPB)[9] was also accused of anti-regime activities, an allegation not helped by the meeting held between Andzelika Borys – who would become ZPB leader – and EU representatives in Brussels

---

[8] Personal interview: TK02846.
[9] The Związek Polaków na Białorusi (in Polish) or the Sayuz palyakau na Belrusi (in Belarusian) is the Union of Poles in Belarus and acts as cultural and education association for the Polish community in Belarus.

(BelaPAN, 2005). The Belarusian security services 'discovered' a plot between the ZPB and the Polish security services to start a Colour Revolution in Minsk (Ankudo, 2007). Other Polish and Lithuanian 'plots' to remove Lukashenka were 'found' to increase support for the regime (Provalinskaya, 2007; Ankudo, 2006a; 2006b; Gryl', 2005b).

Having located a viable 'enemy' to rouse the public in support of the authorities, the Belarusian regime set about refining other tactics from the Colour Revolutions. For instance, the Belarusian authorities saw the prominence of the youth group Otpor in the 2000 Bulldozer Revolution in Serbia, and so the Belaruski Respublikansky Sayuz Moladzi (BRSM)[10] was created. The BRSM was an amalgamation of two other pro-regime factions: the Belarusian Youth Union and the Belarusian Patriotic Youth Union. The BRSM was created in 2002, a full three years before Nashi in Russia (Gryl', 2012), highlighting that the Belarusian authorities were quicker to draw lessons from the Colour Revolutions than the Kremlin, and that the Kremlin learnt from the Belarusian government (Hall, 2017b: 162). The BRSM was created as a forum to bring young Belarusians into a pro-regime and patriotic organisation (Dovnar, 2003). The organisation was tasked with taking control of squares and streets during protests in Minsk to stop a Belarusian Orange Revolution (Vyachorka, 2004). The creation of the BRSM was one practice the Belarusian authorities devised to restrict a possible Belarusian Colour Revolution. For good measure, the KDB infiltrated the opposition youth group Zubr to neuter Zubr as a viable Belarusian Otpor (Dovnar, 2004).

Although the regime was relatively safe after a 2004 referendum did away with presidential term limits, thereby giving the regime a large measure of security, the demise of a neighbouring authoritarian regime in Ukraine in the same year as this power grab set off fears of instability diffusing into Belarus. Lukashenka is wary of any events that could spiral out of control and result in his loss of power, resulting in the indiscriminate reaction to any protests,[11] and so after events that had seen a close friend in Slobodan Milošević lose power, and the demise of an authoritarian regime in neighbouring Ukraine, the regime used significant repression against demonstrations in 2006 and 2010. The regime only refrained from such coercive practices in 2015 due to the

---

[10] In English – the Belarusian Republican Youth Union.
[11] Personal interview: NF29463.

geopolitical need to improve relations with the EU.[12] Although the Belarusian regime was relatively safe after 2004, the authorities still needed to stop any future bank runs and remain responsive to potential protests. It is why the Belarusian government continued a preventive counter-revolution even when relatively safe (Silitski, 2010), increasing control over media, NGOs, and the education sector to improve regime Security. The Colour Revolutions worried the Belarusian regime and resulted in the authorities attempting to prevent such an eventuality happening in Minsk, and to alleviate a '"pink", "orange" or "banana" revolution in Belarus' (Lukashenka, 2005).

Unlike Belarusian and Russian reactions to the Orange Revolution and wider Colour Revolutions, there is less information on how Moldovan regimes responded. The PCRM regime led by Vladimir Voronin had started to consolidate power almost immediately after coming to power in 2001, placing allies in control of state institutions, increasing patronage access to supporters, and practising *reiderstvo*[13] tactics to take control of businesses. This increased Voronin's wealth and that of his family, while also giving others a stake in the continuation of the regime.[14] The PCRM took control of local government by reducing budgets, thereby making these institutions dependent on PCRM largesse and willing to exert control over the regions for the central government. Also, state-controlled media became little more than a PCRM voice, and the PCRM became a patronage party, dispensing financial incentives to gain the support of other factions, while continually changing the electoral system to ensure the PCRM's control (Rodkiewicz, 2009). The PCRM co-opted opposition parties to create a pliant opposition, and Voronin made it difficult for sustained opposition protests by backing down at key intervals and offering concessions, only to re-calibrate later, which split the protesters (Hale, 2015: 389; Point.md, 2009).

The PCRM regime's position looked safe by 2004 and so the Colour Revolutions – principally the Orange Revolution – had a limited effect. Although in 2009 the regime did lose power due, in part, to mass protests, this was due to the withdrawal of financial support of the PCRM from oligarchs, principally Vladimir Plahotniuc, Vlad Filat, and

---

[12] Personal interview: NJ08269.
[13] *Reiderstvo* involves asset-grabbing to take assets and businesses of others.
[14] Personal interviews: MQ25710, FT36819.

Chiril Lucinschi, resulting in the PCRM being unable to keep supporters onside by offering patronage (Hale, 2013: 490; 2015: 405). There is limited information on the PCRM and Voronin's reactions to the Colour Revolutions, but the consolidation of power that the PCRM attempted was partly due to learning from Yanukovych's failure in 2004.

Another reason for the lack of obvious reaction by Voronin to the Orange Revolution was that by late 2003 Voronin had rejected the Kozak Memorandum,[15] and so relations with the Kremlin had already deteriorated, which made direct cooperation with the Kremlin on countering Colour Revolutions difficult. However, the Colour Revolutions, especially the Orange Revolution, would have worried Voronin, as protests could lead to regime collapse.[16] So, it is likely that the Moldovan regime looked at the failures of the Ukrainian regime in 2004 and Russian reactions. For example, in 2006 the Information and Security Service of the Republic of Moldova (SIS) established Moldova's first anti-terrorist centre to deal with all 'manifestations of extremism' (Point.md, 2006). As seen later, the case studies have a loose definition of what constitutes extremism, and although an oblique reference, it is likely Voronin worried about a possible Colour Revolution in Chișinău. While there was a breakdown in relations between the Voronin regime and the Kremlin, there remained significant links, due to Moldovan membership in the CIS, allowing the Moldovan and Russian regimes to share information. Although relations between Voronin would have closely watched the Orange Revolution in Kyiv and taken lessons from this protest.

Diffusion, linkage, and lesson-drawing were crucial for how the Belarusian and Russian regimes reacted to the Orange Revolution, and to a lesser extent the Moldovan regime as well. Lukashenka was a close ally of Milošević and Milošević's fall in 2000 induced learning by the Belarusian regime for fear that what happened in Serbia might occur in Belarus (Feduta, 2005: 442). The Belarusian and Russian regimes work closely together and would certainly have

---

[15] The Kozak Memorandum was developed by Dmitriy Kozak to solve the Transnistrian conflict. it would have allowed Russia to station troops indefinitely on Transnistrian territory and federated Moldova. Under American and EU pressure Voronin refused to sign the agreement (Hale, 2015: 380).

[16] Personal interview: KH32708.

worked jointly to counteract further Colour Revolutions in the post-Soviet space. As mentioned, Belarus was a testing ground for the Kremlin and having developed an earlier preventive counter-revolution, the Belarusian regime provided lessons for the Kremlin on how to best a Colour Revolution in Moscow (Hall, 2017b). By contrast, Moldovan regimes have been less integrated with the Kremlin and the Belarusian authorities, forcing successive Moldovan regimes to diffuse ideas and draw lessons from afar. Although the PCRM had consolidated power in Moldova by 2004, politics in Moldova does not allow for control on the same level as in Belarus and Russia, and so the PCRM did not have the capacity to counter an Orange Revolution in Chişinău. However, this does not detract from the fact that the PCRM regime did instigate some learning process from the 2004 events in Kyiv. Therefore, the Colour Revolutions highlight the power of linkage, diffusion, and lesson-drawing in explaining authoritarian learning from external failure.

By contrast, the Arab Spring was a group of mass protests across the Middle East and North Africa, which ended in the collapse of some regional authoritarian regimes. As authoritarians are wary of anything leading to power loss, seeing the collapse of some authoritarian regimes known for their long tenure likely caused a seismic shock in the post-Soviet region. Table 3.1 details the key events of the Arab Spring. From there, we analyse how all four case studies learnt from these events through a mix of diffusion and lesson-drawing.

The Arab Spring clearly unsettled the Russian regime, with Putin (2014a) speaking of an 'Arab Spring' being replaced by an 'Arab winter'. Similarly, Dmitry Medvedev (2011) argued that the Arab Spring would 'backfire' for the West. Lukashenka (2011; 2014a) stated that the Belarusian army should prepare for a Western-sponsored coup, such as had happened in the Arab Spring. Therefore, events in the Arab Spring alarmed the Belarusian and Russian regimes and there is evidence that Moldovan and Ukrainian authorities were also concerned. This assumption is investigated here. The secretary of the Russian Security Council, Nikolai Patrushev, regularly met representatives from Middle Eastern and North African Security Councils to discuss the Arab Spring. In 2015, Patrushev visited Cairo and met his Egyptian counterpart, Fayza Abunnaga, to discuss 'Colour Revolutions' and 'their impact on the security of Russia and Egypt', and the failure of the Egyptian regime during the Arab Spring (Security Council of the Russian Federation, 2015c).

Another meeting saw Patrushev meet Egyptian and Emirati officials to discuss how Colour Revolutions were being used 'to divide the Muslim world and at the same time weaken Russia and China' (Security Council of the Russian Federation, 2015b). During the meeting, Patrushev stated that 'over the past decades, Russia has accumulated considerable experience in countering "Colour" revolutions' from passing legislation 'aimed at strengthening the constitutional system, protecting territorial integrity', while 'countering terrorism and extremism', and bringing up a patriotic youth cohort, developing 'civil society institutions, and rallying the nation based on common, spiritual, moral, and historical values. On all these issues, we are ready to provide the necessary advisory assistance to our partners' (Security Council of the Russian Federation, 2015b). It is indicative that Patrushev referred to the Arab Spring as a Colour Revolution, highlighting again that the Kremlin is still affected by the Colour Revolution spectre. However, direct dialogue between Patrushev and members of various Arab security councils highlights that the Kremlin took a direct interest in learning from the Arab Spring and offering support to Arab regimes to restrict the chances of future protests.

Yet, the Kremlin did not need to visit the Middle East and North African region – although first-hand information is always best – as television channels showed the protests allowing lessons to be drawn from the comfort of Moscow. Putin (2012: 3) remarked that the Arab Spring had occurred due to the growth of communication technologies, allowing protesters to use the Internet, social media, and mobile phones to organise protests. While there should be free communication, Putin (2012: 3) argued that it should be restricted so that 'terrorists and criminals' would be unable to use communication devices to organise protests. Due to the NATO intervention in Libya and the ensuing regime change, as perceived by Moscow, the NATO intervention in Libya set a precedent which Putin (2012: 3) warned could result in allowing NATO 'to realise a "Libyan Scenario"' in other countries, a direct reference to NATO regime change in Moscow, and this was a key lesson from failure in the Arab Spring for the Kremlin and for Russian security.

However, the primary lesson for the Kremlin from the Arab Spring became what was known as the so-called Gerasimov Doctrine – named after the current chief of the General Staff of the Armed Forces of the Russian Federation. Gerasimov (2013: 1) argued that the Arab Spring had changed perceptions of how a future war would be conducted, stating that direct military confrontation between armies in the field was being replaced by 'political, economic, informational, humanitarian and other non-military measures implemented with the use of the protest potential of the population'. Such ideas, learnt from events in the Arab Spring, have been used by the Kremlin in the ongoing Ukrainian conflict since 2014 in what has been termed by Galeotti (2015) as 'guerrilla geopolitics'. It is revealing that the 2014 pro-Russian protests that began in south-east Ukraine were called the 'Russian Spring', which in part was a mockery of the alleged American intervention in the Arab Spring (Lauder, 2018).

The Belarusian reaction to the Arab Spring was relatively quick, with Lukashenka (2011) mentioning instability and that elections in Egypt and Tunisia had not brought peace. In 2014, during a visit to the Holy Spirit Cathedral in Minsk, Lukashenka (2014a) stated that the authorities should constantly prepare for something such as the Arab Spring. When addressing the National Assembly in 2014, Lukashenka (2014b) mentioned that the Belarusian regime had already prepared by controlling NGOs and the 'fifth column'.[17] Lukashenka (2014b) stated that poverty had been the catalyst for the Arab Spring, and that the Belarusian regime had learnt that economic pressures could be a catalyst for protest and so the regime needed to continually develop the Belarusian economy to reduce the possibility of protests.

Like the Orange Revolution, where the Belarusian regime devised an 'enemy' in the form of the Polish and Lithuanian governments, the Arab Spring allowed the authorities to re-create the external 'enemy' story. The recreation of past stories to be used in the present situation appears to be a trend in post-Soviet authoritarian regimes. For example, for the Kremlin 'there is nothing better than using the same story again and again',[18] and this is why the Kremlin reverts to blaming the 'West' for all the ills facing Russia, to galvanise public support, as most Russians still view the 'West' with suspicion. The Belarusian discourse of an external enemy was helped by the 2012 Teddy Bear Bombing,[19] an event that allowed the Belarusian authorities to claim that then Swedish ambassador Stefan Eriksson, and by association the

---

[17] Lukashenka's label for the opposition.    [18] Personal interview: AM07019.
[19] A Swedish NGO dropped teddy bears over Minsk. These parachutists carried pro-democracy messages. The escapade resulted in a diplomatic row between Sweden and Belarus and tit-for-tat diplomatic expulsions.

Swedish government, supported radical factions in Belarus to instigate an Arab Spring (Yanushevskaya, 2012). After the Arab Spring, the regime improved its listening capabilities, enhancing the capacity of the Information Analytical Centre (IAC) to poll Belarusians to find issues that could lead to future protests (Inanets, 2017). The authorities developed tactics to better control the Internet and monitor what Belarusians viewed online as a direct lesson from the Arab Spring as events in the Arab world had seen protesters unite and organise protests online (Shraibman, 2015). When the Arab Spring started, the Belarusian government allegedly issued orders to all regional state structures and security services to be ready for potential instability (Gryl', 2016). During 2011, after the Arab Spring, there was a recruitment drive for the police and counter-protest training exercises for interior ministry troops in Hrodna (AFN.by, 2011). The regime monitored opposition movements and constantly detained opposition activists (Tikhonenko, 2011). Phishing emails were sent to the email accounts of opposition activists to freeze their accounts and steal information, allegedly originating from the KDB (Kanygin, 2011). The available evidence points to the Belarusian regime reacting to the Arab Spring and devising practices to restrict copy-cat protests in Belarus. Unlike the Kremlin it appears that the Belarusian government reacted to the Arab Spring from Minsk, rather than sending representatives directly to Arab countries for first-hand information. It is likely that Belarusian representatives visited Arab states after the Arab Spring and were in direct contact, but there is no conclusive evidence of this.

Unlike the Belarusian and Russian regimes, the Moldovan authorities do not have the capacity and aptitude to exert the same level of control and react to the Arab Spring at the same level. It is likely that the Arab Spring highlighted the power of social media to Moldovan civil society, which contributed to the organisation and galvanisation of protesters during the 2015 and 2016 protests (Popşoi, 2015). The Moldovan authorities tried to implement greater media control when the Arab Spring was occurring (Point.md, 2012), although there could have been another reason for such an attempt and the Moldovan authorities did not have the capacity for concerted media control. The Plahotniuc regime attempted to increase control over state institutions to restrict potential protests, coupled with the simulation of reform to reduce the number of potential protesters (Jurnal.md, 2016a; NewsMaker, 2016c). It is likely that the Arab Spring was tracked in Chişinău, but there were no significant changes because Moldovan regimes do not have the capacity for significant change when events happen in other global regions, although this would change if events occurred in the post-Soviet space or Romania.[20]

Like Moldova, there is limited information on the effect of the Arab Spring on Ukraine, however, as with Moldova, Yanukovych tried to consolidate control over state structures at the time of the Arab Spring (Solodky, 2011: 5). The authorities devised new methods to control the electoral system (Minakov, 2011) and increased the number of Berkut and Griffin security personnel, while also procuring weapons, and instigating anti-protest training exercises (Grani.ru, 2017).[21] However, it is likely that these actions were taken because of the coming 2012 parliamentary elections and the need for the Yanukovych regime to limit opposition in parliament and control the streets to restrict the possibility of protests. While it is probable that the Arab Spring played a role in precipitating attempts at consolidation after 2011, Bankova began consolidation immediately after Yanukovych became president in 2010 and was focused on ensuring Yanukovych's electoral victory at the 2015 presidential elections and so was consolidating power for this reason (Kudelia, 2014). Elsewhere (2017a: 163), I have argued that Yanukovych was too busy 'fighting the last war' of the Orange Revolution to acknowledge the Arab Spring, which is why Bankova failed with the Euromaidan, as the Euromaidan shared many similarities with the Arab Spring (Dagaev et al., 2014).

Although there are limitations on information available on how the Arab Spring affected the Moldovan and Ukrainian regimes, evidence points to learning by these regimes but the Arab Spring would have contributed to this learning. However, it is likely that the Arab Spring was too far to directly worry both regimes. There is ample data of Kremlin and Belarusian regime learning from the Arab Spring, with evidence of direct dialogue between the Kremlin and Middle East and North African regimes, highlighting that policy transfer and linkage occurred. The Arab Spring was televised, so representatives of each regime did not need to be on the streets of Cairo, Algiers, or Tunis, which leads to diffusion being a key factor from learning on the Arab Spring. It is likely that the linkage between the four case studies

---

[20] Personal interview: MQ25710.     [21] Personal interview: DF59302.

allowed lessons to be passed between post-Soviet regimes, although evidence is limited that the Moldovan and Ukrainian regimes learnt directly from the Arab Spring.

Nearly a decade after the Orange Revolution in 2013 there were protests in Ukraine again with the Maidan in Kyiv being the main stage for the demonstrations. Table 3.1 summarises the events of what became known as the Euromaidan. This is particularly, but this section addressed responses by the other three case studies. This is particularly so for leaders in Belarus and Russia but is there some evidence pointing to a reaction in Moldova as well. Analysis of learning from the Euromaidan shows that it is again a case of diffusion, lesson-drawing, and to an extent linkage as well.

The Euromaidan's proximity resonated for the Kremlin, and the Belarusian regime and possibly the Moldovan authorities too, as Yanukovych's failure as a fellow authoritarian caused consternation in the post-Soviet region due to the proximity of Kyiv to other post-Soviet capitals (Maltseva, 2016: 144). The Kremlin has had a view that Ukraine is like Russia, which had been a problem during the Orange Revolution with the Kremlin thinking that what worked in Russia would work in Ukraine. Similarly, after the Euromaidan, the Kremlin followed this notion with the Russian authorities relying on an argument by Tamara Guzenkova, deputy director of the *Rossiysky Institut Strategicheskikh Issledovany* (RISI),[22] where the Kremlin followed Guzenkova's argument that Russian intervention would be welcomed in Ukraine, as Ukrainians had always supported Russia since the Treaty of Pereyaslav.[23] Like the Orange Revolution, the Kremlin failed to learn lessons that Ukraine is not Russia, and while possibly the Kremlin continued to fail to learn about Ukraine, there were lessons the Kremlin drew from Bankova's failure during the Euromaidan.

During the Euromaidan, Russian state media quickly created two discourses, arguing, first, that Yanukovych was weak for not having

---

[22] In English – Russian Institute for Strategic Studies.

[23] These allegations were made by former RISI analyst Aleksandr Sytin: www .facebook.com/alexander.sytin/posts/772114072866973. The Treaty of Pereyaslav was a treaty between Hetman Bohdan Khmelnytsky and Muscovy, giving Muscovite support to Khmelnytsky against the Polish-Lithuanian Commonwealth. Eventually, Muscovy incorporated the Hetmanate as part of the Empire.

resorted to violence to disperse protesters, while negotiating with the West and still allowing Western states to fund the protesters and the so-claimed far-right crowds (Shestakhov, 2014: 1). Second, Kremlin media and even Putin (2014c) claimed Yanukovych's fall was a Western-sponsored coup against a legitimately elected president. Such rhetoric was used in 2004 in the aftermath of the Ukrainian Orange Revolution, when the Kremlin claimed it was Western-sponsored regime change (Wilson, 2005: 183), although the coup rhetoric of 2014 was stronger than in 2004.

During the Euromaidan, Bankova used thugs – called the Titushki – to attack protesters, thereby allowing the regime deniability for the attacks and death of protesters (Nemyrych, 2013). Bankova paid each Titushek between €25 and €50 a day to fight protesters (Goncharenko, 2014). The Titushki were 'tracksuited thugs, a mixture of football hooligans, fight-club members and petty criminals', and operated with the Berkut security forces (Reid, 2015: 265). However, the Titushki were unorganised, ill-disciplined, and violent, with the Titushki 'responsible for almost a dozen documented deaths, though many of their victims were among the "disappeared"' (Wilson, 2014c: 79). While the Titushki were notoriously violent, when faced by large numbers of protesters they often fled, such as the forty Titushki who were found hiding in a supermarket, after losing a fight with football hooligans from Dynamo Kyiv and Dnipro football clubs (Kyiv Post, 2014; Ukrainskaya Pravda, 2014b).

Bankova relied on the Titushki, but this was a problem as the Titushki fled when the going got tough and the regime could not rely fully on the Berkut as the numbers of Berkut numbers were insufficient to counter mass protests. The principal lesson from the Maidan for the Kremlin was the need for well-equipped, well-trained, and numerous regime fighters. The Euromaidan precipitated the creation of Russia's new security forces, the Rosgvardiya, which had been formed after the 2011–12 protests in Moscow, but was rapidly equipped and trained, with more personnel hired after the Euromaidan (Zygar, 2016: 181). Rosgvardiya is a separate entity to existing security services, giving the Kremlin a well-equipped armed force without relying on the army and 'constitutional rules' (E'kspert, 2016: 7; The Moscow Times, 2016a). Rosgvardiya was expanded to include the *Otryad Mobilny Osobogo Naznacheniya* (OMON), the Special Rapid Response Unit, and interior ministry troops who had all failed to counteract protesters in Moscow between 2011 and 2012. This led to the Rosgvardiya reaching 340,000 personnel (Falaleev, 2016: 7; The Moscow Times, 2016b; Sozaev-Guriev, 2016: 2), which was over 100 times bigger than the Berkut forces of 3,250 that Bankova had during the Euromaidan.

Ostensibly, the Rosgvardiya was created to fight terrorism, although the Kremlin is increasingly wary of the perceived enemy within (Sinitsyn and Zheleznova, 2016), and the Rosgvardiya has been used against protesters rather than terrorists since its inception (Odissonova, Dokshin, and Artem'eva, 2019). A video of the Rosgvardiya training in Lyubertsy – just outside Moscow – highlights tactical development of methods against protesters (Otkrytaya Rossii, 2016; Standish, 2016). Under legislation Rosgvardiya personnel can shoot protesters (Interfax, 2016), and Rosgvardiya is only accountable to the president, giving it a stake in Putin's survival (Baidakova, 2016a). The failure of the Ukrainian regime to coerce protesters emphasised to the Kremlin the need for a large, heavily equipped, repressive force. Many former Berkut officers from Ukraine, and not just those living in annexed Crimea, fled to Russia, and the Kremlin re-created the Berkut and placed it with the Rosgvaridiya in 2016. This provided the Rosgvardiya with personnel with direct knowledge of the Euromaidan and the failures of these events. People such as Sergey Kusyuk, who is wanted in Kyiv for his actions during the Euromaidan, have become part of the Rosgvardiya and have been used against protesters in Moscow (Bershidsky, 2019b).

The Belarusian regime took lessons from the Euromaidan, such as the perception that Bankova had not constructed a national identity acceptable to most Ukrainians, and with Belarusian identity weak, the Belarusian regime remains fearful that it is possible that a Donbas scenario could occur primarily in a Belarusian region like Mahileyskaya voblast'. Therefore, the Belarusian authorities began a soft-Belarusianisation policy to differentiate Belarus from Russia to internal and external audiences after the Euromaidan.[24] The regime promoted Belarusian in schools (Astapenia, 2014) and endorsed a new history – although it did not stop promoting Belarus's role in the Great Patriotic War – incorporating the Polish-Lithuanian Grand Duchy. The regime began emphasising figures such as Grand Duke Algirdas, who beat Muscovy in the fourteenth century, and Algirdas was recast as

---

[24] Personal interviews: NF29463, RW64293, HA20938.

a Belarusian freedom fighter (Mojeiko, 2015). The centenary of the first independent Belarusian state in 1918 was celebrated in 2018, a date traditionally recognised by the non-regime opposition. The principality of Polotsk was given a makeover as an entity distinct from Kyivan Rus' and, therefore, a separate Slavic unit, and the Grand Duchy of Lithuania was recast as a quasi-Belarusian state (Wilson, 2018: 8).

Similarly, Russianisation, which had in the past served Lukashenka well in maintaining public support, was reduced, with Soviet-sounding street names replaced with the names of historic Belarusians to decrease Soviet nostalgia and promote Belarusian identity (Astapenia, 2014). Security personnel deemed too close to the Kremlin were replaced by personnel considered loyal to Belarus, although these people remain pro-Russian, having trained in Russia and having kept close ties with Russian security personnel.[25] During an address to the National Assembly, Lukashenka (2014b) spoke about maintaining a strategic partnership with Russia while preserving Belarusian identity. While Lukashenka (2015) has stated that there is a growing need to protect the Belarusian language, and Belarusian history and culture, there has only been limited Belarusianisation (Shraibman, 2016a). The regime cannot alienate the Kremlin too much,[26] and some proto-Belarusian figures, such as Kastus' Kalinouski and Tadevsh Kastsyushka,[27] are too revolutionary for Lukashenka. Kalinouski and Kastsyushka have been claimed by Poland, a state seen as enemy number one for the Belarusian regime (Karbalevich, 2019).

This lesson from the Euromaidan about the need to differentiate Belarus from Russia to an internal and an external audience has caused difficulties with the Kremlin, as pro-Russian groups perceive this Belarusianisation policy as a precursor to a Ukraine scenario with the Belarusian regime infringing on the rights of Russians (Fadeyev, 2015; Instituta stran SNG, 2016; Kachurka, 2014). For instance, in December 2016, pro-Russian activists were arrested for claiming that Belarus was not a separate nation with a distinct language, history, or culture (Shraibman, 2016b). Fearing that the Kremlin could use these pro-Russian cliques to stage protests that the Belarusian authorities would repress, giving the Kremlin justification either to directly

---

[25] Personal interviews: HA20938, KG84027, RW64293, GY69350.
[26] Personal interview: VW28501.
[27] Kastus' Kalinouski and Tadevsh Kastsyushka are better known as Konstanty Kalinowski and Tadeusz Kościuszko in Polish.

intervene in Belarus or use other subversive measures, the Belarusian security services arrested this pro-Russian faction in a pre-emptive strike.[28] This shows learning by the Belarusian authorities from the Euromaidan. Firstly the regime began to differentiate Belarusian culture from Russia to strengthen Belarusian identity, Secondly knowing that the Kremlin justified Crimea's annexation and Donbas intervention based on protecting Russians from nationalist Ukrainian groups, the Belarusian authorities did not overtly crack down on pro-Russian protesters, but was quick to react to any external activisim in Minsk linked to Moscow.

However, further Belarusinisation is unlikely, as it will cause friction with Russia,[29] and the Kremlin retains economic leverage over Belarus, thereby limiting distancing by the Belarusian authorities (Hansbury, 2016). The Kremlin has tightened the screws in the energy and banking sectors, with Russian banks refusing to lower interest rates, which has affected Belarusian monetary policy. The Kremlin has withdrawn funding for projects and constructed border controls, all of which ties Belarus closer to Russia and limits any possibility of further distancing from Russia (Bohdan, 2017b; Hansbury, 2017; Preiherman, 2017b).

The Belarusian authorities took another lesson from the Euromaidan about the claim made by Bankova that the protesters were fascists. During the 25 March 2017 protests, the Belarusian regime contended that a clandestine military-sports-club known as the Bely Legion – which had dissolved in 2000 – had re-emerged (Smok, 2017). The Bely Legion reappeared in Belarusian state media after the social parasite protests (Smok, 2017), and state-media linked Bely Legion to Pravy Sektor (BelGazeta, 2017a), a Ukrainian far-right grouplet that had received undue attention in the Russian media during the Euromaidan. The Belarusian authorities learnt that the story of a far-right terrorist group could justify repression and get Kremlin support, and it would also likely lessen condemnation from Western states. It is unlikely Bely Legion was real. As the Belarusian authorities had used the Bely Legion as the terrorist organisation that perpetrated the 2011 Minsk bombings to justify a further crack-down on the opposition after the 2010 presidential elections (Pankovets, 2017). The regime resuscitated Bely Legion for two

---

[28] Personal interview: VW28501.    [29] Personal interview: VW28501.

reasons. First, Belyi Legion could be portrayed as a similar organisation to Pravy Sektor and was a message to the Kremlin to support Lukashenka (Lukashuk, 2017; Hansbury, 2017). Second, the coercion against the Bely Legion was a message to Belarusians that future protests would be met with repression.[30]

As with the Arab Spring, there is less evidence on how the Moldovan regime reacted to the Euromaidan, although the Moldovan authorities got first-hand experience of the Euromaidan by meeting the Yanukovych-era Ukrainian ambassador Serhiy Pyrozhkov to find out what practices Bankova was using against protesters during the protests. The Moldovan security services devised practices to counteract a possible Maidan in Chişinău (Tristan, 2014). The Plahotniuc regime could not be seen to be cracking down on the opposition, as it needed EU funds. However, the Moldovan regime increased control over state structures and reduced 'the protesters mobilization capacity to a manageable size'.[31] Media outlets controlled by Plahotniuc did not give much coverage to the Euromaidan to reduce potential protests in Moldova (TV7.md, 2014), and the Moldovan security services received greater legislative powers to cope with a potential Euromaidan in Chişinău as well as receiving updated riot gear (Point.md, 2014). During protests in 2015, Plahotniuc used his control of parliament to get an ally, Pavel Filip, appointed prime minister at night to reduce the chance of protesters mobilising (Kazanskiy, 2016: 1). The quick swearing-in of a new government at night left demonstrators with a fait accompli and was a lesson from the Euromaidan that governments needed to act quickly rather than allowing protests to fester.[32] Another lesson for the Moldovan regime was the use of agents provocateurs who were paid well like the Titushki but unlike the Titushki were willing to use violence and did not flee when faced with a fight.[33]

The Euromaidan, due to proximity to other post-Soviet states, induced learning, especially for the Kremlin and the Belarusian regimes, although even the Moldovan regime drew lessons from events in Kyiv. The learning from the failure of Bankova in 2014 by the other three case studies highlights a mixture of diffusion and linkage. The Euromaidan was well publicised. Due to its geographical proximity in Kyiv, other neighbouring authoritarian regimes devised best practices

---

[30]  Personal interview: HW29578.     [31]  Personal interview: FT36819.
[32]  Personal interview: FT36819.      [33]  Personal interview: FT36819.

to counter a domestic Euromaidan. Due to the linkage between Bankova – and especially the Kremlin – but also the Belarusian and Moldovan regimes, there was significant lesson-drawing from events in Kyiv in 2013 and 2014.

## 3.3 Conclusion

The chapter investigated the extent of learning from external failure among the four cases studied. Reactions to the Orange Revolution, the Arab Spring, and the Euromaidan in the four case studies show that each regime drew lessons from these events, although the Belarusian and Russian regimes appeared more adept. As both states have authoritarian leaders with long tenure, both governments have established fuller learning capabilities than the regimes in Moldova and Ukraine. Yet, there is evidence that the Moldovan and Ukrainian authorities also learnt from these events. So, there is clear evidence that authoritarian-minded leaders learn from examples of external failure.

# 4 | *Learning from Internal Failure*

The Greatest teacher, failure is.[1]

## 4.1 Introduction

Yoda's quote to Luke Skywalker during the 2019 Star Wars film *The Rise of Skywalker* emphasises that learning from failure is crucial to improving knowledge. Yoda's admonishment to Luke centres on Luke's failure to teach potential future Jedi as he had been taught by Obi Won Kenobi and Yoda. This quote is relevant to authoritarian learning as we argue that learning from internal failure is crucial to helping authoritarian leaders develop best survival practices. If authoritarian-minded leaders do not learn from domestic failure of others – or from their previous mistakes – then they are more susceptible to lose power. Like Luke, who had become the last Jedi by isolating himself and not passing knowledge on, authoritarian leaders cannot afford to isolate themselves and not learn from the past. Although not a perfect representation of learning from internal failure, the lack of new Jedis makes it easier for a new Empire to rise. Similarly, if authoritarian leaders do not learn from previous domestic failure, it is likely that external democratisation efforts will have a better chance of succeeding, resulting in regime collapse.

Having assessed examples of external failure that the four cases learnt from, we now analyse internal examples. We investigate learning from the Soviet period and the 1990s in Belarus and Russia, determining what each government learnt. We then assess learning from image failure for Putin and the evolution from a man in too-large suits to the macho figure that has become a popular meme today. A Twitter Revolution in Moldova is addressed as another example of learning

---

[1] Quote from Yoda in the 2019 Star Wars film *Rise of Skywalker*.

from internal failure. Having been close to Vladimir Voronin in the past, Plahotniuc learnt from Voronin's failure to remain in power in 2009 when faced with protest in 2015, 2016, and 2017. We then address learning from failure in two Ukrainian examples. First, we investigate Yanukovych's learning from failure to become president in 2004 when he became president in 2010. However, Yanukovych was too busy fighting the last war, concentrating on Colour Revolutions, to see new protest techniques epitomised by the Arab Spring. It is why the authorities could not cope with the Euromaidan. Yanukovych had not completed power consolidation, making it harder to use repressive measures to end the 2013–14 protests. Second, we analyse Poroshenko's learning from Yanukovych's failure at the Euromaidan. Poroshenko copied much from Kuchma and refrained from developing the same authoritarian techniques Yanukovych used, as these alienated other key actors. A final example is learning from sub-optimal legislation investigating the Russian monetisation and pension protests in 2004 and 2018, and the Belarusian 2017 social parasite protests.

## 4.2 Learning from Internal Failure in Belarus, Moldova, Russia, and Ukraine

The wider literature on authoritarian learning has largely failed to address internal learning from failure. Thereby, by analysing examples of this in the four case studies, our understanding of authoritarian learning is more complete. Internal learning is a crucial method of learning in Moldova and Ukraine. For instance, Moldovan elites regularly change political allegiance, thus providing them with in-depth knowledge of past regime failures. This allows them to learn from these mistakes. For example, Plahotniuc moved from funding Voronin and the PCRM to financing the Democratic Party of Moldova (PDM) while retaining a close affinity to former president Igor Dodon. How close the Plahotniuc–Dodon axis was remains speculative, but throughout the ascendancy of Plahotniuc from 2009 to 2019 there were rumours that Dodon and Plahotniuc had created a cartel (Całus, 2018). While the fall of Plahotniuc appeared to end the cartel, the emergence of a new government between the PCRM and the PDM – at least briefly – in 2020 pointed to the continuation of the cartel (Batanova, 2020). Plahotniuc learnt from his time in the PCRM and the 1990s as a businessman, highlighting that the past is a place of valuable lessons.[2] In Ukraine, elites are closely tied to previous regimes. For instance, Poroshenko was at the centre of power under Kuchma, Yushchenko, and Yuliya Tymoshenko. He even kept close ties to Yanukovych and Rinat Akhmetov (Hale, 2015: 333). This provided Poroshenko with plenty of learning opportunities.

To better understand learning from internal failure, examples of learning for Belarusian and Russian elites from the Soviet collapse and 1990s are investigated. Another case is image failure. This is relevant in Belarus and Russia, where the leader's image is a key source of legitimacy. Originally, Putin's image was that of a bureaucrat, but the Kursk disaster ended this, as Putin took on a more macho persona after. As will be seen, the Kursk Disaster is an example of learning from failure. A final set of examples are the learning by Plahotniuc from the 2009 Moldovan revolution, Yanukovych's learning from the 2004 Orange Revolution, and Poroshenko's learning after the Euromaidan.

The examples here on learning from the Soviet period and the 1990s, image failure, the 2009 Twitter Revolution in Moldova, and the 2004 Orange Revolution and 2013–14 Euromaidan in Ukraine are but four examples of internal learning. In Chapter 1, we argued that there are types of learning when analysing the internal, which are policy transfer and lesson-drawing. The examples in this chapter have been chosen because they highlight these two types of learning. Belarusian and Russian learning from the Soviet period and the 1990s, coupled with Russian learning from image failure, is lesson-drawing. The image failure did involve a change in policy, but it was not a policy transfer from the Boris Yeltsin era and so we classify this example as lesson-drawing. The example of the Moldovan 2009 Twitter Revolution involves some policy transfer from one government to another, but it is largely one of lesson-drawing. Similarly, learning from the Orange Revolution and Euromaidan does involve some policy transfer, but this is relatively subtle and limited. In this example, lesson-drawing remains a focus of learning from internal examples.

---

[2]  Personal interviews: FD84603, WE39704.

### 4.2.1 Learning from the Soviet Period and the 1990s in Belarus and Russia

The failure of the Soviet Union and the 1990s still resonates for Putin, who has often referenced the failure of both periods during presidential addresses to parliament or in interviews (Malinova, 2011: 108). At a 2016 meeting of the All-Russia People's Front, Putin (2016b) argued that Lenin's federalisation policy for ruling the Soviet Union created 'a time bomb', allowing for possible secession. While there were other reasons for centralisation since 2000, such as taking power from regional leaders and oligarchs and the 2004 Beslan disaster (Gel'man, 2015a: 23–4), Putin saw federalism as having weakened the Soviet Union. By 2005, Putin had centralised power, thus making Russia a federation on paper. This was partly due to the failure of Soviet federalism, but also state weakening in the 1990s.

Economics is another lesson of Soviet failure that the Kremlin has taken on board, with Putin (1999) stating that the Soviet economy had 'doomed' Russia. Therefore, the Kremlin has been averse to a Soviet centrally planned economy, preferring a more capitalist system allowing people to get rich, have the latest technology, and travel. Yet, there is a dichotomy in these policies. On the one hand, the authorities feel an open economy brings prosperity, reducing the likelihood of stagnation as in Soviet times. Many Kremlin personnel today served during the Soviet Union, so the Russian authorities fear 'systemic collapse' and a sluggish economy that would cause wide public dissatisfaction. Fears over economic malaise are why the Kremlin retains a large repressive capacity (Galeotti, 2019b) to reduce possible future protests.

On the other hand, the Russian authorities have turned the economy over to close Kremlin allies to allow them to increase their wealth and support the regime (Dawisha, 2014; Makeev, 2017; Murtazaev, 2012). The private sector is largely controlled by the state from behind shell companies.[3] Therefore, the Kremlin must perform a constant balancing act, weighing the needs of the wider populace to increase their wealth while increasing the wealth of close allies to maintain loyalty. With only finite resources, the

---

[3] Personal interview: HF29751.

economy is stagnating, which is why repressive forces have been built up recently, as the authorities look to maintain allied loyalty rather than popular support.[4] While the Kremlin is struggling economically in 2022, the idea of a Soviet-style economy is one that has been learnt from and viewed as a failure.

While Putin largely missed Glasnost and Perestroika, East Germany was a good learning environment. Having been abandoned by the Soviet Union, the East German authorities were left with a crumbling economy and ideology (Hill and Gaddy, 2015: 114). This was like the Soviet Union – but witnessing it in Dresden – Putin concluded that ideology was insufficient for regime survival (Gevorkyan, Timakova, and Kolesnikov, 2000: 71–2). A final lesson was that Glasnost allowed ordinary citizens to speak out (Aron, 2012: 43), which for a KGB officer was anathema. Allowing the public a voice resulted in questions about the legality and support for the Soviet Union.

The so-called wild 1990s, which has long been a Kremlin analogy for instability, has been the principal example of failure for Putin. Putin (2015) blamed Yeltsin for the Soviet collapse, which fits with his often-misunderstood address to the federal assembly that Soviet failure was the greatest geopolitical disaster the world ever saw. Putin (2005) stated that it was the 1990s that brought instability, oligarchs, and mass poverty, all against a 'dramatic economic downturn, unstable finances, and the paralysis of the social sphere'. During the Millennium Message, Putin (1999) argued that now Russia needed patriotism and state strengthening, and the wild capitalism under Yeltsin would end. Other lessons of the 1990s 'failure' were that the regional parade of sovereignties and personal fiefs, such as Karelia and Tatarstan (Gel'man, 2010: 9–10; Prokhanov, 2013), could not happen again. In 1993 and again in 1999, Yeltsin could have been impeached (Sakwa, 2008: 123, 136), so after becoming president in 2000, Putin set about making certain impeachment could never happen again. It is one reason why by the end of his first term in 2004, he had coerced the media, other parties, and the oligarchs into either accepting Kremlin control or 'political oblivion'.[5] State weakness under Yeltsin was epitomised by defeat in the First Chechen War (1994–96) and is one reason why during the Second Chechen War (1999–2009), Putin showed a strongman persona (Moscatelli, 2011). The 1990s were 'defamed'

---

[4] Personal interview: HF29751.    [5] Personal interview: TM26801.

by the Kremlin for instability. The need to create a stable façade is a direct lesson from the 1990s (Prokhorova, 2017; Troitsky, 2017).

The 1990s instability is a similar mantra of the Belarusian regime, with Lukashenka learning from the failure of Prime Minister Vyacheslau Kebich to win the 1994 presidential election. The failure of Kebich to get elected as president in 1994 was a lesson, as Kebich, through media control and the use of electoral fraud, had the resources to win the 1994 presidential elections. However, Kebich had never contested a truly competitive election, and so was unprepared for it. Lukashenka used the media and his running of a corruption commission to good effect, and increased his popularity in the run-up to the election (Way, 2012: 629–31, 636). Kebich knew how to manipulate the media and use electoral fraud in the 1980s, but he had never experienced a fully competitive election. Kebich failed to keep regional elites onside, attacked other candidates, and failed to take Lukashenka seriously until days before his electoral defeat.[6]

Lukashenka (2002) referred to the Kebich period (1991–94) as a 'nightmare' and later that corruption was extreme (Lukashenka, 2014c). Highlighting learning, Lukashenka has stated that elites should not take too much (EJ.BY, 2018), although the system has constructed hidden corrupt activities (Smok, 2015). Another lesson for Lukashenka from Kebich was that while Kebich had Russian support, Kebich and Stanislav Shushkevich, the former head of the Supreme Soviet, constructed a Belarusian identity allied to the West, which upset most Belarusians. Lukashenka portrayed himself as a person who would return Belarus to a close alliance with Russia, or even integrate it into a new Soviet Union.[7]

The Kremlin took lessons from the Soviet period, learning from the failure of Soviet federalism and the economy to implement a centralised political system and capitalist economy. The regime also took lessons from the 1990s, seeing this decade as one of failure and instability. Similarly, the Belarusian regime viewed the 1990s as unstable, with Lukashenka learning from Kebich's failure to get elected as president in 1994. Lukashenka also learnt the value of keeping corruption hidden from public view, something that Kebich failed to do, allowing Lukashenka to win the presidency as an unknown.

---

[6] Personal interview: HA20938.     [7] Personal interview: NJ08269.

### 4.2.2  *Learning from Image Failure*

Another area of authoritarian failure is the failure of leader image, which is an issue for personalised regimes, as with Belarus and Russia, as the regime receives legitimacy from the perception among the populace that there is a leader in power who is a man of the people. The Kremlin has adapted to consistently keep Putin popular and maintain the so-called Putin majority.[8] Likewise, Lukashenka's image is consistently maintained by the regime and even though he has been in power for nearly thirty-six years he still manages to have a close link to the people,[9] although in the build-up to the 2020 presidential elections in August there was a need among some in the regime and electorate for an alternative. However, it is likely that Lukashenka will retain power through the *siloviki*,[10] although the regime is not as able to use its historic repression (Shraibman, 2020). The possible growing competition in elections means it remains to be seen what the future holds for Lukashenka. For now, this is speculation, and the leader image remains important in Belarus. Therefore, the leader's image is maintained constantly, as image collapse will lead to questions about legitimacy.

One example of image failure occurred during the early days of Putin's first presidency. Putin flew a helicopter at the beginning of the Second Chechen War in 1999 and famously promised to kill Chechen terrorists by 'wasting them in the outhouse',[11]. This which turned him from a little-known prime minister into a Russian superhero with most Russians, significantly contributing to his presidential election victory in 2000. While Putin has often framed himself with a tough-man persona, there was in the first years of his presidency a balance between this tough-guy persona and bureaucratic Putin. The Kursk disaster finally confirmed that a macho persona was required rather than a bureaucratic image if Putin was to continue to be popular. Since the Kursk disaster, bureaucratic Putin has been replaced by macho, or even superman Putin, a result of Kremlin learning. The sinking of the K-141 Kursk nuclear submarine – the pride of the

---

[8]  Personal interview: GR69301.
[9]  Personal interviews: JL96420, BN61592, YR52870.
[10]  The term '*siloviki*' refers to personnel in the so-called power ministries of the armed forces, interior ministry, and the security services.
[11]  A link is here: www.youtube.com/watch?v=rPFDp4KdJ0M.

Russian Navy – threatened the nascent tough-guy image and was the death knell for bureaucratic Putin.

Initially, during the Kursk disaster the authorities blamed a collision with another naval vessel of an unidentified state, the machinations of a foreign power, while also internally blaming 'the guilty' (Rossiskaya Gazeta and INTAR-TASS, 2000: 1) without stating who they were. The sinking of the submarine was compounded by the fact that the crew were poorly trained, and the submarine did not have an escape hatch, which would have allowed the seamen to evacuate. The Navy refused to acknowledge there was an incident for nine hours, with Russian ships in the vicinity failing to come to the rescue, and when a rescue team was finally sent, the rescue was bungled as they were poorly trained (Gessen, 2014: 164–6).

Putin initially refused to go to Viyayevo, the Kursk's home base, stating that his presence would only get in the way of specialists (Rossisskya Gazeta and ITAR-TASS, 2000: 1). Ten days after the sinking, he visited Viyayevo but was accosted by angry relatives of the sailors (Gessen, 2014: 168–70), a situation that was compounded by a television interview with Larry King, where Putin, when asked what happened to the submarine, merely responded with the caustic 'It sank'. This CNN interview, which went viral in Russia, coupled with the verbal abuse Putin suffered in Viyayevo, which was publicised in the Russian media (Burrett, 2011: 40; Shevtsova, 2005: 117), resulted in the image of Putin taking a direct hit and increased public dissatisfaction with the regime.

Although there were other reasons for the change of Putin's image, the Kursk disaster and Putin's failure to deal effectively with the situation contributed to the Kremlin changing Putin's image to one of mystique and a macho-man persona (Arutunyan, 2014; Goscilo, 2011, 2013) capable of getting things done and protecting Russians. Since the Kursk sinking in 2000, Putin has quickly been on the scene of all crises. For instance, with the Dubrovka Theatre siege, when Chechen terrorists took an audience hostage on 23 October 2002, Putin cancelled a meeting with then American president George W. Bush (BBC, 2002), emphasising he had learnt he needed to be on the scene of a crisis. During the 2004 Beslan school disaster, when Chechen terrorists took control of a school, Putin was very visible, orchestrating the rescue plan (Toal, 2017: 90). Such a learning curve from the Kursk disaster was further seen after the explosion at the

Sayano-Sushkenia hydroelectric plant in 2009, where Putin not only visited the plant but held a visual conference call with relatives immediately after the explosion (Gerasimenko, 2009).

Another example in the change of Putin's persona was the public dressing down of oligarch Oleg Deripaska by Putin to force him to re-open his factory in Leningrad Oblast and pay the factory's employees. It was broadcast on television, showing Putin arriving by helicopter and forcing an oligarch to re-open a factory and pay his workers. It was the personification of the tsar looking after his people, and while an agreement had already been reached in Moscow the day before, the televised dressing down of Deripaska played well to the crowd (Badanin et al., 2009). The public dressing down of Deripaska was a further continuation of the *dramaturgiya*,[12] which has personified Putin's rule from 'Putin versus the Chechens' to 'Putin versus the oligarchs' (Wilson, 2012). Therefore, the Kursk disaster is an example of the Kremlin learning from internal failure as the regime looked to develop the image of Putin and re-cast him as an all-man action hero, which has continued to be the image of choice for the regime.

Although, the presidential direct line (*pryamaya liniya*)[13] is a lesson from the failure of the Soviet Union to speak with its citizens, the Kursk disaster was a factor, as Putin had appeared distant during the Kursk sinking. The *pryamaya liniya*, as Putin (2001) stated at the first event in 2001, provided the Kremlin with knowledge about the problems faced by Russians, and the first *pryamaya liniya* occurred soon after the Kursk disaster, pointing to learning. Although, less popular than it once was (Korchenkova, 2015: 2; Korchenkova and Samokhina, 2015: 2), the *pryamaya liniya* is still watched by about 60 per cent of Russians (Korchenkova and Miller, 2015: 3) and is a controlled environment allowing the Kremlin to show that Putin deals with citizens' problems, while being seen by millions of viewers (Hill and Gaddy, 2015: 76). The *pryamaya liniya* shows that Putin is close to most Russians and is in part a direct lesson from Putin's ambivalence over the Kursk disaster.

---

[12] The Kremlin often uses dramatic or grand narratives to increase popular support in crisis times or elections.

[13] The *pryamaya liniya* is a heavily circumscribed event, where for about four hours Putin answers questions of the public. These questions are often vetted beforehand (Davies, K, 2017).

### 4.2.3 A Moldovan Twitter Revolution

One interviewee[14] argued that Plahotniuc learnt much from domestic examples as he was concerned with finding the best practices to govern Moldova, and as someone who was – until 2009 – close to President Voronin and the PCRM leadership, he has kept this as his point of reference. While Putin was the model to which to aspire, much of what Voronin did to consolidate power was taken up by Plahotniuc. Although it is considered by many would-be autocrats to be the model par excellence, the difference in governing Russia compared to Moldova is acute, and so in Voronin – a home reference – there was more that could be applied. Moldovan elites have known one another for many years. Allegiance to a political party is negligible and elites are close regardless of their current political allegiance.[15]

The 2009 Twitter Revolution was caused by the PCRM trying to steal the 2009 election and stop opposition parties from forming a governing coalition that excluded the PCRM. Without power, the PCRM would be unable to elect the president and thus lose control of both the legislature and executive (Harding, 2009; Mungiu-Pippidi and Munteanu, 2009: 138–9; Wilson, 2009). Under pressure from the EU, Voronin did not use as much repression as he had the capacity. While protesters were jailed, there was a perception that the authorities were unable – or unwilling – to clear the streets.[16] This had the effect of bringing more people out into central Chișinău. However, later during the protests, the police did use excessive coercion, which left the leadership isolated internationally.[17] The PCRM's failure in 2009 resonated with Plahotniuc as an example of what not to do.

The lessons from the 2009 Twitter Revolution were used effectively during protests in 2015, 2016, and 2017. The leadership knew that the repression used under Voronin in 2009 would affect relations with the EU and possibly result in Brussels cancelling the association agreement Moldova had signed in 2014. Therefore, the repressive practices used in 2009 were not implemented during the 2015, 2016, and 2017 protests.[18] The interior minister and director of the

---

[14] Personal interview: PD59726.    [15] Personal interview: WE39704.
[16] Personal interview: ST93601.    [17] Personal interview: GH26850.
[18] Personal interviews: GH26850, WE39704.

General Police Inspectorate at the time of the 2015, 2016, and 2017 protests, Alexandru Jizdan and Alexandru Pânzari, were both involved in the 2009 repression and used their tactical know-how from it (Jurnal.md, 2016e). Whereas the police in 2009 had attacked protesters in central Chişinău under the cameras of Western journalists, the leadership during the 2015–17 protests were subtler. By the standards of Moldovan politics, an excessive police presence was deployed, and protesters were stopped from reaching Chişinău, with buses and trains cancelled and police cordons set up every thirty kilometres throughout Moldova. Many of the 2015–17 leaders were members of the PCRM regime and so had inside experience of the Twitter Revolution.[19]

## 4.2.4 Bankova Learning from the Orange Revolution and the Euromaidan

### 4.2.4.1 Yanukovych and the Orange Revolution

Yanukovych's learning after the 2004 Orange Revolution encapsulates the need for leaders with authoritarian tendencies to learn from failure. As Treisman (2020) has shown, authoritarian regimes collapse not so much because of mass protests but because of the implementation of the wrong policies, resulting in failure. Authoritarian leaders do not want to fail because to do so results in the likely loss of everything including power, property, and political immunity. Few authoritarian leaders pass away in their beds as Francisco Franco did in Spain. Rather, it is more likely to end like al-Gaddafi in Libya or in arrest, conviction, and execution like Saddam Hussein in Iraq. To reduce the likelihood of a violent end, authoritarian leaders are constantly learning, although they do not necessarily learn the correct lessons. The example of Viktor Yanukovych learning from the 2004 Orange Revolution when he became president in 2010 is a good example of learning from internal failure. It is also an excellent illustration of learning the wrong lessons. Hall (2017a: 163) argued that during Yanukovych's presidency from 2010 to 2014 he was 'fighting the last war' devising best practices to reduce the chance of a new Orange Revolution forcing him from power after 2010. Focusing on the last

---

[19] Personal interview: DW48620, CR52981.

war meant that Yanukovych was unprepared for the Euromaidan, which was a different type of protest to the Orange Revolution, needing different counter-revolutionary methods. We tabulate the eight lessons in Table 4.1 that Yanukovych learnt from the Orange Revolution, although many of these lessons precipitated the Euromaidan. This is a challenge for authoritarian leaders. Concerned with staying in power, they are constantly learning and adapting, but are not always effective learners of the practices used and so precipitate another crisis.

Rather than list all the lessons that Yanukovych took from the Orange Revolution, we tabulate the learning linking this to the argument that internal learning follows lesson-drawing and policy transfer. We argue that there are eight learning instances that Yanukovych drew from his failure to become president in 2004 after he became president in 2010. The implementation of learning occurred even before Yanukovych became president. One key factor that had made him unelectable in 2004 to enough of the electorate was because he was perceived as little more than a thug. To get elected after 2004, Yanukovych changed his image. This is one example of learning for Yanukovych post-2004. We argue that policy transfer refers to the sharing of legislation between states, and as elites are often members of previous governments, policy transfer can occur in the same country. Table 4.1 draws out these lessons, linking them to the idea that learning from internal sources is one of either policy transfer or learning.

While Yanukovych learnt from the failure of 2004, the lessons he took, and his implementation of those lessons contributed to the Euromaidan. The growing authoritarianism and control of state structures created a zero-sum game between the regime and the opposition (Haran, 2013) that resulted in growing opposition unity in the build-up to the 2015 presidential elections, just in time for the Euromaidan. The emergence of the Yanukovych 'family', which stripped $8 billion annually from the Ukrainian economy (Wilson, 2014b), alienated established factions, who perceived that their resource access was being threatened, resulting in their support for the Euromaidan (Neef, 2014). Although Yanukovych learnt from the 2004 failure, many of those lessons directly contributed to the Euromaidan, highlighting that learning is not always successful.

Table 4.1 *Yanukovych's learning from the 2004 Orange Revolution*

| Learning type | Examples |
|---|---|
| Policy transfer | • Reversion back to the 1996 Constitution, as this provided Yanukovych with greater power as president. Doing so allowed him to take greater control over state institutions. |
| | • Political technology had been a key part of the Kuchma presidency – creating political parties to compete in elections and weaken the vote for opposition parties. Yanukovych took this into overdrive. |
| | • 2004 legislation that had allowed for the creation of political blocs was terminated in 2010. |
| Lesson-drawing | • Image change: having been widely seen as a thug – epitomised by vocally calling on Kuchma to clear protesters from the streets during the Orange Revolution – he changed his tune in the 2010 presidential election campaign, stating that the Orange Revolution was an example of democratic will. He employed American public relations specialists to change his image, including a new wardrobe of Western-style suits. |
| | • Kuchma had not tried to create a party of power, rather relying on multiple parties to support his policies. However, Yanukovych used the financial resources of backers – such as Rinat Akhmetov – to create a party of power in Party of Regions. This was used to co-opt other politicians and increase support for Yanukovych. |
| | • Similarly, Kuchma had not tried to create a broad coalition of elites willing to support him in a time of crisis. By contrast, Yanukovych formed a governing coalition with the Communist Party and Lytvyn Bloc to create a wider coalition that would support him during times of crisis. Although once Yanukovych's chosen prime minister Mykola Azarov was elected, the Communists and Lytvyn Bloc were largely excluded from the coalition. |

- In 2004, Kuchma had not used pro-regime supporters as a force on the streets. The creation of the Titushki by elites under Yanukovych was a way to get pro-regime foot-soldiers to counteract potential protests in the future. The Titushki were a pro-regime rent-a-mob and the new Berkut paramilitary force was given greater legislative powers to deal with protesters. Kuchma simply did not have sufficient repressive capacity in 2004 and Yanukovych was trying to create such capacity.
- The creation of a family – centred not on blood ties, but political alliances – was another lesson that Yanukovych took from Kuchma's failure. Kuchma had relied on different clans who looked out for their own interests before supporting Kuchma. The family gave Yanukovych control of the tax inspectorate, which was used against opposition groups.

### 4.2.4.2  Poroshenko and the Euromaidan

Yanukovych made some mistakes during the Euromaidan, which Poroshenko learnt from, as Unlike Yanukovych, who attempted to create what Putin has achieved in Russia since 2000,[20] Poroshenko took a quieter approach to power consolidation with control of the prosecutor general's office going under the radar. Unlike Yanukovych, whose jailing of Tymoshenko shocked the West, as Tymoshenko was the main opposition leader, Poroshenko only temporarily jailed confidantes of Kolomoisky and politician Oleh Lyashko without attempting to eviscerate the opposition, meaning Poroshenko's consolidation of power did not receive condemnation from Western states (Sukhov, Grytsenko, and Zhuk, 2016). While Poroshenko copied Yanukovych in placing allies in control of key state institutions (BusinessViews, 2017), Poroshenko was subtler in terms of pace and the number of allies in control of state institutions.[21]

While Poroshenko's power consolidation can be attributed to Russian actions in Crimea and Eastern Ukraine, these events have been used as an excuse for power consolidation. Civil servants and politicians from the regions were banned from criticising central politicians. One example was the ban on civil servants criticising the government, and legislation was used against Mikheil Saakashvili, who had gained quite a following with his criticisms of then prime minister Arseniy Yatsenyuk. There was fear in Bankova that Saakashvili could use his popularity to mount a political challenge to Poroshenko (Melkozerova, 2017). Poroshenko's aversion to criticism was highlighted by one interviewee[22] who argued that Poroshenko did not accept any criticism and only used the formal *vi* (you) form with ministers.

During his presidency, Poroshenko instigated media restrictions, which can be linked to the Euromaidan, during which social media played a significant role in organising protesters and sharing information. Under Poroshenko, journalists were attacked. On the day that journalist Pavel Sheremet was killed in July 2016, another journalist, Maria Rydvan, was stabbed, and five days after Sheremet's death another journalist was beaten (Interfax-Ukraine, 2016; Liga.net, 2016; Miller, 2016). Sheremet's death remains unsolved, although CCTV footage showed two people loitering by his car at about 2:40

---

[20]  Personal interview: MQ37492.    [21]  Personal interview: DF59302.
[22]  Personal interview: ZD49618.

a.m., with one spending about twenty seconds kneeling by the car (Obozrevatel', 2016). While the footage should have allowed the security services to find the perpetrators, the Organized Crime and Corruption Reporting Project (OCCRP) and their Ukrainian partner Slidstvo found that the police investigation was flawed. The OCCRP and Slidstvo's own investigation pointed to *Sluzhba Bezpeki Ukraini* (SBU) collusion in the death of Sheremet (Organized Crime and Corruption Reporting Project, 2017a). While it is uncertain whether the SBU wanted Sheremet dead, he was investigating people close to the Poroshenko regime, and the failure to find his killers (Ukrayinska Pravda, 2018c) leads to questions of complicity and incompetence on the part of at least some in the Poroshenko regime.

After the Euromaidan, Ukrainian television channels have had 'content supervisors', which are the channels' owners dictating what content their channels show with the approval of Bankova (Detektor, 2016), This Fitted the argument of one interviewee[23] that the media had a gentleman's Agreements with the presidential administration not to criticise Poroshenko. This trend has continued under the Zelensky regime, with Agreements and television channels owned by Rinat Akhmetov, Viktor Pinchuk, and Ihor Kolomoisky to not criticise the government and run programmes praising the work of Zelensky (Sorokin, 2020b), However it is also likely to be three oligarchs trying to gain favour rather than there actually being a formal agreement. During his presidency, Poroshenko created the ministry of information, which in a similar practice to the Kremlin used trolls to promote Poroshenko. As in Russia, these trolls attacked journalists online for publishing information detrimental to Poroshenko. Head of the Ministry of Information Policy Yuriy Stets' stated at the time that he would create a Ukrainian Internet army, to promote and praise Poroshenko (Sukhov, 2016c). The trolls could be a lesson from Russia, but they could also be a lesson from Yanukovych's failure, as the Yanukovych regime did not try to win the media war during the Euromaidan. Another lesson from Yanukovych's failure was his media regulation, which while attempting to control the media could not control the whole narrative. Poroshenko took a softer approach, by not trying to regulate the media, but rather reaching agreements with other oligarchs to control the narrative.[24]

---

[23] Personal interview: RK36829.      [24] Personal interview: LG52071.

### 4.3 Not Learning from Failure? Sub-optimal Legislative Failure in Russia and Belarus

Having analysed internal failure from the Soviet collapse and the 1990s, we analyse two further instances of learning from failure in Belarus and Russia. Regarding Russia, we analyse the monetisation reforms of 2004 and the 2018 pension protests. As will be seen, the Russian authorities did not learn from their failure in the mid-2000s when implementing a similar policy in 2018. Affected by an economic downturn in both periods, the government attempted to reform pension and other state-aid initiatives to save money. However, both attempted reforms ended in failure. The example from Belarus addresses the 2017 social parasite law – which saw the regime attempting to raise money by taxing the unemployed. This led to mass riots that the authorities did not see coming, and there does not appear to be much learning from this event other than to not create state-wide protests. However, the protests after the fraudulent re-election of Lukashenka in 2020 belies this view that the authorities had learnt not to antagonise the public. Both examples highlight learning from internal failure. However, this learning failed.

As authoritarian leaders are constantly learning to survive it is highly likely that they are not always successful at learning and as Treisman (2020) has remarked authoritarian regimes do not collapse just because of protests, but because they make mistakes. While the protesters only must be lucky once, authoritarian elites must be lucky all the time. This constant adaptation to ensure survival results in at least some failure and it is how elites react to this that ensures their survival or not. Internal learning from failure is not always successful and these two examples emphasise this point.

### 4.3.1 Russian Pension Protests: 2004 and 2018

On 25 August 2004, legislation to monetise benefits – giving people a set amount monthly – passed its third reading in the State Duma (Vinogradov, 2004: 1). The law gave 35 million people 450 roubles monthly, drastically reducing state benefits and making it unclear what the money covered (Ivanova, Grozovsky, and Bekker, 2005). Whether planned or not, the legislation became active during the New Year celebrations, so it was not until 11 January 2005 that the first protests began. Protests occurred in St Petersburg, Moscow, Moskovskya Oblast, Kazan, Penza, and Samara (Moshkin et al., 2005: 3; Pol'gueva, 2005: 1; Shleinov, 2005: 2). Protesters blocked the Moscow–St Petersburg Road, the Nevsky Prospekt in St Petersburg, and attempted to stop Putin's motorcade near Pulkovo airport in St Petersburg (Andreev, 2005: 3; Ivanov, 2005: 1; Pol'gueva, 2005: 1; Rotkevich, 2005: 2).

For a few weeks, the authorities appeared unable to deal with protests across the country, with some police units refusing to oppose the protesters (Ampelonsky and Meteleva, 2005: 4; Ivanova et al. 2005). Fissures occurred among the elite with former Patriarch Aleksey II stating that the law was unjust (Moskovsky Komsomolets, 2005: 3). In parliament, United Russia stalled against a concerted effort by systemic-opposition parties, like the Communist Party of the Russian Federation (KPRF) and Rodina, to discuss the protests (Horvath, 2013: 52–53). The systemic opposition even managed to get a no-confidence vote in the government tabled with the support of three United Russia deputies, who only backed down once party leader Boris Gryzlov threatened them (Guseva, 2005: 2; Rodin, 2005: 2). While the authorities eventually managed to control the situation using a mixture of repression and concessions, the government learnt from this failure. It re-introduced the original benefit system and afterwards retained close ties to pensioners, seeing them as a crucial source of support.[25]

Reform to the pension system was very quietly announced by the government on the opening day of the 2018 football World Cup in Russia, when most Russians were watching the opening ceremony and Russia's 5–0 destruction of Saudi Arabia in the opening game. Due to United Russia's majority in the State Duma, the legislation to raise the retirement age for both men and women[26] was passed on the first reading, even though all the systemic-opposition parties voted against the proposed law. There was dissatisfaction that Putin had not mentioned any reform of the pension system during his presidential election campaign in 2018, and that there was little attempt to engage in dialogue with the public during the campaign. Believing that victory

---

[25] Personal interview: PY29735.
[26] The retirement age was raised for men from 60 to 65 and for women from 55 to 63.

for Putin in 2018 signalled approval for touted structural reforms, the authorities were unprepared for the protests that occurred after changes to the pension system were announced.[27]

There was confusion as to what the reforms would mean and fear that they would result in a loss of existing benefits. As previous monetisation, health care, and education reforms had all resulted in the loss of benefits, there was a real fear that these 'reforms' would have a negative effect on a population that felt they had got poorer over the last few years (Alekseeva et al., 2018). Social media played a crucial role in organising protests and in providing information to protesters about when demonstrations would occur and to provide information to a wider audience. Protests themselves tended to differ across regions but were particularly high in European Russia, where many people were at pensionable age, and in Siberia, the Far East, and the North Caucasus, where people lived below the subsistence level (Mukhametshina, 2018).

Having in the 2000s created wealth and a growing middle class, the authorities had developed a society that while still supportive of the government – at least to some extent – wanted more focus on social issues and justice. Russian public opinion had increasingly changed from the militaristic tone of Crimea's annexation and wars in Syria and Ukraine to one focused on domestic issues.[28] Economic modernisation in Russia was gradual, but there was a trickle-down effect of money reaching the populace. On the one hand there was a sense that life had improved for many, but on the other hand that improvement had resulted in poverty for many. There was a growing demand that the state provide better social benefits, while allowing the public to go about their business (Kolesnikov, 2018d). The pension reforms highlighted not only that the authorities were secretive, but they had little regard for the citizenry. The social contract had been about increasing Standards of living for voting for the authorities. However, it was felt that the government had reneged on its part of the bargain (Kolesnikov, 2018a).

With a slowing economy, the authorities attempted to raise money and had developed new taxes against the private business sector (Kolesnikov, 2018e). Stagnation meant that there was less of a pie for the elites to share and in a system in which elite factions compete for

---

[27]  Personal interview: BD29641.     [28]  Personal interview: AM01079.

access to resources,[29] the authorities had to look for new sources of money generation. Pension reform was one way to generate revenue and keep elite factions onside supporting the government. The presidential administration, which regularly sends political strategists to the regions to gauge what may lead to protests, did not consider that a secret sharp increase in the pension age would result in protests (Kolesnikov, 2018b). But there were mitigating circumstance. Initial protests were low and earlier polling had shown that Russians appeared to accept such changes.[30] This shows the effectiveness – or lack thereof – of polling in more authoritarian states. It appeared that by passing the pension reform the authorities wanted to test how the public would react and then make concessions if there were protests (Bocharova and Mukhametshina, 2018). This tactic allowed the government to see how apathetic the population were and then be seen to make concessions – thereby gaining legitimacy – if there was a reaction.

There appeared to be division among elite factions. Medvedev had hoped that once the legislation was passed Russians would accept the new law. Putin himself did not comment on the reforms, thereby distancing himself from Medvedev. Similarly, Head of the State Duma Vyacheslav Volodin called for an enquiry thereby keeping the issue in the limelight to local elections. This was seen as an attempt by Volodin to weaken Medvedev, as if United Russia did badly at regional elections, then Medvedev would be the obvious scapegoat (Rustamova, Shamina, and Kozlov, 2018). While elite factions used the pension debacle for their own purposes in competing for power, there remained a real fear of protest (Bocharova et al., 2018) and United Russia quickly developed concessions to lessen the pain of the policy (Fontanka, 2018). In a televised address during the protests, Putin (2018) called for concessions to reduce the proposed retirement age for women from sixty-three to sixty. He also called for further changes to the law that would see more existing benefits preserved.

However, these calls for concessions did not appear to work, as protests continued (Kommersant, 2018; Meduza.io, 2018). A common tactic of the authorities is to be seen to make concessions to protesters to split demonstrators. Knowing that not all protesters are hardcore but are protesting on one issue, the authorities offer changes to placate enough people. This isolates hardliners and reduces protest

---

[29] Personal interview: AM01079.    [30] Personal interview: BD29641.

numbers. The concessions brought out after the pension reforms in 2018 was a similar tactic to that used during the protests in 2011 and 2012 against falsified elections. However, in 2011 and 2012, protesters had largely been isolated in Moscow. The pension reforms hit people across the country and affected a core group of regime supporters – the elderly.

With concessions not working, the authorities chose to ignore the protests and continued with making the pension reforms law. The State Duma quickly put the legislation through the second and third readings. The Upper House, the Federation Council, quickly read it and sent it to Putin for signature and it became law relatively speedily. By pushing through the pension reforms (Polutba, 2018), the authorities ignored the protests and did not engage with the public, presenting the pension reforms as an irreversible change. The government calculated that once the law was passed, most of the public would be dissuaded by further protest as there was no chance to change the situation (Mukhametshina and Didkovskaya, 2018). It was a tactic that worked. Once the pension reforms became law, there was little incentive to continue the protests and most demonstrators stopped attending.

It appears that there was limited learning from the 2004 monetisation changes when the 2018 pension reforms were implemented. Certainly, there is little that the authorities learnt from the failure of 2004. Rather it appears that the 2018 pension reforms were implemented out of necessity, rather than because of any learning. With a stagnating economy and the need to keep elites onside, the government tried to raise money in a very inefficient way by increasing the pension age, which would antagonise a sector of key support for the authorities, pensioners. It appears that the proposed pension reforms were a test to gauge how the public would react (Bocharova et al., 2018). Putin's popularity had fallen since the 2014 heyday with Russia's annexation of Crimea, and it is possible that people in the presidential administration calculated that publishing stringent pension reforms that would allow Putin to step in and make concessions (Kolesnikov, 2018c). This would improve the legitimacy of the authorities and increase Putin's approval rating. The authorities consist of competing factions and are often allowed to run their own policies,[31] with the system running on the practice of *otmashka* (Pavlovsky,

[31]  Personal interview: ND30192.

2016). Putin will not openly state that he believes in a proposed policy, merely saying 'I agree' and leaving it to the person to implement the policy as they think Putin wants it to be. This allows Putin to step in when a policy fails (Pavlovsky, 2016) and look like he is tackling inefficiencies. This increases Putin's popularity, which is the basis of the authorities' legitimacy.

There was limited learning by the authorities from the 2004 monetisation legislation during the formulation of the pension reforms in 2018. The elites who had initialled the 2004 law had mostly retired by 2018 and so there was a process of institutional forgetting from events that occurred fourteen years ago. The government also thought that the legitimacy that the authorities had gained from the Crimean annexation still existed and that pension reform would be accepted by enough of the public to negate possible protest.[32] If we draw the conclusion that the reform was implemented gradually and the authorities passed the reforms quietly, which limited the possibility of protest, then 2018 can be construed as learning from the 2005 protests. However, the pension reforms reduced the support base of the government. The anti-corruption protests in 2017 had reduced the support of the youth – a sector of society that had largely supported the regime – and the 2018 protests reduced the support of another key electorate, pensioners. If elites had truly learnt from the 2004 monetisation laws and the resulting protests in 2005, then they would not have done anything to undermine their support base.[33] Consequently, there was only limited learning between events in 2004 and 2018, but because there were few protests in 2018, with no demands for political change, the authorities were unaffected.

## 4.3.2 Taxing the Unemployed Belarusian Style

On 2 April 2015, presidential decree no. 3 'On Prevention of Social Dependency' was signed into law by Lukashenka. After putting this decree into law, Lukashenka notified parliament that an estimated 500,000 Belarusians were unemployed, and with the continued economic crunch in Belarus since 2010 (Wilson, 2021: 258) the authorities created decree no. 3 to get most of these 500,000 people into

---

[32] Personal interview: AM01079.
[33] Personal interviews: AM01079, BD29641.

employment by reducing their state benefits. During his address to the National Assembly, Lukashenka (2018) stated that the new decree was taken from the experience of the Soviet period, emphasising the authorities' reliance on ideas from the Soviet past. The connotations of the Soviet period were not lost on many Belarusians, especially as the preamble to the decree referred to freeloaders.

The new tax proposed to fine all able-bodied people who had not worked for 183 days a year 360 Belarusian roubles ($250). While the proposed legislation exempted such sectors of society as students and pensioners, the law included those living abroad, young mothers, and those looking after the infirm. An estimated 470,000 people – or 10 per cent of the population – were newly designated as freeloaders (Murphy, 2017) out of a working population of 4.5 million. Letters notifying the newly designated freeloaders were sent out in late 2016 and early 2017, which is when people began to become aware of the legislation. Even the authorities began labelling people social parasites and using the Soviet term for 'scrounger'.[34]

For the first time, protests in Belarus were state-wide and not just limited to central Minsk. The authorities were hamstrung in terms of limited finances to buy off enough protesters and were caught between a rock and a hard place geopolitically. With the Russian annexation of Crimea and the real fear among Belarusian elites that Belarus – or parts of the country – might be next, the leadership sought some rapprochement with the European union (EU) and Western states. With Western sanctions having only just been lifted in 2016, Lukashenka did not want to close off a source of much-needed investment, so was unable to crack down hard on the protesters like in 2006 and 2010 (Wilson, 2021: 267).

The authorities did resuscitate an old enemy in the Belyi Legion[35] as a justification for a crackdown on 25 March – a day traditionally linked with the opposition. The Belyi Legion featured prominently in Belarusian state media after the social parasite protests (Smok, 2017). The Belarusian authorities had used it as justification for a crackdown after the Minsk bombing in 2010 and now it was used again as the enemy within (Pankovets, 2017). The re-emergence of the Belyi Legion

---

[34] The Soviet term was *tuneiadets*.

[35] White Legion in English. This group of alleged nationalists and fascists were used by the regime to tarnish the opposition and re-appeared as the embodiment of evil whenever the authorities felt threatened.

was a case of learning from the Euromaidan. While the Ukrainian protests had not been the fascist coup that the Russian government painted these events as, there had been small groups of right-wing paramilitaries at the protests, such as Pravy Sektor. On the one hand, the crackdown on 25 March was a signal to the EU that the authorities were reacting to a political opposition – rather than the citizenry – as 25 March is a traditional day of opposition protest. However, the crackdown was not as extreme as in the past (Preiherman, 2017a; 2017b; Shraibman, 2017a).

On the other hand, the link between Belyi Legion and Pravy Sektor was a signal to Russia that the Belarusian authorities remained a close ally and were dealing with a possible Belarusian Maidan. Even before 25 March, the KDB had 'discovered' the Belyi legion and had begun arresting opposition activists (Meduza.io, 2017). At the same time, the authorities ran programmes on television linking the Euromaidan in Ukraine and the current war in Donbas – coupled with montages of the 1991–2001 war in Yugoslavia – to emphasise that protests lead to violence (Shraibman, 2017b). This was an effective tool in reducing the numbers of people who would go protest.

While the 2017 protests were the first state-wide demonstrations since Lukashenka became president in 1994, the authorities appear not to have learnt much from these events. Improved relations with the EU coupled with reticence at closer integration with Russia meant that a full crackdown was something beyond the regime. The leadership could not afford to alienate the EU and leave itself isolated and further dependant on Russia. There were further restrictions placed on media outlets and, in late 2017, Internet users had to prove their identity when posting a comment online (Wilson, 2021: 268). There was an increase in spending on security – although that had begun with the annexation of Crimea in 2014 – and this spending was focused on stopping little green men[36] or Colour Revolutions, both of which would be considered to have Russian involvement (Wilson, 2021: 270).

The limited repression instigated by the authorities created an issue for the future as the crackdown was not as coercive as it had been in the past. This created the sense that the regime was becoming milder and

---

[36] This is the name given Russian soldiers who led the Crimean annexation but did not wear Russian army markings allowing plausible deniability and making it harder for the new Ukrainian government to react effectively.

more willing to allow public involvement in politics.[37] Another change
that had begun before 2017 but highlighted that the regime was chan
ging was the policy of soft-Belarusianisation. To differentiate Belarus
from Russia in the opinion of Western audiences, and reduce the view
among Belarusians that they are the same as Russians, the authorities'
hijacked a soft-Belarusianisation project that had been a bottom-up
initiative to promote Belarusian identity (Boulègue, Lutsevych, and
Marin, 2018) giving Belarusians an identity dissimilar to Russia.
Belarusian history became less Sovietised, with Lithuanian grand
dukes re-cast as proto-Belarusian freedom fighters against Muscovy
and the city of Polotsk re-cast as proto-Belarusian, thereby giving
Belarus over 1,000 years of statehood (Mojeiko, 2015; Wilson,
2018). Soft-Belarusianisation and the 2017 protests instigated the
creation of civil society organisations distinct from the government
(Mojeiko, 2019; Pierson-Lyzhina and Kovalenko, 2020).

While there was some learning by the authorities from the 2017
protests regarding greater control over the Internet, we contend that
the authorities were less able to adapt as previously in preventing
Colour Revolutions. The economic situation meant that the regime
had less money to maintain security resources and co-opt enough
people into supporting the regime. The geo-political situation put the
authorities in a difficult situation, balancing relations with the West
and Russia. Increasingly distrusting Russia and wanting to continue the
rapprochement with the EU, the regime began limited liberalisation.
Yet, in a country where any change is significant,[38] this changed the
perception in society that the regime was exclusively repressive.

Having not experienced any major protests since 2010 and believing that the opposition was defeated after 2015,[39] it appears
Lukashenka and his inner circle became isolated from societal
changes. For most of his time as president, Lukashenka had known
what the average Belarusian wanted.[40] However, increasingly after
2015 it appeared that Lukashenka no longer has this knowledge.
The regime failed to see the changes in society – and the demands
that society was now making – and still followed the formula that
Belarus was little more than a collective farm managed by

---

[37] Personal interview: KW37410.    [38] Personal interview: VW28501.
[39] Personal interview: IR39203.    [40] Personal interview: BN61592.

Lukashenka.[41] Another issue was the change in focus for the regime. Lukashenka's press secretary, Natallya Eysmant, seeing the role social media played in the Arab Spring and Euromaidan, began to initiate a programme to win the hearts and minds of Belarusians through an online campaign.[42]

However, to complete this agenda, Eysmant closed the Information Analytical Centre (IAC), a structure in the presidential administration that regularly ran opinion polls and tested the reactions of Belarusians to proposed legislation. While there will always be questions as to how effective public opinion polling can ever be in an authoritarian regime, the IAC had been the eyes of the authorities. This structure's polling had been effective in the past by gauging what could lead to protest.[43] It is unclear quite when the IAC was closed but it appears to have been before 2015 when decree no. 3 was signed into law. As one foreign ministry employee speaking off the record once said, 'This law was crazy, absolutely crazy. It put the limited forward momentum we'd made with Belarusians here back to the beginning. It has destroyed what little trust we had established.'[44]

The social parasite law protests appear not to have been a lesson that the authorities have learnt from. While no further attempt has been made to pass such legislation, the authorities have stumbled in the past four years from crisis to crisis. Like the Russian government, who appeared to learn little in 2018 from the 2005 protests – and little after the 2018 protests as well – it appears that the Belarusian leadership has failed to learn from the 2017 protests. However, there are differences. Protests were small in 2004 and 2018 in Russia, and demonstrations were not political in nature. By contrast, there has been a range of crises in Belarus that culminated in the year-long protests of 2020–2021. Hamstrung by financial woes, a deteriorating geopolitical arena, the evolution of society, and a leadership increasingly out of touch, this appears to be a fragile moment for the Belarusian regime. There have been predictions of Lukashenka's fall before and we are not going to make such forecasts here, but it does appear – for now at least – that the Belarusian regime is no longer adept at adaptive authoritarianism as Frear (2019) argued. Rather, it is

---

[41] Personal interview: NF29463.   [42] Personal interview: KW37410.
[43] Personal interview: KW37410.   [44] Personal interview: ZP73618.

increasingly becoming a regime reliant on accessing enough repressive resources to keep control.

## 4.4 Conclusion

The chapter showed that the four case studies learnt from internal examples of authoritarian failure, from Russian learning from Soviet failures and both Russian and Belarusian learning from the failures of the 1990s. In Moldova, Plahotniuc learnt from the 2009 revolution and the ensuing loss of power for the PCRM. Similarly, Yanukovych and Poroshenko took lessons from the Orange Revolution and the Euromaidan, although Yanukovych's lessons from 2004 contributed to failure at the Euromaidan, and Poroshenko's subtle consolidation of power after the Euromaidan did not save him from electoral defeat in the 2019 presidential elections. However, as the analysis of sub-optimal legislation highlights, the cases studied do not always learn from previous failure. For the Belarusian elite, this is particularly an issue as the previous adaptive nature of the regime appears to be diminished and there is increasing reliance on repressive structures to keep power. There is evidence that authoritarian leaders are as likely to learn from internal failure as external failure and that they learn from internal examples as well as external examples.

# 5 | *Learning from External and Internal Success*

It's hard for an authoritarian to admit they learnt from success. Learning from failure gives you credit.[1]

## 5.1 Introduction

In Chapter 4, we investigated examples of authoritarian leaders learning from external and internal failure. As mentioned, learning from failure is a crucial part of survival for authoritarian leaders especially if the failure occurs in a neighbouring state. However, because authoritarian leaders are concerned with their survival at all costs, they will always learn from any available opportunity. This includes learning from examples of success. As Treisman (2020) contended, authoritarian regimes begin a democratic transition because the elite made a mistake. Yet, there is nothing to say that an authoritarian-minded leader in a neighbouring state will not make a different mistake reacting to the collapse of the government next-door. This is particularly so if the regime is reacting to events that have recently happened. The Arab Spring is an excellent example of this process. Authoritarian regimes that had protests soon after the collapse of the regime in Tunisia reacted in a similar way and lost power, but those regimes that did not have protests almost immediately had sufficient time to develop effective practices to ensure survival. Therefore, authoritarian leaders may learn from failure, but they do not always learn the right lessons.

However, there is a problem when analysing authoritarian learning from success. Unlike failure – which is relatively easy to track, as examples of authoritarian regime failure can be easily followed in media coverage such as with the Euromaidan – success tends to go

---

[1] Personal interview: SS20641.

under the radar. As the quote at the start of this chapter highlights, few authoritarian leaders would willingly admit that they learnt from the success of other authoritarians. It is much better to be the first to learn from the failure of others and develop the successful methods that others follow. This gives an authoritarian leader kudos among similar regimes, and few want to admit they copied and pasted the survival tactics from somewhere else. While former Uzbek president Karimov is a success to Putin, according to Zygar (2016: 107), as he learnt first from the failure of earlier authoritarian regimes during the Colour Revolutions, Putin has not publicly admitted his admiration for Karimov's success.

To draw conclusions that authoritarian leaders learn as much from success as they do from failure, we address examples of learning from success here. The first example of learning from external success analyses how China and Singapore, and to a lesser extent Kazakhstan, are models for the four case studies (Section 5.2.1). Another example analyses the copying of restrictive NGO legislation across the post-Soviet region and even in China, particularly following Russian legislation in 2012 (Section 5.2.2). The chapter then addresses learning from examples of internal success, analysing historical figures that play a role in the implementation of ideas in the present, which is particularly the case for the Kremlin (Section 5.3.1). The other examples of learning from internal success are the lessons Plahotniuc and Poroshenko took from their roles in previous Moldovan and Ukrainian regimes (Section 5.3.2).

## 5.2 Learning from External Success in Belarus, Moldova, Russia, and Ukraine

Due to the lack of evidence in some cases, not every example that is analysed in the chapter includes the four case studies. However, the examples analysed here all highlight that success is as crucial for authoritarian learning and survival as learning from failure is. When analysing learning from external success it is important to refer to the topics of lesson-drawing, policy transfer, and diffusion. While many of the examples used here represent the most crucial aspect of authoritarian learning – diffusion – the other aspects of learning are also crucial. As shown in the examples here, it is a strong form of diffusion that sees direct cooperation between elites and personnel. It is likely that emulation is also crucial, but it is difficult to measure, and the examples show that there is direct cooperation, which is stronger than emulation. Lesson-drawing, which involves drawing from external policies, and policy transfer, which involves the sharing of legislation, are also relevant to examples of learning from success. Linkage between regimes is likely to make the sharing of information easier, thereby playing a crucial role in trust and the decision of where ideas will be diffused from.

One example of learning from external success is Kremlin learning from regimes that stopped a revolution during the Arab Spring. For instance, Patrushev visited the Algerian director of external security, Rachid Lallali, to discuss 'the prospects for the development of the situation in the Middle East and North Africa' (Security Council of the Russian Federation, 2012b). By talking with the Algerian regime about Algerian successes during the Arab Spring, the Kremlin learnt the practices developed by the Algerian government to stop protests. This dialogue with Algerian counterparts would give the Kremlin first-hand knowledge of events and development of best practices to survive the protests. The Kremlin could use these, to counter protests, on the streets of Moscow if necessary. Similarly, in 2016, Patrushev met the chief of the Moroccan counter-espionage and police service to get details about 'the situation in the Middle East and North Africa' (Security Council of the Russian Federation, 2016b). As with Algeria, the Moroccan regime had successfully devised practices to stay in power, countered demonstrations, and not become another Arab Spring casualty like the Egyptian and Tunisian regimes. The Russian authorities would be interested to understand the successful practices the Moroccan regime used and contrast these with Algerian tactics, to ascertain if similar methods could be used in Russia. Therefore, learning from success is likely to be essential to authoritarian learning and the examples used in the rest of the chapter will highlight this.

### 5.2.1 *China, Singapore (and Kazakhstan?): Authoritarian Models for the Four Case Studies?*

Kneuer and Demmelhuber (2016) have argued that some authoritarian regimes act as authoritarian gravity centres for authoritarian-minded leaders in other states. While this representation is a little too hierarchical – failing to acknowledge that authoritarian learning is far more horizontal – certainly some authoritarian regimes do serve as models for others. While not all learning comes from these centres, as the authoritarian gravity centres paradigm advocates for – with the satellites providing learning opportunities for the centre – authoritarian leaders will look at successful examples and copy these. There are successful authoritarian models in Asia that serve as examples of authoritarian state-building for authoritarian-minded elites in the four case studies. China and Singapore are models, but it is possible that Kazakhstan is too. Consequently, analysis of these three models and their effect on the four case studies are examples of diffusion and emulation. There is a growing assertion in the literature that the Chinese authoritarian model is one that other authoritarian-minded personnel are copying and aspire to build (Ambrosio, 2012; Bader, J., 2015a, 2015b, 2015c; Breslin, 2011; Horesh, 2015; Kurlantzick, 2013; Lai, 2016; Nathan, 2016; Zhao, 2010). However, Ortmann and Thompson (2014, 2016) assert that the Chinese regime learnt from the Singaporean regime's economic and political model. Therefore, it is pertinent to analyse the role that a Singaporean model plays in the four case studies as well. Kazakhstan could possibly be a model for other post-Soviet countries, having created a relatively strong economy – although perhaps too dependent on natural resources – and an authoritarian political model.

### 5.2.1.1 China as a Model?

As an effective combination of an authoritarian political system with market capitalism that has seen the Chinese authorities maintain power while seeing exceptional economic growth, China is a model that other authoritarian-minded leaders want to copy. Having developed state structures that allow the authorities to better keep control and gain legitimacy by improving the economic well-being of the populace, China is a model for others to copy. Diffusion and emulation are key to the copying of this model, although as will be seen, there are direct lessons between the Chinese authorities and those of the four case studies. This is particularly the case regarding Belarus and Russia, but it is also so in Moldova and Ukraine.

Russian–Chinese relations have been conceptualised as an axis of convenience (Lo, 2008), or a 'cosplay alliance' with more form than substance (Galeotti, 2019a). For instance, during the military exercises

Vostok-2018, the Chinese military contingent only played a minimal role, lest they gain information on new Russian weaponry (Galeotti, 2019a). While the Russian and Chinese elites appear closer today, there is still mistrust there, in part due to conflict during the Soviet period and the continued Russian belief that China has eyes on Russia's far east and competes for control over Central Asia. However, this marriage of convenience has been relatively successful, and while China is the dominant partner, it has not made Russia subservient. Although Russia's economic weakness is of limited value for China, both regimes have forged a stable relationship together. There remain existing tensions, but these tensions are not being allowed to affect cooperation (Lubina, 2017: 283, 290; Kaczmarski, 2015: 165). For now, it appears that any alliance between China and Russia is on a limited scale. For many in the Russian elite, China is the embodiment of what the Soviet Union should have been had Gorbachev only instigated economic reforms – or had Andropov not died and been able to initialise his own economic reforms. Consequently, for this faction in the Kremlin, China is the model to copy in building an effective authoritarian capitalist state.[2]

The Russian and Chinese authorities have developed political, economic, and military contacts and delegations for personnel from each country to meet regularly. There are various inter-governmental commissions covering a wide range of topics, regular consultations between delegations from various ministries, and frequent meetings of the security services (Kaczmarski, 2015: 18). This points to something stronger than diffusion – if perceived as the spread of ideas that requires limited interaction – and emulation. It is likely that policy ideas are shared, although there is limited direct evidence on this. While Ambrosio (2017: 138) found that the connections between Chinese and Russian personnel remain relatively weak compared to Russia's relations with post-Soviet regimes, this is so because the Russian authorities perceive the post-Soviet space as their exclusive neighbourhood. But the Chinese and Russian partnership is growing with increased collaboration. This cooperation and integration enhances the learning capacity of both governments through direct learning, diffusion, lesson-drawing, and probably policy transfer. China and Russia use the Shanghai Cooperation Organisation (SCO) to counter

---

[2] Personal interview: AM01079.

American infringement on their interests in Asia, with the SCO criticising 'the West's propensity to use force, its disrespect for international law and infringement of other states' sovereignty' (Kaczmarski, 2015: 96). The SCO – along with other regional organisations in the post-Soviet space – are arenas for the spread of information and close collaboration between authoritarian-minded elites, thereby increasing the likelihood that learning happens.

In an article in *Kommersant*, the head of the Kremlin's Investigative Committee, Aleksandr Bastrykin (2016), stated that American involvement in Russia's neighbours' affairs was democracy promotion. Consequently, for Bastrykin, the Kremlin should counter American democracy promotion by not following Western 'pseudo-liberal values', stop 'playing with false democracy', and construct an ideology where the 'common good' overrides individual needs. This, according to Bastrykin, would allow the Kremlin to construct a distinctive Russian political system with popular support. Apart from forging a Russian form of democracy, the Kremlin should look to Chinese methods to maintain regime stability against American pressures and Chinese legislation that restricts foreign media operating in China to stop Western states influencing the Russian public (Bastrykin, 2016). This fits with assertion[3] that at least some factions in the Russian government are focused on learning from China. Bastrykin has been a close associate of Putin since their school days in Leningrad. Therefore, it is likely that Bastrykin's *Kommersant* article was approved by others in the Kremlin and highlights that the Kremlin believes Western democracies are trying to destabilise Russia through hybrid war. To alleviate the 'information war' emanating from America, Bastrykin (2016) argued that the Kremlin needed to copy Chinese practices to better consolidate control. To do this, the Russian government should increase control over the media and NGOs and increase surveillance to cope with American-sponsored protests. The *Kommersant* article gives a blueprint for increased Kremlin control, with examples of authoritarian consolidation from China seen as crucial for the Kremlin to copy, to limit American machinations against Russia.

China has perfected a system of Internet control, and the Russian authorities have selectively copied from this playbook. The Chinese

[3] Personal interview: AM01079.

system of Internet regulation is popularly known as China's Great Firewall and comes under the wider Golden Shield Project.[4] The Great Firewall was started in 1998 and finished in 2003. It is the most sophisticated system of surveillance in the world. The creation of the Great Firewall is direct learning on the part of the Chinese regime learning from American businesses – such as Cisco – who had developed a closed network to stop employees accessing blacklisted websites on company time in the 1990s. This technology, which was first developed in America, was used to develop a system to block any website deemed inappropriate. The Chinese authorities went further than in America by employing an army of censors to expunge comments seen as harmful to the Chinese government. While VPNs are used by some in China to circumnavigate the Great Firewall, these are convoluted processes and the censors are constantly expanding the Great Firewall, thereby creating a battle between censors and those wanting to look over the wall. The Chinese authorities are adept at deploying hackers to attack websites, politicians, organisations, and even states deemed to have upset or misrepresented China.

The trappings of the Great Firewall have been exported to countries like Russia, with Chinese personnel helping their Russian counterparts develop a 'walled Internet' that the Kremlin can control (Yang, 2019). Russian oligarch Konstantin Malofv arranged a conference in Moscow in 2016 with the deputy head of the Chinese Propaganda Department, Lu Wei, and the head of the Central Leading Group for Internet Security and Informatisation, Fang Biuxing, to learn about Chinese Internet control and how it would be useful in a Russian context (Seddon, 2016; Wade, 2016). This points to a strong form of diffusion with direct dialogue and meetings. Malofeyev set up the Safe Internet League, which has trialled several Chinese methods, such as white wall software to stop non-approved websites being viewed (Seddon, 2016), and the Kremlin has begun using Chinese technology requiring users to sign identity forms prior to posting content on any website (Rudolph, 2017).

Russian attempts to restrict access to Facebook and Twitter and banning LinkedIn follow Chinese practices (Zelensky, 2016). The Yarovaya

---

[4] The Golden shield is a 'transformative software that enabled the government to inspect any data being received or sent, and to block destination IP addresses and domain names' (Economy, 2018).

package of laws, which greatly increased the powers of the Russian security services to monitor the Internet, was passed in 2016 after a year of meetings between the Chinese and Russian delegates (Soldatov and Borogan, 2016). This example points to some form of policy transfer and lesson-drawing. In 2019, the Kremlin analysed methods to create an autonomous Internet, based on the Chinese model, which would be independent of American root servers, where all Internet traffic passes (Maçães, 2019). This example points to diffusion and emulation of Chinese methods in Russia. In April 2019, Putin signed legislation to create a truly independent Russian Internet. While these laws surpassed existing Chinese systems, the legislation was done in close collaboration with the Chinese authorities (Kovachich, 2019). This is a direct example of policy transfer, and again highlights a strong form of diffusion occurring between authoritarian-minded elites.

It is interesting to note that, in this case, it appears that Russia was used as a testing ground to gauge what restrictions could be put in place and ascertain the response of Western states. If the reaction from Western states is limited – as appears to be the case at the time of writing in 2021 – then the Chinese authorities may follow and increase overall control of the Internet in China, although existing restrictions are more than sufficient. If this is the case and Russia was a testing ground for gauging the reaction of Western states to Internet control for China to learn from, then this points to strong cooperation between both governments. The collaboration between the Chinese and Russian regimes over the Internet highlights direct learning, and is a solid example of authoritarian learning.

If it is the case that some in the Russian elite perceive China as the embodiment of what the Soviet Union should have accomplished, then it is likely that at least in the late 1990s and early 2000s the Belarusian authorities looked to China as the example of what the Soviet Union should have been. Although an exaggeration that Lukashenka wanted to create a mini Soviet Union in Belarus, his point of reference remains the Brezhnev period and a Sovietised economy.[5] Therefore, an example of a successful authoritarian political system – and to a lesser extent a market capitalism – that retains a communist ideology is a model that fits with Lukashenka's perception of the best form of state.

---

[5] Personal interview: HW29578.

While the relationship between Belarus and China is largely economic, as Lukashenka tries to diversify Belarus's economy away from Russia, there are political aspects to the relationship, with the Chinese regime supporting the Belarusian authorities from interfering outside forces (Koch-Weser, 2011). Lukashenka wants to copy aspects of the Chinese model, but rather than economic liberalisation, Lukashenka favours Chinese practices of restricting human rights and achieving annual GDP growth of 8 to 10 per cent (Dubina, 2017). Achieving that kind of growth is difficult, as Lukashenka also wants control of the economy and a prominent place for state business – a hard circle to square. While the Chinese model has state businesses, and the private sector has to follow government requests, the Chinese model's main success is that the economy includes private enterprises. These enterprises are given some leeway, and the Belarusian regime would be unwilling to allow any independence for fear that the authorities would lose control by privatising the economy.[6] Privatisation would lead to greater independence for business and employees would not be reliant on the state. It could even create independent entities to challenge the state. A strong private state would have the independence to raise or lower wages and possibly sack workers. This would especially be the case initially if inefficient state-controlled businesses were privatised. Low wages and mass unemployment would affect the social contract, ending reliance on the state and affecting the legitimacy of the government, leading to potentially more protests. The social contract of guaranteed jobs, a wage, and pensions for non-intervention in politics is the agreement between the government and the people, and the very basis of regime legitimacy. Therefore, the authorities would be unwilling to sacrifice the social contract for greater – but uncontrolled – economic prosperity.

The Belarusian and Chinese regimes collaborate on Internet control. For example, after Belarusian presidential administration head Viktar Sheyman visited China in 2005 there was a spurt of Internet censorship orchestrated by the Belarusian regime (Naviny.by, 2005), pointing to Sheyman having held talks with the Chinese authorities about Internet censorship. As with the Russian example on the Internet, this points to a strong form of diffusion, lesson-drawing, and possibly policy-transfer – although there is no evidence of direct copying of Chinese

---

[6] Personal interview: YR52870.

legislation. In 2015, the Belarusian government issued a tender for equipment to censor the Internet and block websites, which Chinese manufacturers won (Petrovskaya, 2015). After the 2017 protests in Belarus, both head of the presidential administration Stanislau Zas and Lukashenka flew to Beijing on separate occasions, and it is likely both Belarusian delegations discussed information security and how the Chinese authorities used the Internet to reduce potential state-wide protests (Mitskevich, 2017). Although evidence is lacking as to quite what was discussed, this example points to direct cooperation and lesson-drawing. Under former prime minister Michail Myasnikovich, Belarus worked with the Chinese regime to enhance media and telecommunication control, and the KDB copied Chinese telecommunication practices. Again, this points to direct cooperation. While for the most part there is little direct collaboration between the two governments, there is direct Belarusian copying of Chinese Internet practices. Therefore, diffusion seems to play a greater role in Belarusian learning from China, although there is also dialogue pointing to at least some form of cooperation.

The relationship between the Moldovan and Chinese authorities is based on economic integration, with Dodon (2017, 2018) advocating for Chinese investment and Moldovan involvement in China's One Belt – One Road initiative. Much of the relationship between Moldova and China involves Chinese investment in Moldova from agriculture to energy and roads (Svitrov, 2019). There is evidence that the Chinese regime invested in the Moldovan interior ministry (NewsMaker, 2016b), although it is unclear what the Moldovan regime spent the money on. While there is economic linkage, the Chinese authorities do not view Moldova as a strategic partner (Larson, 2018; Popşoi, 2018). However, it is probable that China serves as a model of emulation for some Moldovan elites.

Like Moldova, Ukraine's relationship with China is largely economic, with successive Ukrainian governments interested in Chinese investment (Larson, 2018). However, the Yanukovych regime went further than just economic collaboration trying to strengthen political control over Ukraine by copying Chinese policies (Umland, 2011). This points to emulation, rather than direct cooperation. The Chinese model may resonate for Ukrainian authorities – like Yanukovych – but for China Ukraine is 'a door to the European market' (Hiymol', 2014). Although Yanukovych implemented aspects of the political part of the

Chinese model, the relationship between Ukraine and China is largely economic, pointing to linkage, which induces diffusion and emulation, rather than direct cooperation and learning.

### 5.2.1.2 A Singaporean Model?

It is possible that Singapore is another authoritarian model for the four case studies. Like China, Singapore has created an effective authoritarian political system that incorporated market capitalism. While elections exist, the party of power in Singapore – the People's Action Party – has not lost an election since independence in 1965 and serves as a model of a successful party of power that the Russian government could copy with United Russia. The Singaporean authorities have developed an effective systemic opposition and electoral system, which can be adapted to ensure the People's Action Party dominance at elections. The authorities have developed control mechanisms to cope with protest and pioneered facial recognition technology to maintain public order. This is likely to be something that authoritarian-minded elites in other countries would want to copy. It is likely that other authoritarian-minded leaders would want to copy Singapore's political model. As mentioned, China looked to Singapore's model of an authoritarian polity combined with market capitalism as an example to follow (Ortmann and Thompson, 2014; 2016). It is likely that if Singapore were a model for China, then it will be for other authoritarian-minded elites as well.

Kremlin representatives have met Singaporean counterparts[7] to ascertain if the Singaporean model can be transferred from a small island state to the world's largest country (Tsepliaev, 2010). The Singaporean model provides an example of a rich state ruled by the same small circle for decades, thereby making it an excellent example for any authoritarian regime concerned with remaining in power. Singapore is also an example of a country that caught up with more economically developed states – such as America – thereby serving as an example for Russia. However, Singapore achieved this without natural resources, and it is unlikely that Russia will develop its economy away from natural resources. Due to the difference in size between Russia and Singapore, it is also difficult to imagine how the Russian

---

[7] Personal interview: TW28643.

authorities could follow the Singaporean model. However, China which is nearly as big as Russia, did copy the Singaporean model. It is likely that while there is no direct learning, Singapore serves as a model to be emulated by Russian elites in terms of the economy and political control.

There is limited evidence of direct learning from Singapore, with modernisers in the Belarusian regime interested in Singapore as a developed authoritarian state, which may be relevant to Belarus in the future (BelGazeta, 2017b). However, if Lukashenka remains president, any implementation of a Singaporean model is unlikely. Regime modernisers have initiated reforms taken from the Singaporean play-book, but any change must be gradual and incremental, testing the water to ascertain what Lukashenka and the inner circle in the regime will accept (Shraibman, 2017c). However, since the protests at the 2020 presidential election fraud, most modernisers have been removed from government, thereby weakening any movement towards a Singaporean model. Another issue with the current Belarusian government has implementing the Singaporean model is that Singapore has a relatively free judiciary and private sector. It is hard to believe that Lukashenka would allow an independent judiciary and business sector to exist, for fear that either sector would weaken his hold on power. Therefore, the Singaporean model is one that only a small faction in the Belarusian government looks to emulate. Now, any implementation of this model appears unlikely, but it could be implemented in the future.

Although the Moldovan authorities are enamoured by Singapore's economic development, there is limited contact between the Moldovan and Singaporean governments (NewsMaker, 2018). At a meeting between then president Igor Dodon and Singaporean prime minister Li Xianlong, Dodon (2019b) thanked Xianlong for the Singaporean government's training of Moldovan foreign ministry personnel and increased political dialogue between the two governments. In 2014 then president Nicolae Timofti (2013), when meeting his Singaporean counterpart Tony Tan Ken Yam, referred to Moldovan attendance at the Singaporean Cooperation Programme Training Award (SCPTA). The SCPTA is a training programme that covers how Singapore successfully built a strong economy, political system, and judiciary. Moldovan attendance of this programme points to learning by the Moldovan authorities of the Singaporean model. Analysis of the presidential portals of Belarus, Russia, and Ukraine does not mention

SCPTA attendance, pointing to this being a programme that only Moldova uses, demonstrating the importance of Singapore to Moldova. Both are geographically small countries that had viability issues upon their independence – although for different reasons, with Singapore not experiencing secession – and Singapore's success is a reference point for Moldova to copy.

The Ukrainian political elite have long seen Singapore as a model of economic prowess to emulate (Lossovskaya, 2015). The Yanukovych regime studied the tactics that the Singaporean regime used to keep power (Ukrainskaya Pravda, 2011). The Singaporean government has created a less corrupt, relatively open political system, but one that is controlled by the regime. Various Ukrainian regimes have tried to emulate this model (Tkachuk, 2014), but have so far failed to effectively tackle corruption. The anti-corruption success of Singapore is one reason why Poroshenko sent anti-corruption employees to study in Singapore in 2014 (Ukrainskaya Pravda, 2014d). However, a concerted fight against corruption is unlikely, as corruption permeates the system and provides opportunities for factions to get kompromat on others by prosecuting corrupt members (Grabovsky, 2012). There is less linkage between Ukraine and Singapore than with Ukraine and China, so it is clearly a process of emulation and diffusion, although regarding corruption it could involve policy transfer and lesson-drawing.

### 5.2.1.3 A Kazakh Model?

Kazakhstan may not appear an obvious model for authoritarian-minded elites, but the authorities have established an authoritarian political system with a relatively vibrant economy largely from scratch. The longevity of Nazarbaev's time in power and his controlled transition of placing an ally as president and becoming head of an empowered security council is likely a model for would-be authoritarians. The protest events in 2022 may have rather tarnished the model for other authoritarian-minded elites, with Nazarbaev's carefully crafted system of power behind-the-scenes having appeared to fail at the time of writing. However, Kazakhstan serves as a model of political longevity and the creation of a strong economic system.

When first contemplating changing term limits, Lukashenka regularly spoke with Nazarbaev about how best to achieve such a change.[8]

---

[8]  Personal interviews: HA20938, HW29578.

Kazakhstan is a close ally of Russia and member of numerous post-Soviet regional organisations, allowing it to share best experiences. Due to the influence of China and Russia in Central Asia – coupled with mistrust of Kazakhstan and foreign influence in the other Central Asian republic – it remains to be seen whether Kazakhstan will become a model. Russia retains significant influence in the region and in Kazakhstan as well. Consequently, it is unlikely Kazakhstan is much of a model for the Russian authorities to copy (Del Sordi and Libman, 2020). But it may be that Kazakhstan serves as a model of emulation to other post-Soviet states of a regime that has established longevity and a market economy, which others may look to copy. It is probable that this is done through diffusion and emulation, although it is likely there is direct collaboration as well. For instance, modernisers in the Russian government often look at Kazakhstan as a source of 'liberal economic reforms and ... learning for Russia' (Del Sordi and Libman, 2020: 140).

There are examples that make Kremlin learning from Kazakhstan a likely scenario, one of which is the Russian government changing extremism legislation in 2012 – which made media outlets responsible for the content that is posted on their websites. This was directly taken from existing Kazakh legislation that was passed in 2009 (Savchenko, 2016). The longevity of Nursultan Nazarbaev's tenure (1991 to 2019), his personality cult, economic development, construction of a new capital, and strengthening of presidential power while maintaining a relatively open economy (Gusev, 2010: 7; Nezavisimaya Gazeta, 2007: 2; Solntseva, 2008: 9; Vedomosti, 2010: 4) give authoritarian-minded elites in other countries ideas. It is a model of authoritarian regime capabilities. It is likely that the Kremlin drew lessons from how former Kazakh President Nazarbaev seemingly successfully retained power as chairman of the Kazakh Security Council. It seemed that this was once an option for Putin after 2024, when he is constitutionally barred from standing as president again (Bershidsky, 2019a).

However, the 2022 protests may have ended this possible option for Putin to retain power after 2024. Nazarbaev had himself seen what happened in Uzbekistan in 2016 when Islom Karimov died and did not leave a designated successor, with elites competing for power and Karimov's family having to give up many of their businesses (Gabuev and Umarov, 2022). Fearful of such an eventuality, Nazarbaev began planning his succession, placing a close associate – Karim Massimov – as head of the security services and Kassym-Jomart as president, while retaining the leadership of a much more politically strengthened Security Council. Massimov, who is perceived as a Uighyur, is unelectable in Kazakhstan and Tokaev lacked a network that could oppose Nazarbaev. Therefore, both were perceived by Nazarbaev to be people he could trust without them wanting to take power, thereby allowing Nazarbaev to keep control of formal and informal institutions. Yet, Nazarbaev's failing health and the sudden state-wide protests in early 2022 allowed Tokaevto to develop his own network and remove Nazarbaev allies, including Massimov, from power (Gabuev and Umarov, 2022).

Until 2022, Kazakhstan was a possible model of how Putin could step back from the presidency while keeping overall control. The 2022 protests and the difficulty of ensuring that those below Nazarbaev did not establish their own networks has probably put an end to such an option occurring in Russia. Yet for a while at least, Nazarbaev's plan of leaving front-line politics while holding overall power as head of the Security Council was an option seriously considered by the Russian presidential administration as a solution for a possible retirement plan when until Constitutional changes in 2020 Putin was affected by term limit in 2024 (Gabuev and Umarov, 2022). Kazakhstan as a model highlights the argument that the hierarchy of authoritarian learning is flatter than widely considered. While Russia, as the regional hegemon, does dominate learning, as it dominates in so many other respects the post-Soviet region, it is willing to learn from other post-Soviet authoritarian regimes, as the elite want to ensure their survival.

Lukashenka is less interested in the model of Kazakh economic development and more in copying how presidential power was strengthened in Kazakhstan. While it was Lukashenka who did away with presidential term limits in 2004, before Nazarbaev did, in 2007 Lukashenka consulted Nazarbaev on how best to implement such a process.[9] Kazakhstan and Belarus are post-Soviet states that both have a long history of authoritarianism. Each is a member of many of the same regional organisations. This makes it likely that both states cooperate with one another, which makes learning through dialogue and collaboration more than likely. While there is little direct evidence of cooperation and learning, it is likely to exist (though well hidden), and emulation is likely to occur as well.

---

[9] Personal interviews: HA20938, HW29578.

Diffusion is crucial to Moldovan learning from Kazakhstan as it appears to be a case of Moldovan elites seeing what happens in Kazakhstan and trying to implement these ideas and policies. During a meeting with current Kazakh president Qasym-Jomart Toqaev,[10] Dodon (2019a) stated that Moldova and Kazakhstan had achieved high levels of political communication between state departments. While the statement is vague, it highlights collaboration, learning, and sharing of best practices, pointing to direct cooperation. Though it is likely that Putin and Lukashenka were the models Plahotniuc emulated when he changed the electoral system in 2018, there were many similarities in electoral changes to how Nazarbaev kept control in Kazakhstan (Jurnal.md, 2018), pointing at emulation of Kazakhstan. Although, Moldovan and Kazakh representatives meet and attend meetings at regional organisations such as the CIS, it appears that emulation and diffusion are as important as direct dialogue to Moldovan learning from Kazakhstan.

Since the Soviet collapse, Ukraine and Kazakhstan have retained close ties, especially regarding economic cooperation (Forina, 2013). Even with Russia stopping Ukrainian exports onto Russian territory, which affects Kazakh–Ukrainian trade, both governments retain close ties (Melkozerova and Talant, 2016). Having successfully turned itself 'into the Singapore of Central Asia', Kazakhstan is an example for other post-Soviet states to emulate, which Ukrainian governments' have looked to do (Raikhel', 2015). While direct evidence of cooperation is limited, there are strong ties between the Ukrainian and Kazakh governments. Personnel of each government regularly meet bilaterally and multi-laterally at regional organisations such as at the CIS. These meetings allow for the sharing of best practices and information gathering between the personnel of each country.

### 5.2.2  NGO Legislation: A Helpful Trend of Authoritarian Learning?

Another aspect of learning from success is NGO legislation and the passing of foreign agents legislation, which portrays certain NGOs – generally those involved in politics as defined by the government – as financed from abroad. This type of legislation is certainly a case of

---

[10]  We give the Kazakh spelling of his name.

emulation and diffusion. However, it is also likely an example of policy transfer. Lemon and Antonov (2020) have shown that post-Soviet states, through the auspices of the CIS, share legislation. Since 2012, with the advent of the Russian foreign agents law, many other governments have passed similar legislation, some of which copies the 2012 Russian law almost word for word, including the law passed in China in 2018.[11] This trend of foreign agents legislation across the globe points to direct cooperation and policy transfer.

The 2012 Russian foreign agents law expanded on previous 2006 Belarusian legislation.[12] The Belarusian legislation had restricted the capacity of Western NGOs to operate in Belarus and constrained the activities of Belarusian NGOs that were supported externally. The Belarusian authorities had developed legislation that increased the bureaucratic work of NGOs – requiring notification of all activities and finances – but after the 2006 protests harsher legislation seriously curtailing the activities of Western NGOs and domestic NGOs sponsored from abroad was enacted. Before 2012, the Russian authorities relied on legislation that was very similar to the older 2006 Belarusian law.[13] Yet, with the 2011–12 Russian protests, the authorities looked for harsher legislation. As with the copying of previous Belarusian laws, the Russian authorities copied the newer legislation. With regular meetings through the Union State of Belarus and Russia between personnel of both regimes, it is hard to believe that the Russian authorities were unaware of such legislation. However, it was only when protests occurred that the Kremlin incorporated a Belarusian import, with the Russian law copying much of the older Belarusian law.[14] This is a direct example of direct discussions and likely policy transfer.

The 2012 Russian legislation restricted foreign funding of NGOs and placed limitations on the activities of NGOs engaged in political activity. For good measure in 2014, the law was changed, allowing the Kremlin to register NGOs as foreign agents for being involved in political activities as defined by the authorities (Lyons and Rice-Oxley, 2015). The 2012 Russian NGO legislation precipitated a trend of restrictive NGO legislation across the post-Soviet space and further afield. Similar laws were passed in Azerbaijan (2013),

---

[11] Personal interview: DX52073.
[12] Personal interviews: MU19837, CN20491.
[13] Personal interview: MU19837.
[14] Personal interviews: MU19837, CN20491.

Tajikistan (2014), and Kazakhstan (2015). While Belarus had already passed NGO legislation that limited the activities of Western NGOs in Belarus and Western state funding for Belarusian NGOs, Moldova and Ukraine attempted to copy Russian legislation on NGOs after 2012. In August 2017, the Moldovan justice ministry nearly got the power to force NGOs receiving foreign money and engaging in ill-defined political activities to submit quarterly audits and disclose funding origins, spending, and employee salaries. The proposed legislation had some key similarities to the 2012 Russian legislation and used remarkably similar language (Popşoi, 2017). But, after EU threats to stop funding, the proposed legislation was dropped (Jurnal.md, 2017b). While EU pressure stopped the Moldovan authorities from passing such legislation, the EU was unable to compel Bankova from signing legislation in 2017, which forced anti-corruption NGOs to file asset declarations. This expanded the time NGOs had to spend completing asset declarations, thereby stopping them working effectively (Sukhov, 2017b). Although different from the 2012 Russian foreign agent law, this legislation shared many similarities with previous Russian 2006 anti-NGO legislation.[15] The NGO legislation analysed here points to a strong source of diffusion (direct discussion), emulation to an extent, and policy transfer, all of which are crucial aspects of learning.

## 5.3 Learning from Domestic Success in Belarus, Moldova, Russia, and Ukraine

This section investigates learning from domestic success, and there are several areas that highlight that internal success is relevant to authoritarian learning. Finding examples of learning from internal success is difficult. Authoritarian-minded leaders do not willingly emphasise external success or that past leaders were successful. To best analyse examples of learning from internal success, we assess learning from the Soviet past in Belarus and learning from previous regimes for Plahotniuc and Poroshenko. Both were members of previous regimes in Moldova and Ukraine and have drawn lessons from others to use these practices when in power. By analysing internal aspects of learning, we analyse lesson-drawing and policy transfer, which are the two aspects of authoritarian learning from internal sources.

---

[15] Personal interview: JH58291.

### 5.3.1 *Living the Soviet Highlife in Minsk*

In 2016, Lukashenka (2016b) stated that the Soviet collapse was due to it producing insufficient good-quality consumer products. With this in mind, according to Lukashenka (2016a), the Belarusian regime has established an updated Soviet economy. The Soviet economy is viewed by Lukashenka as a success story, and it is why the Belarusian economy has remained largely Sovietised. This contrasts with the Kremlin, which has done away with the Sovietised economy, although the Russian economy remains kleptocratic in nature and controlled by Putin allies. Allegedly, when Lukashenka came to power in 1994, there was a meeting in which Lukashenka asked his advisors if anyone knew how to build a capitalist system. When no one answered in the affirmative, he asked if they knew about the Soviet economy, which was answered positively. Allegedly, Lukashenka said, 'Okay we shall go with what we know then.' While an analogy, it explains the strong late-Soviet elements existing in the Belarusian economy today, with the state maintaining control over most industries.[16] Lukashenka remains Sovietised, wanting to construct a modernised Soviet state (Ioffe, 2014: 125; Karbalevich, 2010: 50).[17] Like Putin, Lukashenka (2016c) has stated that the Soviet collapse was a cataclysm. In 2021, at a meeting of the CIS, Lukashenka (2021) devoted time in his speech about the positives of the work of the CIS to the collapse of the Soviet Union, which he said was 'forced'. Lukashenka (2021) went on to reiterate that 'everyone knows my negative attitudes to these events'. In the past Lukashenka has consistently reiterated that his was the only negative vote in the Belarusian Soviet parliament, but this is an embellishment, as Lukashenka was not even in the hall when the vote was cast (Feduta, 2005: 55–6).

After the Second World War, Belarus's economy surged. While the country was the poorest part of Western Russia in the Tsarist period, its Soviet history was positive, at least economically (Ioffe, 2004). The Soviet rebuilding of Belarus into a hi-tech economy – by Soviet standards – left excellent infrastructure and good universities.[18] As Lukashenka (2016a) has alluded to, the Belarusian regime has established an updated Soviet economy, rather than changing the economic system to resemble a more

---

[16] Personal interview: YR52870.
[17] Personal interviews: YR52870, VW28501, NF29463, HA20938.
[18] Personal interview: UR24751.

modern economy. Lukashenka retains an idealised view of the Soviet Union and does not see the Soviet economy as a failure, but in need of reform.[19]

The Belarusian authorities took a further lesson from the Soviet period, integrating the relatively effective Soviet power vertical into an updated Belarusian model, although the present system is arguably more effective due to Belarus's geographical compactness and Lukashenka's longevity in power.[20] The power vertical gives Lukashenka the power to even tell the collective – another Soviet copy – farm tractor drivers how to drive their tractors. As one interviewee[21] quipped, for Lukashenka, Belarus is his farm. The authorities copied Soviet government administration structures, with many current Belarusian state institutions either copied directly from the Soviet period or given a makeover but based on previous Soviet structures.[22]

Hall (2017b: 173–4) argued that the Belarusian regime was a testing ground for the Kremlin to ascertain how certain practices worked against protesters, the media, NGOs, and external efforts at democratisation. The Belarusian authorities began their preventive counter-revolution against the Colour Revolutions earlier than the Kremlin. Two examples of the Kremlin copying practices developed in Belarus are the Belarusian Republican Youth Union being the precursor to the Kremlin's Nashi, and Belarusian NGO legislation being copied by the Kremlin. As one of the first regimes to implement a preventive counter-revolution, the Belarusian authorities became an example for other authoritarian-minded elites on how to develop repressive measures. Belarusian actions allow other post-Soviet authoritarian leaders to gauge the reaction of Western states and international organisations before acting accordingly.[23] Lukashenka has been in power since Bill Clinton's first term and has seen attempts to impeach him in 1995 and 1996, protests in 2001, 2006, 2010, 2017, and 2020–2021, and many economic crises.[24] However, he has survived them all and learnt from them.[25]

Lukashenka's longevity – rather than his economic policies – and his pragmatism and ability to quickly adapt to situations could be

---

[19] Personal interview: YR52870.  [20] Personal interview: TK02846.
[21] Personal interview: NF29463.  [22] Personal interviews: SD35107, VF64893.
[23] Personal interview: TK02846.  [24] Personal interview: MU19837.
[25] Personal interview: TK02846.

models for other authoritarian- minded leaders.[26] The idea that Lukashenka is a model for others can be seen by Moldovan president Dodon – apparently on Lukashenka's advice – trying to pass four resolutions to increase his own presidential power in Moldova in 2017 (UDF.by, 2017). Dodon justified this proposed consolidation of power by arguing it would strengthen the state, as Lukashenka had done in Belarus. However, unlike Lukashenka, Dodon had not taken control of the Supreme Court, which struck the legislative changes down (UDF.by, 2017). Lukashenka may be an example of success for other authoritarian leaders, as his longevity would be welcome. There are pointers to Lukashenka being a successful model for Dodon, who, if he could have, would implement a similar model to Lukashenka in Moldova.

### 5.3.2 Learning from Previous Regimes: Plahotniuc and Poroshenko

It is likely politicians learn from the successes of regimes which they were a part of in the past. While it is unlikely that this learning is advertised, it is probably crucial, as authoritarian-minded elites do not want to lose power and so will learn from an example of success. This is especially so if that success is domestic, as the strategy clearly works in the context. Both Plahotniuc and Poroshenko were members of various governments before becoming the main players in regimes. Poroshenko was something of a bell-weather having served under Kuchma, before joining with Yushchenko and then having ties to Yanukovych before being elected president in 2014. Plahotniuc had a complete political change in 2009; from being a member and financier of the PCRM, he joined and financially supported the PDM. Having been in important roles in previous regimes, Plahotniuc and Poroshenko likely used these experiences to gauge and learn from the successes and failures of their times in past regimes to help shape their current thinking and how each reacted to events during their tenure in power. As argued in Chapter 1, this is an aspect of habitus. The example of Plahotniuc and Poroshenko learning from failures and, in this case, success highlights the importance of internal learning well.

---

[26] Personal interviews: HA20938, IP28037, KR48280.

Plahotniuc was a businessman and supported Vladimir Voronin's regime financially. Plahotniuc was trusted by Voronin to increase Voronin's business portfolio using *reiderstvo* practices.[27] These practices were used by Voronin and Plahotniuc before 2009 to pressure other elites to support Voronin for fear that they may lose their businesses, and Plahotniuc continued these methods to ensure the support of other elites and most politicians in parliament.[28] Many representatives in the Alliance for European Integration (AEI) coalition were politicians under the PCRM and were schooled to use repression, as the PCRM regime did, when threatened.[29]

Poroshenko was a part of every regime since the 1994 Kuchma presidency, and according to Sukhov (2017b), Poroshenko shares characteristics of previous presidents, borrowing behavioural patterns from Kuchma. Poroshenko wanted to create a scenario similar to how Kuchma kept control of state structures and competing factions in the regime, but, after the Euromaidan, Poroshenko was hampered by greater checks on him by civil society than in previous regimes.[30] Kuchma was less thuggish than Yanukovych, using softer coercive tools, rather than naked repression, although the death of journalist Heorhy Honhadze showed that Kuchma would use violence when necessary. Poroshenko followed this relatively soft coercion path laid down by Kuchma, balancing competing clans and oligarchs, while using kompromat to keep control.[31]

Poroshenko exerted control over other elites using kompromat and by 2016 had established a close relationship with former Yanukovych allies (Romanyuk and Kravets, 2016; Sukhov, 2016b). Former prime minister Volodymyr Hroysman was a Poroshenko loyalist, thereby allowing Poroshenko to keep some control of parliament (Romanyuk, 2016; Synovitz, 2016). Like Yanukovych – who made secret deals with oligarchs and parliamentarians to get support – Poroshenko used backroom deals to increase his power (Romanyuk, 2016). Poroshenko, using similar methods to Yanukovych, tried to control institutions, but unlike Yanukovych, he was subtler in how he achieved consolidation. Another area of learning from success is in the 1990s, when Poroshenko started his business, learning the

---

[27]  Personal interview: FD84603.     [28]  Personal interview: CR52981.
[29]  Personal interviews: PD59726, DW48620, KH32708.
[30]  Personal interview: WU39568.     [31]  Personal interview: JH58291.

appropriate survival skills to survive and flourish. As with Plahotniuc in Moldova, Poroshenko used practices learnt in the 1990s to control others, which allowed him to maintain power.[32]

## 5.4 Discussion: Success or Failure and Internal or External?

Having investigated examples of failure, we turned to analysing examples of learning from success. As authoritarian leaders are concerned with their survival at all costs, we argue that they will learn from any example that ensures their survival. Consequently, authoritarian leaders are just as likely to learn from examples of success as from failure. Existing literature has largely concentrated on authoritarian learning from failure. This is because failure is easier to track as it generally makes the news, such as with the Euromaidan. However, examples of learning from success are crucial to authoritarian learning, as they also provide cases of what do. While failure shows authoritarian leaders what not to do, these examples do not tell them exactly what. By contrast, success provides a clear path of what to do and survive. For instance, the Eurasian Economic Union (EAEU), which was constructed in 2015, used the EU as the example to copy,[33] and the Kremlin borrowed the German and New Zealand electoral systems when designing an electoral system. However, there were nuances that allowed the Russian authorities to tweak both systems to ensure regime control of elections. Similarly, the Moldovan constitution is based on the French one,[34] although again the Moldovan constitution gives the incumbent regime more power than in France. However, examples of success are harder to find than regime failures. As the quote at the start of the chapter highlights, authoritarian leaders do not like to admit that they copied someone else. While conducting research for this book, we were told pointedly by someone close to the Russian government that the authorities do not learn anything from Belarus. This is part of the reason there is limited evidence of learning from success, but another factor is that it does not make the news. As mentioned, the Arab Spring and Euromaidan are striking moments of popular uprisings against authoritarians.

[32] Personal interviews MU19837, ES74082.   [33] Personal interview: KR48280.
[34] Personal interviews: LD03148, CR52981.

Moldovan learning from Singapore is less likely to be noticed and does not come with an easy good-versus-bad narrative. Evidence is lacking to conclusively show that success is as pertinent to authoritarian learning as failure. However, as the examples highlighted here show, there are instances of direct learning, policy transfer, diffusion, and emulation, pointing to the relevance of success in better understanding authoritarian learning.

While the four case studies learn from success, there are examples of a lack of success in learning from others. This is particularly the case for the Kremlin, although this could be attributed to the fact that there is more evidence of Kremlin learning. However, this does not detract from the fact that authoritarian leaders learn equally from both failure and success, although they may not necessarily learn the right lessons. Authoritarian leaders are as likely to learn from external examples as from internal examples and learning from internal examples is crucial for authoritarian learning. Consequently, authoritarian elites learn from both success and failure, and they learn equally from internal and external examples. But it is harder to highlight cases of success and examples of internal learning than external cases and learning from failure.

# 6 | *The Role of Regional Organisations in Authoritarian Learning*

These organisations have ... provided mechanisms for participating states to enhance and streamline their cooperation, especially when it comes to collaboration among security organisations.[1]

## 6.1 Introduction

The quote at the beginning of this chapter refers to post-Soviet regional organisations and the opportunities that they provide for cooperation between member states. The purpose of this chapter is to test how crucial regional organisations are in explaining authoritarian learning in the four case studies. The post-Soviet region has an array of regional organisations to deal with economic and political issues that cross state borders, such as recessions, the environment, and terrorism. Organisations like the European Union (EU) and other democratic regional organisations (DROs) have received much attention regarding how they lock member states into democracy and liberal reforms (Pevehouse, 2005). However, increasingly, there is another side to regional organisations, what Debre (2021) calls 'the dark side of regionalism'. This growing literature investigates how regional organisations are being used by elites with authoritarian tendencies to re-shape international norms, entice others, help support incumbents by giving them greater legitimacy than internal challengers, offer protection in troubled times, and, in the case of the analysis here, offer opportunities for learning.

Regional organisations provide opportunities for cooperation between member states and thus help shape learning. Post-Soviet regional organisations are no exception to providing learning opportunities for member states. Through an array of structures, these organisations offer opportunities for regular meetings, informal

---

[1] Cooley and Schaaf, 2017.

discussions, sharing of best practices, and regular training exercises to ascertain what works effectively in each situation. Obydenkova and Libman (2019) found that post-Soviet regimes who were members of the Commonwealth of Independent States (CIS), the Eurasian Economic Union (EAEU), and the Shanghai Cooperation Organisation (SCO) had increased chances of survival, as members collaborate. It is likely that the other two regional organisations – the Collective Security Treaty Organisation (CSTO) and the Union State of Belarus and Russia (hereafter the Union State) – help member cooperation and survival. Existing literature has posited that it is possible regional organisations consisting of authoritarian-minded elites provide opportunities for member states to learn, thereby increasing their survival chances (Libman and Obydenkova, 2018: 153).

The regional organisations that are investigated here have formal structures that help member states develop best practices for survival. However, these organisations also offer opportunities to develop informal networks that exist inside these institutions. While formal cooperation and working together is an important part of authoritarian learning, of similar relevance – if not more so – are networking aspects. These regional organisations offer formal structures but also plenty of opportunities on the side-lines to develop individual networks for the sharing of best practices and learning. While finding evidence of those informal networks and meetings is difficult, it is possible to do an in-depth analysis of these organisations and locate examples of the importance of post-Soviet regional organisations in enabling the four case studies to learn and develop best practices for consolidating power.

Much of the existing literature on the role of authoritarian regional organisations and learning contends that the regional hegemon dominates such structures. Obydenkova and Libman (2019) have argued that post-Soviet regional organisations are dominated by Russia, which uses them to enhance Russian interests in the region and potentially further afield. Similarly, the literature on authoritarian gravity centres (Kneuer and Demmelhuber, 2016; Kneuer et al., 2019) posits that some authoritarian regimes act as models for other authoritarian regimes. These role models create regional organisations to enhance emulation by bringing potential emulators together to copy the model of the authoritarian gravity centre.

We do not refute that some authoritarian regimes are more likely to act as role models to others and have the resources to invoke emulation and the devising and sharing of best practices, using regional organisations – or creating them – to share best practices more. However, we perceive authoritarian learning as more horizontal than the literature on authoritarian gravity centres accounts for. As authoritarian-minded elites are concerned about their survival chances, they are unlikely to only focus on one possible lesson that may or may not work. Rather, learning is likely to come from multiple sources with member states in authoritarian regional organisations bringing their own ideas to the table and ascertaining what works most effectively through discussion and observation. While Russia is the post-Soviet regional hegemon and is likely a key source of learning and emulation for other post-Soviet states, Russian elites – concerned with their survival – are likely to take ideas from other sources As Hall (2017b) showed, much of Russia's preventive counter-revolution after 2004 to deal with Colour Revolutions had been taken from the already existing playbook developed in Belarus in the early 2000s.

Kneuer and colleagues (2019) see regional organisations as part of the arsenal that authoritarian gravity centres use to develop models for emulation. They correctly state that authoritarian regional organisations are learning rooms for the sharing of best practices and increasing survival chances. For Kneuer and colleagues (2019: 452), these learning rooms are places for authoritarian gravity centres to 'function as role models for the other states that face similar problems and are therefore looking for policy solutions and best practice examples'. While they correctly offer the representation of the learning room, as will be shown here, learning in post-Soviet regional organisations is more of a team effort.

The role regional organisations play in providing opportunities for learning among member states may – at least in part – account for why authoritarian-minded elites have been unable to consolidate power in Moldova and Ukraine. Moldova is a member of the CIS and has observer status of the EAEU, but the current government of Maia Sandu is focused on obtaining EU membership – or at least a close alignment with the EU. This has negated Moldovan involvement in post-Soviet regional organisations and while this may change later, Moldova's political elite is divided as to whether to integrate in a Western or post-Soviet direction. Even if the next government were to reduce cooperation with the EU and integrate with post-Soviet organisations, it is unlikely such a stance would last, as power consolidation remains difficult for Moldovan governments. There is a similar scenario in Ukraine. Since 2014 and the Russian annexation of Crimea and war in the Donbas, Ukrainian governments have reduced any integration with post-Soviet regional organisations. The Poroshenko government formally removed Ukraine from the CIS, although Ukrainian representatives have attended CIS meetings since then. Similarly, the Zelensky government has not returned to the CIS and – like Poroshenko – it has concentrated on integrating Ukraine with the EU and NATO.

Post-Soviet regional organisations offer member states learning rooms – where regular discussions can be held, best practices shared, and even tactics developed in real-time – membership of these structures helps with authoritarian consolidation. It is likely that one crucial reason why Moldovan and Ukrainian elites with authoritarian tendencies have been unable to consolidate power – unlike their Belarusian and Russian counterparts – is in part due to not belonging to many post-Soviet regional organisations. Without being members of regional organisations, Moldovan and Ukrainian elites do not have access to sharing of information but must rely on emulation – particularly of Russia – and using practices used by previous domestic regimes. However, what may work in Russia or in the past may not work in the present. Membership of regional organisations would provide opportunities for Moldovan and Ukrainian elites to learn from multiple sources. Joining these organisations would be an obvious solution for authoritarian-minded elites, but, unable to consolidate power and take enough of the elite and electorate with them, they cannot join these structures. This creates a catch-22, where authoritarian-minded elites do not have the power to get sufficient domestic support to join these regional organisations, but cannot consolidate power without membership.

As mentioned, learning is perceived here as one of constant adaptation and although authoritarian-minded elites may make mistakes – leading to failure as Treisman (2020) argues – these elites are concerned with survival. Therefore, they will constantly learn to ensure their survival. Regional organisations are used as collaborative structures to make it easier for the right lessons to be learnt. Regional organisations are a mix of formal and informal networks allowing for learning. They have official structures, such as council bodies or parliaments, and offer informal opportunities for the sharing of best practices.

Regional organisations mix formal and informal networks. While the latter overlay themselves on formal structures – such as council meetings – they operate differently, allowing for ideas to be expressed and shared away from formal proceedings and recordings.

By providing opportunities for regular meetings, both formal and informal regional organisations offer chances for consistent networking between personnel from member states to learn and share best practices. This helps authoritarian-minded elites develop the best practices for consolidating and retaining power. Consequently, member states of these regional organisations have a much better chance of increasing their survival chances as they can meet regularly, share information, and develop appropriate tactics. While we argue that authoritarian learning is largely horizontal, networks do have a vertical structure and we do not deny that – regarding the post-Soviet space – Russia plays a crucial role in the survival of other authoritarian regimes. However, these informal networks allow for all member states to bring ideas to the table and share ideas, thereby making existing vertical structures flatter than widely considered in the literature.

## 6.2 Regional Organisation Collaboration: Vehicles for Learning?

To determine the role regional organisations play in learning for post-Soviet authoritarian regimes, we investigate four institutions: the CIS, the CSTO, the SCO, and the Union State. These organisations provide significant opportunities for learning, with regular formal and informal meetings and chances to develop networks. As we are concerned here with learning, we do not include the EAEU in this analysis. This is because, as an economic organisation, the EAEU is used to bolster members and non-member sates. Bolstering – another term for support – is a way to enhance the chances of authoritarian survival. However, it is not the same as learning, and the EAEU does not provide avenues for learning and the sharing of best practices. Rather, it concentrates on economic integration and development. As the EAEUs principal remit is to offer support, rather than help with learning, we do not include it here.

In Chapter 1, we addressed potential networks for external and internal learning. One of the structures mentioned was regional organisations that we perceive as crucial for learning from external examples.

Figure 6.1 represents the learning types that regional organisations engage in providing best survival practices and "learning rooms" (Kneuer et al., 2019) for authoritarian regime members states. By collaborating, member states of these post-Soviet regional organisa- tions – consisting of authoritarian regimes and authoritarian-minded elites – can share experiences, engage in discussions, and participate in training exercises. Consequently, the role regional organisations play in authoritarian learning is crucial to explaining how these regimes and elites develop best survival practices.

As shown in Figure 6.1, regional organisations provide myriad opportunities for learning for authoritarian-minded elites. There is regular dialogue between the elites of member states, allowing them to develop best practices for survival through a range of activities. This points to a strong version of diffusion and lesson-drawing from the experiences of others, coupled with viewing training exercises. By regularly attending meetings in regional organisations, authoritarian- minded elites develop links with one another. Authoritarian learning is more likely to occur with these strong links as inter-personal connec- tions develop trust. Regular meetings in regional organisations allow for information exchange. As will be seen, the Commonwealth of Independent States Inter-Parliamentary Assembly (CIS-IPA) provides information on all legislation existing in member states. Therefore, policy transfer is also a crucial learning type for authoritarian learning that is offered by membership of regional organisations. Having

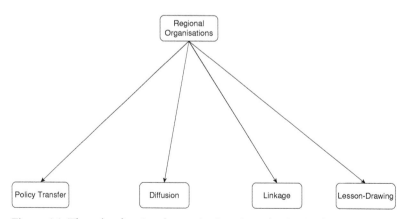

**Figure 6.1** The role of regional organisations in authoritarian learning

documented the different learning types that regional organisations offer, we turn to the evidence of the importance of these structures to authoritarian learning.

### 6.2.1 The Commonwealth of Independent States

The CIS was created in 1991 to keep the post-Soviet states together in a loose confederation and potentially as an alternative to the Soviet Union. However, with the Soviet Union's demise and political elites favouring independence, the CIS became a regional organisation bringing members together to counter common issues such as environmental degradation, terrorism, migration, and cross-border trade. Political integration has largely failed, with most of the focus of the CIS being on economic cooperation (Obydenkova and Libman, 2019: 122–3). There are open and closed meetings within the CIS, so tracking discussions in the closed meetings is difficult, and information on closed meetings is often limited in scope and detail.

However, CIS members collaborate and share information, and the organisation publishes journals which provide information about what was discussed at meetings (Commonwealth of Independent States, 2001a), allowing some information to be gleaned. The CIS provides 'a common information space' expanding to an 'interstate information exchange' (Commonwealth of Independent States, 2001b), again allowing some information to slip out. As will be seen, much of the learning of best practices is conducted by CIS structures devoted to anti-terrorism, and like other post-Soviet regional organisations, these institutions have a broad definition of what constitutes terrorism. However, there are instances of other bodies, such as the Council of Foreign Ministers, that discuss protests. One example of this was the 2009 Moldovan protests, where the Council analysed events in Chișinău in detail (Commonwealth of Independent States, 2009).

Another crucial CIS institution for learning is the CIS-IPA. As mentioned by Lemon and Antonov (2020), the CIS-IPA is a body that harmonises the legislation of member states and provides forums for discussion among member delegations. Lemon and Antonov showed how laws on rights to assembly, civil society, and political participation found in Kazakhstan, Kyrgyzstan, Russia, Tajikistan, and Uzbekistan were very similar. It is possible each government wrote legislation individually. But it is likely that representatives of each held discussions with one another. The CIS-IPA provides a venue for delegates from these member states to meet and discuss legislation. This institution also records all legislation from member states, thereby making it easier for member states to find appropriate laws and use them in their own legislation. The CIS-IPA allows member deputations to share best practices and legislation to improve regime consolidation and tackle protests, civil society, NGOs, and the media in their own countries. While much legislation found across the post-Soviet space is copied from pre-existing Russian legislation, the CIS-IPA allows other member states to bring their laws to the table. As Lemon and Antonov (2020) show, regarding the Central Asian states, minus Turkmenistan but including Russia, the Kremlin does not dominate the legislative field.

Members collaborate extensively on security issues, enhancing 'operational and technical capabilities ... their analytical work, exchange information and professional experience' (Commonwealth of Independent States, 2013b), thereby developing the necessary best practices to enhance regime survival. The CIS has developed structures such as the anti-terrorist centre, the Council of Ministers of Internal Affairs, and the Council of Security Authorities and Special Services of the CIS (CSASS). These structures allow member states to collaborate and share information and best practices, and train together, which increase opportunities for learning. We will analyse the CIS's CSASS and anti-terrorist centres structures as these provide excellent examples of how the CIS aids authoritarian learning and the sharing of best practices among members.

The CSASS has had many meetings that discuss how to improve collaboration between the security forces of member states and how to continue effective cooperation. One example of this effort is a 2011 meeting at which increasing 'the effectiveness of cooperation between security agencies and special services of the CIS member states' (Commonwealth of Independent States, 2011) was discussed. At a CSASS meeting in 2017, delegates analysed how to limit the 'radicalisation of youth' (Commonwealth of Independent States, 2017) within the post-Soviet region. That this occurred soon after the Euromaidan and protests, in Russia, Moldova, and Belarus, which had all seen young people feature prominently in the protests, points to learning to stifle future young protesters. In 2015, CSASS members discussed how to stop 'neo-Nazi groups ... and their participation in the realisation of technologies of "colour revolution"' (Commonwealth of Independent States, 2015), a direct reference to the Euromaidan, which had been portrayed in state media across the post-Soviet space as a neo-Nazi coup. As is to be expected of an institution centred on security, there is limited information about the activities of the CSASS. However, there is evidence that this CIS structure provides opportunities for members to learn, engage in dialogue, and share best practices.

Another CIS institution that provides evidence for the notion that regional organisations are crucial for learning and the sharing of best practices is the anti-terrorist centre. During the 2011 Donbas anti-terrorist training, one exercise dealt with countering mass riots and coordinated 'activities to identify and prevent terrorist acts being prepared at mass rallies' and the development of tactics to counter 'flash mobs used to destabilise the situation and organise social unrest' (Anti-terrorist Centre of the Member States of the Commonwealth of Independent States, 2011). This highlights that the anti-terrorist centre equates protesters with terrorists, and the member states collaborate to develop best practices to counter demonstrators. The 2011 Donbas anti-terrorist training exercise was led by the Ukrainian security services, pointing to the idea that learning in post-Soviet regional organisations represents more of a flattened hierarchy than widely considered in the existing literature. In 2012, the anti-terrorist centre conducted training to counter terrorists who 'organise riots and cause social unrest' and demonstrate outside government buildings (Anti-terrorist Centre of the Member States of the Commonwealth of Independent States, 2012). A 2013 meeting saw a discussion of tactics that had been used in the 'Arab Revolutions', and the need to 'suppress the activity of radical youth groups' (Commonwealth of Independent States, 2013a), again highlighting learning about the development of the necessary methods to counter protesters.

Since the Colour Revolutions of the early 2000s in Serbia, Georgia, and Ukraine, NGOs have been seen by authoritarian-minded elites as dangerous. These organisations have often been effective at covering elections and showing that the official results are fraudulent. At a 2014 meeting of the CIS's Anti-Terrorist Centre (ATC-CIS), the Kazakh interior ministry presented a report on 'NGO activities in Central Asia'. While this could be construed as harmless the other report at the meeting was on 'ISIS as a new terrorist phenomenon'

(Anti-Terrorist Centre of the Member States of the Commonwealth of Independent States, 2014). Putting two presentations in the same forum points to the likelihood that NGOs are considered by the ATC-CIS to be a danger, if not quite on the same level as ISIS. That the forum was on terrorism and extremism emphasises the view taken by ATC-CIS members on the role NGOs play.

The examples from the CSASS and anti-terrorist centre emphasises that Belarusian, Moldovan, Russian, and Ukrainian regimes learn in these settings, as all four case studies have had regular delegations at these CIS structures. Therefore, the CIS provides opportunities for the four case studies, and although Ukraine has withdrawn from the CIS officially since 2014, there appear to be back-doors. While Poroshenko announced that Ukraine would formally withdraw from the CIS in 2018, he contradicted himself by stating that Bankova would follow some treaties and work with other members (Kizilov, 2018; Ponomarenko, 2018b), pointing to continued, if limited, dialogue with other members. The CSASS and the anti-terrorist centre provides CIS members with opportunities to engage in dialogue, learn, and share best practices, thereby helping incumbent regimes consolidate power. There is some evidence that regional organisations provide the chance for a more flattened learning hierarchy, with all members bringing ideas and practices to the table. However, the CIS does not only provide a venue for learning for post-Soviet regimes, but also bolsters members. Not only does the CIS offer economic support to bolster the economies of members, thereby reducing the possibility of protest, but it has also stated that it would counter instability in any member state (Commonwealth of Independent States, 2012), which is another bolstering practice.

### 6.2.2 The Collective Security Treaty Organisation

The CSTO grew out of earlier CIS structures and became an independent entity in 1992, with the CSTO encompassing military and security matters in the post-Soviet space. Like NATO, the CSTO is a defence pact that views an attack on one member as an attack on all. The CSTO has a Parliamentary Assembly (CSTO-PA) and this body operates in a similar fashion to the CIS-IPA, as a venue for collaboration and cooperation. One of the main purposes of the CSTO-PA is to bring member states together, discuss issues that are occurring and harmonise legislation. For example, in a tweet on the CSTO Twitter account, CSTO-PA executive secretary Sergey Pospelov reported[2] to the Committee Council of the Defence and Security Program that member states had successfully harmonised national legislation. Therefore, the CSTO is something more than a security body, it is also an institution that provides opportunities for learning and the development of best practices for authoritarian regimes to keep power.

The CSTO provides training exercises to members, and the many informal meetings that the CSTO holds annually make it an essential structure for dialogue and sharing best practices. The problem of new Colour Revolutions occurring in the post-Soviet space remains a large issue for CSTO members. For instance, a December 2013 meeting of the CSTO Secretariat was entitled 'Interaction between Authorities and Society to Counter External Interference and Colour Revolutions' (Collective Security Treaty Organisation, 2013b). This meeting involved the internal, military, and foreign affairs ministries of member states, the Russian security services, and the CIS anti-terrorist centre, and it addressed 'the role of NGOs, the media, the Internet, social networks and the blogosphere in the destabilisation of the socio-political situation' in the region, as well as analysing 'provocateurs ... as an element of the organisational system of external interference' and 'technologies to counteract "colour revolution"' (Collective Security Treaty Organisation, 2013b).

This worry about Colour Revolutions has led the CSTO to organise training exercises for the interior ministry troops of member states to counteract 'mass riots' on several occasions (Collective Security Treaty Organisation, 2012, 2014a, 2017). These training exercises develop best practices for stopping protests quickly and effectively. Yet it is not just the Colour Revolutions that worry CSTO member states, as seen by a 2014 meeting that pointed to lessons learnt from the Arab Spring, which had been 'an essential factor in destabilising the political landscape' (Collective Security Treaty Organisation, 2014b). During the CSTO's Unbreakable Brotherhood 2013 exercises, the Russian

---

[2] Tweet is here: https://twitter.com/paodkb/status/1222533036761341953.

OMON forces Zubr[3] and their *Spetsialny otryad bystrogo reagirova-niya* (SOBR)[4] counterparts Rys,[5] along with troops of other member states' interior ministries, undertook 'peacekeeping' by using 'special means and water cannon, split the aggressively-minded crowd and detained the leaders of the "mass riots"' (Collective Security Treaty Organisation, 2013a). That two units tasked with countering terrorism in Russia were involved in a training exercise to counteract protests highlights that terrorism is a loose label for CSTO members.

Although the CSTO has been in existence for thirty years, the organisation was perceived more as a place for discussion than action. During the 2021 Nagorno-Karabakh war, which saw Azerbaijan effectively re-incorporate the region and the territories taken by Armenia in 1994, the CSTO did not involve itself in the conflict, even when Azerbaijani forces crossed into Armenia proper (Khachatrian, 2021). As mentioned, the CSTO is a defensive pact viewing an attack on one member as an attack on all. That the CSTO did not intervene in the Nagorno-Karabakh war emphasised that the organisation was more of a talking-shop than a place for action.

However, during the current protests (at the time of writing in 2022) in Kazakhstan, the CSTO did intervene after President Kassym-Jomart Tokaev asked the organisation to send peacekeepers to counter a terrorist threat funded from external sources. While some of the protesters did resort to violence, there remain questions as to whether they were agents provocateurs funded by the government to tarnish the protests, allowing the authorities to show that the demonstrations were violent. During an extraordinary meeting of the CSTO Collective Security Council, the leaders of the member states spoke about terrorism and 'congregations of militants around the President's residence' (Collective Security Treaty Organisation, 2022). This discussion of protesters and the situation in Kazakhstan was the focus of the meeting. However, the use of 'Maidan technologies' was also considered (Collective Security Treaty Organisation,

---

[3] This is the Russian word for the European Wissent. The Zubr forces in Russia's OMON are the unit tasked with counteracting riots. They have the latest weaponry, armoured personnel carriers, and sniper units.

[4] The Special Rapid Response team are part of Rosgvardiya and tasked with rapid response to criminal threats.

[5] Like Zubr, Rys' (lynx) are an elite SOBR unit and are well-equipped and well-trained to deal with extremism and terrorism.

2022). While the protests have ended in Kazakhstan, it is possible that if the CSTO is perceived as successful, then the organisation may become a rapid reaction force to protect member states from mass protests.

Like the CIS, the CSTO not only provides training exercises and structures for the sharing of best practices, but also attempts to bolster member states. The CSTO is largely a military and security organisation, and so the institution provides avenues for learning for member states on security issues. This can be seen in the meetings that the CSTO organised to offset Colour Revolutions or Arab Spring events occurring in the post-Soviet region, as well as the training exercises to thwart such potential protests. In a similar scenario to the CIS, the CSTO has a loose definition of what constitutes terrorism, with interior ministry troops, whose official remit is to offset terrorism, being used to deal with protesters. Therefore, the CSTO provides structures for learning.

### 6.2.3 The Shanghai Cooperation Organisation

Although, the SCO is not a purely post-Soviet institution, we include it here as it provides one case study member, Russia, with opportunities to share best practices and learn from the tactics of other authoritarian regimes, and some democracies like India, within and outside the post-Soviet space. Belarus is an observer at the SCO and so regularly attends meetings, providing the regime with dialogue and learning opportunities. Documents from the SCO repeat the mantra of stability and non-interference in the internal affairs of member states, such as with the fifth-anniversary declaration, which stated that if stability was threatened, members would militarily intervene in other states.[6] As Ambrosio (2014, 2018) has argued, the SCO helps member states limit the pressures of democratisation from external powers such as America. With the SCO mantra of stability, the organisation attempts to reduce the potential for regime change through close collaboration of member states. The SCO provides opportunities for the Kremlin, and to a lesser extent the Belarusian regime, to collaborate with China and utilise its

---

[6] Source is here: http://rus.sectsco.org/documents/. Scroll to 2006 and click on the document entitled "*Deklaratsiya pyatiletiya Shankhaiskoi Organizatsii Sotrudnichestva.*"

financial, technological, and military strength in supporting their regimes (Ambrosio, 2017). The SCO provides member states with opportunities to share ideas, develop tactics to reduce democratisation pressures and consolidate power (Ambrosio, 2008), and learn from one another.

Like the CIS and CSTO, the SCO conducts training exercises for security and police forces on terrorism, and as with the other two regional organisations, the SCO's definition of terrorism is loose and encompasses devising best practices against protesters. The broad SCO definition of terrorism can be seen in the documents detailing the SCO's 2013 Kazygurt anti-terror exercises, which attempted to 'curb terrorist activities on mass gathering sites' (Shanghai Cooperation Organisation, 2013). For the most part, these are military training exercises. Yet, as the 2013 Kazygurt example highlights, these training exercises can some-times deal with anti-terror training that could be construed as developing best practices against opposition groups.

Another structure of the SCO is its Regional Antiterrorist Structure (SCO-RATS), which holds meetings between member security councils and is, therefore, another structure for learning and dialogue. For example, a 2015 meeting of the SCO-RATS discussed 'Nazism' and the rise of neo-Nazi protests (Security Council of the Russian Federation, 2015a). Due to the classification in Russian media of protesters at the Euromaidan as fascists and Nazis, this can be con-strued as a direct reference to devising best practices against mass protests. In 2009, the SCO passed the counter-terrorism convention, which allows for the security services of member states to pursue suspects on the territory of other members (Cooley and Schaaf, 2017). While not constituting learning itself, a 2019 SCO document on countering extremism requires that member states share informa-tion with one another about groups deemed extremist. Similarly, the convention requires that member states share information about groups deemed extremist in one state but residing on the territory of another member (Shanghai Cooperation Organisation, 2019a). This points to close cooperation and learning between member states on dealing with opposition groups. SCO-RATS has produced blacklists of extremist organisations in member states and this list has grown expo-nentially since it was first created in 2009 (Cooley and Schaaf, 2017).

While again not strictly learning, it does highlight that member states regularly talk with one another and cooperate.

The Internet played a crucial role in spreading the message of state corruption and authoritarian failure during the Arab Spring. The Euromaidan had a founding myth that it was started by a single Facebook post. Yet, there were many social media posts that called for protest (Onuch, 2015: 171). Therefore, during an SCO forum on Central Asia and the Internet, delegates discussed how the Internet should not be used 'to interfere in the internal affairs of other states'. While delegates agreed that the Internet should remain open to everyone, regulation should ensure 'the sovereign rights of states to manage the Internet in their national segment' (Shanghai Cooperation Organisation, 2019b). The SCO-RATS ran a conference on the Internet, where participants discussed how the Internet can be used for 'political purposes' and how it has contributed to 'severe political and socio-economic consequences in entire regions' (Regional Anti-terrorist Structure of the Shanghai Cooperation Organisation, 2011), pointing to learning best practices to restrict the Internet in SCO member states.

In a similar scenario to the CIS and the CSTO, the SCO provides forums for member states to discuss best practices and share tactics, and the SCO provides member states with the opportunity to harmonise legislation (Shanghai Cooperation Organisation, 2008a). This allows member and observer states to discuss existing legislation and copy one another if necessary. The SCO has many structures within the organisation that are devoted to certain individual areas of state governance, such as a structure where member states' interior ministry personnel meet. Therefore, the SCO provides openings for member states to collaborate at the ministerial level, as well as structures for ministry personnel of member states to work closely together (Shanghai Cooperation Organisation, 2008b). Therefore, the SCO provides bolstering opportunities for member states and more importantly plenty of chances for dialogue, engaging in policy and legislative transfer, the sharing of best practices to consolidate power, and learning.

### 6.2.4 The Union State

There is limited information on the workings of the Union State of Belarus and Russia (its official title – we will refer to as the 'Union State'), thereby making it difficult to highlight that X causes Y and that there is learning taking place. However, there are pointers to the learning capacity and structures for dialogue created by the Union State for the Belarusian and Russian regimes. Although relations between the two regimes have often been difficult, with numerous trade wars and gas disputes (Gretsky, 2018: 157–8), both co-ordinate foreign and security policy. There are regular inter-departmental meetings with personnel from the ministries other than minsters and deputies frequently gathering to discuss best practices.

The Union State highlights authoritarian learning, as the organisation provides experience sharing through monthly meetings between ministries at all levels, and one crucial task of the Union State is to discuss legislative harmonisation between Russia and Belarus.[7] For instance, during a 2005 Union State meeting, former Russian parliamentary speaker Boris Gryzlov advocated collaboration between the Belarusian and Russian authorities on counteracting Colour Revolutions (Veretennikova, 2005) and this has been a key aspect of the Union State ever since.[8] During the 2004 Ukrainian Orange Revolution, representatives from Belarus and Russia discussed the effects of such an event happening in either Belarus or Russia, and how to react to Belarusian opposition personnel who had been on the Maidan during the Orange Revolution (Standing Committee of the Union State, 2004). To counteract the diffusion of protest back into Belarus, the Union State agreed to increase collaboration against Colour Revolutions (Standing Committee of the Union State, 2005). This example of counteracting a Colour Revolution points to the sharing of best practices on counter-revolutions. Another example is that in 2016, a new Union State military doctrine specifically addressed the possibility 'of a Colour or Arab Revolution' occurring in Belarus and Russia (Standing Committee of the Union State, 2016).

Combined Security Council meetings happen biannually, and other ministries meet monthly with representatives meeting at all levels.[9] Although there is limited information about the activities of the Union State there is evidence that this organisation serves as a venue for learning. There is close cooperation between all Belarusian and Russian ministries and there are regular meetings of these structures within the Union State. The Union State allows for the discussion of

---

[7] Personal interviews: SD35107, KG84027.     [8] Personal interview: SD35107.
[9] Personal interviews: SD35107, KG84027.

best practices, dialogue about the problems that each regime faces, learning from the experiences of each regime, and cooperation over pressing issues, such as dealing with Colour Revolutions. The Union State operates to allow the Kremlin and the Belarusian regime to devise best practices together to counter threats, collaborate, and learn from one another.[10]

## 6.3 Conclusion

The chapter addressed post-Soviet regional organisations, with these structures providing extensive opportunities for dialogue, the exchange of ideas, the sharing of best practices, and learning. One area of interest was the discussions and actions taken within the organisations on countering protests, with member states collaborating to find the most appropriate tactics to overcome protests and learn from the successes and failures of each other. What can be clearly seen is that regional organisations offer a range of learning opportunities for members, from sharing legislation to exchanging ideas and ascertaining what works best through training exercises. At least regarding the post-Soviet space, regional organisations play a crucial role in authoritarian learning. It is likely that membership of a regional organisation – which offers a range of learning opportunities – partially explains why some post-Soviet states have consolidated authoritarian regimes. States that are not members of many of these structures have seen authoritarian-minded elites less able to consolidate power as they do not have access to as much information. Another point raised here is that while Russia, as the regional hegemon, plays a crucial role in bringing learning opportunities through these institutions, there is evidence that other member states also bring ideas to the table. This highlights that authoritarian learning is more horizontal rather than vertical, as the existing literature – particularly on authoritarian gravity centres – argues.

[10] Personal interviews: SD35107, CN20491, KG84027.

# 7 | *External and Internal Learning in State Institutions*

Much of what is learnt probably occurs in the Banya.[1]

## 7.1 Introduction

Thirty-one years after the Soviet collapse, many post-Soviet elites remain in power. This chapter investigates relations between elites and how this helps authoritarian learning. In Chapter 1, we highlighted that much authoritarian learning occurs in networks in formal state institutions. This chapter highlights learning – both externally and internally – in state networks in the four cases. Krackhardt and Stern (1988: 123) see networks as those that are 'of friends, contacts, and accidental communications' and we use this definition here when discussing learning networks. We investigate how elites work together in external and internal groups and their importance for authoritarian learning.

## 7.2 Ties That Bind: Inter- and Intra-Elite Links

Elite relationships in the four cases studies are extensive. Personnel regularly work together, exchange ideas, engage in dialogue, and learn from others' failures and successes. Analysis of institutions emphasises how crucial these relationships are for learning. For example, close economic and political ties between Russian and Ukrainian elites existed for nearly thirty years before the Crimean annexation and war in Donbas.[2] The Ukrainian gas apparatchiks Dmytro Firtash, Serhy Lovochkin, Valery Khoroshkovsky, and Yury Boyko, or the 'Moscow quartet' (Kondratov, 2010), were until 2014 dominant players in Ukrainian politics. With business

---

[1] Personal interview: YR52870.    [2] Personal interview: TD38463.

and political interests in Russia, this clique pushed successive Ukrainian regimes towards Moscow.[3] By investigating relations between regime personnel, one can locate evidence of learning in the cases.

As shown in Chapter 1, there are a range of institutions involved in learning from external and internal examples. The institutions investigated here are presidents, presidential administrations, security services, security councils, governments, foreign and internal ministries, and ambassadors. Each brings elites together, enabling discussion, exchanges of ideas, learning, and the development of best practices to maintain power. Referring to Figures 1.1 and 1.2 in Chapter 1, all structures analysed here are involved in external learning.

Figure 1.1 shows the different structure types analysed in this chapter, and the different types of learning that each brings to developing best survival practices for authoritarian-minded elites. Having investigated regional organisations in the previous chapter, we exclude those structures here. Most of the structures analysed here engage in diffusion, linkage, and lesson-drawing. In Chapter 1, we argued that policy transfer refers specifically to legislative development and the spread of laws between states. This more rigorous definition provides nuance to a term that otherwise would see all structures engage in using it if it was defined loosely. Having shown the structures to be assessed regarding external learning and the types of learning each is involved in, we turn to addressing networks of internal learning.

Figure 1.2 provides a representation of the different state networks involved in learning from internal examples. Domestic learning involves policy transfer and lesson-drawing. All six structures learn best survival practices from both learning types. It is possible that other networks are involved in internal learning, but Figure 1.2 represents the structures that we believe are involved in learning from internal examples. However, by analysing the different networks, we will ascertain how representative Figures 1.1 and 1.2 are. Having represented the internal learning networks, we turn to analysing the evidence in the next section.

---

[3] Personal interview: TD38463.

### 7.2.1 Presidents

Presidential meetings show concealed links and learning. For instance, in the early 1990s, Lukashenka regularly visited Uzbek president Islom Karimov to discuss how Karimov consolidated power.[4] A clear learning presidential example is the meetings between Yanukovych and Putin during the Euromaidan in October and December 2013, at which Putin advised Yanukovych on how to stop the protests.[5] Putin reiterated that if Ukraine signed the EU's association agreement, it could not join the Eurasian Customs Union[6] (Ukrainskaya Pravda, 2013b). Putin also offered Yanukovych support in the 2015 presidential election and a better loan than the International Monetary Fund and EU could offer (Gorchinskaya, 2013; Silina, 2013: 1). Another financial incentive was to buy $15 billion of Ukraine's debt (Eremenko et al., 2013: 1; Gorchinskaya and Marchak, 2013), although the loan came in tranches, allowing the Russian authorities to stop payment if Yanukovych did not clear the Maidan (Pasochnik, 2013: 1). After a January 2014 meeting at an airfield outside Moscow, Yanukovych instigated the dictatorship laws. These were translated from Belarusian and Russian legislation (Coynash, 2014; Koshkina, 2015: 173; Snyder, 2014; Wilson, 2014a). Putin offered personnel to develop appropriate methods to crush the Euromaidan (Leshchenko, 2014b). While Russian tactics ultimately failed as its plans re-invigorated demonstrations, the Euromaidan is replete with secret meetings between Yanukovych and Putin.

Putin and Lukashenka consulted one another in St Petersburg on 3 April 2017, after widespread protests in Belarus in March, with Lukashenka (2017) stating that they discussed 'internal issues'. This points to likely discussions about the Belarusian protests (Kot, 2017). In another example, there was the green light given by Medvedev to Lukashenka that he had Russian support during the 2010 presidential elections, giving the Belarusian regime support to crack down hard on protesters during any likely protest over fraudulent election results (Padhol and Marples, 2011: 7; Wilson, 2021a: 234–5).

Face-to-face meetings do not need to occur. The telephone conversation remains an important information-sharing tool. During the 2018 Armenian protests, Lukashenka spoke with then president Armen Sargsyan. Sargsyan provided information on events occurring in

---

[4] Personal interview: IR39203.    [5] Personal interview: BK07421.
[6] This was the EAEU's predecessor.

Yerevan. Sargsyan and Lukashenka 'agreed on a schedule for further action' (Lukashenka, 2018b), with the Belarusian authorities likely learning from these events and providing advice. Lukashenka (2018a) alluded to providing advice during his National Assembly address, stating that he had advised Sargsyan on what to do. Similarly, Sargsyan and Prime Minister Karen Karapetyan spoke separately with Putin about the situation (Kremlin.ru, 2018a; 2018b), thereby allowing the Kremlin to advise and learn.

Emulation is a pertinent aspect of authoritarian learning and presidents often emulate one another. For instance, Dodon tried to emulate Putin, stating during the 2016 presidential election that he wanted to be 'a dictatorial leader, the same as Putin', and 'Moldova immediately needs an iron fist, a strong vertical of power' (Nemtsova, 2016). Dodon praised Lukashenka, seeing him as an example to follow. At a meeting with Lukashenka in Chişinău in 2018, Dodon stated that he was 'envious' of Belarus and that 'we would have a dictatorship as you have' (Levchenko, M, 2018). Presidents regularly meet – or are in frequent contact – allowing them to impart information and learn. Case presidents support one another and engage in learning. This is particularly so for the Kremlin, supporting Lukashenka in repression after his 2010 re-election and the repression and financial and legislative support given Yanukovych during the Euromaidan.

## 7.2.2 Presidential Administrations

### 7.2.2.1 External Networks
Presidential administrations play different roles in the four cases. As Moldova is a parliamentary republic with a weak presidency, the presidential administration does not play a significant role. By contrast in Belarus, the presidential administration is the main institution devising legislation and helping Lukashenka formulate his will.[7] While the four presidential administrations have different roles, we argue that this institution is crucial for authoritarian learning. For example, head of the Russian presidential administration Sergey Naryshkin (2008–11) visited Chişinău, meeting opposition and PCRM leader Voronin, to discuss the Moldovan political situation and how Voronin could undermine the pro-European coalition (Savina, 2010).

---

[7] Personal interview: HA20938.

Viktor Medvedchuk, who headed the Ukrainian presidential administration between 2002 and 2005, along with many other roles in
various Ukrainian regimes, has consistently been close to Putin. Putin
is Medvedchuk's daughter's godfather (Roldugin, 2013). Medvedchuk
was labelled the 'main lobbyist of Russia's interests in Ukraine' (Silina,
2003), with one interviewee[8] stating that Medvechuk is 'clearly
a Russian agent'. During a 2003 meeting with Putin, Medvedchuk
discussed Ukraine's situation and which candidates Russia could support in the 2004 Ukrainian presidential elections (Zaets, 2003: 2).
During 2004, Medvedchuk met Kremlin representatives to discuss the
difficulties the Kuchma regime experienced during the Orange protests
(Ukrainskaya Pravda, 2004). While Medvedchuk is under house arrest
in 2022, he remains the Kremlin's man in Ukraine.

### 7.2.2.2 Internal Networks
The Belarusian presidential administration concentrates on making
sure the power *vertikal* is effective and that regional leaders get the
electorate out to vote, so that Lukashenka is re-elected and government
policies are implemented state-wide. In 2007, the head of the presidential administration, Henadz Nyavyhlas (2006–8), held seminars with
personnel from Belarus's six regions to ensure that the power *vertikal*
was effective and implemented fully (Gritsanov, 2007; Lazyuk, 2007).
Nyavyhlas's successor, Natallya Kochanava (2016–), created response
loops between the people and local government to feedback any possible regional protest (Ivanov, 2017; Lebedko, 2017; Pechenko, 2017).
Having experienced state-wide protests in 2017 over the parasite law,[9]
Kochanava's attempt to strengthen the power *vertikal* which was likely
a direct lesson from these protests. However, the current protests
highlight that policy implementation was ineffective. Ensuring the
effectiveness of the power *vertikal* allows the authorities to learn
about what is occurring regionally.

[8] Personal interview: HU30571.
[9] This was legislation taxing the unemployed for being jobless. It is an example of
learning as the Belarusian parasite law was taken from earlier Soviet laws. We
have it on good authority – although the person was not officially interviewed
and remains anonymous – that even people in the presidential administration
thought this law would lead to protests. But higher-ups thought it was an
effective money-making scheme. This highlights that the presidential
administration is not homogenous and can be ineffective in policy creation.

The presidential administration appoints personnel in other ministries, giving it control over other state structures through personnel loyalty as their first allegiance is to the presidential administration.[10] In the run-up to the 2010 presidential election, then first deputy head of the presidential administration Natallya Pyatkevich (2009–11) created a Public Advisory Council 'to discuss topical issues of the development on the state and society', and gauge what actions the regime should take to guarantee Lukashenka victory and what problems could appear that would lead to protests (Gryl', 2009). The Belarusian presidential administration advises state-media on which stories to run and how to portray Lukashenka.[11] By knowing what the public thinks the regime can learn what could cause protests, although recently this has been less successful.

The Russian presidential administration is the 'command centre from which the Kremlin manages politics at all levels' (Ananyev, 2018: 33), employing *Kuratory*[12] in the domestic policy unit. *Kuratory* work with pro-regime politicians and parties to ensure a positive electoral outcome, and that regional governors follow orders on how to conduct elections. Regional elections are used to develop different practices to ascertain which work effectively to be used in the future (Bocharova et al., 2018), pointing to continuous learning. With the growing unpopularity of United Russia, the presidential administration is developing appropriate electoral tactics to maintain its dominance and creating new parties in case the Kremlin disbands United Russia (Samokhina and Inyutin, 2018). In the build-up to the 2019 local elections, the head of the domestic unit of the presidential administration, Andrei Yarin, worked with pro-regime politicians to tailor individual regional electoral strategies to ensure best results for Kremlin candidates (Karpenko, 2019). Therefore, the presidential administration continually adapts, learns, and develops best practices to guarantee electoral victory.

Head of the presidential administration between 2011 and 2016 Sergey Ivanov collected kompromat on corrupt regime personnel that he used to ensure compliance in following regime orders (Gazeta.ru, 2012). This is probably what happened to former defence minister

---

[10] Personal interview: KW37410.   [11] Personal interview: KW37410.
[12] *Kuratory* are Russian officials who are set a task, such as keeping Ukraine close to Russia. These officials have to make this project work and bypass official institutions, relying on established relationships to achieve success.

Anatoly Serdyukov, who was officially sacked for corruption but was Ivanov's rival. It is likely Ivanov leaked Serdyukov's corruption. After the 2011–12 protests, Ivanov and first deputy head of the presidential administration Vyacheslav Volodin (2011–16) ran training exercises so regional governors knew the Kremlin's requirements for upcoming elections (Kostenko, Kornya, and Khimshiashvili, 2012). In November 2016, Sergey Kirienko spoke with political technologists about electoral system problems. Therefore, Kirienko could see potential problems before the election and ascertain which regional governors were ineffectual (Vinokurov, 2016a, 2016b). The authorities are continually devising best practices, ascertaining what is and is not effective, and learning accordingly.

There is competition between the presidential administration and other institutions, with the presidential administration placing personnel in powerful positions in other institutions. For example, in 2001, head of the presidential administration Aleksandr Voloshin appointed former prosecutor general employee Nazir Khapsirokov as his assistant to gain control over the prosecutor general's office (Arutyunova, 2001: 1). The presidential administration tries to play other factions off against one another by allying with some to weaken others (Levchenko, 2006). Putin regularly moves people from position to position as he only trusts a small group but does not want personnel to hold too much power independently.[13] As one interviewee[14] stated, with only a small coterie of trusted individuals, personnel are moved regularly to stop continual fires or try to make institutions more efficient. The authorities may continually adapt and learn, but it is often inefficient, resulting in having to continually deal with serious disorganisation.

Kompromat is kept in Ukraine as well, with the head of the Ukrainian presidential administration between 2006 and 2009, Viktor Baloha, referred to as the 'all-seeing eye', taking information on regime personnel and storing it for later use, when personnel try to exert too much power (Mostovaya, 2006). As in Russia, the head of the Ukrainian presidential administration between 2010 and 2014, Serhy Lovochkin, regularly tested how effective regional representatives were at getting out the vote for Yanukovych and Party of Regions (Ukrainskaya Pravda, 2010g). As in Russia, the Ukrainian presidential

---

[13] Personal interview: ND30192.    [14] Personal interview: QI40827.

administration under Viktor Medvedchuk (2002–5) regularly dictated to television chiefs what they could present and who they could interview (Ukrainskaya Pravda, 2003b). There are allegations that the presidential administration under Poroshenko agreed with oligarchs that criticism of Poroshenko on television be kept to a minimum,[15] although in the build-up to the 2019 presidential election, this agreement appeared to end. Controlling personnel and the media helps maintain control over the system, making it easier for an incumbent to keep power.

There are many examples of interlinkage between political elites, with one such example being former deputy of the presidential administration Olena Lukash, who was close to both Yanukovych and Firtash (Batherin, 2014: 1; Bolotny, 2014: 6). Lovochkin has been in politics since Kuchma's presidency, building relations across the political spectrum (Ukrainskaya Pravda, 2010i), and learning from previous successes and failures. Even though deputy of the presidential administration Oleksy Ishchenko (2002–5) masterminded the 2004 electoral fraud for Kuchma – which precipitated the Orange Revolution – this little infraction did not stop Tymoshenko employing him when she became prime minister after the Orange Revolution (Ukrainskaya Pravda, 2008b). Having worked for Yushchenko as deputy of the presidential administration, Yuriy Bohutsky (2007–10) became a Yanukovych adviser (Ukrainskaya Pravda, 2013c). Similarly, presidential administration deputy Andry Honcharuk (2008–10) worked for Yushchenko but became Yanukovych's foreign policy adviser (Ukrainskaya Pravda, 2014c). All this elite intra-linkage enables best practices to be shared.

First deputy of the presidential administration Vitaly Kovalchuk (2014–19) was a Poroshenko ally, known as the grey cardinal because of his electoral manipulation (Mostovaya, 2016: 1). Head of the presidential administration Borys Lozhkin (2014–16) was appointed by Poroshenko to head the National Reform Council as well. Under his tenure, it proposed greater presidential powers (Den', 2015; Dubrovyk-Rohova, 2015). This was an attempt to build an alliance willing to support these so-called reforms and help ensure Poroshenko's 2019 electoral victory (Koshkina, 2017a). When Poroshenko was elected president in 2014 the

---

[15] Personal interview: RK36829.

presidential administration began working on Poroshenko's re-election in 2019 immediately (Koshkina, 2016). However, this failed because Bankova cannot stop support leaching for an incumbent once it seems the officeholder is unlikely to remain in power. Links between personnel in the presidential administrations are strong with regular external and internal meetings, making learning likely. The limited powers of the Moldovan presidential administration may partially explain why Moldovan authoritarian-minded elites have been less able to consolidate power. However, this does not explain why Ukrainian authoritarian-minded elites have been less successful at consolidating power too.

### 7.2.3  The Security Services

#### 7.2.3.1  External Networks

Belarusian and Russian security service personnel share rest and recuperation facilities, thereby allowing for informal meetings in places such as the sauna.[16] Both closely collaborate in training exercises and hold monthly meetings on issues faced.[17] This allows both to train together, hold discussions, and learn from successes and failures. Until 2015 the Belarusian security forces did not have a training school, so personnel went to Russian security service training schools, thereby increasing already strong links.[18] Although, Belarus now has its own school, it only offers a few courses. So, any KDB officer wishing to progress must go to the Federalnaya Sluzhba Bezopasnosti's (FSB) Moscow school.[19] Many Belarusian security personnel remain close to Russia. Many were born or were educated there and remain close to Russian counterparts (Kalinkina, 2014), so improving learning opportunities for both.

Many KDB personnel were in the Belarusian military – which does not have a military training academy – and so already have close ties to Russian regime personnel.[20] Ties are strong between the Belarusian and Russian security services, resulting in sharing of best practices and learning. In 2005, the KDB claimed to have tracked American money in a Ukrainian bank account for use in a Colour Revolution in Belarus by Serbian, Georgian, and Ukrainian activists who were prominent in

---

[16]  Personal interview: YR52870.    [17]  Personal interview: YR52870.
[18]  Personal interview: UR24751.    [19]  Personal interview: KW37410.
[20]  Personal interviews: UR24751, KW37410.

previous Colour Revolutions (Kovalenko, 2006a: 1, 2006b: 2). Poland and the Baltic States were perceived to be funding a Belarusian Colour Revolution (Ankudo, 2006a, 2006b; Gryl', 2005b; Provalinskaya, 2007). Much of the information the KDB acted on came directly from FSB intelligence that a 'flower revolution' would happen in Belarus (Snegin, 2005: 2).

During a Moscow press conference in 2012, head of the KDB Vadzim Zaitsau (2008–12) spoke about how both security services shared anti-terror practices (Budkevich, 2012). One example of the KDB and FSB's close collaboration is the FSB's abduction of Pavlo Hryb in Belarus. Hryb, the son of a Ukrainian border guard, was lured to Homel in August 2017 after talking with a girl on VKontakte.[21] She was forced by the FSB to entice Pavlo to Homel. Upon arrival, Pavlo was arrested and charged by the FSB with planning a terrorist act in Crimea (BBC Ukrainian Service, 2017a, 2017b; Belsat, 2017a; 2017b; Gordonua.com, 2017b, 2017c; TSN.ua, 2017). It is inconceivable that the KDB was unaware of the FSB's actions, which emphasises the integration of both security services.

Ukrainian president Viktor Yushchenko created inter-departmental meetings and discussion forums between Ukraine and Russia. One structure was about SBU and FSB cooperation (Ukrainskaya Pravda, 2008a). SBU chief Valery Khoroshkovsky (2010–12) stated that he was modelling the SBU on the FSB (Ukrainskaya Pravda, 2010e, 2010a). Head of the SBU Oleksandr Yakimenko (2013–14) was a member of the Russian military (Ukrainskaya Pravda, 2013b). That Yakimenko was appointed SBU head emphasises Yanukovych's closeness to the Kremlin, and the SBU and FSB at this time. It is likely that this relationship led to sharing of best practices and learning. The Kuchma regime had close links to the Russian security services. There is evidence that the FSB was involved in poisoning opposition candidate Yushchenko during the 2004 presidential elections. Two Russians – with FSB links – were arrested in Boryspil Airport on false passports (Wilson, 2005: 100). Yushchenko was poisoned by dioxin.[22] While there is no concrete evidence of FSB involvement, dioxin is hard to obtain and Russian Laboratory 12, known for the development of poisons such as dioxin,

---

[21] VKontakte is the Russian-language Facebook.
[22] These are highly toxic chemical compounds, like Agent Orange or Yellow Rain.

is the closest provider to Kyiv. Consequently, it is likely that someone in the Kremlin approved the dispatch.

During the Euromaidan, there is evidence the Kremlin gave weapons to Bankova (Ukrainskaya Pravda, 2014b). However, even before the Euromaidan, the FSB was heavily involved in Ukraine, and some SBU members worked for the FSB (Ukrainskaya Pravda, 2015a, 2015b). The SBU did not oppose Russian operations in Crimea or Donbas under Yanukovych (Kapsamun, 2014; Melkozerova, 2015). During the Yanukovych presidency, Serhy Lovochkin ran a bank – used by the FSB – for Russian operations in Ukraine, and Lovochkin worked with Russian criminal gangs, using these to help FSB operations in Ukraine (Ivanchenko, 2012). When Yanukovych fled in February 2014, the FSB, who had employees working in the government (Balachuk, 2018), took, or destroyed, all pertinent information on intelligence and actions perpetrated by the authorities. This weakened the SBU, as it lost much intelligence and was unaware which SBU personnel worked for the FSB (Miller, 2014). The SBU was further affected by 1,391 personnel joining the FSB after Crimea's annexation[23] and the discovery that the second-in-command of the Anti-Terrorist Operation[24] was a Russian spy (TSN.ua, 2016b). During the Euromaidan, SBU factions sent information to Russia about protester and regime tactics and failures.[25] This helped the Kremlin draw lessons from the Euromaidan. Similarly, many Berkut personnel after 2014 joined the Russian security services, sharing information with the Kremlin on Bankova's failures (Bershidsky, 2019b).

There is evidence of learning between the security services in the case studies, although learning and sharing of best practices are dominated by the FSB. This is likely because there is more information available on FSB operations and practices. Certainly, the Kremlin uses the FSB to infiltrate other regimes and uses personnel from other security services for Russian interests. This is particularly the case in Ukraine, but it is so in Belarus too. The extensive collaboration shown between the KDB

---

[23]  Names are here: https://psb4ukr.org/532062-spisok-kolishnix-spivrobitnikiv-sb-ukra%D1%97ni-yaki-zradili-prisyazi-i-perejshli-na-bik-voroga/#more-532062.

[24]  This is the term the Ukrainian government gave the Donbas conflict for political reasons.

[25]  Personal interview: CM29876.

and FSB and the FSB and SBU emphasises dialogue, tactic sharing, and learning between security services in the four case studies.

### 7.2.3.2 Internal Networks

Although the KDB has been weakened recently, with people removed for close ties to the Kremlin as Lukashenka fears a Donbas scenario in Belarus,[26] the Belarusian regime has fourteen different security services. While the regime rules by dividing these different structures and playing them against one another, these services adapt and learn to try to guarantee regime survival.[27] The KDB plays on Lukashenka's fears of losing power to maintain their pre-eminence.[28] KDB personnel regularly meet other ministry personnel to discuss issues in these ministries, thereby allowing the KDB to keep abreast of issues and learn.[29] Current and former KDB members oversee other ministries, allowing the KDB to control other institutions and learn from failures or successes.[30] Through close collaboration with other ministries, the KDB shares best practices and learns about problems faced by other structures, allowing the KDB to adapt, learn, and rectify problems.

Although there are nine security services in Russia, the FSB is the most prominent security service (Soldatov and Borogan, 2010: 20) and has increased its powers by inventing threats, which it presents to Putin as real issues (Soldatov, 2013). For example, head of the FSB Aleksandr Bortnikov (2008–) created stories to keep the FSB relevant, like the story that claimed that forest fires in 2012 were Al-Qaeda terror attacks (Preobrazhensky, 2012). Bortnikov worked closely with Igor Sechin to set up minister of economic development Aleksey Ulyukaev on corruption charges to weaken the moderniser faction (Galeotti, 2017; The Moscow Times, 2017). Ulyukaev was found guilty – and given an eight-year prison sentence – for taking a $2 million bribe. He had met Sechin, who gave him a briefcase containing money rather than documents (Galeotti, 2017). The case against Ulyukaev was created to weaken the moderniser faction and stop this group getting Putin's approval for modernisation reforms that would weaken the FSB (Galeotti, 2018b). This highlights intra-

---

[26] Personal interviews: NF29463, GK80361.     [27] Personal interview: KG84027.
[28] Personal interviews: KW37410, HA20938.     [29] Personal interview: IR39203.
[30] Personal interview: KW37410.

institutional rivalry and factionalism. While factions share best practices and learn, it is incorrect to see these groups as homogenous and sharing similar interests. Factions are fluid and centred around protecting a resource or collaborating on a certain issue. Cliques that worked together previously may well be rivals in the next crisis,[31] with Putin being the final arbiter (Galeotti, 2018a: 9).

Moldovan SIS leaders have traditionally been affiliated to the incumbent government, so the organisation is politicised and used against regime opponents.[32] For example, head of the SIS Artur Reşetnicov (2007–9) used the organisation to prepare an electoral victory for the PCRM in 2009. Under Reşetnicov's tenure, the SIS monitored media and opposition parties, and scrutinised donations from domestic and foreign sources (Point.md, 2007, 2008c, 2008d, 2008b). In 2019, Dodon gained control over the SIS as part of negotiations with the ACUM coalition over forming a government. This allowed him to appoint the SIS director and deputy director. Dodon appointed Aleksandr Esaulenko and Artur Gumeniuc, who both had close ties to the Kremlin, giving him control of the SIS (Gorchak, 2019; Stepanov, 2019). Gumeniuc was Dodon's advisor and apart from being SIS deputy director he was Secretary of the Security Council (NewsMaker, 2017).

The 2009 protests were discussed between interior minister Aleksey Roibu (2011–12), head of the SIS Gheorghe Mihai (2009–11), and the Alliance for European Integration (AEI) government to learn from these events (Vesti.md, 2011). Although the AEI government was 'pro-European', many members had been PCRM members before 2009. Learning from the 2009 protests allowed elites to adapt lessons from the protests to the present.[33] Although it is likely that former PCRM members in the AEI coalition would have already developed methods to reduce the chances of the 2009-like protests re-occurring, it is always best to have a refresher course. SIS head Mihai Bălan (2012–19) advocated widening the SIS's role and allowing SIS personnel to work in other ministries, giving the SIS greater ministerial control and allowing for learning (NewsMaker, 2015). Bălan met Prime Minister Filip and Interior Minister Jizdan (2016–19) to discuss the 2016 protests. As a direct

[31] Personal interview: AM07019.    [32] Personal interview: KH32708.
[33] Personal interviews: DW48620, CR52981.

response to this meeting – in August 2016 – Bălan requested increased anti-terror powers (NewsMaker, 2016d, 2016a). The SIS remains highly politicised, and was used by Plahotniuc to control regime opponents (NewsMaker, 2016d).

SBU Chief Ihor Drizhchany (2005–6) worked for Yushchenko but kept his options open by maintaining close ties to Yanukovych (Trofimova, 2006). Similarly, SBU chief Valery Koroshkovsky (2010–12) had close ties to Kuchma, Firtash, Lovochkin, Boyko, and Tymoshenko (Ukrainksya Pravda, 2010d, 2010f). SBU chief Oleksandr Yakimenko (2013–14) supervised Yanukovych's growing business empire and Akhmetov's assets before being appointed head of the SBU (Ukrainskaya Pravda, 2013a). Yakimenko was close to the 'family' and worked with Yanukovych in Donetsk as an adviser (Kapsamun, 2013). During the Euromaidan, Yakimenko used the SBU to gather intelligence on the opposition, NGOs, and protesters, and he developed a plan to use the SBU's anti-terrorist units to clear the Maidan. Some of the units were involved in the death of 100 protesters on 20 February 2014 (Ukrainskaya Pravda, 2015c). Poroshenko increased the SBU's power while placing allies in key positions (Ponomarenko, 2018a), giving him control.

Control of the security services is a necessity for authoritarian-minded elites to preserve power. The closeness of the security services to the leadership and other institutions enhances learning potential. Placing allies in charge of the security services increases the likelihood of preserving power, as these allies have a vested interest in keeping the incumbent leader in power. This is almost the first step any new leader makes in Belarus, Moldova, Russia, and Ukraine. Although regimes are harder to consolidate in Moldova and Ukraine, authoritarian-minded elites across the cases use the security services to tie in other institutions, thereby increasing learning potential.

## 7.2.4 Security Councils

### 7.2.4.1 External Networks
During the Kuchma presidency, the Ukrainian and Russian Security Councils regularly met and discussed pressing issues (Ukrainskaya Pravda, 2001a), highlighting the role of Security Councils in learning. Head of the Belarusian Security Council Nyavyhlas (2001–8)

increased cooperation between the KDB, FSB, and interior and defence ministries to devise applicable methods to counter Colour Revolution (Mazaeva, 2004). This collaboration continued between the Belarusian and Russian Security Councils with Belarusian Security Council chairman Leanid Maltsau (2009–13) meeting his Russian counterpart Nikolai Patrushev twice in 2012 to discuss cooperation and experience sharing (BELTA, 2012a, 2012b). Regular meetings occur biannually to discuss national security issues (Security Council of the Russian Federation, 2017). Therefore, there are several avenues between both security councils that precipitate learning opportunities.

There is evidence of cooperation between the Russian and Ukrainian security councils, although this is not at the same level as the Belarusian and Russian security councils. Russian Security Council head Igor Ivanov (2004–7) met Ukrainian parliamentary chairman Oleksandr Moroz (2006–7) to discuss political cooperation in 2006 (Security Council of the Russian Federation, 2006). This was likely an attempt to co-opt Moroz and use him to weaken or terminate the Orange government. In 2013, Patrushev discussed with Andry Klyuyev (2012–14) about increasing joint Security Council cooperation (Security Council of the Russian Federation, 2013). This would have given the Yanukovych regime greater learning possibilities had the Euromaidan not stopped this support.

Evidence to support learning in security councils is seen in the examples of Belarus, Russia, and Ukraine. However, information on Ukrainian Security Council activities remains limited, as does information about the Moldovan Security Council. While Dodon (2017b) tried to strengthen the security council's role to help consolidate his power, there is limited evidence of collaboration with other cases. The lack of cooperation for the Ukrainian and Moldovan security councils can partially explain why authoritarian-minded elites have never consolidated power in either country. Nevertheless, there is evidence that security councils help dialogue, sharing of best practices, and learning.

### 7.2.4.2 Internal Networks

A Russian Security Council meeting of permanent members is held weekly and discusses international and domestic issues (Levchenko, 2007), allowing top personnel to exchange ideas and learn. For example, Putin (2014b), at a 2014 Security Council meeting, spoke about how the Ukrainian protests and resulting 'fascism' could cause instability in Russia, so the authorities needed to stop such events reaching Moscow. A working commission of the Security Council discussed the anti-terrorist problems faced by Russia in 2016. The main anti-terror issue discussed was one where 'people stayed in one place'. This points to developing anti-protest measures, rather than anti-terror measures as protesters tend to congregate on a square or single space, whereas terrorists are more likely to try to take control of state institutions or assassinate elites or members of the public. Other anti-terrorist matters discussed were how to stop protesters controlling space and how to better equip the Rosgvardiya (Security Council of the Russian Federation, 2016a, 2016c).

Head of the Belarusian National Security Council Viktar Sheyman (2006–8) has been close to Lukashenka since 1994 and has been a constant in the regime.[34] During the 1994 presidential elections, where Lukashenka competed against Vyacheslau Kebich, Sheyman staged an assassination attempt to increase Lukashenka's vote (Wilson, 2021: 161–2). Sheyman remains a crucial figure developing practices to guarantee continued regime survival. After the Euromaidan, the head of the Belarusian National Security Council, Stanislau Zas (2015–), spoke on the situation, potential spill-over, efficiency of Belarusian law enforcement units, and how Ukraine's association agreement with the EU might destabilise Belarus (TUT.by, 2015). Zas devised a new military doctrine giving equal emphasis to internal and external threats (BELTA, 2016), pointing to learning from the Ukrainian situation.

Head of the Ukrainian Security Council Yevhen Marchuk (1999–2003) regularly met members of all parties – including the opposition – to get their support for Kuchma (Ukrainskaya Pravda, 2001b). After the Security Council, Marchuk became defence minister, an adviser to Yanukovych, and currently works in the security sub-group of the Minsk peace agreement under Zelensky. So, Marchuk is trusted across the political spectrum and uses his experience to pass on information for learning. Possibly Marchuk and his successor Volodymyr Radchenko (2003–5) knew of the Melnychenko tapes[35] and approved

---

[34] Personal interview: NF29463.
[35] Recordings by Major Mykola Melnychenko of Kuchma speaking with other regime members about killing a journalist, repressing opponents, and selling weapons to Saddam Hussein.

their recording and publication of conversations to serve their own interests (Urainskaya Pravda, 2004; Wilson, 2005: 52), possibly about changing allegiance and joining Yushchenko.

Head of the Ukrainian Security Council Anatoly Kinakh (2005–6) tried to construct an effective power *vertikal* to stop an Orange Revolution-type event re-occurring (Ukrainskaya Pravda, 2006). Like Marchuk, after leaving the Security Council, Kinakh advised Yushchenko, Yanukovych, and Poroshenko, showing that Kinakh could cross political divides and bring his experience to help incumbent leaders. As head of the Security Council, Andry Klyuyev (2012–14) was close to Lovochkin, who headed the presidential administration. This brought the Security Council under the presidential administration umbrella. There were regular private meetings between Klyuyev and Lovochkin (Ukrainskaya Pravda, 2012c, 2012e), allowing for effective best practice sharing and learning.

Both Klyuyev and Lovochkin surreptitiously supported Pravy Sektor[36] and used this group as foot soldiers against protesters on the Maidan.[37] Lovochkin approved the idea of Pravy Sektor supporting Poroshenko and Maidan demonstrators, allowing Bankova to label Poroshenko and the protesters as fascists. Klyuyev apparently gave a million dollars to Pravy Sektor to stop defending the Maidan when the Berkut tried to storm it in January 2014. Others in the Yanukovych regime also financed Pravy Sektor. Its leader, Dmytro Yarosh, allegedly had close ties to the SBU (Nayem, 2014). Klyuyev – with Yanukovych's support – created a secret unit with experience of national security issues (Ukrainskaya Pravda, 2012b), allowing Klyuyev to learn from previous episodes of unrest. Klyuyev ran the 2012 parliamentary campaign of Party of Regions and visited parliament to convince opposition deputies to support Yanukovych (Ukrainskaya Pravda, 2012a). After Yanukovych fled in February 2014, Klyuyev and his brother Serhy ran money-laundering schemes, taking loans from Ukrainian banks, and sending the proceeds through their companies to Austrian bank accounts. This nearly created a banking collapse (Ekonomicheskaya Pravda, 2017). Having worked closely with Yanukovych, Klyuyev had

---

[36] Pravy Sektor's leadership had links to the Yanukovych government and were used as agents provocateurs allowing the regime to label the protesters as fascist.

[37] Personal interviews: RK36829, RM29174, JH58291, MQ37492.

links to Poroshenko as the Klyuyev brothers owned shares in Poroshenko's company Roshen (Roshchenko, 2017).

Moldova's Supreme Security Council (CSS) does not have the same level of importance as in Belarus, Russia, and Ukraine. However, there are instances of learning here. In 2015, the CSS discussed domestic security issues (Jurnal.md, 2015b), conveniently as protests began in Chişinău. During the theft of the century and laundromat scandals, the CSS met secretly (Jurnal.md, 2015a) to discuss how both scandals occurred. The 2016 CSS strategic doctrine focused on domestic issues (Jurnal.md, 2016a) and highlighted learning from the 2015–16 protests as the CSS looked to strengthen domestic enforcement structures.[38] Dodon appeared to strengthen the CSS's role as it started running the state. At a 2018 meeting, Dodon (2018) stated that the CSS would devise appropriate tactics to deal with protesters who 'arrive in Chisinau to destabilise the situation', highlighting that Dodon looked to learn from protests between 2015 and 2017 to reduce future destabilisation.

## 7.2.5 Governments

Information about collaboration between prime ministers is limited, as they deal with domestic issues and, like presidents, they tend to be from opposing sides, making cooperation less likely. However, there are pointers to the role prime ministers play in learning. For instance, Russian prime minister Mikhail Fradkov (2004–7) reportedly gave the Kremlin's approval to Lukashenka to overturn the Belarusian constitution and remove presidential term-limits (Gryl', 2004). On 6 June 2017, Moldovan prime minister Pavel Filip (2016–19) held secret meetings with personnel in the Belarusian regime (Otkroi Novost', 2017), although there is no information of what was discussed.

Inter-governmental commissions are a good place for regime personnel to meet and discuss pressing issues and learn from others' experience. The four case studies have established several inter-governmental commissions. While there is limited evidence of their role, the Ukrainian–Russian Intergovernmental Commission regularly met until 2014. During the Euromaidan, the commission discussed economic support for Bankova, which was granted through a $15 million loan. In closed meetings there is evidence that the Euromaidan was discussed, with

---

[38] Personal interview: KH32708.

Kremlin representatives offering advice on quelling protests (BBC Ukrainian Service, 2013; Bilousova, 2013). Inter-parliamentary commissions and parties are crucial learning avenues as they bring representatives together to discuss ideas. One example is the regular meetings between the Russian Federation Council and the Belarusian parliament (Khilko, 2016). Deputies on the Committee of the State Duma for CIS Eurasian Integration and Relations with Compatriots regularly meet representatives of other post-Soviet parliaments to discuss ideas that are not about Eurasian integration or compatriot policy. In 2016, the Belarusian parliament created an international affairs committee, concentrating on the CIS states and bringing representatives together. This allows for discussions, the sharing of best practices, and learning. The Kremlin actively organised inter-party collaboration between United Russia and Party of Regions to coordinate 'political positions, exchanging experience in the election campaign' (Liga.net, 2007). Another example of inter-party collaboration in the four cases studied is the supposedly pro-European and at the time governing party, Plahotniuc's PDM and United Russia. This provided consultations and visiting delegations to help Plahotniuc learn from Russian experiences. Another agreement saw United Russia increase existing close ties with the pro-Russian PSRM (Vlas, 2017), pointing to the Russian authorities having close ties to parties ostensibly across the political divide in Moldova. A 2017 agreement was signed to improve inter-parliamentary relations between the Russian and Moldovan parliaments (A-TV.md, 2017; Bloknot-Moldova.md, 2017).

## 7.2.6 Foreign and Internal Affairs Ministries

### 7.2.6.1 External Networks

The four defence ministries have not been investigated, as the armed forces in three of the case studies are under-funded. In all four cases studied, there is as much investment, or even more, in the interior ministry. While the Kremlin projects military strength the budget of the armed forces was quietly cut in 2016 by 5 per cent (Galeotti, 2016). The Rosgvardiya are as well equipped, if not more so, than the army (Luzin, 2017). The Belarusian army has been consistently scaled down (Bohdan, 2017a, 2017c). With the Belarusian regime more concerned about domestic protests than invasion, police numbers are close to 325,000 *militsiya* for a population of 10 million. This figure excludes other 'sprawling' law enforcement agencies (Charnysh, 2016). Similarly, the Moldovan army is under-financed, whereas the Fulger elite Interior Ministry troops are well equipped for a force of 500 (Minzarari, 2014). Yanukovych stripped the Ukrainian army of equipment, personnel, and training facilities, relying on the Berkut (Euromaidan Press, 2014; Jacobs, 2014). While the Ukrainian military has improved after eight years of conflict with Russia, Bankova retains well-equipped interior ministry forces. With this in mind, we concentrate on interior and foreign ministries, although future studies could assess the military role in authoritarian learning.

Russian interior minister Vladimir Rushailo (1999–2001) met his Ukrainian counterpart Yury Kravchenko (1999–2001) to discuss coordinating law enforcement agencies, focusing on an 'exchange of operational information' (Novye Izvestiya, 2000: 2), an indirect reference to learning. In 2005, all Russian and Ukrainian interior ministry generals discussed conducting 'joint operations and investigations' (Falaleev, 2005: 3), highlighting use of training exercises to determine appropriate tactics for exercising control. Belarusian interior minister Anatol Kulyashou (2009–12) worked for the Russian police in Moscow, before joining the Minsk police in 2008 (Tut.by, 2009). Kulyashou was close to personnel in the Russian interior ministry. After March 2015, Ukrainian interior minister Viktor Zakharchenko worked for the Kremlin, providing further information on Bankova's failure during the Euromaidan. Belarusian interior minister deputy Mikalai Melchanka (2014–) spoke with Russian interior ministry personnel about the Euromaidan (Burmenko, 2014), although what was discussed is not known.

Ukrainian foreign minister Anatoly Zlenko (2000–3) met Russian foreign minister Igor Ivanov in 2003 about security. The meeting went beyond what were diplomatic niceties (Ukrainskaya Pravda, 2003a), emphasising Zlenko's closeness to the Kremlin. Before becoming foreign minister again, Konstyantyn Hryshchenko (2010–12) met Russian elites. Nine days after being appointed he signed a cooperation agreement with the Russian foreign ministry (Ukrainskaya Pravda, 2010b, 2010c, 2010h), pointing to Hryshchenko conducting negotiations before becoming foreign minister. Until 2014, both foreign ministries regularly met to discuss ideas, share best practices, and learn.[39]

---

[39] Personal interview: BO39761.

Belarusian and Russian foreign ministry colleagues meet regularly, bringing staff closer from the beginning of their careers, thereby establishing ties for discussion, sharing, and learning.[40]

Russian first deputy foreign ministers like Vyacheslav Trubnikov (2000–4), Valery Loshchinin (2002–5) and Andrey Denisov (2006–13) worked as *Kuratory* in the post-Soviet region (Bai, 2006: 3; Neglinina, 2004). Their role was to collect information about events in other post-Soviet states, allowing the Kremlin to gauge what was happening and predict potential problems. If there was a possible issue, then Trubnikov, Loshchinin, and Denisov would advise regime personnel in each state, or pro-Russian entities if the incumbent regime was considered anti-Russian. Then Russian deputy foreign minister Grigory Karasin held secret meetings in Chişinău with 'all Moldovan political elites'. However, it appears that the only politician at the meeting was Dodon (Gamova, 2017: 1).

### 7.2.6.2 Internal Networks

Although it is probable that foreign ministers talk, we did not find evidence of this. Consequently, this sub-section focuses on internal ties between interior ministers. In April 2009, protests erupted in Chişinău at electoral fraud by the PCRM to ensure their parliamentary majority, allowing the PCRM to pick the president. The protests began with a flash-mob organised by Natalia Morari on Twitter and evolved into the Twitter Revolution, with 30,000 protesters in central Chişinău, ending in parliament being stormed. Even though the Twitter Revolution led to regime change – after a united opposition denied the PCRM the one seat necessary to form a government – many PCRM personnel switched sides and became pro-European (Point.md, 2019). Plahotniuc's interior minister Alexandru Jizdan was the police chief tasked with crushing the protests (Jurnal.md, 2016e). Plahotniuc and Jizdan were allies since at least 2004 when Jizdan, as head of the General Department of the Judicial Police, stopped a corruption case linked to Plahotniuc's businesses (Jurnal.md, 2016b; Rise.md, 2015).

Interior minister Gheorghe Papuc (2002–8 and 2008–9) was quickly re-appointed after a drug scandal. This emphasised that Papuc was a trusted ally of President Voronin (Point.md, 2008a). Another instance of how Moldovan regimes try to control the interior ministry

---

[40] Personal interview: UR24751.

was a 2012 reform that Plahotniuc initiated, changing the appointment procedure for the interior ministry's head of the Centre for Combating Economic Crimes and Corruption (CCECC). This gave parliament – with most deputies in Plahotniuc's pay – control of the appointment. Control of the CCECC allowed Plahotniuc to blackmail opposition into supporting the authorities. CCECC control meant that opposition members could be targeted through selective corruption cases (Logos-Press, 2012).

Loyalty is crucial in an interior minister. After all, if one runs the risks of protests, as happen from time to time across the four case studies, then having a loyal interior minister willing to keep the regime in power at all costs is beneficial. Dorin Recean (2012–15) had no relevant experience when he became Moldovan interior minister, except loyalty to Prime Minister Filat (Nesterova, 2014). That allegiance was seen in 2013 after telephone intercepts incriminated Recean as well as politician Valery Strelts of the Party of Liberal Democrats of Moldova, Central Electoral Commission chief Iurie Ciocan (2011–), and head of the tax inspectorate Nikolae Vikol (2013–15) over using the tax inspectorate against opposition leaders (Point.md, 2013).

Ukrainian interior minister Yury Lutsenko (2005–6) was close to Prime Minister Tymoshenko. Upon leaving the interior ministry Lutsenko, led the People's Self-Defence (Rakhmanin, 2008), a party in the coalition led by Bloc Yulia Tymoshenko. When Poroshenko became president in 2014, Lutsenko was appointed prosecutor general and quickly became part of the Poroshenko 'family', using his position to promote 'family' interests while prosecuting cases against Poroshenko's enemies (Politeka.net, 2016). Lutsenko regularly brought corruption cases against opposition politicians and NGOs fighting corruption (Sukhov, 2018b, 2016d) and increased pressure on anti-corruption bodies such as the National Anti-Corruption Bureau (Zerkalo Nedeli, 2017). By bringing corruption cases against the opposition, Bankova tried to emphasise that the opposition were more corrupt.[41] Under Poroshenko the prosecutor general's office did not prosecute those responsible for the Euromaidan shootings (Kyiv Post, 2018), pointing to elite collusion and protecting personnel who had changed allegiance from Yanukovych to Poroshenko.

---

[41] Personal interview: JH58291.

There was learning from the Orange Revolution when Yanukovych became president in 2010 and looked to rectify mistakes made in 2004, to consolidate power after 2010. In 2004, interior minister Mykola Bilokon (2003–5) spoke about introducing 'a third force', which was a euphemism for a people's militia to counter opposition during the build-up to the 2004 presidential elections (Zerkalo Nedeli, 2004). The creation of the Titushki was a direct lesson from this failure. The Titushkis's establishment in May 2013 was preparation for the upcoming 2015 presidential elections, with protests expected afterwards.[42] The Titushki were controlled by Viktor Zubrytsky (LB.ua, 2014b). Zubrytsky had close ties to interior minister Viktor Zakharchenko (2010–14). Zubrytsky's control of the Titushki gave Zakharchenko 'deniability and distance' (Wilson, 2014c: 79), allowing Bankova to deny – however unbelievably – that the Titushki were not part of the regime. That Zubrytsky was allowed to work for the television channel 112 – owned by Taras Kozak, who is close to Viktor Medvedchuk (LB. ua, 2017a; Ekonomichna Pravda, 2018) – after he had played such a significant role in the Euromaidan points to elite collusion between Poroshenko, Russia, and Yanukovych era regime elites.

Interior Minister Arsen Avakov (2014–21) allegedly did not reform law enforcement structures because Yanukovych's operational configuration allowed Avakov more control (Sukhov, 2016a). In 2020, Ukrainskaya Pravda (2020) found that Avakov had constructed a new police department tasked with countering economic crimes. This division is a secretive structure taking over from the Department of Economic Defence, which was discredited for targeting of non-regime elites. The new entity's powers are hidden 'behind the screen of "official information"' and can do 'anything Avakov wants'. The unit's tasks go further than countering economic crimes, existing to protect government and maintain public order against perceived threats. Additionally, this division possesses the same powers as the SBU (Sukhov, 2020b).

Belarusian interior minister Yury Sivakou (1999–2001) exerted control over other institutions, bringing him into competition with the KDB (Podolyak, 2000). Sivakou headed a clandestine clique close to Lukashenka, developing 'blitzkrieg tactics' against protesters. There were regular training activities by internal ministry troops in and

---

[42] Personal interview: BK07421.

around Minsk (Kozhenikova, 2000). The closeness of Sivakou to Lukashenka is seen in the prominent role Sivakou played in organising the disappearances of opposition people between 1999 and 2001. Interior minister Uladzimir Navumau (2001–9) headed the president's security service because Lukashenka trusted him (Volanin, 2000). This gave Navumau direct and constant contact with Lukashenka.

During the 2010 protests, the KDB and interior ministry regularly met to discuss best practices and effective measures to end the protests. One result of these discussions was the use of the Almaz anti-terror special unit against protesters (Malashenkov, 2010), emphasising again the broad definition of terrorism for the cases. In the run-up to the 2015 presidential election, Belarusian interior minister Ihar Shunevich said the interior ministry had 'a rich experience in carrying out such events' (BELTA, 2015), a direct reference to measures taken against protesters in 2001, 2006, and 2010. Shunevich's statement was likely a threat to potential protesters that the regime knew what measures to take if protests occurred after the 2015 presidential election. In 2017, the interior ministry introduced 'cameras and special detectors' to monitor state-wide events (BELTA, 2017). That this request occurred during the 2017 protests shows that the ministry was learning from the events.

Rosgvardiya was created in 2014 and its leader Viktor Zolotov was until his appointment Putin's chief bodyguard (Zygar, 2016: 137). While its formation was rushed through due to the Euromaidan, Rosgvardiya's creation was first explored during the 2011–12 Russian protests. Existing structures – like the OMON – were considered ineffective against concerted protests (Baidakova, 2016b: 7). Rosgvardiya regularly trains against protesters, like with a large exercise on 7 April 2016, outside Lyubertsy (Moskovskaya Oblast), where Rosgvardiya practised dispersing a potential Moscow Maidan (Otkrytaya Rossiya, 2016).[43]

Another training exercise in 2006 involved more than 32,000 personnel in an anti-terrorist exercise stopping militants seizing government buildings (Kozlova, 2006: 2; Poletaev, 2006: 13). This points to devising practices to repress protests. That this exercise occurred in 2006 points to learning from the Colour Revolutions. In 2007, over 3 billion roubles was spent re-equipping interior ministry troops (Falaleev, 2007: 3), pointing to preparation for countering a Colour

---

[43] A video of the practice is here: https://openrussia.org/post/view/14173/.

Revolution. A 2008 interior ministry meeting addressed Colour Revolutions (Falaleev, 2008: 2), again highlighting the Kremlin's focus on events in Serbia, Georgia, Ukraine, and Kyrgyzstan. Interior minister Vladimir Kolokoltsev (2012–) worked for the Moscow police before becoming interior minister. One of his roles in Moscow was to run anti-protest training exercises (Bocharova and Savina, 2010; Sumskoi, 2010). In 2014, Kolokoltsev wanted the number of public law enforcement units increased. Although in 2014 there were 402,000 personnel in law enforcement structures (Igorev, 2014a: 1, 2014b: 5), the Euromaidan evidently scared Kolokoltsev. He stated that any Yanukovych-era Berkut forces would be welcome (Gazeta.ru, 2014). This has happened with many ex-Berkut joining Rosgvardiya, thereby giving the Kremlin valuable insider information from the Euromaidan experience (Bershidsky, 2019b) to counter future Russian protests.

Like the security services, interior ministry control is crucial for regime survival as placing a loyal ally in this structure makes it easier for incumbent regimes to use law enforcement for their purposes. There is evidence that the interior ministries of the four cases engage in more learning than the security services. There are training exercises, although there is only evidence that this is a Russian and Belarusian phenomenon. However, in all four case studies, there are attempts to devise best practices to keep control and regularly learn. Consequently, it can be stated with some certainty that all four interior ministries are crucial for learning.

## 7.2.7 *Ambassadors*

Belarusian ambassador to Russia Vladimir Grigor'ev (1997–2006) regularly met Russian ministers to discuss the Colour Revolutions and how best to stop them (Gryl', 2005a). Russian ambassador Aleksandr Surikov (2006–18) worked closely with the Belarusian presidential administration (Reshetnikova, 2006: 1; Tolkacheva, 2018). His successor Mikhail Babich (2018–19), as well as being ambassador, was special trade representative and Putin's personal representative. Having been a member of the Russian Security Council when the decision to annex Crimea was made, Babich's appointment was seen in Belarus as an attempt by the Russian authorities to keep Belarus close (TUT.by, 2018; UDF.by, 2018). Ukrainian ambassador Mykhailo Yezhel (2013–15) often met Belarusian regime personnel secretly to discuss events in both countries (Kryat, 2014: 2; Mendeleev, 2010), which he then sent back to Kyiv, likely allowing Bankova to learn from Belarusian experiences rather than the other way around. Even when Ukraine had no ambassador to Belarus, Ukrainian embassy officials met interior ministry personnel to exchange views (Lavnekevich, 2017).

Viktor Chernomyrdin (2001–9) reportedly recommended possible prime ministers to Kuchma after pressuring Kuchma to remove Yushchenko as prime minister in 2001 (Rudenko, 2001: 2). Chernomyrdin was labelled by the Ukrainian opposition as the real Ukrainian president as he was perceived to make all the decisions (Sokolovskaya, 2001: 1). Chernomyrdin was a reason why Kuchma found a successor for the 2004 presidential elections, as Chernomyrdin made it clear that the Kremlin did not approve of Kuchma's attempt to engineer an unconstitutional presidential third term (Romanova, 2002: 2). Just before Kuchma lost power in 2004, Chernomyrdin orchestrated financial deals giving Russian state-owned companies – and by association the Kremlin – control over key Ukrainian assets (Izvestiya, 2004: 1). This forced the new Orange government to work with the Kremlin as it could not break the contracts (Prokopchuk, 2004: 2).

Russian ambassador to Ukraine Mikhail Zurabov (2009–16), using similar tactics as Chernomyrdin, was a channel between Bankova, the Kremlin, and the Ukrainian opposition (Kravchenko, 2010). Zurabov threatened that if Ukraine did not renew the Kharkiv Pact[44] – signed in 2010 – Russia would withdraw funding and Ukrainian debt would spiral (Podrobnosti.ua, 2010). In 2013 he used the same tactic, stating that if Ukraine signed the EU association agreement it would need to discuss red lines with the Kremlin (LB.ua, 2013). Allegedly Zurabov had close business ties to Poroshenko, having known him since Poroshenko was foreign minister under Kuchma (Argumenty Nedeli, 2014: 2; Dergachev et al., 2016). Zurabov often held late-night meetings with Poroshenko to discuss Ukrainian domestic affairs (LB.ua, 2014a) and likely offer advice on power consolidation.

During the 2010 Belarusian protests, Russian ambassador Aleksandr Surikov (2006–18) supported the Belarusian authorities, stating that

---

[44] These renewed Russia's lease on Crimean naval facilities until 2042. However, Russia's annexation of Crimea ended the Kharkiv Pact.

the government had to use repression to ensure regime survival (Gazeta.ru, 2010). Surikov's lengthy tenure of thirteen years meant that he developed a lasting closeness with people in the Belarusian regime. Surikov was involved in writing policy that became law and was often taken from Russian legislation (Lavnekevich, 2012). In 2018, Surikov stated that he 'respected' Lukashenka for rolling back democracy after 1994 (EurAsia Daily, 2018).

Belarusian ambassador to Moldova Vasil Sakovich (1999–2009) often met parliamentarians to increase 'inter-parliamentary cooperation' (Nezavisimaya Moldova, 2005: 5). Ukrainian ambassador to Moldova Serhy Pyrozhkov (2007–14) was invited to the Moldovan Security Council to discuss the Euromaidan (Tristan, 2014). By inviting Pyrozhkov, the government got in-depth information, rather than relying on other sources. Ukrainian ambassador to Belarus Viktor Tykhonov stated that Ukraine should become like Belarus as the Belarusian regime survived protests and was stable (Unian.info, 2011). After the 2012 parliamentary elections, Belarusian ambassador to Ukraine Valyantsin Velicheka (2011–16) praised Yanukovych for free elections, even though there was significant electoral fraud (Ukrainskaya Pravda, 2012d). After 2014, Velicheka did not help the Poroshenko authorities locate Yanukovych allies who fled to Belarus (UDF.by, 2014).

Pressure that Russian ambassadors exert on Ukraine is also applied to Moldova, with the Kremlin pressuring the current pro-European Moldovan regime or giving support to pro-Kremlin groups. The Russian embassy in Moldova has a large staff, allowing the Russian authorities to infringe on Moldovan statehood and support the de facto Transnistrian government.[45] The Russian ambassador to Moldova Pavel Petrovsky (1999–2003) stated that it was important that Russia had a friendly Moldova and only Russia could solve the Transnistrian conflict. His successor, Yury Zubakov (2003–7), reminded Moldovan authorities that Russia was Moldova's main creditor, and that thousands of Moldovans were guest workers in Russia (Amambaeva, 2004: 16), implying that Moldova should remain close to Russia.

The Russian ambassador Valery Kuzmin (2007–12) was thanked by President Voronin for support during the 2009 protests (Gazeta.ru, 2009), pointing to Kuzmin offering advice on how the Russian authorities dealt with protests. Kuzmin continued supporting politicians who could

---

[45] Personal interview: MQ25710.

become pro-Russian candidates at elections, with one candidate being Dodon (Nezavisimaya Moldova, 2011: 4). Russian ambassador to Moldova Farit Mukhametshin (2012–19) continued to pressure Moldova. As Moldova negotiated the EU association agreement, Mukhametshin stated that further EU integration would lead to difficulties in trade with Russia, which would cause economic harm for Moldova (Logos-Press, 2014). Mukhametshin indicated that most Moldovans wanted Russian integration and the government should accept this (Logos-Press, 2015; Moldavskie Vedomosti, 2016b: 4) although he provided no evidence to support this argument. Mukhametshin argued that the EU association agreement would not make Moldova richer and that the EAEU was a better option (Demidetsky, 2017: 2), although he again provided no evidence for this conclusion.

The Kremlin uses its ambassadors in Moldova to maintain ties with the autonomous region of Gagauzia and the de facto state of Transnistria. By maintaining close ties with the Gagauz leadership, the Russian authorities keep successive Moldovan governments in line, as no Moldovan regime can afford a new Transnistria scenario (Moldavskie Vedomosti, 2016a: 9). Similarly, the Kremlin maintains close ties with the Transnistrian government to exert leverage over Moldovan governments. Although not ambassadors, Dmitry Kozak and Dmitry Rogozin were presidential representatives on developing trade and economic relations. Both focused on improving ties with Tansnistria rather than Moldova (Tul'ev, 2020). The Kremlin maintains inter-governmental cooperation between Russia and Transnistria. There is a Russian ambassador at large in Tiraspol. Russian influence in Gagauzia and Transnistria means Moldova can never fully integrate with the EU (Shimanovskaya, 2017: 10).

On 28 June 2017, the Russian, Belarusian, and Kazakh embassies arranged a conference in the Radisson Blu Leogrand Hotel in Chişinău attended by Dodon and other pro-Russian politicians (Materik.ru, 2017). In August 2017, Dodon and Mukhametshin discussed domestic issues and how to improve cooperation between pro-Russian politicians and the Russian authorities (Gazeta.ru, 2017). Ambassador networks are extensive, and ambassadors forge strong ties, working extensively with regime personnel and imparting knowledge. While Russian ambassadors have been the most effective at this, the other three cases show the importance of ambassadors in imparting knowledge to strengthen authoritarian-minded elites.

## 7.3 Conclusion

The previous chapter analysed the role of regional organisations in the post-Soviet space and their role in learning. Here we addressed the role of networks within the four case studies and how important these are for learning. The external and internal networks that pervade the four cases studied are extensive and crucial to understanding authoritarian learning. We investigated the networks of presidents, presidential administrations, security services, security councils, governments, foreign and internal ministries, and ambassadors, and highlighted that all are key networks aiding learning. Some of these personnel and institutions have a role in both external and internal opportunities for learning, particularly the security services, security councils, and interior ministries. By working closely together, having constant discussions, and in many cases engaging in training exercises, these networks offer extensive learning opportunities. Russian networks with the other three cases studied are particularly extensive and emphasise the role the Russian authorities play in learning. However, there is evidence pointing to how Belarusian and Ukrainian personnel have also been involved in offering learning opportunities. While this is less pronounced than Russian examples, it does highlight that authoritarian learning is less vertical than widely considered in current research.

Consequently, the role of networks is crucial to authoritarian learning in the four cases studied and to helping authoritarian-minded elites consolidate power and survive. As with their lack of membership in regional organisations, the limited networks of Ukrainian governments – and especially Moldovan regimes – may partially explain why authoritarian-minded elites in both countries have been less successful at consolidating power than in Belarus and Russia. As seen in this chapter, these various networks provide extensive opportunities for discussion, sharing of best practices, developing of effective techniques through training exercises, and learning. If authoritarian-minded elites do not have access to such networks, then it makes it harder to consolidate power and survive. Although there are many other factors explaining a lack of authoritarian consolidation in Moldova and Ukraine, access to networks may be a partial factor in the lack of regime longevity in both cases.

# 8 | *How External and Internal Informal Networks Shape Learning in Belarus, Moldova, Russia, and Ukraine*

Networks exist across the post-Soviet region both externally and internally.[1]

## 8.1 Introduction

A crucial aspect of authoritarian learning is the networks between elites that allow for information sharing and learning. As seen in the previous chapter, these networks are extensive. They are internal and external, helping elites learn from numerous sources. By being part of networks, elites can better develop appropriate survival practices. External networks help authoritarian-minded elites share experiences of what worked and failed and learn from others. Internal networks assess what has worked – or not – domestically, thereby allowing elites to draw lessons. Learning from domestic cases – particularly successful examples – is crucial. If something was successful before domestically, it is likely to be so again.

Having looked in the previous two chapters at regional structures and learning in an institutional setting, we turn to analysing external and internal networks in the four case studies. Krackhardt and Stern (1988: 123) see networks as those that are 'of friends, contacts, and accidental communications'. This means that networks do not need to be formal structures. Many networks do indeed follow formal structures. On the one hand, networks overlap with formal structures. On the other hand, these networks are separate from these formal structures and exist in individual relationships. It is to these networks that we turn in this chapter. By analysing Russian links with Moldova and Ukraine, we investigate how Russian elites use networks in both states to support authoritarian-minded elites and pass on information on

---

[1] Personal interview: ND30192.

how to consolidate control. While there are certainly close networks between Russian and Belarusian elites, we felt that to best represent external networks and learning the chapter's focus should be on Russia, Moldova, and Ukraine. As Ambrosio (2009) shows, the Russian authorities bolster the already established authoritarian Belarusian regime and while there is certainly learning from Russia to Belarus, Hall (2017b) has shown it is more of a two-way street. By contrast, the relationship between the Russian, Moldovan and Ukrainian authorities is more likely to be one of one teacher and two pupils. Consequently, to show the importance of informal networks for authoritarian learning we feel an analysis of Russia, Moldova, and Ukraine will better represent this area of learning. After investigating these informal external networks, we address internal informal networks. While formal networks are crucial for authoritarian learning so are the informal kind.

## 8.2  Russian Linkage in Moldova and Ukraine

To gain support for a major decision, Moldovan elites go to Moscow, as seen when former President Petru Lucinschi – and former leader of the Moldavian Soviet Socialist Republic – changed his holiday plans in 2000, detouring to Moscow – on route to Sochi – to get Kremlin approval for a referendum ending presidential term-limits (Chubchenko, 2000: 3; Tarasov, 2000: 4). However, the Kremlin had already backed Voronin and so refused to approve Lucinschi's power grab. Russian support for Gagauzia and especially Transnistria destabilises Moldova. The latter cannot join the EU – and less so NATO – without full control of its de jure territory,[2] thereby making Russia the only alternative for Moldovan regimes (Orenstein and Mizsei, 2014). Some Moldovan elites acquiesce in the status quo between Moldova and Transnsitria because they make money through smuggling. Plahotniuc was allegedly involved in many of these initiatives and had business interests in Transnistria (Kvitka, 2019). Plahotniuc and Victor Guşan – who owns the Sheriff business empire in Transnistria – laundered money from their shared companies through Transnistria and Moldova into EU banks (Rise.md, 2019). Consequently, Moldovan elites have often been largely content with the existing status

---

[2]  Personal interview: MQ25710.

quo. Transnistria's existence increases Kremlin leverage over Moldova and to a lesser extent Ukraine, as a solution cannot happen without the Kremlin, which remains satisfied with the existing status quo (Popşoi, 2016).

Like Transnistria, Gagauzia is another Moldovan region that has a tenuous relationship with the central government. Due to an agreement in 1994 – to stop Gagauzia going the same way as Transnistria – Gagauzia has significant autonomy. The Russian authorities retain close ties to the Gagauz elite. The Kremlin finances Gagauz politicians. This allows the Russian authorities to get the Gagauz elite to demand greater autonomy and independence depending on how acquiescent Moldovan governments are to Kremlin interests.[3] Most Gagauz watch Russian media and are susceptible to these messages, while consistently voting for pro-Russian and nationalist Gagauz politicians.

In a 2014 referendum – which the Moldovan authorities viewed as illegal – 98.4 per cent of the Gagauz populace wanted closer ties with Russia (Calus, 2014a). After the referendum, the Gagauz regional government travelled to Moscow to meet Putin and Medvedev to get approval for the referendum and Russian assistance to enforce it (Calus, 2014b). During the Ukrainian Euromaidan, some Gagauz politicians met Kremlin personnel in Odesa to discuss instigating protests in Gagauzia's capital, Comrat. It was hoped that the Moldovan authorities would attempt to crush it, thereby giving the Russian authorities the chance to intervene.[4] This scheme did not come to fruition, but it emphasises how some Kremlin factions considered using Gagauzia to destabilise Moldova and reverse engineer a Euromaidan. It was hoped that by replacing a pro-European government with a pro-Russian one it would results in a loss for the EU. Gagauz politicians support Russian initiatives, allowing the Kremlin to use these factions to either destabilise Moldovan regimes or increase Moldovan acquiescence.[5]

Some Moldovan politicians have a close affinity with Moscow. President Dodon was a prominent example,[6] although rhetoric was mitigated by inaction on actual integration (Calus, 2016a). Under Dodon, Moldova became an EAEU observer, with Dodon trying to stop further Moldovan integration with the EU (Falyakov, 2017;

---

[3] Personal interview: MQ25710.    [4] Personal interview: FD84603.
[5] Personal interview: KH32708.    [6] Personal interview: MQ25710.

Gordonua.com, 2017a). Voronin used to be an example of a pro-Russian leader, although after failing to sign the Kozak Memorandum, his relationship with the Kremlin visibly deteriorated.[7] However, the Kremlin still supported Voronin at the 2005 parliamentary and presidential elections, perceiving him as a better option to the pro-European opposition leaders.[8] As both are nominally communists, Voronin retained close personal links to Russian KPRF leader Gennady Zyuganov and thus close links to the Russian political elite.[9]

There are rumours that the Kremlin financially supports Moldovan politicians. But if they do exist, these financial dealings are well hidden.[10] In 2014, the Patria party was banned for links to Russian extremist groups (Popșoi, 2014). The leader of Patria, Renato Usatîi, has close business links with the Kremlin (Nuttall, 2017). Usatîi's meteoric rise in Moldovan politics to become mayor of Moldova's second city Bălți increased allegations of close Kremlin links (Ciurea, 2016; Gente, 2015). Plahotniuc had business interests in Russia and Ukraine and was unwilling to lose control over these assets and networks (Calus, 2016b). During his control of state structures until 2019, Plahotniuc drew a balance between the West and Russia. During his tenure of behind-the-scenes control, Plahotniuc owned the rights to broadcast Russian state television, pointing to the likelihood that he signed a deal with the Kremlin to obtain these rights.[11] However, relations visibly deteriorated, as the Kremlin considered Plahotniuc too independent, whereas Dodon was perceived as a more pliable candidate (Solov'ev, 2019). There are links between the Moldovan and Russian political elites that allow the Kremlin to maintain its influence and support pro-Kremlin politicians.

Laundromat is another example of Moldovan-Russian linkage. Laundromat was a money-laundering scheme where Company A loaned money to Company B, who had the loans guaranteed by other companies. Company B would then default on the loan from Company A and a judge would authenticate the debt. Company A would transfer the money it got from the debt into a bank account. From there the money was moved on to a bank in the EU – specifically in Riga – where it disappeared (Harding, 2017). The main protagonists

---

[7]  Personal interview: FT36819.     [8]  Personal interview: MQ25710.
[9]  Personal interview: FT36819.     [10]  Personal interviews: ST93601, PD59726.
[11]  Personal interviews: ST93601.

were based in Russia and Moldova. It was likely some money came from the Russian treasury via businessmen who had state contracts (Organized Crime and Corruption Reporting Project, 2017c). Russian-registered companies took money out and used Moldovan courts to force other Russian companies to pay the debt. The money was deposited in Moldindcombank. This caused liquidity flooding, which allowed the protagonists to remove $8 billion without notice. This and another $5 billion disappeared 'into accounts of ghost companies', and ended up in tax havens (Rise.md, 2017).

Three of the businessmen involved were Aleksey Kripivin, Georgy Gens, and Sergey Girdin, all of whom had links to the Kremlin (Anin, 2017). However, the main protagonist was Moldovan businessman and politician Veaceslav Platon. He, along with American-Moldovan Emmanuil Grinshpun, were previously implicated in defrauding Moldovan banks of $1 billion during the theft of the century banking scandal in 2015 (Radu, Preaşca, and Mako, 2016). The Filat government during Laundromat had questionable links to the Russian mafia (Kontsyu, 2010: 1). This made Laundromat easier to accomplish. Laundromat could only have been possible with political acquiescence (Jurnal.md, 2016f). It is inconceivable that Moldovan political elites were unaware of the fraud.[12] It is highly likely Plahotniuc, former president Nicolae Timofti, and president of the Constitutional Court Alexandru Tănase were involved (Jurnal.md, 2017a). The Moldovan investigation showed that most Russian banks involved in the scandal were directly or partly owned by Igor Putin, Putin's cousin (Organized Crime and Corruption Reporting Project, 2017b). The FSB was heavily linked, which is probably why the Kremlin hampered Moldovan investigations to return some of the money (Galyatkin et al., 2017: 2–5; Tamkin, 2017). As Laundromat highlights, contacts between Moldovan and Russian political elites are extensive, with the Kremlin supporting pro-Kremlin politicians. The Russian authorities support Gagauz and Transnistrian elites to limit Moldovan integration into Western structures. By reducing opportunities for Moldovan democratisation, these networks increase the potential for learning for both the Moldovan and Russian

---

[12] Personal interview: DW48620.

authorities, although it is likely that Moldovan regimes learn from the Kremlin more than the other way around.

Until recently many Ukrainian political elites, such as Firtash, Lovochkin, Khoroshkovsky, Boyko, and Medvedchuk, retained close links with the Kremlin[13] – and likely still do. Even today Medvechuk is seen as a 'Russian agent'.[14] Under Yanukovych, 'all eyes were on Russia'.[15] Everything the Yanukovych regime wanted to implement had to have originated in Russia. The conflict between Russia and Ukraine is helpful for explaining relations between some Ukrainian elites and Russia. Ukraine has not severed diplomatic ties with Russia even with the current conflict. This raises questions about close ties among both regimes (Evropeiskaya Pravda, 2018), although this is partially due to Ukrainian reliance on Russian gas. Even with the ongoing conflict, some Ukrainian elites are close to Moscow. Reducing these links has proved difficult, as often the people with the responsibility for terminating these links have them themselves.[16]

There are questions about oligarch and Donetsk native Rinat Akhmetov's role in organising militias against Kyiv and supporting the Russian invasion during the Donbas conflict (Wilson, 2014c: 130–4). Akhmetov has many business interests in Russia, partially explaining his support for the initial Donbas debacle (Toal, 2017: 255). While Akhmetov backtracked from supporting the Russian invasion, he allegedly spoke with Kremlin representatives about the composition of the initial leadership of the Donetsk People's Republic in 2014 (Apostrophe.ua, 2015; Meduza.io, 2016). As with Akhmetov, Oleksandr Yefremov – former governor of Luhansk – was accused of cooperating with the Kremlin, exemplified by calls for a referendum on Luhansk's status after visiting Moscow in 2014 (Ukrainskaya Pravda, 2014a). Like Akhmetov, Yefremov financed the rebels in the early days (LB.ua, 2015). Politician Andry Artemenko devised a peace plan apparently with Russian backing because the Kremlin believed Artemenko had kompromat on Poroshenko, which the Kremlin wanted (LB.ua, 2017d). Artemenko claimed he spoke with Kremlin personnel about the peace plan (Kravets and Romanenko, 2017). The Radical Party – of which Artemenko belonged – quickly disassociated itself from him (LB.ua, 2017c), but there were questions as to why

---

[13]  Personal interview: TD38463.    [14]  Personal interview: HU30571.
[15]  Personal interview: ZD49618.    [16]  Personal interview: TD38463.

Radical Party leader Lyashko was in Moscow in 2014 (Ukrainskaya Pravda, 2014e). Lovochkin, Boyko, and Medvedchuk were linked to the Artemenko peace plan as well (LB.ua, 2017d).

The political party Opposition Bloc was founded after Yanukovych fled and took up the mantle of the pro-Russian opposition (Olszański, 2014). However, during the 2019 presidential and parliamentary elections Medvedchuk and Akhmetov – likely with Kremlin support – promoted Vadim Rabinovich as a less obvious pro-Russian candidate. Opposition Bloc members were incentivised by Akhmetov to join Rabinovich's party (Kravets, 2018a, 2018b; Miselyuk, 2018). This attempt failed and Rabinovich's For Life! Party merged with Opposition Bloc to become Opposition Bloc – For Life! Most former Party of Regions members joined other parties such as Bloc Petro Poroshenko (Ukrayinska Pravda, 2016) meaning that many parties retained a pro-Russian caucus. After the 2019 parliamentary elections, the Opposition Bloc – For Life! party came second, so there is a strong pro-Russian voice in parliament (Talant, 2019). If a solution to the Donbas conflict is found – likely involving guaranteed parliamentary seats for the Donbas – pro-Russian factions in Ukrainian politics will be even stronger.

Medvedchuk prepared for the 2015 presidential elections – which never came due to the Euromaidan – by helping pro-Russian parties and candidates (Chevordov, 2012) and running conferences on Ukraine's civilizational choice. In 2013, Putin attended one of the conferences, highlighting which vector Medvedchuk hoped to push Ukraine on (LB.ua, 2013). Crimea's annexation has not worried Medvedchuk unduly and he still owns property there (TSN.ua, 2016a). Medvedchuk has been labelled the 'governor of the Kremlin in Kiev' and is the only Ukrainian politician Putin trusts (Kanygin, 2018; LB.ua, 2017d). The current crisis has stopped direct flights between Kyiv and Moscow, but Medvedchuk flew directly to Moscow on three occasions in 2016 alone (LB.ua, 2016). In 2018, it was found that Medvedchuk had flown twenty-one times to Russia with Opposition Bloc politician and ally Taras Kozak, pointing to negotiations with the Kremlin about the 2019 elections (Ukrainskaya Pravda, 2018). Medvedchuk is not the only person directly flying to Moscow. Other officials and law enforcement personnel have done so (LB.ua, 2017b).

There is conclusive evidence of links between Russian and Ukrainian politicians existing since 1991. These links show that at least part of the Ukrainian elite – even today – wants close ties with Russia. This allows the Kremlin to help allies in Ukraine obtain power. This in turn results in attempts at power consolidation.[17] Many Opposition Bloc leaders have business interests in Russia. Therefore, this party advocates for close Kremlin ties.[18] Medvedchuk is the clearest example of someone with close Kremlin links; Putin is even the godfather to his daughter. Medvedchuk's close personal ties to Putin have made him useful to previous Ukrainian presidents – such as Poroshenko – who used Medvedchuk as an interlocutor to the Kremlin,[19] a tactic Zelensky has continued. In late 2018, Medvedchuk held regular meetings with Ukrainian presidential administration representatives, pointing not only to Medvedchuk's growing importance in politics but to negotiations between Poroshenko and Medvedchuk to draw Ukraine closer to Russia (Ukrainskaya Pravda, 2018b). However, in May 2021 Medvedchuk was placed under house arrest for treason, having allegedly supplied Russia with coal from the Donbas and for maintaining close ties with the Kremlin – looking to find ways to bring Ukraine closer to Russia. For good measure, three television channels owned by Taras Kozak – but linked to Medvedchuk – were closed for their pro-Russian stance (Sukhov, 2022). In November 2021, there were claims that Akhmetov had begun to organise a coup. Zelensky announced a coup attempt at a press conference to Western journalists but offered no evidence to support the claim. Increasingly, it seems that Zelensky is at war with the oligarchs over control of the media (Olearchyk and Seddon, 2021) and highlighting the close links between Akhmetov and the Kremlin was an attempt by Zelensky to gain popular support for his moves towards media control. A further example of close ties between Russian and Ukrainian elites is when Poroshenko was elected president in 2014, and Putin was asked by journalists for his reaction. Putin responded that he knew all the people who had got elected, emphasising the close ties between Russian and Ukrainian elites.[20] After all, Poroshenko had been a founder of Party of Regions and was close to Kuchma, so was not someone to alarm the Kremlin.[21]

---

[17] Personal interview: MQ37492.     [18] Personal interview: TD38463.
[19] Personal interview: JH58291.     [20] Personal interview: BO39761.
[21] Personal interview: NJ08269.

Russia remains an attractive model to some Ukrainian elites as it is a consolidated authoritarian regime with little power turnover.[22] Many Ukrainian elites are aware that EU integration will bring too many costs. While they espouse pro-European integration rhetoric, they do not believe it, perceiving that integration with Russia – with no strings attached – is a better option. Bankova will not publicly make overtures to the Kremlin, but it happens in private.[23] President Poroshenko retained links to the Kremlin, for example with his relationship with businessman Kostyantin Hryhoryshin, who made his wealth in Russia and had close links to the Kremlin. Until 2017, Poroshenko's chocolate company Roshen had a factory in Russia and the company paid taxes to the Russian budget. While the Russian Roshen factory was officially closed in 2018, Poroshenko allegedly still owns a starch factory and grain company in Lipetsk. Without close Kremlin ties, Poroshenko – who was leading a country at war with Russia – would have been unable to retain control of these assets (Sukhov, 2018d; TSN.ua, 2018).

## 8.3 Internal Political Networks in Belarus, Moldova, Russia, and Ukraine?

Having investigated the informal networks between Russian, Moldovan, and Ukrainian elites and the importance of these for learning, we turn to analyse internal informal networks between political elites in each case. Understanding internal links between political elites clearly shows learning. Internal networks allow regime members to share information, learn, and develop best survival practices. In Moldova and Ukraine, interlinkage between elites in one regime and previous regimes allows information to be exchanged. Many incumbent elites were in power previously, but regularly change allegiance. This allows them to provide first-hand experiences of successes or failures from past governments. To better understand authoritarian learning nuances and role of internal networks in this, we analyse internal networks in the case studies here.

Although Lukashenka seemingly has a low tolerance for people who disappoint him[24] the inner circle has remained relatively homogenous.

---

[22] Personal interview: TD38463.    [23] Personal interview: JH58291.
[24] Personal interview: NF29463.

While the dominance of the Mahilou group – Lukashenka's original clan – has now diminished,[25] the current dominant faction consists of personnel who are willing to use violence to preserve the regime and have proven themselves, having violently dispersed protesters before.[26] In 2020, Lukashenka put his eldest son Viktar as head of the security services, keeping the coercive capacity with someone he can trust. There are questions as to whether Lukashenka is looking – in an indeterminate future time – to anoint his youngest son Mikalai as successor (Usov, 2020: 75). Lukashenka surrounded himself with family members and those who have everything to lose if the regime collapses, like those who know where the bodies of disappeared opposition leaders are.[27] One person close to Lukashenka is his tennis coach, Syarhei Tsyatseryn. Tsyatseryn acts as a sounding board, gives access to others, and even advises on policy (Vodchyts, 2014). Other close associates are Natallya Pyatkevich, who filters information to Lukashenka, and Viktar Sheyman, who has been around since the beginning.[28] Pyatkevich and Sheyman have leeway to implement policies and run state structures without too much interference by Lukashenka. This shows a level of trust, as Lukashenka is reticent about anyone having independence.[29] It is this small faction of close allies that are in regular contact with Lukashenka and whom he trusts. Most decisions about idea sharing and learning are made in this small faction.

While Lukashenka is influenced by his inner circle, the mystique must be that Lukashenka cannot be influenced and that he makes decisions based on his knowledge of what Belarusians want.[30] Implementation orders are verbalised. This allows Lukashenka the opportunity to deny knowledge of decisions if unpopular or enforced incorrectly, thereby placing the blame on the implementer.[31] Although the presidential administration implements policies across the state, the power *vertikal* is very hierarchical from Lukashenka downwards. Therefore, Lukashenka is involved in most decisions.[32] He allegedly has a folder of all top regime personnel, which he can then use as kompromat to control them and make sure they implement his policies (Belsat, 2018).

[25] Personal interview: NJ08269.     [26] Personal interview: VT48602.
[27] Personal interview: HW29578.     [28] Personal interview: YR52870.
[29] Personal interviews: NF29463, IR39203.     [30] Personal interview: TI93618.
[31] Personal interview: TK02846.     [32] Personal interview: TK02846.

The Informational Analytical Centre (IAC) of the presidential administration effectively tracks potential issues that could result in protests. It has developed 'excellent polling groups to get an idea of what is happening in society',[33] thus allowing the regime to keep track of popular feelings. Consequently, the authorities learn and adapt policies to reduce protests occurring (Inanets, 2017). Through the IAC, the regime has a relatively effective system of gauging public opinion, allowing for learning and adaptation. Due to Belarus's geographical size and extensive power *vertikal*, policies to alleviate the potential for protest are quickly passed throughout the country.[34]

Another faction Lukashenka is close to are *siloviki* structures, with Lukashenka even getting economic policy from the KDB and the interior ministry.[35] Knowing this, the KDB routinely plays on Lukashenka's fears that Western states want to destabilise Belarus and implement regime change.[36] It is why the KDB – like other ministries – engages in intra-institutional factionalism to remain the dominant state structure. However, Lukashenka is the final arbitrator and plays factions against one another. For regime factions to gain prominence, they often create scenarios that play on Lukashenka's fears of being deposed.[37] Therefore, the regime is constantly adapting to scenarios that may not exist, but through the adaptation it is constantly learning and developing best survival practices.[38]

Like in Belarus, there is an inner circle in the Kremlin, with Arkady and Boris Rotenberg, Igor Sechin, Sergey Chemezov, Yury Kovalchuk, and Gennady Timchenko (Galeotti, 2018a: 11) as the principal figures there. For the inner circle, everything is acceptable, so long as loyalty to Putin is maintained.[39] Although some inner-circlers – like Vladimir Yakunin – were removed because they could no longer maintain Kremlin interests above their own,[40] this clique has largely remained together. While more *siloviki* personnel have recently been appointed, these new cadres share similar backgrounds to the inner circle (Litvinova, 2016). Personnel in the presidential administration increasingly only pass information to this faction that they know fits with this group's world view.[41] This affects learning and adaptability as the

---

[33] Personal interviews: KR48280, IP28037.  [34] Personal interview: TK02846.
[35] Personal interviews: CM29876, KW37410.
[36] Personal interview: HA20938.  [37] Personal interview: KW37410.
[38] Personal interview: IR39203.  [39] Personal interview: TM26801.
[40] Personal interview: ND30192.  [41] Personal interview: RW39802.

inner-circlers are increasingly of the same world view and are unable to adapt, thereby making them less likely to learn.[42] However, they are constantly devising ways to adapt (Stanovaya, 2020) although it is questionable how effective this adaptation and learning has been and can be when only one view is considered.[43]

If this is the case, then the Russian authorities have a possible learning problem. There are several ever-changing factions in the regime and all are involved in learning and implementing what they think Putin wants. The authorities use the *otmashka* system, where Putin agrees to an idea without detailing how he wants the decision to be implemented (Pavlovsky, 2016). This provides Putin with deniability should the decision be poorly implemented, and involves factions applying what they think Putin wants to a policy or issue. This leads to poor implementation and problems – which points to inefficient learning at times.[44] This is made worse because Putin is less and less interested in domestic affairs and is only involved in 20 per cent of decisions,[45] becoming isolated and thus reliant on a worldview and closeness to a small group who share the same ideas (Stanovaya, 2020). In particular, the *siloviki* play on Putin's fears that Western states are conspiring against Russia and the mantra 'whoever comes up with the scariest scare gets the money'[46] shapes Kremlin policies. This affects the Kremlin's ability to learn and adapt as the authorities become increasingly linked to *siloviki* structures (Eggert, 2018: 15). This results in an echo chamber. Increasingly this is also the case for Lukashenka. The Belarusian regime closed the IAC sometime around 2015 to try to increase the Internet presence of the authorities and win hearts and minds. But without the IAC – which were the eyes of the regime – and the ability to know what could cause protests, the authorities were blinded. At the same time, Lukashenka increasingly only wanted positive news that followed his existing worldview. It is possible that both regimes are experiencing lethargy that is affecting their learning capacity, and this spells danger for both Lukashenka and Putin.

The Kremlin relies on political consultants[47] and polls to gauge Russian public opinion. The authorities use weekly polls by the

---

[42] Personal interview: QI40827.
[43] Personal interviews: QI40827, ND30192, AM07019.
[44] Personal interviews: ND30192, QI40827, AM07019.
[45] Personal interview: TM26801.    [46] Personal interview: AM07019.
[47] Personal interview: AH91023.

Russian Public Opinion Research Centre (VTsIOM) and the Public Opinion Foundation to assess what problems need to be rectified and then uses state television to alleviate these to show that the authorities take public opinion into account, even if it is a façade (Rogov and Ananyev, 2018: 204–5). Nevertheless, the system does not have free-flowing information, so 'feedback is very twisted. Those in the system have a very specific understanding of what is really going on.'[48] While Kremlin personnel have mostly been in power for over two decades – and know the Russian mindset[49] – increasingly Putin reads what a select few in the presidential administration put in front of him, so they control the information he receives.[50] This affects how the Kremlin learns, and actions are increasingly reactive rather than proactive.[51]

Moldovan and Ukrainian regimes come and go, but while the regimes themselves often collapse, regime personnel are constant. While a person's position in government changes – along with power held and resource access – there is a consistent presence of the same people in Moldovan and Ukrainian governments.[52] Internal elite networks have existed in Moldova and Ukraine since independence. These networks support dialogue, the sharing of best practices, and learning. Although the analogy of Moldova as a 'village'[53] is unfair, it refers to the fact that all elites have known each other for decades. Therefore internal networks are likely crucial in Moldova and Ukraine for learning.

While Moldovan elites know one another – often growing-up together and going to the same schools – there are clans competing to control state resources.[54] But clans are fissiparous – loose structures that constantly change as members compete with one another.[55] However, as individuals are in constant negotiation to get the best deal, this results in dialogue and information sharing, which aids learning. The PCRM under Voronin constructed a system where a small political elite controlled most financial resources. Plahotniuc helped create this system using *reiderstvo* tactics against other businesses to increase Voronin's business portfolio by threatening businessmen who refused to give Voronin their companies.[56] Plahotniuc was one of five 'hunters' who quite literally went hunting with Voronin and

---

[48] Personal interview: AM07019.   [49] Personal interview: AM07019.
[50] Personal interview: RW39802.   [51] Personal interview: QI40827, SS20641.
[52] Personal interviews: WE39704, DP24850.
[53] Personal interviews: WE39704.   [54] Personal interview: KH32708.
[55] Personal interview: WE39704.   [56] Personal interview: WE39704.

his son Oleg and used this time to discuss policies and ideas for keeping power. Plahotniuc was the main funder of the PCRM and was known as Voronin's 'wallet' (Cojocaru, 2019). Voronin kept control because he dominated the PCRM and used his control of the party and placement of allies in key party positions to ensure control of state institutions (Nicolae, 2019). Plahotniuc saw how Voronin put people he could manipulate into powerful positions and followed this part of the Voronin playbook, controlling power from behind the scenes after 2014.[57] He learnt much of what he implemented after 2014 from the 1990s and Voronin. Another key actor – until 2021 – was President Igor Dodon – who owed his political career to Voronin. Voronin picked Dodon first as minister of economy and then as a deputy prime minister from 2006 to 2009 (Nicolae, 2019).

As minister of economy, Dodon was in direct contact with Plahotniuc. Both agreed to give Plahotniuc-owned supermarkets exclusive rights to import products such as fish, allowing Pahotniuc and Dodon to make money by raising the import price.[58] Apart from fish, Plahotniuc bought properties well below market value and Dodon, who had the power to stop such purchases, turned a blind eye, which suggests they both profited from the sales.[59] It was during the PCRM period that Plahotniuc and Dodon formed an alliance, which would from 2014 to 2019 increasingly become a cartel.[60]

One tactic Plahotniuc used to gain control of parliament was to recreate the PCRM's use of financial incentives to get opposition parliamentarians to either join the PDM or vote for PDM legislation.[61] Plahotniuc split the PCRM by paying fourteen PCRM delegates a six-figure bribe each to set up the party 'For Moldova' to support the PDM (Jurnal.md, 2015a). After the arrest and imprisonment of Filat, Plahotniuc – through his munificence – controlled the judiciary, parliament, the prosecutor general's office, the economic and interior ministries, and most judges in the constitutional court (Alaiba, 2011; Gherasimov, 2017; Jurnal.md, 2016c, 2016d; Socor, 2016), although this changed after he fled in 2019. Like Lukashenka, Putin, and most likely Voronin, Plahotniuc relied on people he could manipulate to keep power (Alaiba, 2016).

---

[57] Personal interview: KH32708.     [58] Personal interview: KH32708.
[59] Personal Interview: DW48620.     [60] Personal Interview: DW48620.
[61] Personal interviews: MQ25710, CW25719, ST93601.

However, Plahotniuc's power consolidation and use of kompromat alienated other actors. This resulted in the PSRM and ACUM forming a coalition of convenience to oust Plahotniuc when given the chance at the 2019 parliamentary elections. Plahotniuc used kompromat, such as posting sex tapes of opposition leaders to blackmail these people into acquiescence (Nemtsova, 2017, 2019). However, Plahotniuc overstepped and used kompromat against Dodon to keep him in line during the parliamentary election campaign (Gamova, 2019; Kommersant, 2019). This gave Dodon little alternative but to unite with ACUM and oust Plahotniuc. Like Yanukovych at the Euromaidan, Plahotniuc relied on thuggish practices, epitomised by the suspicious suicide of Yury Lukash. Lukash was a member of the Plahotniuc family – quite literally, he was married to Plahotniuc's sister – and knew where all the money Plahotniuc had stashed away was. His death protected these ill-gotten gains (Efremov, 2019). Like the Kremlin and Yanukovych, Plahotniuc may not have been successful in his learning. But, in a country as divided as Moldova, where governments are short-lived, it is unlikely any dominant player could keep power for any length of time. Plahotniuc learnt lessons from Voronin and used similar practices while continuously talking to Dodon. All this points to learning.

After Plahotniuc fled in 2019, Dodon began to exert more control. Without the financial muscle of Plahotniuc, Dodon was able to use state resources to splinter the PDM, splitting the PDM into a rump anti-PSRM party and those who were happy to vote for any government. Dodon wrested control of some Plahotniuc-owned business and gave them to allies (Point.md, 2020). However, Dodon used similar practices to Plahotniuc (NewsMaker, 2020) and was unable to consolidate power quickly enough, losing the 2020 presidential election to Maia Sandu of the Party of Action and Solidarity. Dodon appeared to make many of the same mistakes as Plahotniuc, which highlights a lack of learning, although he had much fewer resources to help consolidate power than Plahotniuc did.

Due to the vagaries of the Moldovan political system, it seems that once a person is in power, they try to take control as quickly possible, knowing that it is short-lived. However, this makes the situation worse, as other factions, angry at their loss of power, begin to cooperate with one another and undermine the dominant faction. This leads the incumbent to increase repression until they cannot repress an ever-larger opposition, resulting in a loss of power and the re-calibration of the system. Although it is still early days, Maia Sandu appears for now at least to be bucking this trend of power consolidation. This of course may change in the build-up to presidential and parliamentary elections in 2024 and 2025 respectively. Another possibility is if the electoral Bloc of Communists and Socialists can increase its support among the electorate. Currently it has the support of over a quarter of the population. If this increases, then it is possible the Party of Action and Solidarity may begin to consolidate power. For now though, this has not happened.

Like Moldova, Ukraine has seen several regimes since independence, with six presidents in thirty-one years. This is five more than Belarus and three more than Russia, but two below the nine presidents of Moldova if acting presidents are included. Unlike Moldova, there are more competing clans in Ukraine and more oligarchs who invest significantly in parties to ensure their interests are represented in parliament. As mentioned, Ukrainian political elites know one another. Regimes may change but the political elite remains the same. While political elites may not have the same amount of power or resource access depending on the regime, they remain part of the elite and know one another well.[62] This creates internal networks, which facilitates the sharing of best practices and learning. One protest demand during the Euromaidan was the end to the oligarchic-dominated political system. However, this system reasserted itself almost immediately when Petro Poroshenko – who had been close to various presidents and was an oligarch himself – was elected president in 2014 (Leshchenko, 2014a). The re-assertion of the oligarchic system after the Euromaidan led to the stifling of proposed reforms which would have allowed Ukraine to access EU and International Monetary Fund loans.

One of the lessons that Yanukovych took from the end of the Kuchma presidency in 2004 was that there had been too much factionalism, with competing groups only looking out for their own – ever-changing – interests (Hall, 2017a). Yanukovych created a two-ring system of key allies with the outer ring involving cronies – like Akhmetov and other oligarchs – and an inner ring known as the 'family'. Blood ties were less important for 'family' membership, although Yanukovych's sons – Oleksandr and Viktor – were prominent (Motyl, 2012). Along with

---

[62]    Personal interview: DP24850.

Yanukovych's sons this inner network included Oleksandr Klimenko, Serhy Arbuzov, Viktor Zakharchenko, Eduard Stavitsky, and Serhy Kurchenko. 'Family' members were close allies not of Viktor Yanukovych senior, but of Oleksandr Yanukovych (Konończuk, 2016; Korrespondent.net, 2013), who used control of state institutions to run the country behind the seat of the president.[63]

However, there was one fundamental problem with creating a single clan – it kept other elite groups out of accessing resources, which caused resentment. Another major problem was that Yanukovych was greedy and focused on reducing the power of others to consolidate his own. Due to Yanukovych's greed the 'family' asset-stripped $8 billion from the economy between 2010 and 2013 (Wilson, 2014b). This put it in competition with other oligarchic factions. Due to its financial and political power, the 'family' took control of other businesses and encroached on other clan interests. This alienated these groups. With nothing to lose if Yanukovych lost power, these factions openly supported the Euromaidan (Neef, 2014). In part, this explains the staccato repression[64] Bankova was forced to use during the protests (Wilson, 2014c: 76–7). The increasingly deep regime divisions, and lack of financial support from other oligarchic clans meant that Bankova simply did not have the capacity to fully repress protesters. Coupled with a lack of popular support, Bankova did not have the finances to maintain regime support (Coalson, 2013; Wilson, 2014c: 84–5).

Poroshenko employed personnel from the Kuchma and Yanukovych periods,[65] which gave him the opportunity to learn from their experiences in how Kuchma and Yanukovych had operated. Although Poroshenko was a member of each regime, he had never been prominent in either and would not have been party to most decisions. By employing old Kuchma and Yanukovych cadres Poroshenko could learn from past successes and failures. By the end of 2016, a counter-revolution was begun with anti-corruption initiatives curtailed and most reformers removed. This counter-revolution emphasised that Poroshenko was part of the old system, rather than anything new (De Borja Lasheras, 2016: 56–7; Eristavi, 2017; Iwański, 2017: 73).

---

[63] Personal interview: GL31074.
[64] This is repression that is not continuous, but the regime oscillates between hard and softer repression.
[65] Personal interview: LG52071.

Poroshenko had a narrow circle of confidantes as president (Koshkina, 2017b), and a larger group of people who had been a part of his Vinnytsia powerbase (Vishnev'skyy and Pivnev, 2014). Such people became key members of the Poroshenko 'family' and personnel from the Poroshenko 'family' gained control of state institutions (Politeka.net, 2016) to maintain Poroshenko's power and use their state offices to go after the opposition leaders (Zerkalo Nedeli, 2019), becoming a 'tool of the President's political vendettas' (Kyiv Post, 2018). While Poroshenko did attack political rivals and created a 'family' like Yanukovych, there were some differences. Although Poroshenko did try to take control he never went quite as far as Yanukovych, and did not try to usurp resource access for other groups. In short, Poroshenko was not as greedy as Yanukovych.

During his presidency, Poroshenko attempted to consolidate and entrust power to a small number of allies, which was a copying of similar methods by previous presidents, like Kuchma and Yanukovych.[66] Like Kuchma, Poroshenko tried to become a godfather for competing clans and balance between them. However, Poroshenko was less successful than Kuchma because oligarchs like Akhmetov and Kolomoisky did not see him as a godfather; Poroshenko was not the richest oligarch and did not provide the same resource access as Kuchma had done. While Poroshenko did try to balance resource access for all clans – far better than Yanukovych had managed – his 'family' did encroach on the terri-tories of Akhmetov and Kolomoisky,[67] thereby leading them to support other politicians – or in Kolomoisky's case, bring Zelensky into politics. This is a similar scenario to Yanukovych's failed power consolidation and explains why Poroshenko could not get re-elected in 2019. It is an example of failed learning, as Poroshenko did not learn from Yanukovych's many failures in 2014. Like Kuchma and Yanukovych, Poroshenko created his own clan, giving them resource access and control over institutions. Unlike Yanukovych, who removed people outside his inner-circle from power, Poroshenko took time and followed similar methods to Kuchma, reducing the power of other factions one by one.[68]

There are links between Poroshenko- and Yanukovych-era person-nel, who not only re-appeared under Poroshenko but were not pros-ecuted. One example was former Yanukovych aide Olexy Takhtay,

---

[66] Personal interview: BK07421.     [67] Personal interview: DP24850.
[68] Personal interview: MQ37492.

who became an interior ministry secretary under Poroshenko (Vygovsky, 2017: 3). Investment Capital Ukraine is owned by Poroshenko confidante Makar Pasenyuk. It helped Yanukovych launder $1.5 billion in 2014, even after he fled Ukraine (Kalenyuk et al. 2018). The money went into offshore companies owned by Serhy Kurchenko, Yanukovych's 'wallet' (Sukhov, 2018c). While Kurchenko and his company Gas-Alliance were sanctioned by America, both remained off the Ukrainian sanctions list during the Poroshenko presidency, pointing to a close association (Sorokin, 2018).

Yanukovych allies reached an agreement not to work against Poroshenko during his presidency in return for being able to keep their businesses (Sukhov, 2017a). With the re-employment of Yanukovych-era cadres and failure to prosecute Yanukovych allies, links remained strong (Kovensky, 2018; Kyiv Post, 2018; Sukhov, 2017c; Vygovsky, 2017: 3). Since the early 1990s, there has been an agreement between oligarchs that those in power can take others' assets but cannot jail one another. While this agreement was broken by Yanukovych – who jailed Tymoshenko – Poroshenko returned to this gentleman's agreement by not going after former Yanukovych elites. This would have broken the agreement and jeopardised his position.[69] Many Yanukovych-era personnel simply moved to positions under Poroshenko (Sukhov, 2018a, 2018d). This allowed for dialogue to occur, information to be shared, and learning.

However, Poroshenko failed to reform Ukraine and took control of state resources. This created a cycle where public opinion – and the support of other clans – were low when it came to his attempt at re-election in 2019. If a new candidate was to appear who was popular and had not been in politics, then Poroshenko was likely to face a struggle to get re-elected. Enter Zelensky – who had been a television comedian and TV president of Ukraine – who joined the presidential campaign late but won with 75 per cent of the vote. At the beginning of his presidency, Zelensky, some of his advisers, and his party Servant of the People found it hard to work within the reality of Ukrainian politics. This resulted in the authorities flailing to keep control, moving between liberalisation and coercion (Motyl, 2020). Servant of the People had only existed since 2019 and brought people

[69] Personal interview: MQ37492.

from very different backgrounds together. This resulted in competition within the party, as party representatives followed the patron interests. This has led some party factions implementing policy and passing legislation without presidential control and benefitting external elites like Kolomoisky (Sorokin, 2020a). The business links between Zelensky and Kolomoisky are highly entangled. While Zelensky has stated repeatedly that Kolomoisky will not receive preferential treatment, there are questions as to whether this can happen (Nahalyo, 2019) and Kolomoisky's informal control of the lucrative energy distribution company Centrenerho has been increased (Wilson, 2021b). The previous head of the presidential administration, Andry Bohdan (2019–20), was Kolomoisky's lawyer, and the new head of the presidential administration, Andry Yermak (2020–), has close ties to Kolomoisky (Sukhov, 2020a), although the links are less clear than those of Bohdan with Kolomoisky. There is growing competition among oligarchs to gain influence over Zelensky, with Akhmetov making concerted efforts on this front (Olearchyk, 2020).

Like all previous Ukrainian presidents, Zelensky has created an inner circle of people primarily from his television days who now control key state positions (Clark, 2020). Zelensky's childhood friend Ivan Bankov became first deputy head of the SBU and was put in charge of the SBU's efforts to target corruption (LB.ua, 2019), even though had no intelligence experience. This led to questions that was given the position to control the SBU's corruption investigation into Zelensky. Within days of becoming president, Zelensky appointed thirty allies to state offices and another twenty were elected to parliament on the Servant of the People party list. Secret meetings with oligarchs – part of all previous regimes – have continued and the oligarchs are increasingly influencing the government. Ending the network of friends and oligarchic influence which dogged previous governments were campaign promises but these were quickly ignored when Zelensky became president (Sorokin, 2020c).

Judicial and constitutional reforms have at the very least stalled, and court rulings in May 2020 on PrivatBank favoured Kolomoisky allies (Kalymon, 2020). Informal control of the constitutional court has been exerted, with attempts to take formal control by removing the chief judge, Oleksandr Tupytsky. While Tuytsky managed to keep his position – when his attempted removal became too public – his wage was reduced and Zelensky ally Viktor Kryvenko became head of the constitutional court. This has given the presidency some informal control of the court (Wilson, 2021b).

Zelensky brought in many Yanukovych-era personnel (Sukhov, 2019), pointing to learning from the Yanukovych era. Bringing back Yanukovych-era personnel broke another election promise that the political system would face lustration. However, this promise was broken on day one when Andry Bohdan – who had close ties to Yanukovych as head of the presidential administration (Sorokin, 2020c) – was appointed. Zelensky is copying some Poroshenko traits, talking a lot about reform and passing legislation tackling vested interests but maintaining control of institutions that consolidate power, like the prosecutor general's office (Ryaboshapka, 2020). The Zelensky presidency is now three years old and while there have been some reforms there have also been attempts at power consolidation. It is difficult to tackle the myriad vested interests in Ukraine and cope with a war.

Increasingly Zelensky has placed the 'top managers of Ukrainian oligarchs' in positions of power, resulting in the system being much like that of previous governments (Lutsenko, 2020). With a parliamentary majority, Zelensky has much leeway to use state institutions to increase his own power. There are pointers towards populism, which gives Zelensky popular support (Hosa and Wilson, 2019). This gives him leeway in consolidating power as it can be played as a democratic action. This power consolidation is starting to become apparent. There have been claims that Akhmetov was instigating a coup, allowing Zelensky to weaken a key oligarch and financial backer of opposition groups (Olearchyk and Seddon, 2021). Similarly, one opposition leader – Medvedchuk – is under house arrest for apparent treason (Sukhov, 2022), an allegation that has also resulted in Poroshenko being taken to court and possibly facing arrest soon (Kramer, 2022). By bringing Akhmetov, Medvedchuk, and Poroshenko into line, Zelensky has reduced the opposition even more and brought alternative media under control. The use of unlawful powers has seen non-Zelensky media put under threat and a signal has been sent that the regime wants only positive stories about the president (Sukhov, 2021). Zelensky prefers to govern through informal networks and signals and has brought in Yanukovych-era elites to use their experience in exerting control over the system (Wilson, 2021b). Zelensky has created an inner circle, maintained an oligarchic system, kept Yanukovych-era personnel, and learnt from Poroshenko, all of which points to dialogue, the sharing of best practices, and learning.

## 8.4 Conclusion

The informal networks existing between the four case studies are extensive in their nature. There are networks between Belarus and the three other cases studied, but we felt that the best representation of these informal external networks was between Russia, Moldova, and Ukraine. By analysing these links, we investigate Russian networks in Moldova and Ukraine to support authoritarian-minded elites and pass on information on how to consolidate control. While there are close networks between Russian and Belarusian elites and there is certainly learning from Russia to Belarus, it is a two-way street. By contrast, the relationship between the Russia, Moldovan, and Ukrainian authorities is one of a teacher and two pupils. Therefore, to show the importance of informal networks for authoritarian learning, we analysed these countries. It was shown that there are many learning opportunities between these three case studies.

Having analysed links between Moldovan, Russian, and Ukrainian elites, we turned to investigate informal internal networks in the four case studied. It was shown that many of the elites across Belarus, Moldova, Russia, and Ukraine have been in various regimes or in different positions of power. This provides them with opportunities to learn from previous failures and successes and impart this knowledge. Moldova and Ukraine have a history of regime change – where the government changes but the elite merely move from one administration to another, bringing their knowledge to bear for the current government. As the authorities in Belarus and Russia have been in power for at least twenty-two years, there exist inner circles in which learning happens. However as shown here, both regimes appear to be suffering problems with a growing discord between the information the top leadership receives and their capacity to learn. It is too early to state that both regimes will fail, but this friction will affect learning capabilities. This will make it harder for the regimes to develop best survival practices. After all, to hold on to power, the authorities have to be lucky every time, the protesters – or other crisis – has to be lucky just once.

# 9 | *Conclusion*

Autocrats learn and adjust.[1]

## 9.1 Introduction

Learning has become an issue worthy of study in understanding authoritarian regimes and how they collaborate, engage in dialogue, and develop appropriate survival methods. Through learning – involving diffusion, emulation, linkage, lesson-drawing, policy transfer, and extensive networks – authoritarian regimes protect themselves from democratisation pressures and develop suitable power consolidation tactics. As the quote by Kagan (2008) that began this chapter emphasises, authoritarian regimes learn from events and adapt to these to enhance survival. Understanding how authoritarian regimes defend themselves and engage in learning helps Western states and organisations develop new and better tactics to counteract authoritarian persistence and consolidation, and democratic backsliding.

There are several factors making this monograph a significant contribution to existing literature on authoritarianism and authoritarian learning. As the number of authoritarian regimes continues to increase globally, understanding their survival – which principally occurs through learning – will better explain the nuances of authoritarian persistence. By analysing four post-Soviet case studies we offer valuable information on regime inter-connectedness, how lesson-drawing occurs, how engaged these regimes are with one another, and in which institutions and state structures learning occurs. This is invaluable for better understanding authoritarian learning. In this chapter, we address the findings of the book, before raising areas for future research and finally offer policy

---

[1]  Kagan, 2008.

recommendations for states and organisations engaged in democratisation to use to counteract authoritarian learning.

## 9.2 Research Findings

The field of authoritarian learning has been growing, with some
decisive analysis already. However, there remains a lot to be done
and much of what has been classified as authoritarian learning only
briefly touches on the topic or does not address authoritarian learning
at all. For instance, two literatures linked to authoritarian learning
were authoritarian promotion and authoritarian gravity centres, but
both were often vague in analysis. Until now, the field of authoritarian
learning has remained centred on analysis of inter-state relations,
without analysis of internal aspects of authoritarian learning. Much
existing authoritarian learning literature did not provide much in-
depth analysis of authoritarian learning, failing to address how, why,
and when authoritarian regimes learn and what it is they learn and
where they learn from.

   Rather authoritarian learning literature was left underdeveloped, with
the literature stating that because authoritarian states B, C, and
D followed something like state A in a short time-period, learning must
have occurred. While this is perhaps an over-exaggeration, there has been
a shortage of comprehensive studies on authoritarian learning. We have
attempted to increase understanding of authoritarian learning significantly by analysing Belarus, Moldova, Russia, and Ukraine to show
how authoritarian-minded elites learn, what they learn, how they learn,
and to an extent when they learn. The existing literature has suffered
because information does not percolate out of authoritarian regimes as
quickly as in democracies, thereby making gathering evidence difficult.
This affects the argument, so inferences that X causes Y can only be
drawn. However, there is sufficient evidence provided here that there is
authoritarian learning.

### 9.2.1 Authoritarian Learning as an Under-Theorised Topic

Until now, authoritarian learning had been an under-theorised topic
with only a few attempts to conceptualise and explain it. Existing
literature has stuck with the mantra that because authoritarian

states B, C, and D do something like authoritarian state A in a short space of time, learning must have occurred. However, there has been little attempt to conceptualise and theorise authoritarian learning. However, we have attempted to address this issue, expanding the understanding of authoritarian learning. We conceptualise authoritarian learning as a combination of experiential and social learning theories. Although it is unlikely that they are aware of it, authoritarian-minded elites use experiential learning when developing best survival practices, with elites discussing with one another, relying on past experiences, and using observation to draw appropriate conclusions about developing best survival practices. Similarly, social learning is crucial to authoritarian learning, with authoritarian-minded elites observing others, and incorporating examples of success and failure to develop appropriate consolidation methods.

Similarly, the literature on learning was a terminological mess and there had been little attempt to place authoritarian learning within this literature. Existing literature had largely focused on the role diffusion plays in authoritarian learning. However, we felt this did not give the full picture. Sorting through the different learning types allowed for a clear typology of learning to be developed when explaining authoritarian learning. As shown here, it encompasses a combination of policy transfer, diffusion, linkage and leverage, and lesson-drawing. Autocracie have a wide palette and will use different learning aspects when faced with a problem. Authoritarian-minded elites constantly learn and adapt to stay in power and these regimes regularly collaborate with one another to develop a palette of best practices to remain in power. They use all analysed learning types at various points to achieve their survival.

### 9.2.2  *Authoritarian Learning Is Horizontal*

Authoritarian learning is less hierarchical than widely considered in the existing literature. It has been shown that Belarus was a testing ground for the Kremlin to learn from to counter democratisation pressures and stop a Colour Revolution in Moscow. However, existing literature has concentrated on the notion that Russia dominates the post-Soviet region and dispenses diktats that other post-Soviet regimes merely follow. This notion of Russian dominance has resulted in contentions about authoritarian promotion and authoritarian gravity centres. For the literature on authoritarian promotion, the Kremlin promotes authoritarianism into other post-Soviet states. Even if this is true – and this is by no means certain – there does not seem to be much accounting for the Kremlin's seeming lack of interest in promotion, and little to explain how Russia promotes authoritarianism to established authoritarian regimes with a longer permanence than Putin in the Kremlin. Similarly, for the literature on authoritarian gravity centres, some authoritarian regimes act as magnets for other authoritarian regimes to associate with and learn from.

We do not refute the importance of Russia in the post-Soviet space. After all, it is the hegemon, and so other states will naturally look to Russia as a guide and will possibly gravitate towards Russia due to its much larger economy and capacity to bolster smaller authoritarian regimes from external democratisation pressures. However, as shown here, Russia does not dominate learning and the development of best survival practices. Of course, once the Russian authorities instigate a policy, other post-Soviet regimes follow. The NGO law on foreign agents is a prime example of this, although it may not be because the policy originated in Russia but because it was the best legislation to increase survival chances. We have shown plenty of examples in this book that the other three cases studied bring much to the table. While their methods may not be implemented, they are likely listened to – after all, authoritarian-minded elites are concerned with survival and so are unlikely to reject any available practices. Relying on one source of information is dangerous and what may work in Moscow may not necessarily be effective in Chişinău, Kyiv, and Minsk. Therefore, authoritarian learning is more vertical than has previously considered.

## 9.2.3 *Authoritarian Learning Is Networked*

Both external and internal networks of authoritarian learning are extensive, with both network types offering opportunities for dialogue, the sharing of best practices, and learning. Existing literature on authoritarian learning has not delved deeply into the different networks that exist, and which institutions and personnel are engaged in learning. Rather, current literature often focuses on the presidential level and little else. But as shown in this book, much learning occurs in *siloviki* structures like the presidential administration, the security service, interior ministry, and security council. Although evidence is lacking – as information is simply unavailable – it is likely that regular meetings occur between junior personnel in each institution. This allows for learning to occur at many state levels.

Existing literature has focused on the external level when addressing authoritarian learning, and indeed external networks are crucial to it. However, this only offers about a quarter of the picture for understanding authoritarian learning. We have shown here that formal external networks are extensive and encompass a range of institutions from the presidency to ambassadors and from the security councils to prime ministers. The analysis points to the sharing of best practices at a lower level than the ministerial and presidential levels. Similarly, we showed that internal formal networks are an integral aspect of authoritarian learning. Institutions involved in learning from internal examples are fewer than those involved in learning from external sources. But this does not detract from the importance of internal networks for authoritarian learning. Interior ministries, presidential administrations, and security councils are some of the institutions involved in this aspect of learning.

A further crucial set of networks are the informal networks. Whereas learning networks exist within state institutions, there are also informal associations. These are much harder to locate and keep changing as elites compete for access to resources and leadership, and will change allegiances to maintain – or gain – access. We investigated informal networks between Russia, Moldova, and Ukraine and found that these networks are extensive and that these associations are crucial for authoritarian learning. Due to the opaque nature of these connections, locating information is difficult and we can only make inferences from the available evidence. However, we can say that like formal networks in existing institutions, informal associations are as important – if not more so – for authoritarian learning.

## 9.2.4 Regional Organisations Are Important

As shown in this book, regional organisations are central to a better understanding of authoritarian learning. Four post-Soviet organisations – the CIS, the CSTO, the SCO, and the Union State – were investigated. We found that these regional organisations provide a perfect opportunity for dialogue, information sharing, engaging in training exercises, and learning. The CIS, the CSTO, and the SCO bring member states together in training exercises to develop best practices and ascertain which tactics are most effective to survive and consolidate power. The CIS and the CSTO regularly hold training exercises for member states to gauge which methods work best in each scenario. The concept of learning through training is one that the CIS has taken to heart. Through the CIS's anti-terrorist centre – which regularly holds training exercises – it develops tactics to deal with protesters. As seen, these regional organisations have a broad interpretation of what constitutes anti-terrorism, with the development of best practices against protesters being included within the sphere of anti-terrorism. Like the CIS, the CSTO and the SCO also engage in anti-terrorist exercises that include dealing with protesters. Therefore, these organisations develop similar anti-protest methods to the CIS and engage in learning by doing – experiential learning.

These regional organisations hold regular committee meetings, allowing different ministries to meet and discuss what is happening in the region. There are regular inter-departmental meetings – both formal and informal – in the CIS and the CIS-IPA provides member states with opportunities to harmonise legislation. This is so for the CSTO and the SCO as well, with all three regional organisations holding regular meetings and offering places for learning through dialogue, cooperation, and learning. By offering space for discussion, the development of best practices, and learning by doing, these regional organisations are crucial for authoritarian learning. The Union State is another organisation that is crucial for providing opportunities for dialogue and imparting learning. The institution allows Belarusian and Russian regime personnel to regularly meet one another – monthly – and provides opportunities for legislation to be harmonised. This means that the Union State is a crucial place for learning for personnel in both regimes.

The Belarusian and Russian regimes are members or observers of most of these regional organisations. Membership helps both regimes with learning, the sharing of best practices, and power consolidation. By contrast, Moldovan and Ukrainian regimes are not members of many of these regional organisations. Ukraine has not been a member of the CIS since 2018 and was not a member of the other three regional organisations. Consequently, this affects the learning capabilities of Moldovan and Ukrainian regimes, as they do not have access to regular meetings, dialogue, exchange of best practices, engagement in training exercises, and learning. Although there are other factors, it is likely that non-membership of many – or all – post-Soviet regional organisations is one component explaining why authoritarian-minded elites in Moldova and Ukraine have been unable to consolidate power.

### 9.2.5 Learning from Internal Examples Is Crucial

Existing literature on authoritarian learning has concentrated on the inter-state level by analysing interactions between authoritarian regimes, principally learning from external failure. However, this misses a key aspect of authoritarian learning, which is the intra-state or internal level. By analysing intra-state-level learning in Belarus, Moldova, Russia, and Ukraine, we showed that there is significant inter-linkage between factions and clear opportunities for dialogue, best practice sharing, and learning. Due to extensive elite interlinkage – where governments may come and go but elite personnel merely change allegiance – elites in the four cases studied know one another and learn from one another. This makes learning much easier as relations and linkages have been built up over many years. Regarding Moldova and Ukraine, internal learning has been detrimental to the democratisation of both states as elites bring previous experiences into government and implement these. This follows the idea of social learning, which contends that people bring past experiences to bear on the present day. Similarly, personnel in Belarus and Russia use past experiences from the Soviet Union – and survival in the 1990s – in the present. This partially explains why both states are consolidated authoritarian regimes today, although there are other factors at play.

### 9.2.6 Authoritarian Learning Is Mostly about Dialogue

We showed that while diffusion certainly plays a role in authoritarian learning – epitomised by the joke that '90% of what to do can be found on Google' – there is something stronger than it occurring. On the one hand, there is emulation and diffusion, where authoritarian-minded elites decide what to implement and imitate one another by looking at what other authoritarian elites have been doing and the policies that they have implemented. On the other hand, there is actual dialogue and the sharing of best practices. As seen here, authoritarian-minded elites in the cases studied collude with one another.

There are strong pointers towards direct dialogue and cooperation on techniques. This is a stronger concept than looking at what is occurring in another authoritarian state and implementing practices accordingly. Of course, this does not detract from the relevance of diffusion, policy transfer, and emulation, which are integral aspects of authoritarian learning. However, there appears to be a concerted effort by authoritarian-minded elites to talk with one another, share best practices, and learn. We contend that when it comes to diffusion in authoritarian learning, this is a strong form of diffusion with regular meetings, opportunities for discussion, sharing of best practices, and engagement in training exercises.

### 9.2.7  *Learning from Success Is Relevant*

As mentioned above, learning from failure has received much analysis in the existing literature on authoritarian learning. This is partially because it is easier to see failure. As authoritarian regimes do not provide many opportunities for the public to replace them non-violently, the demise of these regimes is often violent. Generally it ends with mass protests or the regime being violently deposed and the leader dead, imprisoned, or on trial. Naturally, other authoritarian regimes do not want to share that fate, so they ascertain the causes of that failure and develop practices to counter such possibilities occurring in their own country.

By contrast, though no less relevant to authoritarian learning, learning from success is harder to measure and see than learning from failure. As shown in this book, internal sources of learning are the main sources of learning from success. For example, Plahotniuc and Poroshenko learnt from the internal success of previous regimes to try to consolidate power. Zelensky has begun to implement certain practices that have been successful for consolidating power in the past, like taking control of key institutions. Providing that Zelensky does not become too greedy or take too much power, like Yanukovych, but is more subtle, like Kuchma and Poroshenko, then it is possible he will be able to consolidate power, at least for a time.

## 9.3 Areas for Future Research

There are several areas that require further analysis to increase understanding of authoritarian learning. A crucial area of future focus is to see whether the findings here on four post-Soviet case studies can be extrapolated into other regions. For instance, one area of focus would be to ascertain if the findings here are likely to be corroborated by cases in Africa, the Middle East, and East Asia; and if not, why not. Another area of focus would be whether authoritarian regimes cooperate with other authoritarian regimes outside their own region. There is evidence pointing to this, but there needs to be deeper research on this topic.

A further area for future study would be to analyse the role played by post-Soviet regimes other than Russia in authoritarian learning. As mentioned, Belarus is an example of an authoritarian regime learning and sharing best practices with other authoritarian regimes. We addressed the likelihood that Moldovan and Ukrainian authoritarian-minded elites do not require the Russian example to learn. It is possible to resist including Russia in future analyses to focus on how the other authoritarian post-Soviet states learn from each other. Similarly, future investigation could analyse the South Caucasus or Central Asia.

Another related topic for future research is the role of regional organisations. We argued here that post-Soviet regional organisations are crucial for authoritarian learning, but is this the case in other regions? There are several questions that future research can address, with the most obvious being whether regional organisations in other regions are engaged in providing opportunities for authoritarian learning. As shown in this book, post-Soviet regional organisations offer opportunities for representatives of authoritarian states to meet regularly, hold discussions, share best practices, engage in training exercises, and develop learning capacity for consolidating power. However, the question remains whether this is the case for regional organisations in regions like Africa and the Middle East. It is likely that further investigation of the SCO – an organisation partially outside the post-Soviet space – would show that regional organisations outside the post-Soviet region are crucial for learning. However, further research on this is needed.

The existing literature has largely focused on the inter-state level and on failure. Learning from success and internal learning remain understudied and need further analysis, even though this monograph has provided extensive analysis of these topics. More work could also be done on understanding if the regional hegemon is significant to authoritarian learning. We showed that in the post-Soviet space the regional hegemon, Russia, does not just teach, but also learns. Investigation of other global regions such as South America, the Middle East, North Africa, or East Asia could shed further light on the role of regional hegemons in authoritarian learning.

Determining *when* authoritarian-minded elites will engage in learning is something that has not been covered here, but it would be a fruitful area for future research. We argue that learning is a survival strategy. As authoritarian regimes must be lucky all the time, they need to gauge the appropriate strategies for enhancing their survival. Consequently, these regimes are likely to engage in learning when they feel threatened. However, what does it mean for an authoritarian regime to be threatened and what threats are likely to lead to learning? This area of research is crucial to understanding authoritarian learning and how authoritarian regimes and authoritarian-minded elites operate. By understanding what threats lead to learning, it is possible to better understand power consolidation.

## 9.4 Policy Recommendations for Democratisers

Having addressed areas for future research, there are several policy-relevant suggestions addressed here. Authoritarian regimes are not only surviving but their numbers are increasing globally. While Western efforts at democratisation have been dominant since the end of the Cold War there is growing push-back against democratisation as authoritarian regimes cooperate and learn to limit democratisation pressures. Learning is a key part of the authoritarian arsenal to protect against democratisation efforts. With an increase in the number of authoritarian regimes globally, democracy is no longer the only game in town. As authoritarian regimes learn to survive and collaborate, some more effective authoritarian regimes are becoming role models for others – and even some democracies – to consolidate power. Ideas diffuse both ways, so democratic values are not the only criteria that may spread between states.

The rise of authoritarian regimes puts pressure on Western states and international organisations, and the promotion of democratisation and market liberal values. The authoritarian model creates a zero-sum game reminiscent of the Cold War. During that period from 1945 to

1991, the West was fearful of communism and so was less concerned with promoting its values to states that had not completed a democratic transition but were anti-Soviet. With the rise of authoritarian regimes like China, the Western model of democratisation and market capitalism is competing with an effective authoritarian model of state power and market capitalism. Western states have suffered numerous crises since the global financial crisis of 2008 – and interventions in Afghanistan and Iraq ostensibly to bring about democracy. The Western model is consequently no longer as attractive, resulting in some democracies weakening and others reneging on democratic promotion and ignoring democratic backsliding. In the EU, Brussels seems less concerned with defending its values than concentrating on keeping neighbouring states away from Russia. Therefore, the EU – and America – are less concerned with defending their values in the interests of geopolitical influence. The rise of China is likely to increase this trend – allowing authoritarian-minded elites to renege on espousing democratic values. Western states and organisations must re-find their values and adhere to these even if it means losing states to other political models.

With authoritarian learning, authoritarian-minded elites can keep power and prevent pressure from Western states and organisations to democratise. Regarding the post-Soviet region, EU policy has become ineffective in helping the Eastern Neighbourhood states modernise. Through collaboration and emulation, authoritarian-minded elites protect themselves from external pressures, thereby affecting the EU's ability to compel democratisation. The EU has faced several crises from 2008 to the present with the financial, refugee, Brexit, and Covid crises. With growing competition from Russia, the EU desperately needs a success story. Therefore, the EU is unlikely to push reforms in candidate states. Regarding the four cases studied, this puts less pressure on Moldovan and Ukrainian elites to reform as the EU does not want to lose two potential success stories after so much investment. Although the conflict in Ukraine makes it almost certain that Bankova will not realign with the Kremlin, greater EU pressure could lead to balancing between Russia and the West. Moldova remains split politically between nominally pro-European parties and pro-Russian parties, although Maia Sandu has put pro-European parties back into the ascendency. However, Moldovan politics is like a pendulum and so while nominally pro-European now it may swing back towards Russia later. The Kremlin will continue to try to strengthen the PSRM and current Bloc of Communists and Socialists coalition. By doing so – and using leverage in Transnistria and Gagauzia – the Kremlin looks to keep Moldova away from further EU integration. This would increase the belief among the Moldovan public that EU integration, while the end goal, is unlikely to occur soon, and Russia is the better alternative in the short and medium term.

Authoritarian learning poses many challenges to Western states and organisations. As the closest neighbour to the four case studies, the EU has several tools at its disposal to get back on track and enforce its values of democratisation and the protection of civil liberties. Russia's sponsored conflict in Ukraine and wider interference in EU states should be counteracted. This can be done through a Russian-language media channel to counter Russian propaganda and strengthen EU support in Eastern Europe. There are services that currently exist, like Deutsche Welle, the BBC, and Radio Free Europe/Radio Liberty, which all offer Russian-language services. However, the EU has left this task to Radio Free Europe/Radio Liberty and the Voice of America's new Russian-language television channel, Current Time. Of course, this is a start, but American media has an ideological taint among many Russian speakers and so the EU needs to create its own Russian-language media outlets. This should not be a propaganda tool – like Russia's international media outlet RT – but should provide news about the EU and member states, giving a fairer picture of what is happening in the organisation and member states than what the Russian media offer. EU member states like Estonia have a Russian-language media outlet – ETV+ – but this should not be an individual member state initiative. ETV+ is also a Russian-language television channel for the Russian minority in Estonia and does not cross into the borders of the case studies. Euronews covers world news from a European perspective – and has a Russian-language channel – but the organisation is not specifically an EU source. However, it can serve as an example of what to do with expansion into radio and social media. Another tactic would be to monitor Russian media sources – on television, radio, and online – to locate fake news and counter such misinformation. Therefore, a more proactive stance from the EU on a universal Russian-language channel to counter Russian propaganda is necessary, and piecemeal actions will not work.

The EU should continue its policy of democratisation in the post-Soviet region. It will be contested, but so be it. Promoting civil society and media is not intervention in the internal affairs of a state, which is an argument by regimes afraid of competition. Democratisation efforts may not weaken regimes – in say Belarus and Russia – but they will show that the EU believes in its proclaimed values. Another option is to stop treating the regimes and people as the same. Young people from Belarus, Moldova, Russia, and Ukraine should have greater opportunity to travel and study in Europe. Visa costs should be reduced, and more scholarships given to allow more to come and live – for a short period – in EU countries. This will not necessarily make them pro-European, but it would give them the experience of what life is like outside the four countries and would also increase linkages between these countries and EU states.

Programmes to train youth activists and future politicians should be increased, and more finances given to these training activities. This can be done by creating more youth parliaments in Brussels or Warsaw or Vilnius to train aspirant politicians in democratic politics and good governance. This would allow them to return to Belarus, Moldova, Russia, and Ukraine and use the skills developed abroad domestically. The EU should aid civil society and activists either through short courses or by supporting their work in their own countries. The EU should stop worrying about losing Moldova and Ukraine. For an organisation that has had several failures recently, losing two signatories to the Association Agreement could be construed as failure. However, the EU must uphold its values. This involves pressurising incumbent governments to continue reforms. Monetary support should be made dependent on modernisation and it should be made clear that backsliding will lead to the withdrawal of financial support, repeatedly, if necessary.

Authoritarian learning, power consolidation, and collaboration between authoritarian-minded elites are here to stay. Western states and organisations should accept this and stand up for values that they espouse as universal. By developing independent civil society and media, and alternative politicians to incumbent regimes, especially in Belarus and Russia, Western states and organisations can show that they stand by these values. Authoritarian regimes cannot be beaten into submission. However, a staunch defence of Western values acts as a beacon for those in authoritarian states in the post-Soviet region who believe in these values. This is the only way to counteract the growing authoritarianism in the post-Soviet region and globally.

This is perhaps a pessimistic view. There is a rise in authoritarian regimes globally and we have shown that there is clear cooperation and learning to develop best survival practices. Authoritarian regimes are on the rise and are offering support to authoritarian-minded elites and opportunities for learning and cooperation. The EU – and Western states – have been in a period of on-off crises, and this has tarnished their image. There is a clear need for Western states and the EU to re-find their mojo and get back to promoting their values. This will probably result in increased authoritarian cooperation against increased democratisation pressures. While the West could just wait for authoritarian regimes and authoritarian-minded elites to lose power – as authoritarian leaders tend to have short tenures – increasingly authoritarian tenure is Rather, by increasing democratisation pressures, Western states are more likely to weaken the current trend of authoritarianism. After all, authoritarian regimes must be lucky all the time and protesters must be lucky just once. Authoritarian-minded elites are constantly learning, but often make mistakes. By increasing external pressure, Western states and organisations can force these regimes into making mistakes and helping protesters take their lucky chance. The people of Belarus, Moldova, Russia, and Ukraine deserve external support in the battle for hearts and minds and eventually help in support of democratisation and the rule of law in their countries. This may have happened in Ukraine due to Russia's invasion, but even here a failure to integrate Ukraine into Western institutions or the failure to reduce presidential powers after the war may have a negative effect. The people of the four states need support from the West to reduce the standing of authoritarianism as a form of government, and to have it consigned to the rubbish bin of history.

# Bibliography

AFN.by. 2011. 'Lukashenko gotovitsya k otrazheniyu "arabskoi vesny".' Inosmi.ru. 11 July. https://inosmi.ru/belorussia/20111107/177237250.html.

Alaiba, D. 2011. 'Procuratura, B*ead*!' Dumitru Alaiba (blog). 10 November. https://alaiba.wordpress.com/2011/11/10/procuratura-bead/.

Alaiba, D. 2016. 'Do What You Must, Just Don't Call This Government "Pro-European"'. Dumitru Alaiba (blog). 24 January. https://alaiba.wordpress .com/2016/01/24/do-what-you-must-just-dont-call-this-government-pro-european/.

Alekseeva, I., Kostyukovsky, A., Timofeeva-Glazunova, O. et al. 2018. 'Reforma Krainego Sroka'. Expert.ru. 11 August. https://expert.ru/rus sian_reporter/2018/16/reforma-krajnego-sroka/.

Amambaeva, E. 2004. 'Tochka zreniya: Yuri Zubakov – "Rossiya ostaetsya glavnym torgovym partnerom Moldovy i ee osnovnym kreditorom"'. *Logos-Press*. 13 February (no. 5), 16.

Ambrosio, T. 2008. '"Catching the 'Shanghai Spirit": How the Shanghai Cooperation Organization Promotes Authoritarian Norms in Central Asia'. *Europe-Asia Studies*. 60(8): 1321–44.

Ambrosio, T. 2009. *Authoritarian Backlash: Russian Resistance to Democratization in the Former Soviet Union*. Farnham: Ashgate Publishing.

Ambrosio, T. 2010. 'Constructing a Framework of Authoritarian Diffusion: Concepts, Dynamics, and Future Research'. *International Studies Perspectives*. 11(4): 375–92.

Ambrosio, T. 2012. 'The Rise of the "China Model" and "Beijing Consensus": Evidence of Authoritarian Diffusion?' *Contemporary Politics*. 18(4): 381–99.

Ambrosio, T. 2014. 'Beyond the Transition Paradigm: A Research Agenda for Authoritarian Consolidation'. *Demokratizatsiya*. 22(3): 471–94.

Ambrosio, T. 2017. 'The Architecture of Alignment: The Russia–China Relationship and International Agreements'. *Europe-Asia Studies*. 69(1): 110–56.

Ambrosio, T. 2018. 'Authoritarian Norms in a Changing International System'. *Politics and Governance*. 6(2): 120–3.

Ambrosio, T., & Tolstrup, J. 2019. 'How Do We Tell Authoritarian Diffusion from Illusion? Exploring Methodological Issues of Qualitative Research on Authoritarian Diffusion'. *Quality & Quantity*. 53(6): 2741–63.

Ampelonsky, V., & Meteleva, S. 2005. 'L'goty. Razreshite zastrelitsya'. *Moskovsky Komsomolets*. 21 January (no. 12), 4.

Ananyev, M. 2018. 'Inside the Kremlin: The Presidency and the Executive Branch'. In *The New Autocracy: Information, Politics, and Policy in Putin's Russia*, edited by D. Treisman (pp. 29–48). Washington, DC: Brookings Institution Press.

Andreev, D. 2005. 'L'gotnoe voskresen'e. Sankt-Peterburg prevratilsya v kolybel' kontrmonetizatsii'. *Vremya Novostei*. 17 January (no. 4), 3.

Anin, R. 2017. 'The Russian Laundromat Superusers Revealed'. OCCRP. 20 March. www.occrp.org/en/laundromat/the-russian-laundromat-superusers-revealed/.

Ankudo, Y. 2006a. 'Partnerstvo v sude'. *BelGazeta*. 12 June (no. 23).

Ankudo, Y. 2006b. 'Zakon i poryadok'. *BelGazeta*. 20 March (no. 11).

Ankudo, Y. 2007. 'Shpiony "spalilis'" na flesh-karte'. *BelGazeta*. 17 September (no. 37).

Anti-terrorist Centre of the Member States of the Commonwealth of Independent States. 2011. 'Sovmestnoe antiterroisticheskoe uchenie "Donbass-Antiterror-2011"'. CISATC. 28–9 September. www.cisatc.org/133/161/377.html.

Anti-terrorist Centre of the Member States of the Commonwealth of Independent States. 2012. 'Sovmestnaya komandno-shtabnaya trenirovka "Don-Antiterror-2012"'. CISATC. 4 September. www.cisatc.org/133/162/506.html.

Anti-terrorist Centre of the Member States of the Commonwealth of Independent States. 2014. '"Aktual'nye voprosy protivodeistviya terrorizmu i ekstremizmy" – kruglyi stol (10 oktyabrya 2014 g.)'. CISATC. 10 October. www.cisatc.org/1289/138/8192.

Apostrophe.ua. 2015. 'V Rossii rasskazali o sekretnykh peregovorakh Akhmetova c Kremlem'. 26 March. https://apostrophe.ua/news/politics/f oreign-policy/2016-03-26/ahmetov-usilenno-dogovarivaetsya-s-puti nyim-o-vozvraschenii-donbass-pod-svoy-kontrol/53621.

Argumenty i Nedeli. 2014. 'Zurabov pakuet chemodany?' *Argumenty i Nedeli*. 21 August (no. 31): 2.

Armstrong, D. A. 2011. 'Stability and Change in the Freedom House Political Rights and Civil Liberties Measures'. *Journal of Peace Research*. 48(5): 653–62.

Aron, L. 2012. *Roads to the Temple: Truth, Memory, Ideas and Ideals in the Making of the Russian Revolution, 1987–1991*. New Haven, CT: Yale University Press.

Arutunyan, A. 2014. *The Putin Mystique: Inside Russia's Power Cult.* Newbold on Sour: Skyscraper Publications.

Arutyunova, V. 2001. 'Pervaya Polosa. Genprokuratura podoshla vplotnuyu k Aleksandru Voloshinu'. *Kommersant-Daily.* 2 February (no. 18), 1.

Astapenia, R. 2014. 'Is Lukashenka Trying to Emancipate Belarus from Russian Culture?' *Belarus Digest.* 3 October. http://belarusdigest.com/st ory/lukashenka-trying-emancipate-belarus-russian-culture-19510.

A-TV.md. 2017. 'Grechanii: Agreement on Cooperation between the PSRM and United Russia Will Help Strengthen Friendship between Both Countries'. A-TV.md. 9 June. http://a-tv.md/eng/index.php? newsid=31598.

Badanin, R., Bocharova, S., Tsvetkova, M., & Borusheva, E. 2009. 'Dlya lyudei i Deripaski'. 4 June. www.gazeta.ru/politics/2009/06/04_a_32067 90.shtml.

Bader, J. 2015a. 'China, Autocratic Patron? An Empirical Investigation of China as a Factor of Autocratic Survival'. *International Studies Quarterly.* 59(1): 23–33.

Bader, J. 2015b. *China's Foreign Relations and the Survival of Autocracies.* London: Routledge.

Bader, J. 2015c. 'Propping Up Dictators? Economic Cooperation from China and Its Impact on Authoritarian Persistence in Party and Non-Party Regimes'. *European Journal of Political Research.* 54(4): 655–72.

Bader, J., Grävingholt, J., & Kästner, A. 2010. 'Would Autocracies Promote Autocracy? A Political Economy Perspective on Regime-Type Export in Regional Neighbourhoods'. *Contemporary Politics.* 16(1): 81–100.

Bader, M. 2014. 'Democracy Promotion and Authoritarian Diffusion: The Foreign Origins of Post-Soviet Election Laws'. *Europe-Asia Studies.* 66(8): 1350–70.

Bai, E. 2006. 'Pervyi zamestitel' ministra inostrannykh del Rossii Andrei Denisov: 'Budu teper' kurirovat' SNG'''. *Izvestiya.* 12 April (no. 64), 3.

Baidakova, A. 2016a. 'Gennady Gudkov: "Natsional'nuyu gvardiyu gotovyat k podavleniyu sotsial'nogo protesta"'. *Novaya Gazeta.* 6 April. www .novayagazeta.ru/articles/2016/04/06/68105-gennadiy-gudkov-171-natsionalnuyu-gvardiyu-gotovyat-k-podavleniyu-sotsialnogo-protesta-187.

Baidakova, A. 2016b. 'Strel'ba na operezhenie'. *Novaya Gazeta.* 8 April (no. 37), 7.

Balachuk, I. 2018. 'Nalvaychenko: Na Maidane byli rossiyskie shevrony'. *Ukrainskaya Pravda.* 7 February. www.pravda.com.ua/rus/news/2018/0 2/7/7170848/.

Bandura, A. 1963. *Social Learning and Personality Development.* New York: Holt, Reinhart & Winston.

Bandura, A. 1971. *Social Learning Theory*. New York: General Learning Press.

Bank, A., & Edel, M. 2015. 'Authoritarian Regime Learning: Comparative Insights from the Arab Uprisings'. German Institute of Global Area Studies Working Papers No. 274. June. www.giga-hamburg.de/de/system/files/p ublications/wp274_bank-edel.pdf.

Bastrykin, A. 2016. 'Pora postavit' deistvennyi zaslon informatsionnoi voine'. 18 April. www.kommersant.ru/doc/2961578.

Batanova, A. 2020. '"My dogovorilis". V Moldove poyavilas' pravyashchaya koalitsiya'. 16 March. https://newsmaker.md/rus/novosti/my-dogovorilis-v-moldove-poyavilas-pravyaschaya-koalitsiya/.

Batherin, S. 2014. 'Musornik' na Reznitskoi?' *Zerkalo Nedeli*. October (no. 39), 1.

BBC. 2002. 'Two Hostages Flee Moscow Theatre'. BBC. 24 October. http://news.bbc.co.uk/1/hi/world/europe/2357729.stm.

BBC Ukrainian Service. 2013. 'Yanukovych v Moskve: kakie soglasheniya podpishut Ukraina i Rossiya'. 16 December. www.bbc.com/ukrainian/uk raine_in_russian/2013/12/131216_ru_s_russia_ukraine_17.

BBC Ukrainian Service. 2017a. 'Chto izvestno ob ischeznovenii v Belarusi ukraintsa Pavla Griba'. BBC. 29 August. www.bbc.com/ukrainian/news-russian-41080609.

BBC Ukrainian Service. 2017b. 'Ukraintsa Pavla Griba vernuli v SIZO'. BBC. 16 September. www.bbc.com/ukrainian/news-russian-41293877.

Beissinger, M. 2007. 'Structure and Example in Modular Political Phenomena: The Diffusion of Bulldozer/Rose/Orange/Tulip Revolutions'. *Perspectives on Politics*. 5(2): 259–76.

BelaPAN. 2005. 'Anzhelica Boris i vitse-spiker pol'skogo Seima Donal'd Tusk vstretilis' s predstavitelyami evropeiskikh mezhdunarodnykh struktur'. Tut. by. 8 September. https://news.tut.by/politics/57567.html.

BelGazeta. 2017a. '"Belyi legion" on "Eurovision"'. *BelGazeta* (no. 15). 18 April.

BelGazeta. 2017b. 'Singapur i Belarus': NPZ, integratsiya, bor'ba so zhvachkoi i porka'. UDF. 2 May. http://udf.by/news/politic/156098-singapur-i-belarus-npz-integraciya-borba-so-zhvachkoy-i-porka.html.

Belsat. 2017a. '17-Year-Old Russian Girl Allegedly Forced to Help Russia's FSB Kidnap Ukrainian Citizen'. Belsat. 29 August. http://belsat.eu/en/ne ws/17-year-old-russian-girl-allegedly-forced-to-help-russia-s-fsb-kidnap-ukrainian-citizen/.

Belsat. 2017b. 'Pavlo Gryb Abducted by FSB in Belarus Has No Access to Doctors'. Belsat. 13 October. http://belsat.eu/en/news/pavel-grib-kidnapped-by-fsb-in-belarus-has-no-access-to-doctors/.

Belsat. 2018. 'Lukashenko spravlyaetsya s krizisom arestami biznesmenov'. UDF. 19 April. https://udf.by/news/economic/172442-lukashenko-spravlyaetsya-s-krizisom-arestami-biznesmenov.html.

BELTA. 2012a. 'Sekretarii Sovbezov Belarusi i Rossii provel konsul'tatsii v Moskve'. Tut.by. 26 June 26. https://news.tut.by/politics/296564.html.

BELTA. 2012b. 'Sovbezdy Belarusi i Rossii obsudyat temy informatsionnoi bezopasnosti'. Tut.by. 1 March. https://news.tut.by/politics/276945.html.

BELTA. 2015. 'Shunevich: MVD k vyboram gotovo'. Tut.by. 15 July. https://news.tut.by/society/456168.html.

BELTA. 2016. '"Zas": V novoi doKtrine aktsenty ot vozmozhnykh vheshnikh ugroz smeshcheny k vnutrennim'. Tut.by. 22 January. https://news.tut.by/politics/481803.html.

BELTA. 2017. 'Shunevich: V strane poyavitsya sistema monitoring obshchestvennoi bezopasnosti'. Tut.by. 27 March. https://news.tut.by/economics/536957.html.

Bernhard, M., Jung, D., Tzelgov, E., Coppedge, M., & Lindberg, S. I. 2017. 'Making Embedded Knowledge Transparent: How the V-Dem Dataset Opens New Vistas in Civil Society Research'. *Perspectives on Politics*. 15(2): 342–60.

Bershidsky, L. 2019a. 'Kazakh Autocrat Shows Putin How to Keep Power'. *The Moscow Times*. 20 March. www.themoscowtimes.com/2019/03/20/kazakh-autocrat-shows-putin-how-to-keep-power-a64879.

Bershidsky, L. 2019b. 'Ukrainian Villain Is Now Cracking Heads in Moscow'. *The Moscow Times*. August 6. www.themoscowtimes.com/2019/08/06/ukrainian-villain-is-now-cracking-heads-in-moscow-a66720.

Bilousova, N. 2013. 'Tretiy – lishniy'. *Den*. 24 December (no. 236).

Bloknot-Moldova.md. 2017. 'Soglashenie o sotrudnichestve PSRM i "United Russia" zaklyuchili Zinaida Greceanii i Dmitriy Medvedev'. 8 June. http://bloknot-moldova.md/news/soglashenie-o-sotrudnichestve-psrm-i-edinoy-rossii-852171.

Bocharova, S., & Mukhametshina, E. 2018. 'Prezidentskaya administratsiya obnovilas' po minimum'. Vedomosti. 24 June. www.vedomosti.ru/politics/articles/2018/06/24/773624-administratsiya.

Bocharova, S., & Savina, E. 2010. 'Preventivnoe nakazanie oppozitsii'. 15 November. www.gazeta.ru/politics/2010/11/15_a_3437933.shtml.

Bocharova, S., Churakova, O., Lomskaya, T., & Mukhametshina, E. 2018. 'V Kremle opasayutsya protestov iz-za povysheniya pensionnogo vozrasta'. 15 June. www.vedomosti.ru/politics/articles/2018/06/15/772958-opasayutsya-protestov.

Bohdan, S. 2017a. 'Minsk Silently Builds a New Army'. *Belarus Digest*. 7 December. https://belarusdigest.com/story/minsk-silently-builds-a-new-army/.

Bohdan, S. 2017b. 'Moscow Erects Border with Belarus, Undermines Its Links With Ukraine And The Baltics'. *Belarus Digest*. 20 February. http://belarus digest.com/story/moscow-erects-border-belarus-undermines-its-links-ukraine-and-baltics-29148.

Bohdan, S. 2017c. 'The Belarusian Army: Scaled Down but Better Trained and Autonomous'. *Belarus Digest*. 23 December. https://belarusdigest .com/story/the-belarusian-army-scaled-down-but-better-trained-and-autonomous/.

Bollen, K. A., & Paxton, P. 2000. 'Subjective Measures of Liberal Democracy'. *Comparative Political Studies*. 33(1): 58–86.

Bolotny, I. 2014. 'Novye "klimenki" I starye "kivalovy" snova v stroyu'. *Zerkalo Nedeli*. 19 May (no. 16): 6.

Boulègue, M, Lutsevych, O., & Marin, A. 2018. 'Civil Society under Russia's Threat: Building Resilience in Ukraine, Belarus and Moldova'. Chatham House. 8 November. www.chathamhouse.org/2018/11/civil-society-under-russias-threat-building-resilience-ukraine-belarus-and-moldova-0/3.

Bourdieu, P. 1972. *Outline of a Theory of Practice*. Cambridge: Cambridge University Press.

Bourdieu, P. 1992. *The Logic of Practice*. Stanford: Stanford University Press.

Bourdieu, P. 2000. *Pascalian Mediations*. Stanford: Stanford University Press.

Brady, A. 2016. 'China's Foreign Propaganda Machine'. In *Authoritarianism Goes Global: The Challenge to Democracy*, edited by M. F. Plattner, L. Diamond, & C. Walker (pp. 187–98). Baltimore: The Johns Hopkins University Press.

Braun, D., & Gilardi, F. 2006. 'Taking Galton's Problem Seriously: Towards a Theory of Policy Diffusion'. *Journal of Theoretical Politics*. 18(3): 298–322.

Breslauer, G. W., & Tetlock, P. E. 1991. 'Introduction'. In *Learning in US and Soviet Foreign Policy*, edited by G. W. Breslauer & P. E. Tretlock (pp. 3–19). Boulder: Westview Press.

Breslin, S. 2011. 'The "China Model" and the Global Crisis: From Friedrich List to a Chinese Mode of Governance?' *International Affairs*. 87(6): 1323–43.

Brookes, J. 1995. *Training and Development Competence: A Practical Guide*. London: Kogan Page.

Brownlee, J. 2017. 'The Limited Reach of Authoritarian Powers'. *Democratization*. 24(7): 1326–44.

Budkevich, V. 2012. 'V Belarusi razrabatyvaetsya kontseptsiya protivideistviya terrorizmu'. 5 October. https://news.tut.by/politics/314370.html.

Burmenko, K. 2014. 'Zhit' bez opasnosti'. *Belarus' Segodnya*. 20 November (no. 221).

Burnell, P. 2010. 'Is There a New Autocracy Promotion?' Fundación para las Relaciones Internacionales y el Diálogo Exterior. Working paper no. 96. March. http://fride.org/descarga/WP96_Autocracy_ENG_mar10.pdf.

Burrett, T. 2011. *Television and Presidential Power in Putin's Russia*. London: Routledge.

BusinessViews. 2017. 'Kakim prezidentom okazalsya Poroshenko v sravnenii c Yanukovichem i chto nam dal'she s nim delat''. Business Views. 24 February. http://businessviews.com.ua/ru/studies/id/kakim-prezidentom-stal-poroshenko-1451/.

Całus, K. 2014a. 'Gaugazia: Growing Separatism in Moldova?' Centre for Eastern Studies. 10 March. www.osw.waw.pl/en/publikacje/osw-commentary/2014-03-10/gagauzia-growing-separatism-moldova.

Całus, K. 2014b. 'Russia Is Playing Harder in Moldova'. Centre for Eastern Studies. 2 April. www.osw.waw.pl/en/publikacje/analyses/2014-04-02/ru ssia-playing-harder-moldova.

Całus, K. 2016a. 'Igor Dodon Has Won the Presidential Election in Moldova'. Centre for Eastern Studies. 14 November. www.osw.waw.pl/en/publikacje/analyses/2016-11-14/igor-dodon-has-won-presidential-election-moldova.

Całus, K. 2016b. 'Moldova: From Oligarch Pluralism to Plahotniuc's Hegemony'. Centre for Eastern Studies. 11 April. www.osw.waw.pl/en/p ublikacje/osw-commentary/2016-04-11/moldova-oligarchic-pluralism-to -plahotniucs-hegemony.

Całus, K. 2018. 'Moldova's Political Theatre: The Balance of Forces in an Election Year'. Centre for Eastern Studies. 31 January. www.osw.waw.pl/en/publikacje/osw-commentary/2018-01-31/moldovas-political-theatre-balance-forces-election-year.

Cameron, D., & Ornstein, M. A. 2012. 'Post-Soviet Authoritarianism: The Influence of Russia in Its "Near Abroad"'. *Post-Soviet Affairs*. 28(1): 1–44.

Carothers, T. 2006. 'The Backlash against Democracy Promotion'. *Foreign Affairs*. 85(2): 55–68.

Charnysh, V. 2016. 'Police in Belarus: Guardian or Threat?' *Belarus Digest*. 4 February. https://belarusdigest.com/story/police-in-belarus-guardian-or -threat/.

Cheibub, J. A., Gandhi, J., & Vreeland, J. R. 2010. 'Democracy and Dictatorship Revisited'. *Public Choice*. 143(1/2): 67–101.

Chevordov, Y. 2012. 'Viktor Medvedchuk. Elitnyi spoiler ili pretendant'. LB. 1 December. https://lb.ua/blog/yuriy_chevordov/180943_viktor_med vedchuk_elitniy_spoyler.html

Chubchenko, Y. 2000. 'Novosti. Luchinskiy boretsya s parlamentom'. *Kommersant-Daily*. 29 July (no. 138): 3.

Ciurea, C. 2016. 'Why a United Opposition in Moldova Is Impossible'. Open Democracy. 4 February. www.opendemocracy.net/od-russia/corneliu-ciurea/why-united-opposition-in-moldova-is-impossible.

Clark, D. 2020. 'Zelenskyy Fails to Deliver on Promise of a New Beginning'. Atlantic Council. 3 May. www.atlanticcouncil.org/blogs/ukrainealert/zel enskyy-fails-to-deliver-on-promise-of-a-new-beginning/.

Coalson, R. 2013. 'News Analysis: Flip-Flops Point to Splits in Yanukovych's Circle'. 12 December. Radio Free Europe/Radio Liberty. www.rferl.org/a/ukraine-analysis-yanukovych-divisions/25198463.html.

Cojocaru, B. 2019. 'Criza politică din Republic Moldova: cine este Vlad Plahotniuc, oligarhul care ține captive un stat – trezorierul democrat al comuniștilor din Republica Moldova, deținătoril unui imperiu media cu puterea de a pune și răpune președinți'. *Ziarul Financiar*. 10 June. www .zf.ro/business-international/criza-politica-republica-moldova-vlad-plahotniuc-oligarhul-tine-captiv-stat-trezorierul-democrat-comunistilor-republica-moldova-detinatorul-unui-imperiu-media-puterea-pune-rapune-presedinti-18164495.

Collective Security Treaty Organisation. 2012. 'Na pervykh mirotvorcheskikh ucheniyakh ODKB pobezhdaet druzhba'. 14 October. http://odkb-csto.org/n ews/detail.php?ELEMENT_ID=1279&SECTION_ID=&sphrase_id=24910.

Collective Security Treaty Organisation. 2013a. 'Vtoroe uchenie Mirotvorche skikh sil ODKB "Nerushimoe Brratstvo-2013", 7–11 Oktyabrya 2013 g., Chelyabinskaya obl.g. Chebarkul". 11 October. http://odkb-csto.org/train ing/detail.php?ELEMENT_ID=2825&SECTION_ID=188& sphrase_id=24909.

Collective Security Treaty Organisation. 2013b. 'Vzaimodeistvie vlasti i obshchestva v tselyakh protivodeistviya vneshnemu vmeshatel'stvu i "tsvetnym revolyutsiyam"'. 20 December. www.odkb-csto.org/associ ation/news/detail.php?ELEMENT_ID=3134&sphrase_id=21524.

Collective Security Treaty Organisation. 2014a. 'Organizatsiya dogovora o kollektivnoi bezopasnosti, SNG, ShOS: V Kyrgystane stranny ODKB provedut ucheniya po vedeniyu mirotvorcheskikh operatsiy'. July 24, 2014. http://odkb-csto.org/obzor-pressy/detail.php?ELEMENT_ ID=3587&sphrase_id=24910.

Collective Security Treaty Organisation. 2014b. 'Ustavnye organy ODKB'. 10 June. http://odkb-csto.org/authorized_organs/detail.php? ELEMENT_ID=3561&SECTION_ID=98.

Collective Security Treaty Organisation. 2017. 'V Kazakhstane Kollektivnye mirotvorcheskie sily ODKB na zaklyuchitel'nom etape ucheniya "Nerushimoe Bratstvo-2017" otrabotali deistviya pri patrulirovanii naselennykh punktov, okhrane vazhnykh ob'ektov, razminirovanii

mestnosti, protivodeistvii massovym besporyadkam'. 20 October. http://
odkb-csto.org/news/detail.php?ELEMENT_ID=11631&SECTION_
ID=91&sphrase_id=24910.

Collective Security Treaty Organisation. 2022. '10 yanvarya v formate
videokonferentsii sostoyalos' vneocherednaya sessiya Soveta Kollektivnoi
Bezopasnosti ODKB. Obsuzhdalas' situatsiya v Respubliki Kazakhstan
i mery po normalizatsii obstanovki v strane'. 10 January. https://odkb-
csto.org/news/news_odkb/10-yanvarya-v-formate-videokonferentsii-
sostoitsya-zasedanie-soveta-kollektivnoy-bezopasnosti-odkb-p/?
clear_cache=Y#loaded.

Commonwealth of Independent States. 2001a. 'Reshenie o doklade o khode
vypolneniya v 2000 godu Mezhgosudarstvennoi programmy gosudarstv –
uchastnikov Sodruzhestva Nezavisimykh Gosudarstv po bor'be
c mezhdunarodnym terrorizmom i inymi proyavleniyami ekstremizma
do 2003 goda'. www.e-cis.info/page.php?id=20415.

Commonwealth of Independent States. 2001b. 'Reshenie ob Analiticheskom
doklade 'Itogi deyatel'nosti SNG za 10 let i zadachi na perspektivu'
i Zayavlenni glav gosudarstv – uchastnikov Sodruzhestva Nezavisimykh
Gosudarstv v svyazi c 10-letiem obrazovaniya SNG'. www.e-cis.info/page
.php?id=20426.

Commonwealth of Independent States. 2009. 'Perechen' dokumentov,
prinyatykh na zasedanii Soveta ministrov inostrannykh del Sodruzhestva
Nezavisimykh Gosudarstv (10 aprelya 2009 goda gorod Ashkhabad)'.
10 April https://e-cis.info/page/3491/80017/.

Commonwealth of Independent States. 2011. 'V stolitse Azerbaidzhana proshlo
zasedanie soveta rukovoditelei organov bezopasnosti i spetsial'nykh sluzhb
gosudarstv sodruzhestva'. 27 October. www.e-cis.info/page.php?id=19560.

Commonwealth of Independent States. 2012. 'Informatsiya ob ocherednom
zasedaniya Soveta ministrov vnutrennikh del gosudarstv – uchastinikov
Sodruzhestva Nezavisimykh Gosudarstv (7-8 Sentyabrya 2012 goda)'.
8 September. www.e-cis.info/page.php?id=22865.

Commonwealth of Independent States. 2013a. 'Informatsiya ob itogakh 34-go
zasedaniya Soveta rukovoditelei organov bezopasnosti i spetsial'nykh
sluzhba gosudarstv – uchastnikov Sodruzhestva Nezavisimykh Gosudarstv'.
15 May. www.e-cis.info/page.php?id=23446.

Commonwealth of Independent States. 2013b. 'Informatsiya ob
ocherednom zasedanii Soveta Ministrov Vnutrennikh Del Gosudarstv –
uchastnikov Sodruzhestva Nezavisimykh Gosudarstv'. 10–11 September.
www.e-cis.info/page.php?id=23673.

Commonwealth of Independent States. 2015. 'Informatsiya ob itogakh 38-
go zasedaniya Soveta rukovoditelei organov bezopasnosti i spetsial'nykh

sluzhba gosudarstv – uchastnikov Sodruzhestva Nezavisimykh Gosudarstv'.
26 May. www.e-cis.info/page.php?id=24693.

Commonwealth of Independent States. 2017. 'Informatsiya ob itogakh 43-
go zasedaniya Soveta rukovoditelei organov bezopasnosti i spetsial'nykh
sluzhb gosudarstv – uchastnikov Sodruzhestva Nezavisimykh
Gosudarstv'. 19 December. www.e-cis.info/page.php?id=26155.

Cooley, A. 2013. 'The League of Authoritarian Gentlemen'. Foreign Policy.
30 January. http://foreignpolicy.com/2013/01/30/the-league-of-
authoritarian-gentlemen/.

Cooley, A. 2015. 'Countering Democratic Norms'. *Journal of Democracy.*
26(3): 49–63.

Cooley, A., & Schaaf, M. 2017. 'The Rise of Authoritarian
Regionalism: Russia and China's Challenge to International Human
Rights and Law'. In *Shifting Power and Human Rights Diplomacy:
Russia*, edited by D. Lettinga and L. von Troost. March. www
.amnesty.nl/content/uploads/2017/03/Strategic-Studies-Russia-
web.pdf?x77572.

Coppedge, M., & Gerring, J. 2011. 'Conceptualizing and Measuring
Democracy: A New Approach'. *Studies in Comparative International
Development.* 9(2): 247–67.

Coppedge, M., Lindberg, S. I, Skaaning, S., & Teorell, J. 2016. 'Measuring
High Level Democratic Principles Using the V-Dem Data'. *International
Political Science Review.* 37(5): 580–93.

Coynash, H. 2014. 'Signed into Dictatorship'. Kharkiv Human Rights
Protection Group. 17 January. http://khpg.org/index.php?
id=1389993373.

Dagaev, D., Lamberova, N., Sobolev, A., & Sonin. K. 2014. 'The Arab
Spring Logic of the Ukrainian Revolution'. Free Policy Briefs. 31 March.
https://freepolicybriefs.org/2014/03/31/the-arab-spring-logic-of-the-
ukrainian-revolution/.

Davies, K. 2017. 'These Uncensored Questions Gatecrashed Putin's Annual
Call-In Marathon'. *The Moscow Times.* June 15. https://themoscowtimes
.com/articles/the-uncensored-questions-gatecrashing-putins-annual-call-
in-marathon-58203.

Dawisha. K. 2014. *Putin's Kleptocracy: Who Owns Russia?* New York:
Simon & Schuster Paperbacks.

de Borja Lasheras, F. 2016. 'Reforming Ukraine in Times of War and
Counter-Revolution'. *New Eastern Europe.* 6: 54–61.

Debre, M. J. 2021. 'The Dark Side of Regionalism: How Regional
Organizations Help Authoritarian Regimes to Boost Survival'.
*Democratization.* 28(2): 394–413.

Del Sordi, A., & Libman, A. 2020. 'Kazakhstan: A Possible Future Authoritarian Gravity Centre?' In *Authoritarian Gravity Centres: A Cross-Regional Study of Authoritarian Promotion and Diffusion*, edited by M. Kneuer & T. Demmelhuber (pp. 138–71). London: Routledge.

Demidetsky, V. 2017. 'Farit Mukhametshin: V rossiysko-moldavskikh otnosheniyakh nametilos' uluchshenie'. *Moldavskie Vedomosti*. 7 April (no. 13): 2.

Den'. 2015. 'Lozhkin naznachen zamestitelem glavy Natssoveta reform'. 3 June. https://day.kyiv.ua/ru/news/030615-lozhkin-naznachen-zamestitelem-glavy-nacsoveta-reform.

Denk, T. 2013. 'How to Measure Polyarchy with Freedom House: A Proposal for Revision'. *Quality and Quantity*. 47(6): 3457–71.

Dergachev, V., Maetnaya, E., & Rozhkova, N. 2016. 'General'skaya uborka'. *Gazeta*. 28 July. www.gazeta.ru/politics/2016/07/28_a_971634 5.shtml?updated.

Detektor. 2016. '"1 + 1", "Era", "112 Ukraina", NewsOne: chi kupuyut' ikh lyudi Poroshenko?' 29 August. http://detector.media/medialife/article/118246/2016-08-29-11-era-112-ukraina-newsone-chi-kupuyut-ikh-lyudi-poroshenka/.

Diamond, L. 2008. 'The Democratic Rollback'. *Foreign Affairs*. 87(2): 36–48.

Diamond, L., Plattner, M. F., & Walker, C. 2016. 'Introduction'. In *Authoritarianism Goes Global: The Challenge to Democracy*, edited by M. F. Plattner, L. Diamond, & C. Walker (pp. 3–19). Baltimore: Johns Hopkins University Press.

Dimitrov, M. K. 2013. 'Understanding Communist Collapse and Resilience'. In *Why Communism Did Not Collapse: Understanding Authoritarian Regime Resilience in Asia and Europe* (pp. 3–39), edited by M. K. Dimitrov. New York: Cambridge University Press.

Dodon, I. 2017a. 'Igor' Dodon provel vstrechu s kitaiskoi delegatsiei pod rukovodstvom gospodina Chizhai Chun'syan'. 6 April. www.presedinte.md/rus/presa/igor-dodon-a-avut-o-intrevedere-cu-o-delegatie-chineza-condusa-de-dl-zhang-chunxian.

Dodon, I. 2017b. 'Prezident Respubliki Moldova obratilsya k chlenam Vysshego Soveta Bezopasnosti s trebovan'em proyavit' otvetstvennost' i predannost' natsional'nym interesam'. 29 August. www.presedinte.md/rus/css-comunicate-de-presa/presedintele-republicii-moldova-a-cerut-membrilor-consiliului-suprem-de-securitate-responsabilitate-si-devotament-intereselor-nationale.

Dodon, I. 2018. 'Prezident strany provel zasedanie Vysshego soveta bezopasnosti'. 7 March. www.presedinte.md/rus/css-comunicate-de-presa/presedintele-tarii-a-prezidat-sedinta-consiliului-suprem-de-securitate.

Dodon, I. 2019a. 'Prezident Respubliki Moldova provel vstrechu s Prezidentom Respubliki Kazakhstan'. 28 May. www.presedinte.md/rus/presa/presedin tele-republicii-moldova-a-avut-o-intrevedere-cu-presedintele-republicii-kazahstan.

Dodon, I. 2019b. 'Prezident Respubliki Moldova provel vstrechu s Prem'r-ministrom Respubliki Singapur'. 30 September. https://presedinte .md/rus/presa/presedintele-republicii-moldova-a-avut-o-intrevedere-cu-prim-ministrul-republicii-singapore.

Dolowitz, D. P., & Marsh, D. 1996. 'Who Learns What from Whom: A Review of the Policy Transfer Literature'. *Political Studies*. 44(2): 343–57.

Dovnar, V. 2003. 'Tri Opory dlya Gosudarstva: Dve uzhe postroeny'. *Belgazeta*. 20 January. www.belgazeta.by/ru/2003_01_20/sobytiya_ot senki/5136/.

Dovnar, V. 2004. 'ZUBRSM'. *Belgazeta*. 8 March. www.belgazeta.by/ru/2 004_03_08/tema_nedeli/7230/.

Dubina, Y. 2017. 'Lukashenko i Kitai: polety vo sne i nayavu'. UDF.by. 5 May. http://udf.by/news/sobytie/156282-lukashenko-i-kitay-polety-vo-sne-i-nayavu.html.

Dubrovyk-Rohova, A. 2015. 'Vladimir Groysman: 'My – parlamentsko-prezidentskaya republika, i eto ne poddaetsya revizii'. *Den*. 17 April (no 67).

Economy, E. C. 2018. 'The Great Firewall of China: Xi Jingpin's Internet Shutdown'. *The Guardian*. 29 June. www.theguardian.com/news/2018/j un/29/the-great-firewall-of-china-xi-jinpings-internet-shutdown.

Efremov, A. 2019. 'Pochemu Ya NE VERYu v samoubiystvo Yuriya Lunkashu, o chernoi metke Vladu Plakhotnyuku, ili kto puskaet nas po lozhnomu sledu'. AVA. 18 August. https://ava.md/2019/08/18/pochemu-ya-ne-veryu-v-samoubiystvo-yuriya/.

Eggert, K. 2018. 'To Challenge Putin's Regime'. *New Eastern Europe*. 2: 14–20.

EJ.by. 2018. '"Myzhiki, lushe bednee, no na svobode". Lukashenko snova vyskalsya o korruptsii'. UDF. 15 November. https://udf.by/news/politic/1 83276-muzhiki-luchshe-bednee-no-na-svobode-lukashenko-snova-vyskazalsya-o-korrupcii.html.

Ekonomicheskaya Pravda. 2017. 'Klyuevy dolzhny ukrainskim gosbankam 28 milliardov – SMI'. *Ekonomicheskaya Pravda*. 15 June. www .epravda.com.ua/rus/news/2017/06/15/626045/.

Ekonomichna Pravda. 2018. 'Soratnik Medvedchuka stav vlasnikom telekanalu "112 Ukraina"'. *Ekonomicheskaya Pravda*. 14 December. w ww.epravda.com.ua/news/2018/12/14/643588/.

E'kspert. 2016. 'Natsional'naya gvardiya'. *E'kspert*. 11 April (no. 15): 7.

Eremenko, A., Silina, T., Skolotyanyi, Y., Izhak, A., & Lantan, A. 2013. 'Zapomni, kak vse nachinalos''. *Zerkalo Nedeli*. 21 December (no. 48): 1.

Eristavi, M. 2017. 'Ukraine Is in the Middle of a Counterrevolution Again: Is Anyone Paying Attention?' Atlantic Council. 29 March. www .atlanticcouncil.org/blogs/ukrainealert/ukraine-is-in-the-middle-of-counterrevolution-again-is-anyone-paying-attention.

EurAsia Daily. 2018. 'Pochemu posol Rossii v Belorussii dolzhen byt' zamenen'. EurAsia Daily. 28 May. https://eadaily.com/ru/news/2018/05/ 28/pochemu-posol-rossii-v-belorussii-dolzhen-byt-zamenyon.

Euromaidan Press. 2014. 'Who Destroyed the Ukrainian Army?' Euromaidan Press. 16 July. http://euromaidanpress.com/2014/07/16/wh o-destroyed-the-ukrainian-army/.

Evropeiskaya Pravda. 2018. 'Poroshenko dolzhen razrovat' dipotnosheniya s Rossei. Argumentov protiv – ne sushchestvuet'. Evropeiskaya Pravda. 26 November. www.eurointegration.com.ua/rus/articles/2018/11/26/708 9847/.

Fadeyev, A. V. 2015. 'A vremeni vse men'she. Lukashenko sam gotovit pochvu dlya belorusskogo maidana?' Materik. 29 January. www .materik.ru/rubric/detail.php?ID=19384.

Falaleev, M. 2005. 'Sobytiya i kommentarii. Nurgaliev prismatrivaetsya k granitse'. *Rossiyskaya Gazeta*. 24 September (no. 214): 3.

Falaleev, M. 2007. 'Nurgaliev sozdaet spetslaboratorii'. *Rossiyskaya Gazeta*. 31 October (no. 243): 3.

Falaleev, M. 2008. 'Nurgaliev vzyalsya za vospitanie'. *Rossiyskaya Gazeta* 2 July (no. 140): 2.

Falaleev, M. 2016. 'Gvardiya rotova'. *Rossii'skaya Gazeta*. 11 November (no. 256): 7.

Falyakov, R. 2017. 'Kishinev prismotrit za Moskvoi'. *Gazeta*. 14 April. w ww.gazeta.ru/business/2017/04/14/10626587.shtml.

Finkel, E., & Brudny, Y. M. 2012. 'Russia and the Colour Revolutions'. *Democratization*. 19(1): 15–36.

Fontanka. 2018. '17 osnovnykh predlozheny no smyagcheniyu pensionnoi reform s zasedaniya "Edinoi Rossii"'. Fontanka. 20 August. www .fontanka.ru/2018/08/20/066/.

Forina, A. 2013. 'Kazakhstan, Ukraine ties survive Soviet collapse'. *Kyiv Post*. 12 September. www.kyivpost.com/article/content/ukraine-politics/ kazakhstan-ukraine-ties-survive-soviet-collapse-329301.html.

Frear, M. 2019. *Belarus under Lukashenka: Adaptive Authoritarianism*. London: Routledge.

Gabuev, A., & Umarov, T. 2022. 'Nur-Sultan bez Nazarbaeva. O prichinakh i posledstviyakh. Krizisa v Kazakhstane'. Carnegie. 7 January. https://car negie.ru/commentary/86147.

Galeotti, M. 2015. '"Hybrid War" and "Little Green Men": How It Works, and How It Doesn't'. In *Ukraine and Russia: People, Politics, Propaganda and Perspectives,* edited by A. Pikulicka-Wilczewska & R. Sakwa. Bristol: E-International Relations Publishing. www.e-ir.info/wp-content/uploads/2015/03/Ukraine-and-Russia-E-IR.pdf.

Galeotti, M. 2016. 'Don't Buy the Hype: Russia's Military Is Much Weaker Than Putin Wants Us to Think'. Vox. 23 February. www.vox.com/2016/2/23/11092614/putin-army-threat.

Galeotti, M. 2017. 'The Ulyukayev Verdict Heralds the End of Putinism (Op-ed)'. 18 December. https://themoscowtimes.com/articles/ulyukayev-verdict-heralds-end-of-putinism-op-ed-59969.

Galeotti, M. 2018a. 'A Tale of Two Putins'. *New Eastern Europe.* 2: 7–13.

Galeotti, M. 2018b. 'Putin Will Elevate Loyalty Over All in His Next Presidency'. Raam op Rusland. 7 January. https://raamoprusland.nl/dossiers/kremlin/823-putin-will-elevate-loyalty-over-all-in-his-next-presidency.

Galeotti, M. 2019a. 'Russia and China's Cosplay Alliance'. *The Moscow Times.* 22 August. www.themoscowtimes.com/2019/08/22/russia-and-chinas-cosplay-alliance-a66973.

Galeotti, M. 2019b. 'Russia's Opposition Has a Long Way to Go'. *The Moscow Times.* 12 August. www.themoscowtimes.com/2019/08/12/russias-opposition-has-a-long-way-to-go-a66810.

Galeotti, M. 2019c. 'The Old Ultra-Violence in Moscow Solves Nothing and Everything'. *The Moscow Times.* 5 August. www.themoscowtimes.com/2019/08/05/the-old-ultra-violence-in-moscow-solves-nothing-and-everything-a66706.

Galyatkin, A., Marokhovskaya, A., Dolinina, I., & Tsybulina, E. 2017. 'Deneg net? Derzhite!' *Novaya Gazeta.* 20 March (no. 28): 2–5.

Gamova, S. 2017. 'Taina vizita Zam.ministra MID Karasina v Kishinev, kazhetsya, raskryta'. *Nezavisimaya Gazeta.* 14 March (no. 50): 1.

Gamova, S. 2019. 'Dodon i Plahotniyuk delyat Moldove'. NG. 9 June. www.ng.ru/cis/2019-06-09/5_7594_moldova.html.

Gat, A. 2008. 'Return of Foreign Great Powers'. *Foreign Affairs.* 86(4): 59–69.

Gazeta.ru. 2009. 'Voronin poblagodaril Medvedeva za podderzhku vo vremya mitingov'. Gazeta. 24 April. www.gazeta.ru/news/lenta/2009/04/24/n_1355483.shtml.

Gazeta.ru. 2010. 'Odin v Minske khozyain'. *Gazeta.* 24 December. www.gazeta.ru/comments/2010/12/24_e_3477174.shtml.

Gazeta.ru. 2012. 'Uvolen genkonstruktor GLONASS Yuriy Urlichich'. *Gazeta.* 11 November. www.gazeta.ru/politics/news/2012/11/11/n_2611761.shtml.

Gazeta.ru. 2014. 'Kolokoltsev: sotrudniki 'Berkuta' budut vostrebovany v Rossii'. *Gazeta*. 19 March. www.gazeta.ru/politics/news/2014/03/19/n _6022257.shtml.

Gazeta.ru. 2017. 'Dodon vstretilsya s rossiyskim poslom v Kishineve'. *Gazeta*. 30 August. www.gazeta.ru/politics/news/2017/08/30/n_105006 92.shtml.

Gel'man, V. 2010. 'The Dynamics of Sub-National Authoritarianism: Russia in Comparative Perspective'. In *The Politics of Sub-National Authoritarianism in Russia*, edited by V. Gel'man and C. Ross (pp. 1–18). Farnham: Ashgate Publishing.

Gel'man, V. 2015a. *Authoritarian Russia: Analyzing Post-Soviet Regime Changes*. Pittsburgh: University of Pittsburgh Press.

Gel'man, V. 2015b. 'Politika strakha: kak rossiiskii rezhim protivostoit svoim protivnikam'. *Kontrapunkt*. 1: 1–11.

Gente, Regis. 2015. 'Bălți's Prodigal Son'. Open Democracy. 28 October. www.opendemocracy.net/od-russia/regis-gente/b-l-is-prodigal-son.

George, A. L., & Bennett, A. 2005. *Case Studies and Theory Development in the Social Sciences*. Cambridge, MA: MIT Press.

Gerasimenko, O. 2009. '"Khorosho, chto ya plavan'em zanimalsya"'. *Gazeta*. 21 August. www.gazeta.ru/social/2009/08/21/3238903.shtml.

Gerasimov, V. 2013. 'Tsennost' Nauki v Predvidenii'. *VPK. Voenno-Promyshlennyi Kur'er*. 27 February (no. 9): 1.

Gershman, C., & Allen, M. 2006. 'New Threats to Freedom: The Assault on Democracy Assistance'. *Journal of Democracy*. 17(2): 36–51.

Gessen, M. 2014. *The Man without a Face: The Unlikely Rise of Vladimir Putin*. 2nd ed. London: Granta Books.

Gevorkyan, N., Timakova, N., & Kolesnikov, A. 2000. *Ot pervogo litsa: razgovory s Vladimirom Putinom*. Moscow: Vagrius.

Gherasimov, C. 2017. 'Moldova: The Captured State on Europe's Edge'. Chatham House. 8 March. www.chathamhouse.org/expert/comment/mol dova-captured-state-europe-s-edge.

Giannone, D. 2010. 'Political and Ideological Aspects in the Measurement of Democracy: The Freedom House Case'. *Democratization*. 17(1): 68–97.

Glasius, M. 2018. 'What Authoritarianism Is... and Is Not: A Practice Perspective'. *International Affairs*. 94(3): 515–33.

Goncharenko, R. 2014. 'Titushki – The Ukrainian President's Hired Strongmen'. Deutsche Welle. 19 February. www.dw.com/en/titushki-the-ukrainian-presidents-hired-strongmen/a-17443078.

Gonzalez-Ocantos, E., & LaPorte, J. 2021. 'Process Tracing and the Problem of Missing Data'. *Sociological Methods & Research*. 50(3): 1407–35.

Gorchinskaya, K. 2013. 'Yanukovych's Trip, Azarov's Comments Indicate New Shift Towards Russia'. *Kyiv Post*. 11 November. www.kyivpost.com /article/content/ukraine-politics/yanukovychs-trip-azarovs-comments-indicate-new-shift-towards-russia-331716.html.

Gorchinskaya, K., & Marchak, D. 2013. 'Russia Gives Ukraine Cheap Gas, $15 Billion in Loans'. 17 December. www.kyivpost.com/article/content/ ukraine-politics/russia-gives-ukraine-cheap-gas-15-billion-in-loans-3338 52.html.

Gorchak, O. 2019. 'SIB postavyat na mesto. Spetssluzhbu vozvrashchayut pod chastichnyi kontrol' prezidenta'. NewsMaker. 25 June. https://newsmaker .md/rus/novosti/sib-postavyat-na-mesto-spetssluzhbu-vozvrashchayut-pod-chastichnyy-kontrol-prezide-44499.

Gordonua.com. 2017a. 'Dodon prizval vlasti Moldovy vernut'sya k strategicheskomu partnerstvu s Rossiei'. Gordon. 27 November. http:// gordonua.com/news/worldnews/dodon-prizval-vlasti-moldovy-vernutsya -k-strategicheskomu-partnerstvu-s-rossiey-219301.html.

Gordonua.com. 2017b. 'Sud v Krasnodare prodlil arrest Gribu do 4 marta'. Gordon. 15 December. http://gordonua.com/news/politics/sud-v-krasno dare-prodlil-arest-gribu-do-4-marta-otec-222311.html.

Gordonua.com. 2017c. 'Ukrainskiy ofitser Grib zayavil, chto FSB pokhitila ego syna v Belarusi'. 28 August. http://gordonua.com/news/localnews/uk rainskiy-oficer-grib-zayavil-chto-fsb-pohitila-ego-syna-v-belarusi-204549 .html.

Goscilo, H. 2011. 'The Ultimate Celebrity: VVP as VIP *objet d'art*'. In *Celebrity and Glamour in Contemporary Russia: Shocking Chic*, edited by H. Goscillo & V. Strukov (pp. 29–55). London: Routledge.

Goscilo, H. 2013. 'Putin's Performance of Masculinity: The Action Hero and Macho Sex-Object'. In *Putin as Celebrity and Cultural Icon*, edited by H. Goscillo (pp. 180–207). London: Routledge.

Grabovsky, S. 2012. 'Yak treba buduvati armiyu ta flot: chomu Ukraina – ne Singapur?' Tyzhden. 6 December. https://tyzhden.ua/World/66824.

Grani.ru. 2017. 'Pervoaprel'skoe vozbuzhdenie'. Grani.ru. 4 January. http s://grani-ru-org.appspot.com/Society/Law/m.259916.html.

Greer Meisels, A. 2012. 'What China Learned from the Soviet Union's Fall'. The Diplomat. 27 July. https://thediplomat.com/2012/07/what-china-learned-from-the-soviet-unions-fall/.

Greer Meisels, A. 2013. 'Lessons Learned in China from the Collapse of the Soviet Union'. University of Sydney. January. https://sydney.edu.au/china_ studies_centre/images/content/ccpublications/policy_paper_series/2013/ Lessons-learned-in-China-from-the-collapse-of-the-Soviet-Union.shtml.pdf.

Gregory. P., & Zhou, K. 2009. 'How China Won and Russia Lost'. *Policy Review*. 158: 35–51.

Gretsky, I. 2018. 'Belarus in a Post-Crimean Deadlock'. *New Eastern Europe*. 6: 157–62.

Gritsanov, A. 2007. 'Byurokratizm: uzhe, no glubzhe'. *BelGazeta*. 16 July. www.belgazeta.by/ru/2007_07_16/mneniya/14434/.

Gryl', Y. 2004. 'Gadanie na uglevodorodnoi gushche'. *BelGazeta* 14 June (no. 23).

Gryl', Y. 2005a. 'Den' pominoveniya edineniya'. *BelGazeta*. 4 April (no. 13).

Gryl', Y. 2005b. 'V shineli zheleznogo feliksa'. *BelGazeta*. 26 September (no. 38).

Gryl', Y. 2009. 'Komu nalevo, komu napravo'. *BelGazeta*. 2 February (no. 4).

Gryl', Y. 2012. 'Molodo. Krasno-zeleno'. *BelGazeta*. 17 September. www .belgazeta.by/ru/2012_09_10/event/24802/.

Gryl', Y. 2016. 'Otkude priletit'. *BelGazeta*. 28 July. www.belgazeta.by/ru/ 1056/topic_week/33194/.

Guihai, G. 2010. 'The Influence of the Collapse of the Soviet Union on China's Political Choices'. In *China Learns From the Soviet Union, 1949 – Present*, edited by T. P. Bernstein & H. Li. Lanham, MD, Boulder, CO, New York (pp. 505–16). Plymouth: Lexington Books.

Gunitsky, S. 2015a. 'How Do You Measure "Democracy"?' *Washington Post*. 23 June. www.washingtonpost.com/news/monkey-cage/wp/2015/0 6/23/how-do-you-measure-democracy/.

Gunitsky, S. 2015b. 'Lost in the Gray Zone: Competing Measures of Democracy in the Former Soviet Republics'. In *Ranking the World: Grading States as a Tool of Global Governance*, edited by A. Cooley & J. Snyder (pp. 112–50). Cambridge: Cambridge University Press.

Gusev, L. 2010. 'Eliksir politicheskogo dolgoletiya Nursultana Nazarbaeva'. *Tribuna*. 28 October (no. 42): 7.

Guseva, D. 2005. 'Pokazatel'naya parka. Duma obeshchaet ustroit' Mikhailu Fradkovu "khoroshuyu banyu"'. *Vremya Novostei*. 8 February (no. 20): 2.

Haas, E. B. 1991. 'Collective Learning: Some Theoretical Speculations'. In *Learning in U.S. and Soviet Foreign Policy*, edited by G. W. Breslauer & P. E. Tretlock (pp. 62–99). Boulder: Westview Press.

Haase, K. 2012. 'Dvor vmesto politbyuro: Chto proiskhodit s okruzheniem Putina'. Carnegie. 25 August. http://carnegie.ru/com mentary/72910.

Hale, H. E. 2013. 'Did the Internet Break the Political Machine? Moldova's 2009 Twitter Revolution that Wasn't'. *Demokratizatsiya*. 21(4): 481–505.

Hale, H. E. 2015. *Patronal Politics: Eurasian Regime Dynamics in Comparative Perspective*. New York: Cambridge University Press.

Hall, S. G. F. 2017a. 'Learning from Past Experience: Yanukovych's Implementation of Authoritarianism after 2004'. *Journal of Eurasian Studies*. 8(2): 161–71.

Hall, S. G. F. 2017b. 'Preventing a Colour Revolution: The Belarusian Example as an Illustration for the Kremlin?' *East European Politics*. 33 (2): 162–83.

Hall, S. G. F., & Ambrosio, T. 2017. 'Authoritarian Learning: A Conceptual Overview'. *East European Politics*. 33(2): 143–61.

Hansbury, P. 2016. 'Brothers In Arms: Russia In Belarus's New Military Doctrine'. *Belarus Digest*. 5 September. http://belarusdigest.com/story/brothers-arms-russia-belarus%E2%80%99s-new-military-doctrine -27104.

Hansbury, P. 2017. 'Bringing Belarus Back Into Line?' New Eastern Europe. 12 April. www.neweasterneurope.eu/articles-and-commentary/2326-bringing-belarus-back-into-line.

Haran, O. 2013. 'President Yanukovych's Growing Authoritarianism: Does Ukraine Still Have European Prospects?' PONARS Eurasia Policy Memo no. 265. July 2013. www.ponarseurasia.org/sites/default/files/policy-memos-pdf/Pepm_265_Haran_July2013_0.pdf.

Harding, L. 2009. 'Moldova Forces Regain Control of Parliament After "Twitter Revolution"'. *The Guardian*. 8 April. www.theguardian.com/w orld/2009/apr/08/moldova-protest-election-chisinau.

Harding, L. 2017. 'The Global Laundromat: How Did it Work and Who Benefited?' *The Guardian*. 20 March. www.theguardian.com/world/201 7/mar/20/the-global-laundromat-how-did-it-work-and-who-benefited.

Heilmann, S. 2008. 'Policy Experimentation in China's Economic Rise'. *Studies in Comparative International Development*. 43(1): 1–26.

Hill, F., & Gaddy, C. G. 2015. *Mr. Putin: Operative in the Kremlin*. Washington, DC: Brookings Institution Press.

Hiymol', A. 2014. 'Kitais'ka perspektiva'. *Ukrains'kiy Tizhden*. 27(347).

Horesh, N. 2015. 'The Growing Appeal of China's Model of Authoritarian Capitalism, and How It Threatens the West'. *South China Morning Post*. 19 July. www.scmp.com/comment/insight-opinion/article/1840920/growing-appeal-chinas-model-authoritarian-capitalism-and-how.

Horvath, R. 2013. *Putin's Preventive Counter-Revolution: Post-Soviet Authoritarianism and the Spectre of Velvet Revolution*. London: Routledge.

Hosa, J., & Wilson, A. 2019. 'Zelensky Unchained: What Ukraine's New Political Order Means for Its Future'. European Council on Foreign Relations. 25 September. https://ecfr.eu/publication/zelensky_unchained_what_ukraines_new_political_order_means_for_its_future/.

Igorev, A. 2014a. 'Vladimir Kolokol'tsev osvobodil kresla vokrug sebya'. *Kommersant-Daily*. 31 May (no. 97): 1.

Igorev, A. 2014b. 'Vladimir Kolokol'tsev sobiraet druzhiny'. *Kommersant-Daily*. 25 September (no. 173): 5.

Inanets, S. 2017. 'Interv'yu s Viktorom Shenderovichem. Pro belorusskie korni, Lukashenko, Putina i "kukly" nashego vremeni'. Tut.by. 25 July https://news.tut.by/society/544566.html.

Instituta stran SNG. 2016. 'Vlasti Respubliki Belarus' protiv Georgievskoi lenty i "Bessmertnogo polka"'. Ross-bel.ru. 12 May. http://ross-bel.ru/ab out/news_post/vlasti-respubliki-belarus-protiv-georgiyevskoy-lenty-i-bess mertnogo-polka.

Interfax. 2016. 'Natsgvardeitsam razreshat strelyat' bez preduprezhdeniya'. Interfax. 6 April. www.interfax.ru/russia/502287.

Interfax-Ukraine. 2016. 'Editor of Forbes Ukriane Attacked in Kyiv Park'. Interfax. 20 July. http://en.interfax.com.ua/news/general/358830.html.

Ioffe, G. 2004. 'Understanding Belarus: Economy and Political Landscape'. *Europe-Asia Studies*. 56(1): 85–118.

Ioffe, G. 2014. *Reassessing Lukashenka: Belarus in Cultural and Geopolitical Context*. Basingstoke: Palgrave Macmillan.

Ivanchenko, K. 2012. 'Sergei Levochkin: krysinyi korol''. Argument. 26 January. http://argumentua.com/stati/sergei-levochkin-krysinyi-korol.

Ivanov, K. 2017. 'Kazus Kochanova'. UDF. 5 July. http://udf.by/news/pol itic/159036-kazus-kochanovoy.html.

Ivanov, S. 2005. 'Na nevskom pyatachke'. *Sovetskaya Rossiya*. 18 January (no. 4): 1.

Ivanova, S., Grozovsky, B., & Bekker, A. 2005. 'Pensionery khvatilis' l'got'. *Vedomosti*. 12 January (no. 2).

Iwański, T. 2017. 'The Oligarchs Strike Back'. *New Eastern Europe*. 2: 73–9.

Izvestiya. 2004. 'Viktor Chernomyrdin, posol Rossii na Ukraine: Yan ad aforizmami ne razmyshlyayu, oni u menya sami vyletayut'. *Izvestiya*. 9 April (no. 64): 1.

Jacobs, H. 2014. 'Why Ukraine's Berkut Special Police Force Is So Scary'. Business Insider. 27 January. www.businessinsider.com/meet-the-ukraines-brutal-berkut-police-force-2014-1?IR=T.

James, O., & Lodge, M. 2003. 'The Limitations of "Policy Transfer" and "Lesson Drawing" for Public Policy Research'. *Political Studies Review*. 1 (2): 179–93.

Jurnal.md. 2015a. 'Memoriu: Spălări de mld. De $ şi atacuri raider prin justiţia din RM'. *Jurnal*. 4 November. www.jurnal.md/ro/justitie/2015/11/ 4/memoriu-spalari-de-mld-de-i-atacuri-raider-prin-justi-ia-din-rm-11763 56/?fb_comment_id=1013330022022305_1047832431905397#f30f15 f78e2e938.

Jurnal.md. 2015b. 'Şeful statului a convocat de urgenţă Consiliul Suprem de Securitate'. *Jurnal* 28 May. http://jurnal.md/ro/politic/2015/5/28/seful-statului-a-convocat-de-urgenta-consiliul-suprem de-securitate/.

Jurnal.md. 2016a. 'Deutsche Welle: Lipsa reformelor poate conduce la o "primăvară araba" în Moldova'. *Jurnal.* 16 April. www.jurnal.md/ro/politic/2016/4/16/deutsche-welle-lipsa-reformelor-poate-conduce-la-o-pri mavara-araba-in-moldova/.

Jurnal.md. 2016b. 'Jizdan and Pănzari, Who Serve Plahotniuc Are Accused and Summoned to Resign: On August 27 the Police Exceeded Any Limit, It Applied Force Against Women, Children, Old Men and Invalids'. *Jurnal.* 29 August. http://jurnal.md/en/social/2016/8/29/jizdan-and-panzari-accused-that-serve-plahotniuc-and-summoned-to-resign-on-august-27-the-police-exceeded-any-limit-it-applied-force-against-women-children-old-men-and-invalids/.

Jurnal.md. 2016c. 'Noua strategie a securităţii naţionale, adoptată la şedinţa Consiliului Suprem de Securitate: Când urmează să fine pus în aplicare documentul'. *Jurnal.* 21 June. www.jurnal.md/ro/politic/2016/6/21/noua-strategie-a-securitatii-nationale-adoptata-la-sedinta-consiliului-suprem-de-securitate-cand-urmeaza-sa-fie-pus-in-aplicare-documentul/.

Jurnal.md. 2016d. 'Plahotniuc vrea să-l facă ministru de Interne pe controversatul colonel de poliţie Alexandru Jizdan, demis anterior de la MAI'. *Jurnal.* 20 January. www.jurnal.md/ro/social/2016/1/20/plahot niuc-vrea-sa-l-faca-ministru-de-interne-pe-controversatul-colonel-de-politie-alexandru-jizdan-demis-anterior-de-la-mai/.

Jurnal.md. 2016e. 'Regimul care renaşte monştri: Torţionarii din 7 aprilie 2009, promovaţi de actuala guvernare în funcţii de conducere şi puşi să facă legea în Republica Moldova'. *Jurnal.* 7 April. www.jurnal.md/ro/social/2016/4/7/regimul-care-renaste-monstri-tortionarii-din-7-aprilie-2009-promovati-de-actuala-guvernare-in-functii-de-conducere-si-pusi-sa-faca-legea-in-republica-moldova/.

Jurnal.md. 2016f. 'Russian Laundromat: The Laundering of 20 Billion USD Through the Banking System of the RM Was Possible Through Legislative Amendments and the Permission of Politicians'. *Jurnal.* 12 December. www.jurnal.md/en/economic/2016/12/12/russian-laundromat-the-laundering-of-20-billion-usd-through-the-banking-system-of-the-rm-was-possible-through-legislative-amendments-and-the-permission-of-the-politics/.

Jurnal.md. 2017a. 'Dezvăliuri: Cifra reală a banilor spălaţi prin Laundromat este de 30 de miliarde de euro; Totul a fost coordonat de Plahotniuc, cu ajutorul lui Timofti, Platon şi Tănase (DOC)'. *Jurnal.* 15 May. www .jurnal.md/ro/economic/2017/5/15/radiografia-jafului-bancar-intr-undemers-catre-dodon-mihail-gofman-face-dezvaluiri-despre-plahotniuc-shor-si-timofti-doc/.

Jurnal.md. 2017b. 'Şeful PD Vladimir Plahotniuc, a anunţaat că legea ONG-urilor nu va mai fi modificată'. Jurnal. 12 September. http://jurnal.md/ro/politic/2017/9/12/seful-pd-vladimir-plahotniuc-a-anuntat-ca-legea-ong-urilor-nu-va-mai-fi-modificata/.

Jurnal.md. 2018. 'Lyudmila Kozlovska: Democraţia se prăbuşeşte în RM cu o viteză fără precedent; În spatele corupţiei sunt nume concrete, iar sancţiunile nominale impuse de UE autorităţilor – unica soluţie // INTERVIU'. *Jurnal.* 2 January. http://jurnal.md/ro/politic/2018/2/1/lyud mila-kozlovska-democratia-se-prabuseste-in-rm-cu-o-viteza-fara-precedent-in-spatele-coruptiei-sunt-nume-concrete-iar-sanctiunile-nominale-impuse-de-ue-autoritatilor-unica-solutie-interviu/.

Kachurka, R. 2014. 'Pro-Russian Groups Become More Active In Belarus'. *Belarus Digest.* 26 November. http://belarusdigest.com/story/pro-russian-groups-become-more-active-belarus-20470.

Kaczmarski, M. 2015. *Russia-China Relations in the Post-Crisis International Order.* London: Routledge.

Kagan, R. 2008. 'The End of the End of History'. New Republic. 23 April. https://newrepublic.com/article/60801/the-end-the-end-history.

Kalenyuk, D., Peklun, T., Moiseenko, A., Dyenkov, D., & Musayeva, S. 2018. '"Myl'nyi puzyr'" ili "konfiskatsiya veka" genpokurora Lutsenko'. *Ukrainskaya Pravda.* 10 January. www.pravda.com.ua/rus/articles/2018/01/10/7167931/.

Kalinkina, S. 2014. 'Yanychary'. UDF. 9 April. http://udf.by/news/main_news/99926-yanychary.html.

Kalymon, B. 2020. 'What Zelensky Must Do to Regain Credibility'. *Kyiv Post.* 4 April. www.kyivpost.com/article/opinion/op-ed/basil-kalymon-what-zelensky-must-do-to-regain-credibility.html.

Kanygin, P. 2011. 'Bat'ka Lukashenko: eto kakoi-to nemoi narod'. *Novaya Gazeta.* 24 June (no. 67): 1.

Kanygin, P. 2018. '"Bozvrashchat" nuzhno ne territorii, a lyudei'. *Novaya Gazeta.* 13 February. www.novayagazeta.ru/articles/2018/02/13/75504-vozvraschat-nuzhno-ne-territorii-a-lyudey.

Kapsamun, I. 2013. 'Tri naznacheniya i pyat' vyvodov…' *Den.* 11 January (no. 3).

Kapsamun, I. 2014. 'O "linii vodorazdela"'. *Den.* 19 June (no. 111).

Karbalevich, V. 2010. *Alexander Lukashenka: Politicheskiy Portret.* Moscow: Partizan.

Karbalevich, V. 2019. 'Prorossiyskie sily v okruzheniya Lukashenko prizvali ideologicheskiy "spetsnaz"'. UDF. 27 September. https://udf.by/news/pol

itic/199740-prorossijskie-sily-v-okruzhenija-lukashenko-prizvali-ideologicheskıj-specnaz.html.

Karpenko, M. 2019. '"Ya tozhe sidelv priemnoi: Na rybok smotrel"'. *Kommersant*. 26 February. www.kommersant.ru/doc/3895593?query=я%20тоже%20сидел%20в%20приемной%20на%20рынок%20смотрел.

Kazan'sky, D. 2015. 'Oligarch Turf Wars 2.0'. *Tyzhden*. 20 November. www.m.tyzhden.ua/publication/151993.

Keane, J. 2018. 'Phantom Democracy: Puzzle at the Heart of Chinese Politics'. *South China Morning Post*. 25 August. www.scmp.com/week-asia/politics/article/2161276/phantom-democracy-puzzle-heart-chinese-politics.

Khachatrian, M. 2021. 'Yerevan Unhappy With CSTO Response To Armenian-Azeri Border Dispute'. Azatutyun. 9 August. www.azatutyun.am/a/31401516.html.

Khilko, K. 2016. 'Prodolzhaetsya podgotovka k tret'emu forumu regionov'. *Belarus' Segodnya*. 26 February (no. 37).

Kizilov, E. 2018. 'Vykhod iz SNG: u Poroshenko zayavili, chto polnost'yu sotrudnichestvo ne prekratyat'. *Ukrainskaya Pravda*. 16 April. www.pravda.com.ua/rus/news/2018/04/16/7177801/.

Kneuer, M., & Demmelhuber, T. 2016. 'Gravity Centres of Authoritarian Rule: A Conceptual Approach'. *Democratization*. 23(5): 775–96.

Kneuer, M., Demmelhuber, T., Peresson, R., & Zumbrägel, T. 2019. 'Playing the Regional Card: Why and How Authoritarian Gravity Centres Exploit Regional Organisations'. *Third World Quarterly*. 40(3): 451–70.

Koch-Weser, I. 2011. 'What Drives China-Belarus Relations'. *Belarus Digest*. 26 March. https://belarusdigest.com/story/what-drives-china-belarus-relations/.

Koehler, K., Schmotz, A., & Tansey, O. 2016. 'Why It's Good for Dictators to Have Dictator Friends'. *Washington Post*. 15 September. www.washingtonpost.com/news/monkey-cage/wp/2016/09/15/why-its-good-for-dictators-to-have-dictator-friends/.

Kolesnikov, A. 2018a. 'Bednye v rayu'. *Gazeta*. 2 October. www.gazeta.ru/comments/column/kolesnikov/12003967.shtml.

Kolesnikov, A. 2018b. 'Kirogennaya ekonomika'. *Vedomosti*. 2 October. www.vedomosti.ru/opinion/columns/2018/10/02/782625-kriogennaya-ekonomika.

Kolesnikov, A. 2018c. 'Kovboi Mal'boro kremlevsky remeik'. Carnegie. 4 September. https://carnegie.ru/2018/09/04/ru-pub-77196.

Kolesnikov, A. 2018d. 'Nelevye povorot: kak ne sputat' sotsial'nyi protest s sotsialistichesky'. *RBC*. 29 October. www.rbc.ru/opinions/politics/29/10/2018/5bd5a2cf9a79470e474b4988?from=center_53.

Kolesnikov, A. 2018e. 'Prishla povestka: kak biznes vybiraet mezhdu dumua versiyami goskapitalizma'. *RBC*. 27 August. www.rbc.ru/opinions/polit ics/27/08/2018/5b8285ab9a79471f2a851fef?from=center_5.

Kommersant. 2018. '"Putin slishkom uzh otkrovenno vzyal vse na sebya"'. *Kommersant*. 29 August. www.kommersant.ru/doc/3726480.

Kommersant. 2019. 'Moldavskie SMI opublikovali kompromat na Dodon'. *Kommersant*. 6 August. www.kommersant.ru/doc/3997626.

Kondratov, V. 2010. 'Chornovil: Esli tak poidet dal'she, to v 2015-m posadyat Yanukovicha'. *Liga.* 24 December. http://news.liga.net/inter view/politics/498579-chornovil-esli-tak-poydet-dalshe-to-v-2015-m-posa dyat-yanukovicha.htm.

Kononczuk, W. 2016. 'Oligarchs after the Maidan: The Old System in a "New" Ukraine'. *Point of View*. August (no. 59).

Kontsyu, M. 2010. 'Moldavskiy prem'er uzhe stal golovnoi bol'yu i dlya Evropy'. *Nezavisimaya Moldova*. 29 April (no. 57): 1.

Korchenkova, N. 2015. '"Pryamaya liniya' v stolichnom vospriyatii'. *Kommersant Daily*. 18 April (no. 69): 2.

Korchenkova, N., & Miller, L. 2015. 'Pryamaya liniya Vladimira Putina prodemonstrirovala stabil'nost". *Kommersant Daily*. 17 June (no. 107): 2.

Korchenkova, N., & Samokhina, S. 2015. 'Pryamaya liniya sobrala ne vsekh'. *Kommersant Daily*. 30 April (no. 76): 2.

Korosteleva, E. 2012. 'Questioning Democracy Promotion: Belarus' Response to the "Colour Revolutions"'. *Democratization*. 19(1): 37–59.

Korrespondent.net. 2013. 'Istoriya odnoi Sem'i. Korrespondent vyyasnil secret stremitel'nogo kar'ernogo rosta okruzheniya syna Yanukovicha'. Korrespondent.net. 8 February. https://korrespondent.net/ukraine/polit ics/1497612-istoriya-odnoj-semi-korrespondent-vyyasnil-sekret-stremitelnogo-karernogo-rosta-okruzheniya-syna-yanu.

Koshkina, S. 2015. *Maidan: Nerasskazannaya istoriya*. Kyiv: Brait Star Pablishing.

Koshkina, S. 2016. 'Igor Rainin: "Vtoroi srok Poroshenko? A chto, est' al'ternativa?"' LB. 16 October. https://lb.ua/news/2016/10/16/347922_i gor_raynin_vtoroy_srok.html.

Koshkina, S. 2017a. 'Imenem vtorogo sroka: Konstitutsiya – izmenit' nel'zya ostavit". LB. 13 April. https://lb.ua/news/2017/04/13/363845_imenem_v torogo_sroka_konstitutsiya-.html.

Koshkina, S. 2017b. 'Konservatsiya'. LB. 27 January. https://lb.ua/news/20 17/01/27/357039_konservatsiya.html.

Kostenko, N., Kornya, A., & Khimshiashvili, P. 2012. 'Trening Volodina'. *Vedomosti*. 24 August (no. 159).

Kot, G. 2017. '"Marsh netuneyadtsev": otkuda vzyalsya rost protestov v Belorussi'. BBC. 15 March. www.bbc.com/russian/other-news -39277515.

Kovachich, L. 2019. 'Russia Flirts with Internet Sovereignty'. *The Moscow Times*. 1 February. www.themoscowtimes.com/2019/02/01/russia-flirts-with-internet-sovereignty-op-ed-a64369.

Kovalenko, I. 2006a. 'Na ulitse igra ne dovodit do dobra'. *Belarus' Segodnya*. 17 March (no. 50): 1.

Kovalenko, I. 2006b. '"Revolyutsiya" otmenyaetsya…' *Belarus' Segodnya* (no. 41): 2.

Kovensky, J. 2018. 'Upcoming Manafort Trial to Spotlight Ukrainian Oligarchs, Politicians'. *Kyiv Post*. 10 September. www.kyivpost.com/ukr aine-politics/upcoming-manafort-trial-to-spotlight-ukrainian-oligarchs-politicians.html.

Kozhenikova, G. 2000. 'Yuri Sivakov snova v oboime. Proshlo chut' bolee polugoda, i byvshiy ministr vnutennikh del RB, uvolennyi s formulirovkoi – po sostoyaniyu zdorov'ya, opyat' prizvan na sluzhbu gosudarevu'. Tut.by. 15 November. https://news.tut.by/society/971.html.

Kozlova, N. 2006. 'Nurgaliyev otsenil spetsnaz'. *Rossiyskaya Gazeta*. 29 September (no. 218): 2.

Krackhardt, D., & Stern, R. N. 1988. 'Informal Networks and Organizational Crises: An Experimental Simulation'. *Social Psychology Quarterly*. 51(2): 123–40.

Kramer, A. E. 2022. 'Poroshenko, Ex-President, Returns to Ukraine, Roiling Politics'. *New York Times*. 17 January. www.nytimes.com/2022/01/17/ world/europe/petro-poroshenko-russia-ukraine.html.

Krastev, I. 2006. 'Democracy's "Doubles"'. *Journal of Democracy*. 17(2): 52–62.

Kravchenko, V. 2010. 'Posol iz "piterskikh"'. *Zerkalo Nedeli*. 30 January (no. 3).

Kravets, R. 2018a. 'Akhmetov, L'ovochkin i Medvedchuk, abo Troe v partii, ne rakhuyuchi Rabinovicha'. *Ukrainskaya Pravda*. 26 September. www .pravda.com.ua/articles/2018/09/26/7193198/.

Kravets, R. 2018b. 'Treti lishniy. Pochemu Levochkin s Medvedchukom gotovyatsya k vyboram bez Akhmetova'. *Ukrainskaya Pravda*. 20 November. www.pravda.com.ua/rus/articles/2018/11/20/7198714/.

Kravets, R., & Romanenko, V. 2017. 'Artemenko podtverdi, chto letal v Moskvu'. *Ukrainskaya Pravda*. 27 February. www.pravda.com.ua/rus/ news/2017/02/27/7136598/.

Kremlin.ru. 2018a. 'Telefonnyi razgovor c ispolnyayushchim obyazannosti Prem'er-ministra Armenii Karenom Karapetyom'. April 26, 2018. http:// kremlin.ru/events/president/news/57368.

Kremlin.ru. 2018b. 'Telefonnyi razgovor c Prezidentom Armenii Armenom Sarkisyanom'. April 25, 2018. http://kremlin.ru/events/president/news/ 57365.

Kryat, D. 2014. 'Razgovor na odnom yazyke'. *Narodnaya Gazeta.* 16 May: 2.

Kudelia, S. 2014. 'The House That Yanukovych Built'. *Journal of Democracy.* 25(3): 19–34.

Kurlantzick, J. 2013. 'Why the "China Model" Isn't Going Away'. *The Atlantic.* 21 March. www.theatlantic.com/china/archive/2013/03/why-the-china-model-isnt-going-away/274237/.

Kvitka, Z. 2019. 'Kto takoi Vladimir Plakhotnyuk, kak on svyazn s Poroshenko i pochemu sbezhal iz Moldovy'. UA Portal. 28 July. www .uaportal.com/news/kto-takoj-vladimir-plahotnyuk-kak-on-svyazan-s-po roshenko-i-pochemu-sbezhal-iz-moldovyi.htm.

Kyiv Post. 2014. 'Opposition Leaders Call for People to Join Self-Defense Teams to Protect EuroMaidan'. *Kyiv Post.* 9 February. www .kyivpost.com/article/content/ukraine-politics/kyivs-weekly-sunday-rally-under-way-as-several-thousand-euromaidan-demonstrators-gather-3365 51.html.

Kyiv Post. 2018. 'Lutsenko Must Go'. *Kyiv Post.* 12 January. www .kyivpost.com/article/opinion/editorial/lutsenko-must-go.html.

Lai, H. 2016. *China's Governance Model: Flexibility and Durability of Pragmatic Authoritarianism.* London: Routledge.

Lankina, T., Libman, A., & Obydenkova, A. 2016. 'Authoritarian and Democratic Diffusion in Post-Communist Regions'. *Comparative Political Studies.* 49(12): 1599–629.

Larson, K. 2018. 'China's Belt and Road Initiative Finds Shaky Ground in Eastern Europe'. Medium post. https://medium.com/@Smalltofeds/chinas-belt-and-road-initiative-finds-shaky-ground-in-eastern-europe-acca69a62b32.

Lauder, M. A. 2018. '"Wolves of the Russian Spring": Examination of Night Wolves as Proxy for Russian Government – Analysis'. Eurasia Review. 7 July. www.eurasiareview.com/07072018-wolves-of-the-russian-spring-examination-of-night-wolves-as-proxy-for-russian-government-analysis/.

Lave, J., & Wenger, E. 1991. *Situated Learning: Legitimate Peripheral Participation.* New York: Cambridge University Press.

Lavnekevich, D. 2012. 'Seichas interesy Putina, Lukashenko i Nazarbayeva sovreshenno identichny'. *Gazeta.* 26 June. www.gazeta.ru/politics/2012/ 06/26_a_4642705.shtml.

Lavnekevich, D. 2017. 'Yuriy Tsarik: "Na 99% vse zavisit ot deistviy vlastei"'. *BelGazeta.* 26 March (no. 11).

Lazyuk, V. 2007. 'Sistemnyi analiz'. *Belarus' Segodnya*. 24 July (no. 135).

LB.ua. 2013. 'Putin posetil konferentsiyu Medvedchuka'. LB. 27 July. https://lb.ua/news/2013/07/27/215936_putin_posetil_konferentsiyu .html.

LB.ua. 2014a. 'K Poroshenko noch'yu prikhodili Kernes i Zurabov'. LB. 22 August. https://lb.ua/news/2014/08/22/276991_poroshenko_nochyu_ prihodyat_kernes.html.

LB.ua. 2014b. 'Pokhishcheniya i izbieniya aktivistov Maidana proiskhodil v tesnoi koorinatsii s militsiei Avakov'. LB. 3 April. https://lb.ua/news/20 14/04/03/261814_pohishcheniya_izbieniya_aktivistov.html.

LB.ua. 2015. 'Landikin v sude rasskazal, kak Efremov platil separatizm'. LB. 25 February. https://lb.ua/news/2015/02/25/296807_landik_sude_rasska zal_efremov.html.

LB.ua. 2016. 'Medvedchuk pozvolyayut letat'' v Moskvu v obkhod zapreta na pryamoe aviasoobshchenie (obnovleno)'. LB. 18 November. https://lb.ua/n ews/2016/11/18/351095_medvedchuku_pozvolyayut_letat_moskvu.html.

LB.ua. 2017a. 'Byshiy kreativnyi prodyuser kanala "112 Ukraina" stal instructorom Kremlya po Ukraine, - Yashin'. LB. 21 January. https://lb .ua/news/2017/01/21/356503_bivshiy_kreativniy_prodyuser_kanala .html.Former.

LB.ua. 2017b. 'Dopros Nalivaichenko v SBU svyazan s poletami Medvedchuka v Moskvu'. LB. 21 September. https://lb.ua/news/2017/09 /21/377148_dopros_nalivaychenko_sbu_svyazan.html.

LB.ua. 2017c. 'Lyashko potreboval ot Artemenko slozhit' mandat'. LB. 20 February. https://lb.ua/news/2017/02/20/359134_lyashko_potrebova l_artemenko.html.

LB.ua. 2017d. 'Lyashko soobshchil o vizite Artemenko v Moskvu pered obnarodovaniem "mornogo plana"'. LB. 22 February. https://lb.ua/new s/2017/02/22/359386_lyashko_soobshchil_vizite_artemenko.html.

LB.ua. 2019. 'Galva predvybornogo shtaba Zelenskogo poluchil dolzhnost' pervogo zamglavy SBU'. LB. 22 May. https://lb.ua/news/2019/05/22/427 529_glava_predvibornogo_shtaba.html.

Lebedko, A. 2017. 'Kochanova trollit Lukashenko'. UDF. 31 October. htt p://udf.by/news/politic/164289-kochanova-trollit-lukashenko.html.

Ledeneva, A. V. 2013. *Can Russia Modernise? Sistema, Power Networks and Informal Governance*. Cambridge: Cambridge University Press.

Lemon, E., & Antonov, O. 2020. 'Authoritarian Legal Harmonization in the Post-Soviet Space'. *Democratization*. 27(7): 1221–39.

Leshchenko, S. 2014a. 'Ukraine's Oligarchs Are Stilll Calling the Shots'. Foreign Policy. 14 August. http://foreignpolicy.com/2014/08/14/ukraines-oligarchs-are-still-calling-the-shots/.

Leshchenko, S. 2014b. 'Yanukovych's Secret Diaries'. Euromaidan Press. 11 March. http://euromaidanpress.com/2014/03/12/yanukovychs-secret-diaries/.

Levchenko, A. 2006. 'Kremlevskaya skleika'. *Gazeta*. 26 July. www.gazeta.ru/2006/07/26/oa_209572.shtml.

Levchenko, A. 2007. 'Preemnik vsplyvet v SovBeze'. *Gazeta*. 9 July. www.gazeta.ru/2007/07/09/oa_243930.shtml.

Levchenko, M. 2018. '"Nam vy takuyu diktaturu": kak v Kishineve prinyal Lukashenko'. UDF. 25 April. https://udf.by/news/politic/172756-nam-by-takuyu-diktaturu-kak-v-kishineve-prinyali-lukashenko.html.

Levitsky, S., & Way, L. A. 2005. 'International Linkage and Democratization'. *Journal of Democracy*. 16(3): 20–34.

Levitsky, S., & Way, L. A. 2006. 'Linkage versus Leverage: Rethinking the International Dimension of Regime Change'. *Comparative Politics*. 38(4): 379–400.

Levitsky, S., & Way, L. A. 2010. *Competitive Authoritarianism: Hybrid Regimes after the Cold War*. New York: Cambridge University Press.

Levy, J. 1994. 'Learning and Foreign Policy: Sweeping a Conceptual Minefield'. *International Organization*. 48(2): 279–312.

Libman, A., & Obydenkova, A. V. 2018. 'Understanding Authoritarian Regionalism'. *Journal of Democracy*. 29(4): 151–65.

Liga.net. 2007. 'Partiya regionov i "Edinaya Rossiya" ukreplyayut druzhbu'. Liga. 8 June. http://news.liga.net/news/politics/345167-partiya-regionov-i-edinaya-rossiya-ukreplyayut-druzhbu.htm.

Liga.net. 2016. 'V Kieve izbit zhurnalist Sergei Golovnev'. Liga. 26 July. http://news.liga.net/news/incident/11867628-v_kieve_izbit_zhurnalist_sergey_golovnev.htm.

Lindberg, S. I., Coppedge, M., Gerring, J., & Teorell, J. 2014. 'V-Dem: A New Way to Measure Democracy'. *Journal of Democracy*. 25(3): 159–69.

Litvinova, D. 2016. 'Putin's Game of Thrones: The Men in Epaulets Take Over'. *The Moscow Times*. 29 July. www.themoscowtimes.com/2016/07/29/game-of-thrones-russian-regions-and-districts-get-new-leaders-in-epaulets-a54782.

Lo, B. 2008. *Axis of Convenience: Moscow, Beijing, and the new Geopolitics*. Baltimore: Brookings Institution Press.

Logos-Press. 2012. 'Reforma TsBEPK: popytka N 10'. *Logos-Press*. 13 July (no. 25).

Logos-Press. 2014. 'Farit Mukhametshin: "Posle podpisaniya dogovarivat'sya budet slozhnee"'. *Logos-Press*. 11 April (no. 13).

Logos-Press. 2015. '"Rossiyskaya strona ne namerena vozvodit' vokrug sebya steny i tem bolee, otgorazhivat'sya ot moldavskogo naroda" – Mukhametshin'. *Logos-Press*. 5 February (no. 5).

Lossovskaya, N. 2015. 'Mozhet li "Singapurskaya model" byt' primenima v nashei strane?' *Den'*. 18 August (no. 147).

Loushnikova, E. 2015. 'The "Parasite Law" in Belarus'. Open Democracy. 16 June. www.opendemocracy.net/en/odr/parasite-law-in-belarus/.

Lubina, M. 2017. *Russia and China: A Political Marriage of Convenience – Stable and Successful*. Opladen: Barbara Budrich Publishers.

Lukashenka, A. 2002. 'Fragmenty iz vyctupleniya Prezidenta Republiki Belarus' pri predstavlenii ezhegodnogo Poslaniya Parlamentu Respubliki Belrus". 16 April. http://president.gov.by/ru/news_ru/view/fragmenty-iz-vystuplenija-prezidenta-respubliki-belarus-pri-predstavlenii-ezhegodnogo-poslanija-parlamentu-5784/.

Lukashenka, A. 2005. 'V Belarusi budut sokhraneny mir, spokoistvie i stabil'nost". 8 January. www.president.gov.by/ru/news_ru/view/v-belar usi-budut-soxraneny-mir-spokojstvie-i-stabilnost-2117/.

Lukashenka, A. 2011. 'Press-konferentsiya predstavitelyam Belorusskikh i zarubezhnykh SMI'. 23 December. http://president.gov.by/ru/news_ru/vie w/press-konferentsija-predstaviteljam-belorusskix-i-zarubezhnyx-smi-5967/.

Lukashenka, A. 2012. 'Aleksandr Lukashenko provel soveshchanie o sostoyanii raboty po privedeniyu Vooruzhennykh Sil i Gospogrankomiteta Belarusi v sootvetstvie s sovremennymi trebovaniyami'. 26 July. http://president .gov.by/ru/news_ru/view/aleksandr-lukashenko-provel-soveshchanie-o-sos toyanii-raboty-po-privedeniyu-vooruzhennykh-sil-i-3907/.

Lukashenka, A. 2014a. 'Aleksandr Lukashenko v prazdnik Paskhi posetil minskii Svyato-Dukhov kafederal'nyi sobor'. 20 April. http://president .gov.by/ru/news_ru/view/aleksandr-lukashenko-v-prazdnik-pasxi-posetit -minskij-svjato-duxov-kafedralnyj-sobor-8544/.

Lukashenka, A. 2014b. 'Poslanie Prezidenta belarusskomu narodu i Natsional'nomu sobraniyu'. 22 April. http://president.gov.by/ru/news_r u/view/aleksandr-lukashenko-obraschaetsja-s-ezhegodnym-poslaniem-k-belorusskomu-narodu-i-natsionalnomu-sobraniju-8549/.

Lukashenka, A. 2014c. 'Press-Konferentsiya Preszidenta Respubliki Belarus' A. G. Lukashenko zhurnalistam rossiiskikh regional'nykh spedstv massovoi informatsii'. 17 October. http://president.gov.by/ru/news_ru/vi ew/press-konferentsija-prezidenta-respubliki-belarus-aglukashenko-zhurnalistam-rossijskix-regionalnyx-sredstv-10025/.

Lukashenka, A. 2015. '42-oi s'ezd Belorusskogo respublikanskogo soyuza molodezhi'. 20 January. http://president.gov.by/ru/news_ru/view/42-oj-sjezd-belorusskogo-respublikanskogo-sojuza-molodezhi-10682/.

Lukashenka, A. 2016a. 'Aleksandr Lukashenko: Belorusam i rossiyanam nuzhno derzhat'sya vmeste, byt' sil'nymi'. 28 November. www.sb.by/art icles/aleksandr-lukashenko-belorusam-i-rossiyanam-nuzhno-derzhatsya-vmeste-byt-silnymi.html.

Lukashenka, A. 2016b. 'Lukashenko o belorusskikh gastarbaiterakh, prichine raspada SSSR i lyubimom chisle'. Tut.by. 17 November. https://news.tut.by/society/520278.html.

Lukashenka, A. 2016c. 'Zavtra dolzhno byt' lushe, chem vchera'. SB.By. 27 June. www.sb.by/articles/zavtra-dolzhno-byt-luchshe-chem-vchera-sobranie.html.

Lukashenka, A. 2017. 'Interv'yu mezhgosudarstvennoi teleradiokompanii "Mir"'. 6 April. http://president.gov.by/ru/news_ru/view/intervjju-mezhgosudarstvennoj-teleradiokompanii-mir-15957/.

Lukashenka, A. 2018. 'Poslanie belorusskomu narodu i Natsional'nomu sobraniyu'. 24 April. http://president.gov.by/ru/news_ru/view/poslanie-k-belorusskomu-narodu-i-natsionalnomu-sobraniju-18594/.

Lukashenka, A. 2018. 'Telefonnyi razgovor s Prezidentom Armenii Armenom Sarkisyanom'. 25 April. http://president.gov.by/ru/news_ru/view/telefon nyj-razgovor-s-prezidentom-armenii-armenom-sarkisjanom-18599/.

Lukashenka, A. 2021. 'Uchastie v zasedanii Soveta glav gosudarstv SNG'. 15 October. https://president.gov.by/ru/events/uchastie-v-zasedanii-soveta-glav-gosudarstv-sng-1634286101.

Lukashuk, Z. 2017. 'Osnovatel' "Belogo legiona": Kto-to sozdaet kartinku spetsial'no dlya Lukashenko'. 22 March. http://udf.by/news/politic/1541 28-osnovatel-belogo-legiona-kto-to-sozdaet-kartinku-specialno-dlya-lukashenko.html.

Lutsenko, I. 2020. 'Noviy uryad starikh oligarkhiv?' *Ukrainskaya Pravda.* 3 March. https://blogs.pravda.com.ua/authors/lutsenko/5e5ec91b3ad4d/.

Luzin, P. 2017. 'The Ominous Rise of the Russian National Guard'. Intersection Project. 21 July. http://intersectionproject.eu/article/security/ominous-rise-russian-national-guard.

Lyons, K., & Rice-Oxley, M. 2015. 'Harassed and Shunned, the Russians Labelled Foreign Agents by the Kremlin'. *The Guardian.* 26 April. www.theguardian.com/world/2015/apr/26/harassed-and-shunned-the-russians-labelled-foreign-agents-by-kremlin.

Mações, B. 2019. 'Why Russia Wants to Break the Internet'. *The Moscow Times.* 14 May. www.themoscowtimes.com/2019/05/14/why-russia-wants-to-break-the-internet-a65570.

Makeev, N. 2017. '"Druz'yami Putina" dali "dobro" na ukhod v ofshory'. MK.ru. 26 March. www.mk.ru/economics/2017/03/26/druzyam-putina-dali-dobro-na-ukhod-v-ofshory.html.

Malashenkov, V. 2010. 'KGB: obstanovka v Belarusi nakanune vyborov absolyutno kontroliruemaya'.Tut.by. 17 December. https://news.tut.by/e lections/208708.html.

Malinova, O. 2011. 'Tema proshlogo v ritorike prezidentov Rossii'. *Pro et Contra*. (May–August): 106–22.

Maltseva, E. 2016. 'Lost and Forgotten: The Conflict Through the Eyes of the Donbass People'. In *The Return of the Cold War: Ukraine, the West and Russia*, edited by J. L. Black and A. D. Theriault (pp. 143–59). London: Routledge.

Marin, E. 2015. 'Experiential Learning: Empowering Students to Take Control of Their Learning by Engaging Them in an Interactive Course Simulation Environment'. *Procedia-Social and Behavioural Sciences*. 180: 854–59.

Materik.ru. 2017. 'Mezhdunarodnyi forum "Sovremennye intergratsionnye protsessy: opyt i perspektivy"'. Materik.ru. 28 June. www.materik.ru/co untry/detail.php?ID=16686&print=Y.

Mazaeva, O. 2004. 'KGB Belarusi i FSB Rossii nachnut sotrudnichat' eshche aktivnee'. Tut.by. 8 October. https://news.tut.by/politics/44980.html.

Meduza.io. 2016. 'Khozyain Donbassa Biznesmen Ronat Akhmetov perezhil voinu i gotovitsya vernut'sya v politiku'. 25 March. https://meduza.io/fea ture/2016/03/25/hozyain-donbassa.

Meduza.io. 2017. 'V Belorussii nakanune Massoviy aktsii protesta zaderzhivayut oppozitsionerov. Nekotorye schitayut, chto vinovata Rossiya'. 24 March. https://meduza.io/feature/2017/03/24/v-belorussii-nakanune-massovoy-aktsii-protesta-zaderzhivayut-oppozitsionerov-nekotorye-schitayut-chto-vinovata-rossiya.

Meduza.io. 2018. 'Teleobrashchenie Putina o pensionnoi reforme: kak na nego otreagirovala Rossiya. Khronika'. Meduza. 29 August. https://med uza.io/live/2018/08/29/teleobraschenie-putina-o-pensionnoy-reforme-onlayn.

Medvedev, D. 2011. 'Vstrecha s musul'manskim dykhovenstvom'. 19 November. http://kremlin.ru/events/president/news/13592.

Melkozerova, V. 2015. 'Ukraine Tries to Catch Up to Russia in Intelligence War'. *Kyiv Post*. 19 August. www.kyivpost.com/article/content/war-against-ukraine/ukraine-tries-to-catch-up-to-russia-in-intelligence-war-3 96107.html.

Melkozerova, V. 2017. 'Past Tragedy Casts Shadow on Ukraine's Relations with Poland'. *Kyiv Post*. 16 February. www.kyivpost.com/ukraine-politics /past-tragedy-casts-shadow-ukraines-relations-poland.html.

Melkozerova, V., & Talant, B. 2016. 'Ukraine Seeks to Bolster Ties with Kazakhstan in Industrial Sector'. *Kyiv Post*. 22 December. www

.kyivpost.com/business/ukraine-seeks-bolster-ties-kazakhstan-industrial-sector.html.

Melnykovska, I., Plamper, H., & Schweickert, R. 2012. 'Do Russia and China Promote Autocracy in Central Asia?' *Asia Europe Journal.* 10(1): 75–89.

Mendeleev, D. 2010. 'Chto dlya Ezhel' Balaklava, to dlya Ivashchenko – tyu'ma?' *Zerkal Nedeli.* 4 September (no. 32).

Miller, C. 2014. 'Ukraine's Top Intelligence Agency Deeply Infiltrated by Russian Spies'. Mashable. 30 December. http://mashable.com/2014/12/3 0/russian-vs-ukrainian-spies/#pzGivmXELOq3.

Miller, C. 2016. 'In Ukraine, Attacks On Journalists Chill Media Landscape'. Radio Free Europe/Radio Liberty. 16 August. www .rferl.org/a/ukraine-attacks-on-journalists-media-landscape-press-freedom/27923284.html.

Minakov, M. 2011. 'Izbiratel'nye perspektivy v svete problemnoi legitimnosti'. *Ukrainskaya Pravda.* 7 June. www.pravda.com.ua/rus/art icles/2011/06/7/6277319/.

Minchenko Consulting. 2017. 'Politbyuro 2.0 i gubernatorskiy korpus'. Minchenko Consulting. 29 September. www.minchenko.ru/netcat_files/u serfiles/2/Dokumenty/PB_2.0_I_GUBERNATORSKIY_KORPUS_29 .09.pdf.

Minzarari, D. 2014. 'Moldovan Armed Forces Train for Hybrid Warfare the Wrong Way'. *Eurasian Daily Monitor.* 11(194).

Miselyuk, A. 2018. 'Kremlevskiy revansh-2019: instrumenty novye, oshibki – starye'. *Ukrainskaya Pravda.* 20 October. www.pravda .com.ua/rus/columns/2018/10/20/7195638/.

Mitskevich, D. 2017. 'What Does Belarus Want from China?' *Belarus Digest.* 23 May. https://belarusdigest.com/story/what-does-belarus-want-from-china/.

Mojeiko, V. 2015. 'Soft Belarusianization: A New Shift In Lukashenka's Domestic Policy?' *Belarus Digest.* 21 April. http://belarusdigest.com/stor y/soft-belarusization-new-shift-lukashenkas-domestic-policy-22434.

Mojeiko, V. 2019. 'Civil Society: Between Repression and Collaboration with Business'. Belarusian Institute for Strategic Studies. 20 June. https://belinsti tute.com/en/article/civil-society-between-repression-and-collaboration-business.

Moldavskie Vedomosti. 2016a. 'Dar ot pravitel'stva Moskovskoi oblasti peredal posol Rossii Farit Mukhametshin'. *Moldavskie Vedomosti.* 13 May (no. 33): 9.

Moldavskie Vedomosti. 2016b. 'Farit Mukhametshin: v EAES ne storyat razdelitel'nykh liniy'. *Moldavskie Vedomosti.* 11 November (no. 76): 4.

Monaghan, A. 2016. *The New Politics of Russia: Interpreting Change.* Manchester: Manchester University Press.

Moscatelli, O. 2011. 'First Chechen Campaign As A Reflection Of The Russian Authorities' Frailty In The Early 1990s'. Valdai Club. 23 August. http://valdaiclub.com/a/highlights/the_first_chechen_cam paign_as_a_reflection_of_the_russian_authorities_frailty_in_the_ear ly_1990s/?sphrase_id=88545.

Moshkin, M., Valieva, S., Anokhina, E., & Eremina, N. 2005. 'L'goty. Boi za proezd'. *Moskovsky Komsomolets.* 12 January (no. 4): 3.

Moskovsky Komsomolets. 2005. 'L'goty. Patriarkh nedovolen'. *Moskovsky Komsomolets.* 15 January (no. 7): 3.

Mostovaya, Y. 2006. 'Viktor Baloga: "Prezident ne zanimaetsya politicheskim barterom"'. *Zerkalo Nedeli.* 18 November (no. 44).

Mostovaya, Y. 2016. 'Za shirmoi'. *Zerkalo Nedeli.* 5 February (no. 4): 1.

Motyl, A. J. 2012. 'Ukraine: The Yanukovych Family Business'. World Affairs Journal. 23 March. www.worldaffairsjournal.org/blog/alexan der-j-motyl/ukraine-yanukovych-family-business.

Motyl, A. J. 2020. 'Ukraine's Naive President is in Serious Trouble Already'. Atlantic Council. 5 March. www.atlanticcouncil.org/blogs/ukrainealert/ ukraines-novice-president-is-in-serious-trouble-already/.

Mukhametshina, E. 2018. 'Vlasti eshche dolgo pridetsya rasplachivat'sya na vyborakh za pensionnuyu reform'. *Vedomosti.* 19 November. www .vedomosti.ru/politics/articles/2018/11/19/786856-vlasti-esche-dolgo- rasplachivatsya-pensionnuyu.

Mukhametshina, E., & Didkovskaya, A. 2018. 'Chislo zhelayushchikh protiv pensionnoi reform rezko snizilos"'. *Vedomosti.* 27 September. www .vedomosti.ru/politics/articles/2018/09/26/782135-protiv-pensionnoi- reformi.

Munck, G. L., & Verkuilen, J. 2002. 'Conceptualising and Measuring Democracy: Evaluating Alternative Indices'. *Comparative Political Studies.* 35(1): 5–34.

Mungiu-Pippidi, A., & Munteanu, I. 2009. 'Moldova's "Twitter Revolution"'. *Journal of Democracy.* 20(3): 136–42.

Murphy, M. P. 2017. 'Tax On "Social Parasites" Stirs Up Public Angst In Belarus'. *Belarus Digest.* 2 March. http://belarusdigest.com/story/tax-%E 2%80%9Csocial-parasites%E2%80%9D-stirs-public-angst-belarus -29298.

Murtazaev, E. 2012. 'Gvardiya Putina: kak rabotaet vertikal' vlasti'. *Forbes.* 27 August. www.forbes.ru/sobytiya/vlast/102436-gvardiya-putina-desyat -klyuchevyh-biznes-figur-putinskoi-vertikali.

Nahalyo, B. 2019. 'The Craft of Kolomoisky'. Atlantic Council. 12 August. www.atlanticcouncil.org/blogs/ukrainealert/the-craft-of-kolomoisky/.

Nathan, A. J. 2016. 'China's Challenge'. In *Authoritarianism Goes Global: The Challenge to Democracy*, edited by L. Diamond, M. F. Plattner & C. Walker (pp. 23–39). Baltimore: Johns Hopkins University Press.

Naviny.by. 2005. 'Internetu skazhut "tsai dian"?' Tut.by. 22 November. ht tps://news.tut.by/it/60547.html.

Nayem, Mustafa. 2014. 'The Right Sector: An Inside View'. Euromaidan Press. 2 April. http://euromaidanpress.com/2014/04/02/the-right-sector-an-inside-view/#arvlbdata.

Neef, C. 2014. 'The Power of Ukraine's Billionaires'. *Spiegel International*. 25 February. www.spiegel.de/international/europe/how-oligarchs-in-ukraine-prepared-for-the-fall-of-yanukovych-a-955328.html.

Neglinina, E. 2004. 'Novyi agent Kremlya'. *Gazeta*. 12 October. www .gazeta.ru/politics/2004/10/12_a_183976.shtml.

Nemtsova, A. 2016. 'Igor Dodon is Vladimir Putin's Moldovan Mini-Me'. The Daily Beast. 29 October. www.thedailybeast.com/igor-dodon-is-vladimir-putins-moldovan-mini-me.

Nemtsova, A. 2017. 'Inside the Uprising Against Moldova's Donald Trump'. The Daily Beast. 13 April. www.thedailybeast.com/inside-the-uprising-against-moldovas-donald-trump.

Nemtsova, A. 2019. 'By Pushing Out Filthy Rich Vladimir Plahotniuc, Moldova Takes the Lead in Ending the Era of the Oligarchs'. The Daily Beast. 21 August. www.thedailybeast.com/by-pushing-out-filthy-rich-vladimir-plahotniuc-moldova-takes-the-lead-in-de-oligarchization? ref=author.

Nemyrych, S. 2013. 'Konets zolotogo spokoistviya'. *Gazeta*. 20 December. https://gazeta.zn.ua/internal/konec-zolotogo-spokoystviya-_.html.

Nesterova, O. 2014. 'Chego khotya liberaly i kommunisty'. *Logos-Press*. 19 December (no. 47).

NewsMaker. 2015. 'Kak SIB na golovu: v rukovodstve gosuchrezhdeniy mogut poyavit'sya sotrudniki gosbezopasnosti'. 10 December. http://news maker.md/rus/novosti/kak-sib-na-golovu-v-rukovodstve-gosuchrezhdeniy-mogut-poyavitsya-sotrudniki-gosbez-20605.

NewsMaker. 2016a. 'Antiterror opravdyvaet sredstva. SIB khotyat nadelit' bezotkaznymi polnomochiyami'. 5 August. http://newsmaker.md/rus/no vosti/antiterror-opravdyvaet-sredstva-sib-hotyat-nadelit-bezotkaznymi-polnomochiyami-26589.

NewsMaker. 2016b. 'Na realizatsiyu trekh proektov Kitai vydelit Moldove grant v razmere €2,6 Mln'. 21 June. https://newsmaker.md/rus/novosti/na-realizatsiyu-treh-proektov-kitay-vydelit-moldove-grant-v-razmere-2-6-ml n-25782/.

NewsMaker. 2016c. '"Naibol'shaya opasnost' – v tom, chto pravitel'stvo prodolzhaet imitirovat' reformy'.' 29 March. http://newsmaker.md/rus/n

ovosti/naibolshaya-opasnost-v-tom-chto-pravitelstvo-prodolzhaet-imitirovat-reformy-23642.

NewsMaker. 2016d. 'V khode protestov postradal 31 chelovek, 11 politseiskikh gospitalizirovany'. 21 January. http://newsmaker.md/rus/no vosti/v-hode-protestov-postradal-31-chelovek-11-politseyskih-gospitalizirovany-21776.

NewsMaker. 2017. 'Novym sekretarem Vysshego soveta bezopasnosti stal Artur Gumenyuk'. 3 March. https://newsmaker.md/rus/novosti/novym-sekretarem-vysshego-soveta-bezopasnosti-stal-artur-gumenyuk-30076/.

NewsMaker. 2018. 'Itogi dnya: o tom, pochemu v Moldove ne Singapur, za chto posol SShA pokhvalil Plakhotnyuka i zachem evakuirovali parlament'. 20 September. https://newsmaker.md/rus/novosti/itogi-dnya-o-tom-pochemu-v-moldove-ne-singapur-za-chto-posol-ssha-pohvalil-plahotn-39215/.

NewsMaker. 2020. 'Rezhim po interesam. Vladislav Kulminskiy o "tenevom gosudarstve" Igora Dodona'. 4 May. https://newsmaker.md/rus/novosti/r ezhim-po-interesam-vladislav-kulminskiy-o-tenevom-gosudarstve-igorya -dodona/.

Nezavisimaya Gazeta. 2007. 'Kul't lichnosti Nazarbaeva'. *Nezavisimaya Gazeta*. 23 May (no. 98): 2.

Nezavisimaya Moldova. 2005. 'Posol Belarusi vstretilsya s Moldavskimi parlamentariyami'. *Nezavisimaya Moldova*. 9 November (no. 213): 5.

Nezavisimaya Moldova. 2011. 'Posol Rossii Valeriy Kuzmin: 'Khoroshim primerom potentsial'nykh vozmozhnostei i effektivnosti otnosheniy nashikh stolits govoryat rezultaty peregovorov mera Moskvy Sergeya Sobyanina i kandidata na gost general'nogo primara Kishineva Igorya Dodina'. *Nezavisimaya Moldova*. 10 June (no. 79): 4.

Nicolae, C. 2019. 'Tot ce trebuie să ştii despre criza din Republic Moldova şi greşelile făcute de România'. *Vice*. 11 June. www.vice.com/ro/article/7xg ded/ce-trebuie-sa-stii-despre-criza-din-republica-moldova.

Novye Izvestiya. 2000. 'Vladimir Rushailo i Yuriy Kravchenko druzhat v Kieve'. *Novye Izvestiya*. 19 June (no. 127): 2.

Nuttall, C. 2017. 'Interview: Moldova's Populist Pro-Russian "Hand Grenade"'. Intellinews. 24 March. www.intellinews.com/interview-moldova-s-populist-pro-russian-hand-grenade-118209/.

Obozrevatel'. 2016. 'Killerom okazalas' zhenshchina: opublikovano video zakladki vzryvchatki pod avtomobil' Sheremeta'. Obozrevatel. 22 July. www.obozrevatel.com/crime/70936-ubijstvo-pavel-sheremet-video-zakladka-vzryivchatka-vzriv-killer-zhenshina.htm.

Obydenkova, A. V., & Libman, A. 2019. *Authoritarian Regionalism in the World of International Organizations*. New York: Oxford University Press.

Odissonova, V., Dokshin, V., & Artem'eva, A. 2019. 'Kak politsiya i Rosgvardiya tselyi den' bili moskvichei'. *Novaya Gazeta*. 27 July. www .novayagazeta.ru/articles/2019/07/27/81396-27-iyulya-fotografii.

Olearchyk, R. 2020. 'Ukraine's Oligarchs Jostle for Influence with President Zelensky'. *Financial Times*. 19 February. www.ft.com/content/1821b882-4366-11ea-abea-0c7a29cd66fe.

Olearchyk, R., & Seddon, M. 2021. 'Ukraine Has Uncovered Russia-Backed Coup Plot, Says President'. *Financial Times*. 26 November. www.ft.com /content/9d4a999e-2ac3-4887-934a-0c30b20809fe.

Olszański, T. A. 2014. 'Ukraine's Political Parties at the Start of the Election Campaign'. Centre for Eastern Studies. 17 September. www.osw.waw.pl/ en/publikacje/analyses/2014-09-17/ukraines-political-parties-start-election-campaign.

Onuch, O. 2015. '"Facebook Helped Me Do It": Understanding the EuroMaidan Protester "Tool-Kit".' *Studies in Ethnicity and Nationalism*. 15(1): 170–84.

Orenstein, M. A., & Mizsei, K. 2014. 'Moldova in the Middle'. Foreign Affairs. 14 April. www.foreignaffairs.com/articles/russian-federation/20 14-04-14/moldova-middle.

Organized Crime and Corruption Reporting Project. 2017a. 'Killing Pavel'. 10 May. www.occrp.org/en/documentaries/killing-pavel/.

Organized Crime and Corruption Reporting Project. 2017b. 'The Russian Banks and Putin's Cousin'. 22 August. www.occrp.org/en/laundromat/th e-russian-banks-and-putins-cousin/.

Organized Crime and Corruption Reporting Project. 2017c. 'The Russian Laundromat Exposed'. 20 March. www.occrp.org/ru/laundromat/the-russian-laundromat-exposed/.

Ortmann, S., & Thompson, M. R. 2014. 'China's Obsession with Singapore: Learning Authoritarian Modernity'. *The Pacific Review*. 27 (3): 433–55.

Ortmann, S., & Thompson, M. R. 2016. 'China and the "Singapore Model"'. *Journal of Democracy*. 27(1): 39–48.

Otkroi Novost'. 2017. 'Pavel Filip v Belarusi // Zona svobodnoi torgovli s ES otkryvaet novye vozmozhnosti dlya biznesa'. Deschide. 6 June. https://de schide.md/ru/russian_news/politic_ru/12789/Павел-Филип-в-Беларуси–3 она-свободной-торговли-с-ЕС-открывает-новые-возможности-для-бизне са.htm.

Otkrytaya Rossii. 2016. 'Tainye ucheniya Natsgvardii v Podmoskov'e 7 aprelya 2016 goda'. Open Russia. 8 April. https://openrussia.org/post/vie w/14173/.

Padhol, U. M., & Marples, D. R. 2011. 'The 2010 Presidential Election in Belarus'. *Problems of Post-Communism*. 58(1): 3–16.

Palmer, J. 2016. 'What China Didn't Learn From the Collapse of the Soviet Union'. Foreign Policy. 24 December. http://foreignpolicy.com/2016/12/24/what-china-didnt-learn-from-the-collapse-of-the-soviet union/.

Pankovets, Z. 2017. 'Za lager' boevikov vydayut ofitsial'no zaregistrirovannyi patriotiocheskii lager' pod Osipovichami'. 22 March. http://udf.by/news/so bytie/154107-za-lager-boevikov-vydayut-oficialno-zaregistrirovannyy-patrioticheskiy-lager-pod-osipovichami.html.

Pasochnik, V. 2013. 'Proekt gosbyudzheta-2014: son razuma prodolzhaetsya'. *Zerkalo Nedeli*. 21 December (no. 48): 1.

Pavlovsky, G. 2016. 'Russian Politics under Putin'. *Foreign Affairs*. 95(3): 10–17.

Pechenko, S. 2017. 'Ekspert: Sistema belorusskoi vlasti porochna'. UDF. November 22. http://udf.by/localelections20128/analitika-mestnye-vybory -2018/165482-ekspert-sistema-belorusskoy-vlasti-porochna.html.

Perry, E. J., & Heilmann, S. 2011. 'Embracing Uncertainty: Guerrilla Policy Style and Adaptive Governance in China'. In *Mao Invisible's Hand: The Political Foundations of Adaptive Governance in China*, edited by E. J. Perry & S. Heilmann (pp. 1–29). Cambridge, MA: Harvard University Press.

Peshkov, V. 2016. 'The Donbas: Back in the USSR'. European Council on Foreign Relations. 1 September. www.ecfr.eu/article/essay_the_donbas_back_in_the_ussr.

Petrovskaya, G. 2015. 'Belorusskii segment internet: pod kolpakom gosudarstva'. Deutsche Welle. 24 September. www.dw.com/ru/белорусс кий-сегмент-интернета-под-колпаком-у-государства/a-18731953.

Pevehouse, J. C. 2005. *Democracy from Above? Regional Organizations and Democratization*. New York: Cambridge University Press.

Pierson-Lyzhina, E., & Kovalenko, O. 2020. 'The Coronavirus Outbreak in Belarus, Russia and Ukraine: Responses by the State, Business and Civil Society'. East Center. October. https://east-center.org/wp-content/upload s/2020/10/The-coronavirus-outbreak-BLR-RU-UKR.pdf.

Plantan, E. 2017. 'Comparing Recent NGO Laws in Russia and China'. China File. www.chinafile.com/ngo/analysis/comparing-recent-ngo-laws-russia-and-china.

Podolyak, M. 2000. 'Reklamshchik dlya prezidenta'. *BelGazeta*. 24 July (no. 28).

Podrobnosti.ua. 2010. 'Zurabov: V sluchae denonsatsii "Kharkovskogo dogovora" Ukraina prevratitsya ma stranu-izgoi'. 30 April. https://lb.ua/n ews/2010/04/30/42703_zurabov_v_sluchae_denonsatsii_ha.html.

Point.md. 2006. 'V Moldove budet sozdan Tsentre po bor'be s terrorizmom'. 2 November. https://point.md/ru/novosti/obschestvo/v-moldove-budet-sozdan-centr-po-borjbe-s-terrorizmom.

Point.md. 2007. 'Kishinev: Spetssluzhby pereshli v ruki neprofessionala?!' 2 November. https://point.md/ru/novosti/politika/kishinyov-specsluzhbi-pereshli-v-ruki-neprofessionala.

Point.md. 2008a. 'George Papuk vernulsya v kreslo ministra vnutrennikh del Moldovy'. 28 October. https://point.md/ru/novosti/politika/george-papuk-vernulsya-v-kreslo-ministra-vnutrennih-del-moldovi.

Point.md. 2008b. 'Kishinev. Oppozitsiya sebya vydala?! Spetssluzhby vzyali sled!' 21 February. https://point.md/ru/novosti/politika/kishinev-oppoziciya-sebya-vidala-specsluzhbi-vzyali-sled.

Point.md. 2008c. 'Moldova. Voronin brosil spetssluzhby na SMI i partii!' 5 February. https://point.md/ru/novosti/politika/moldova-voronin-brosil-specsluzhbi-na-smi-i-partii.

Point.md. 2008d. 'SIB budet borot'sya s oppozitsionnymi partiyami'. 5 February. https://point.md/ru/novosti/politika/sib-budet-borotjsya-s-oppozicionnimi-partiyami.

Point.md. 2009. '"Oranzhevaya revolyutsiya" v Moldove lopnula myl'nym puzyrem – Leonid Radzikhovskiy'. 15 April. https://point.md/ru/novosti/obschestvo/oranzhevaya-revolyuciya-v-moldove-lopnula-miljnim-puzirem—leonid-radzihovskij.

Point.md. 2012. 'Moldova nakhoditsya na 116 meste v reitinge svobody pressy'. 2 May. https://point.md/ru/novosti/obschestvo/moldova-nahoditsya-na-116-meste-v-rejtinge-svobodi-pressi.

Point.md. 2013. 'Rechan o zapisi telefonnykh razgovorov: "Da, eto moi golos"'. 1 October. https://point.md/ru/novosti/politika/rechan-o-zapisi-telefonnih-razgovorov58-quotda-eto-moj-golosquot.

Point.md. 2014. 'Proevropeiskiy Kishinev ishchet strakhovku ot Maidana'. 23 January. https://point.md/ru/novosti/politika/proevropejskij-kishinev-ischet-strahovku-ot-majdana.

Point.md. 2019. 'Natal'ya Morar' o sobytiyakh 7 aprelya 2009: Ya chuvstvuyu sebya ispol'zovannoi'. 8 April. https://point.md/ru/novosti/politika/natalia-morar-o-sobytiiakh-7-aprelia-2009-ia-chuvstvuiu-sebia-ispolzovannoi.

Point.md. 2020. 'Tri lidera DPM proveli tainuyu vstrechu s chelovekom iz okruzheniya Dodona'. 4 May. https://point.md/ru/novosti/politika/tri-lidera-dpm-proveli-tainuiu-vstrechu-s-chelovekom-iz-okruzheniia-dodona.

Poletaev, V. 2006. 'Obshchestvo. Nurgaliev rukovodit ucheniyami'. *Rossiyskaya Gazeta*. 26 April (no. 87): 13.

Pol'gueva, E. 2005. 'Na gorodskikh ploshchadyakh'. *Sovetskaya Rossiya*. 13 January (no. 1): 1.

Politeka.net. 2016. 'Partnery, druz'ya i kumov'ya: iz kogo sostoit "sem'ya" Poroshenko'. 17 May. https://politeka.net/news/219078-partnery-druzya-i-kumovya-iz-kogo-sostoit-semya-poroshenko/.

Polutba, A. 2018. 'Vlast' "prodavila" pensionnuyu reformu i rasteryalas".
27 September. *Svobodnaya Pressa*. https://svpressa.ru/society/article/211582/.

Ponomarenko, I. 2018a. 'Reform of State Security Service Gets Lost in
Bureaucratic Maze'. *Kyiv Post*. 11 May. www.kyivpost.com/ukraine-
politics/reform-state-security-service-gets-lost-bureaucratic-maze.html.

Ponomarenko, I. 2018b. 'Ukraine Withdraws All Envoys from CIS Bodies'.
*Kyiv Post*. 19 May. www.kyivpost.com/ukraine-politics/ukraine-
withdraws-envoys-cis-bodies.html.

Popşoi, M. 2014. 'The Rise and Fall of Renato Usatii: Politics in Moldova
2.0'. Moldovan Politics. 27 November. https://moldovanpolitics.com/20
14/11/27/the-rise-and-fall-of-renato-usatii/.

Popşoi, M. 2015. 'Moldovan Political Activism on Social Media'. Moldovan
Politics. 14 September. https://moldovanpolitics.com/2015/09/14/moldo
van-political-activism-on-social-media/.

Popşoi, M. 2016. 'Transnistria: Change of Leadership, but Not Policy'.
*Eurasia Daily Monitor*. 13(198).

Popşoi, M. 2017. 'Moldova's Civil Society Braces for Another Attack'. Open
Democracy. 22 August. www.opendemocracy.net/od-russia/mihai-popsoi
/moldova-s-civil-society-braces-for-another-attack.

Popşoi, M. 2018. 'State of Play Ahead of Moldova's Parliamentary
Elections'. *Eurasia Daily Monitor*. 15(177).

Preiherman, Y. 2017a. 'Illusions and Lack of Reason Revealed by New
Protests in Belarus'. *Eurasia Daily Monitor*. 14(41).

Preiherman, Y. 2017b. 'Why the EU Should Engage With Belarus'. Carnegie.
3 April. http://carnegieeurope.eu/strategiceurope/68495.

Preobrazhensky, I. 2012. 'Spetssluzhby otzhigayut'. Politcom. 4 October. h
ttp://politcom.ru/14629.html.

Prokhanov, A. 2013. 'Foundations Of Russia's National Ideal'. Valdai Club.
9 August. http://valdaiclub.com/a/highlights/foundations_of_russia_s_na
tional_idea/?sphrase_id=88545.

Prokhorova, I. 2017. 'The First Post-Soviet Decade Was the Happiest Time
of My Life (Op-Ed)'. *The Moscow Times*. 13 October. www
.themoscowtimes.com/2017/10/13/1990s-territory-of-freedom-a59196.

Prokopchuk, S. 2004. 'Viktor Chernomyrdin: ulitsa daleko zabedet...' *Trud*.
15 December (no. 237): 2.

Provalinskaya, N. 2007. 'Dernuli za cheku'. *BelGazeta*. 23 July (no. 29).

Putin, V. 1999. 'Rossiya na rubezhe tystacheletii'. NG. 30 December. www
.ng.ru/politics/1999-12-30/4_millenium.html.

Putin, V. 2001. 'Stenogramma pryamogo tele- i radioefira ("Pryamaya liniya
s Prezidentom Rossii")'. 24 December. http://kremlin.ru/events/president/
transcripts/21457.

Putin, V. 2005. 'Poslanie Federal'nomu Sobraniyu Rossiiskoi Federatsii'. 25 April. http://kremlin.ru/events/president/transcripts/22931.

Putin, V. 2012. 'Putin ob "arabskoi vesne"'. *Rossiyskaya Gazeta*. 1 March (no. 45): 3.

Putin, V. 2014a. 'Obrashchenie Prezidenta Rossiiskoi Federatsii'. 18 March. http://kremlin.ru/events/president/news/20603.

Putin, V. 2014b. 'Po voprosam obespecheniya suvereniteta i territorial'noi tselostnosti Rossiyskoi Federatsii'. 22 July. www.scrf.gov.ru/council/ses sion/2058/.

Putin, V. 2014c. 'Vladimir Putin otvetil na voprosy zhurnalistov o situatsii na Ukraine'. 4 March. http://kremlin.ru/events/president/news/20366.

Putin, V. 2015 'Zasedanie Mezhdynarodnogo diskussionnogo kluba "Valdai"'. 22 October. http://kremlin.ru/events/president/news/50548.

Putin, V. 2016a. 'Rasshirennoe zasedanie kollegii Minsterstva oborony'. 22 December. www.kremlin.ru/events/president/news/53571.

Putin, V. 2016b. 'Zasedanie mezhregional'nogo foruma ONF'. 25 January. http://kremlin.ru/events/president/news/51206.

Putin, V. 2018. 'Obrashchenie Prezidenta k grazhdanam Rossii'. 29 August. http://kremlin.ru/events/president/news/58405.

Radu, P., Preaşca, I., & Mako, Ş. 2016. 'Platon's Money'. Organized Crime and Corruption Reporting Project. 7 September. www.occrp.org/en/inves tigations/5617-platon-s-money.

Raikhel', Y. 2015. 'Kazakhstan rvetsya v 'tigry' Tsentral'noi Azii'. *Den'*. 23 July (no. 129).

Rakhmanin, S. 2008. 'Yuriy Lutsenko: "Esli trudoustroistvo vozhdei stanovitsya glavnoi komandnoi zadachei, to byt' chlenom takoi komandy nezachem"'. *Zerkalo Nedeli*. 4 October (no. 37).

Regional Anti-terrorist Structure of the Shanghai Cooperation Organisation. 2011. 'Ob uchastii predstavitelya ispolnitel'nogo komiteta RATC ShOS v subregional'nom seminare "protivodeistvie ispol'zovaniyu internet v terroristcheskikh tselyakh"'. 2011. https://ecrats.org/ru/cooperation/con ferences/2262.

Reid, A. 2015. *Borderland: A Journey through the History of Ukraine*. London: Weidenfield & Nicolson.

Reshetnikova, N, 2006. 'Soyuz: Belarus' – Rossiya. Posol iz Sibiri'. *Rossiyskaya Gazeta*. 16 February (no. 32): 1.

Rise.md. 2015. 'Omul lui usatîi, propus de Plahotniuc adjunct la SIS'. Rise. 28 September. www.rise.md/audio-omul-lui-usatii-propus-de-plahotniuc-adjunct-la-sis/.

Rise.md. 2017. 'Clienţii din Laundromat'. Rise. 20 March. www.rise.md/a rticol/clientii-din-laundromat/.

Rise.md. 2019. 'Interv'yu / Evgeniy Shevchuk: Pridnestrov'e – eto khalifat, u kotorogo religiya – den'gi'. Rise. 25 June. www.rise.md/rusa/евгений-шевчук-приднестровье-это-x/?lang=ru.

Rodin, I. 2005. 'Votum nedoveriya sobral podpisi dumtsev. Deputaty vyzhidayut nadeyas' na novye aktsii protesta'. *Nezavisimaya Gazeta*. 25 January (no. 12): 2.

Rodkiewicz, W. 2009. 'From "Virtual" to European Democracy – The Origins and Consequences of the Political Breakthrough in Moldova'. Centre for Eastern Studies. December 2009. www.osw.waw.pl/sites/defa ult/files/prace_32_1.pdf.

Rogov, K., & Ananyev, M. 2018. 'Public Opinion and Russian Politics'. In *The New Autocracy: Information, Politics, and Policy in Putin's Russia*, edited by D. Treisman (pp. 191–216). Washington, DC: Brookings Institution Press.

Roldugin, O. 2013. 'Krestyi otets, Vladimir Putin'. Sobesednik. 4 May. https:// sobesednik.ru/politika/20130304-krestnyi-otets-vladimir-putin.

Romanova, L. 2002. 'Benefis Viktora Chernomyrdina: Posol Rossii na Ukraine snova zagovoril'. *Nezavisimaya Gazeta*. 4 December (no. 73): 2.

Romanyuk, R. 2016. 'Vesyane peresadzhuvannya: Prem'er Groisman i kabmin bez koalitsii'. *Ukrainskaya Pravda*. 14 April. www.pravda.com.ua/articles/ 2016/04/14/7105548/.

Romanyuk, R., & Kravets, R. 2016. 'Prokurorskiy blitskrig: Lutsenko stal general'nym prokurorom'. *Ukrainskaya Pravda*. 12 May. www.pravda .com.ua/rus/articles/2016/05/12/7108281/.

Roshchenko, A. 2017. 'Za aktsiyami v 'Roshene' stoyat Klyuyev i Oleynik – Gritsak'. *Ukrainskaya Pravda*. 25 May. www.pravda.com.ua/rus/news/2 017/05/15/7143932/.

Rotkevich, E. 2005. 'Peterburzhtsy trebuyut otmeny zakona o monetizatsii l'got'. *Izvestiya*. 17 January (no. 5m): 2.

Rudenko, G. 2001. 'Novosti. Posol Chernomyrdin nachal s oshibok'. *Kommersant-Daily*. 31 May (no. 93): 2.

Rudolph, J. 2017. 'New Regulations Reinforce Real Name Verification'. 29 August. http://chinadigitaltimes.net/2017/08/new-cyber-regulations-reinforce-real-name-verification/.

Rustamova, F., Shamina, O., & Kozlov, P. 2018. 'Vse v ukrytie: Medvedev i ego zamestiteli proignoriruyut osudzhdenie pensionnoi reform'. BBC. 17 August. www.bbc.com/russian/news-45219695.

Ryaboshapka, R. 2020. 'Zelens'kiy peretvoryuet'sya na Poroshenka?' *Ukrainskaya Pravda*. 6 May. https://blogs.pravda.com.ua/authors/ria boshapka/5eb2704b63d91/.

Sakwa, R. 2008. *Russian Politics and Society*. 4th ed. London: Routledge.

Samokhina, S., & Inyutin, V. 2018. 'Kadry ONF prigodilis' partii vlasti'. *Kommersant* (no. 51): 3.

Savchenko, I. 2016. 'Kazakhstan: The Oppression of Journalists and Bloggers'. Open Dialogue. 22 January. http://en.odfoundation.eu/a/7228 ,kazakhstan-the-oppression-of-journalists-and-bloggers1.

Savina, E. 2010. 'Kreml' ne pomog'. *Gazeta*. 6 December. www.gazeta.ru/ politics/2010/12/06_a_3456937.shtml.

Schedler, A. 2002. 'The Logic of Electoral Authoritarianism'. In *Electoral Authoritarianism: The Dynamics of Unfree Competition*, edited by A. Schedler (pp. 1–23). Boulder: Lynne Reinner Publishers.

Security Council of the Russian Federation. 2006. 'O peregovorakh Sekretarya Bezopasnosti Rossiyskoi Federatsii I.S. Ivanov s Predsedatelem Verkhovnoi Rady Ukrainy A.A. Morozom'. 13 Ocotber. www.scrf.gov.ru/news/allnews/ 27/.

Security Council of the Russian Federation. 2012a. 'Interv'yu Sekretarya Soveta Bezopasnosti Rossiyskoi Federatsii N. P. Patrusheva: "Oranzhevaya" revolyutsiya v Rossii ne proidet' ("Komsomol'skaya Pravda" ot 18.12.2012g.)' 18 December. www.scrf.gov.ru/news/allnews/761/.

Security Council of the Russian Federation. 2012b. 'O vstreche Sekretarya Soveta Bezopasnosti Rossiyskoi Federatsii N.P. Patrusheva s Rukovoditelem Direktsii dokumentatsii i vneshenei bezopasnosti Ministerstva Natsional'noi bezopasnosti Alzhirskoi Narodno-Demokraticheskoi Respubliki A. Lallali'. 17 January. www.scrf.gov.ru/news/allnews/692/.

Security Council of the Russian Federation. 2013. 'Sostoyalsya ocherednoi raund rossiysko-ukrainskikh konsul'tatsiy po voprosam bezopasnosti'. 16 October. www.scrf.gov.ru/news/allnews/799/.

Security Council of the Russian Federation. 2015a. '14 aprelya 2015 goda v Moskve pod predsedatel'stvom Rossiyskoi Federatsii sostoyalas' desyataya Vstrecha Sekretarei Sovetov bezopasnosti gosudarstv-chlenov Shankhaiskoi organizatsii sotrudnichestva'. 14 April. www.scrf.gov.ru/n ews/allnews/879/.

Security Council of the Russian Federation. 2015b. 'Interv'yu Sekretarya Soveta Bezopasnosti Rossiyskoi Federatsii N. P. Patrusheva 'Komsomol'skoi Pravde.' 15 March. www.scrf.gov.ru/news/allnews/855/.

Security Council of the Russian Federation. 2015c. 'Sekretarya Soveta Bezopasnosti Rossiyskoi Federatsii N.P. Patrushev posetil s rabochim vizitom Arabskuyu Respubliku Egipet'. 2 March. www.scrf.gov.ru/news/ allnews/853/.

Security Council of the Russian Federation. 2016a. 'Aktual'nye voprosy obsepecheniya antiterroristicheskoi zashchinshchennosti ob'ektov i territoriy rassmotrenny na zasedanii sektsii nauchnogo coveta pri Sovete Bezopasnosti Rossiyskoi Federatsii'. 7 November. www.scrf.gov.ru/news/allnews/2119/.

Security Council of the Russian Federation. 2016b. 'Sekretar' Soveta Bezopasnosti Rossiyskoi Federatsii segodnya v Moskve vstretilsya

c Rukovoditelem Slyzhby kontrrazvedki i politsii Korolevstva Marokko'.
5 April. www.scrf.gov.ru/news/allnews/1055/.

Security Council of the Russian Federation. 2016c. 'Vladimir Putin provel
operativnoe soveshchanie s postoyannymi chlenami Soveta Bezopasnosti'.
8 April. www.scrf.gov.ru/news/allnews/1058/.

Security Council of the Russian Federation. 2017. 'Sekretar' Soveta Bezopasnosti
Rossiyskoi Federatsii provel rabochuyu vstrechu s Gosudarstvennym
sekretarem Soveta Bezopasnosti Respubliki Belorussiya'. 30 November. www
.scrf.gov.ru/news/allnews/2325/.

Security Council of the Russian Federation. 2019. 'Interv'yu zamestitelya
Sekretarya Soveta Bezopasnosti RF Rashida Nurgalieva "Rossiyskoi
Gazeta"'. 3 July. www.scrf.gov.ru/news/allnews/2613/.

Seddon, M. 2016. 'Russia's Chief Internet Censor Enlists China's Know-
How'. *Financial Times*. 27 April. www.ft.com/content/08564d74-0bbf-1
1e6-9456-444ab5211a2f.

Shanghai Cooperation Organisation. 2008a. 'Vystuplenie General'nogo
sekretarya ShOS na 3-M Soveshchanii Predsedatelei Verkhovnykh sudov
gosudarstv-chlenov ShOS'. 19 May. http://rus.sectsco.org/news/2008051
9/497.html.

Shanghai Cooperation Organisation. 2008b. 'Vystuplenie General'nogo
sekretarya ShOS na kruglom stole "ShOS – sovremennaya model'
regional'nogo sotrudnichestva"'. 19 May. http://rus.sectsco.org/news/20
080519/543.html.

Shanghai Cooperation Organisation. 2013. 'Ob uchastii v sovmestnykh
antiterroristicheskikh ucheniyakh kompetentnykh organov gosudarstv-
chlenov ShOS "Kazygut-Antiterror-2013"'. 13 June. http://rus
.sectsco.org/news/20130613/4434.html.

Shanghai Cooperation Organisation. 2019a. 'Konventsiya Shankhaiskoi
organizatsii sotrudnichestva po protivodeistviyu ekstremizmu'. 26 July.
https://docs.cntd.ru/document/542655220.

Shanghai Cooperation Organisation. 2019b. 'Ob uchastii ShOS v 4-om
Tsentral'no-Aziatikom forume po upravleniyu Internetom "Internet dlya
rashireniya vozmozhnostei Tsentral'noi Azii"'. 16 May. http://rus
.sectsco.org/news/20190516/540610.html.

Shestakhov, Y. 2014. 'Yanukovicha proveli v Evropu – vokrug pal'tsa'.
*Rossiyskaya Gazeta*. 24 February (no. 43): 1.s

Shevtsova, L. 2005. *Putin's Russia*. 2nd ed. Washington, DC: Carnegie
Endowment for International Peace.

Shimanovskaya, M. 2017. 'Posol Rossii Farit Mukhametshin s suprugoi
vruchili podarki zhitelyam Gagauzia'. *Moldavskie Vedomosti*. 6 October
(no. 35): 10.

Shleinov, R. 2005. 'Zakolebalis' vse. Yadernye reaktory mogut ostat'sya bez okhrany'. *Novaya Gazeta*. 17 January (no. 3): 2.

Shraibman, A. 2015. 'O chem posylal prezident? Samye yarkie fragmenty poslednikh 10 poslaniy Lukashenko'. Tut.by. 28 April. https://news.tut.by /politics/445681.html.

Shraibman, A. 2016a. 'Pochemu Lukashenko polyubil belorusskii yazyk i natsiestroitel'stvo'. UDF. 27 December. http://udf.by/news/sobytie/15012 6-pochemu-lukashenko-polyubil-belorusskiy-yazyk-i-nacstroitelstvo.html.

Shraibman, A. 2016b. 'Stanet li Belaya Rus' pravyashchei partiei Lukashenko'. Ostro.by. 29 April. http://ostro.by/politics/stanet-li-belaya-rus-pravyashhej-partiej-lukashenko/.

Shraibman, A. 2017a. 'Novoe kachestvo protesta. Pochemu belorusy nachali vykhodit' na ulitsy'. Carnegie. 2 March. http://carnegie.ru/commentary/? fa=68119.

Shraibman, A. 2017b. 'Ottepel' na pause. Kak Minsk sovmeshchaet razgon protestov i sblizhenie s Zapadom'. Carnegie. 28 March. http://carnegie.ru /commentary/?fa=68415.

Shraibman, A. 2017c. 'Singapur Lukashenko. Smozhet li Belorussiya preiti na bitkoiny i angliiskoe pravo'. Carnegie. 25 December. https://carnegie.ru /commentary/75102.

Shraibman, A. 2018. 'The House that Lukashenko Built: The Foundation, Evolution, and Future of the Belarusian Regime'. Carnegie Endowment. April 2018. https://carnegieendowment.org/files/CP328_Shraibman_Bela rus_FINAL.pdf.

Shraibman, A. 2020. 'Vybory pered novoi eroi. Pochemu vykhodtsy iz elity brosil vyzov Lukashenko'. Carnegie. 27 May. https://carnegie.ru/commen tary/81916.

Silina, T. 2003. 'Viktor Chernomyrdin: "Nikto nikogo ugovarivat" ne budet'. *Zerkalo Nedeli*. 23 August (no. 32).

Silina, T. 2013. 'Vse, chem mogu…' *Zerkalo Nedeli*. 16 November (no. 42): 1.

Silitski, V. 2010. 'Survival of the Fittest: Domestic and International Dimensions of the Authoritarian Reaction in the Former Soviet Union Following the Coloured Revolutions'. *Communist and Post-Communist Studies*. 43(4): 339–50.

Simmons, B. A., & Elkins, Z. 2004. 'The Globalization of Liberalization: Policy Diffusion in the International Political Economy'. *American Political Science Review*. 98(1): 171–89.

Sinitsyn, A., & Zheleznova, M. 2016. 'Ministerstvo vnutrennikh vragov'. *Vedomosti*. 5 April. www.vedomosti.ru/opinion/articles/2016/04/06/636 562-ministerstvo-vragov.

Smok, V. 2015. 'Iskusstvo kontrabandy v Belarusi'. UDF. 26 February. http://
udf.by/posrednik/iz-za/118254-iskusstvo-kontrabandy-v-belarusi.html.

Smok, V. 2017. 'Was the White Legion Really Planning an Armed Attack?'
*Belarus Digest*. 17 April. http://belarusdigest.com/story/was-white-legion-
really-planning-armed-attack-29810.

Snegin, S. 2005. 'Agressiya zla'. *Belarus' Segodnya*. 14 May (no. 90): 2.

Snyder, T. 2014. 'Ukraine: The New Dictatorship'. 18 January. www
.nybooks.com/daily/2014/01/18/ukraine-new-dictatorship/?insrc=wbll.

Socor, V. 2016. 'Plahotniuc's Power Base in Moldova: Allies and Instruments
(Part One)'. *Eurasia Daily Monitor*. 13(7).

Sokolovskaya, Y. 2001. 'Viktor Chernomyrdin: Pozirovaniem ne
zanimayus''. *Izvestiya*. 7 May (no. 118): 1.

Soldatov, A. 2013. 'FSB razvyazali ruki v sfere informatsionnoi bezopasnosti'.
EJ. 12 December. www.ej.ru/?a=note&id=23966.

Soldatov, A., & Borogan, I. 2010. *The New Nobility: The Restoration of
Russia's Security State and the Enduring Legacy of the KGB*. New York:
PublicAffairs.

Soldatov, A., & Borogan, I. 2016. 'Putin Brings China's Great Firewall to
Russia in Cybersecurity Pact'. *The Guardian*. 29 November. www
.theguardian.com/world/2016/nov/29/putin-china-internet-great-firewall
-russia-cybersecurity-pact.

Solnick, S. L. 1998. *Stealing the State: Control and Collapse in Soviet
Institutions*. Cambridge, MA: Harvard University Press.

Solntseva, A. 2008. 'Tsentral'noaziatskaya model''. *Vremya Novostei*.
15 September (no. 169): 9.

Solodky, Sergei. 2011. 'Arabskaya vesna. Ukrainskie zamorozki'. *Zerkalo
Nedeli*. 12 March (no. 9): 5.

Solov'ev, V. 2019. 'Ot zakhvata do pobega. Kak rossiya i Zapad vmeste
osvobodili Moldoviyu ot oligarkha-samoderzhtsa'. Carnegie. 19 June.
https://carnegie.ru/commentary/79322.

Sorokin, O. 2018. 'As Ukraine Imports Most of Its Coal from Russia, "Russia
Sells Coal Stolen from Ukraine to EU"'. *Kyiv Post*. 10 December. www
.kyivpost.com/ukraine-politics/as-ukraine-imports-most-of-its-coal-from-
russia-russia-sells-coal-stolen-from-ukraine-to-eu.html.

Sorokin, O. 2020a. 'Party Crashers: Internal Divides Crack Zelensky's
Ruling Party in Parliament'. *Kyif Post*. 4 May. www.kyivpost.com/ukrai
ne-politics/party-crashers-internal-divides-crack-zelenskys-ruling-party-
in-parliament.html.

Sorokin, O. 2020b. 'Ukrainian TV Channels Air Adulatory Film About
Zelensky's First Year in Office'. *Kyiv Post*. 23 April. www.kyivpost.com/
ukraine-politics/ukrainian-tv-channels-air-adulatory-film-about-zelenskys-
first-year-in-office.html.

Sorokin, O. 2020c. 'Zelensky's First Year: Checking Status of President's Campaign Promises'. *Kyiv Post*. 21 May. www.kyivpost.com/ukraine-politics/zelenskys-first-year-checking-status-of-presidents-campaign-promises.html.

Sozaev-Guriev, E. 2016. 'V Rossii poyavitsya Natsional'naya Gvardiya'. *Izvestiya*. 6 April (no. 59): 2.

Standing Committee of the Union State. 2004. 'Analiz vozmozhnostei eksporta "oranzhevoi revolyutsii" v Belarusi'. 12 November. www.postkomsg.com/news/various/168394/.

Standing Committee of the Union State. 2005. '"Tsvetnye revolyutsii" kak sledstvie setevoi voiny: Novye geopoliticheskie realii Soyuznogo Gosudarstva'. 18 May. www.postkomsg.com/news/various/169905/.

Standing Committee of the Union State. 2016. 'Belarus' i Rossiya primut novuyu Voennuyu doktrinu Soyuznogo Gosudarstva'. 17 February. www.postkomsg.com/expert_opinion/206930/.

Stanovaya, T. 2020. 'Pyat' putinskikh elit na frone tranzita'. Carnegie. 27 February. https://carnegie.ru/2020/02/27/ru-pub-81158.

Stepanov, G. 2019. 'Zayavlenie: Srybu – protiv Ukrainy'. Noi.md. 27 June. https://noi.md/ru/obshhestvo/zayavlenie-syrbu-protiv-ukrainy.

Strang, D. 1991. 'Adding Social Structure to Diffusion Models: An Event History Framework'. *Sociological Methods Research*. 19(3): 324–53.

Strzelecki, J. 2016. 'The Eurasian Economic Union: A Time of Crisis'. Centre for Eastern Studies. 1 February. www.osw.waw.pl/en/publikacje/osw-commentary/2016-02-01/eurasian-economic-union-a-time-crisis.

Sukhov, O. 2016a. 'Exit Reformers'. *Kyiv Post*. 17 November. www.kyivpost.com/ukraine-politics/exit-reformers.html.

Sukhov, O. 2016b. 'Little Hope So Far that Lutsenko Will Bring Change'. *Kyiv Post*. 20 May. www.kyivpost.com/article/content/ukraine-politics/little-hope-so-far-that-lutsenko-will-bring-change-414150.html.

Sukhov, O. 2016c. 'Oleg Sukhov: Poroshenko's Troll Army Borrows Kremlin Techniques'. *Kyiv Post*. 19 April. www.kyivpost.com/article/opinion/op-ed/poroshenkos-troll-army-borrows-kremlin-techniques-412279.html.

Sukhov, O. 2016d. 'Onyshchenko Makes Sweeping Claims About Poroshenko Graft'. *Kyiv Post*. 9 December. www.kyivpost.com/ukraine-politics/onyshchenko-makes-sweeping-claims-poroshenko-graft.html.

Sukhov, O. 2017a. 'Oleg Sukhov: Poroshenko, Ukraine's "Putin Wannabe", Reveals His True Face'. *Kyiv Post*. 29 March. www.kyivpost.com/article/opinion/op-ed/oleg-sukhov-poroshenko-ukraines-putin-wannabe-reveals-true-face.html.

Sukhov, O. 2017b. 'Parliament Approves Controversial Restrictions on NGOs'. *Kyiv Post*. 23 March. www.kyivpost.com/ukraine-politics/parliament-approves-controversial-restrictions-ngos.html.

Sukhov, O. 2017c. 'Prosecutors Strike Secret Deals with Yanukovych Allies, Lawmaker Says'. *Kyiv Post*. 18 May. www.kyivpost.com/ukraine-politics /prosecutors-strike-secret-deals-yanukovych-allies-lawmaker-says.html.

Sukhov, O. 2018a. 'Onyshchenko Releases Alleged Recording of Poroshenko, Zlochevsky in Graft'. *Kyiv Post*. 20 April. www.kyivpost.com/ukraine-politics/onyshchenko-releases-alleged-recording-implicating-poroshenko-zlochevsky-graft.html.

Sukhov, O. 2018b. 'Powerful Suspects Escape Justice on Lutsenko's Watch'. *Kyiv Post*. 13 April. www.kyivpost.com/ukraine-politics/powerful-suspects-escape-justice-lutsenkos-watch.html.

Sukhov, O. 2018c. 'Ruling Exposes Poroshenko Allies' Ties to Yanukovych'. *Kyiv Post*. 12 January. www.kyivpost.com/ukraine-politics/ruling-exposes-poroshenko-allies-ties-yanukovych.html.

Sukhov, O. 2018d. 'Saakashvili's Party Starts Poroshenko Impeachment Process'. *Kyiv Post*. 25 April. www.kyivpost.com/ukraine-politics/saakashvilis-party-starts-poroshenko-impeachment-process.html.

Sukhov, O. 2019. 'Yanukovych's Old Guard is Staging a Comeback'. *Kyiv Post*. 30 August. www.kyivpost.com/ukraine-politics/yanukovychs-old-guard-is-staging-a-comeback.html.

Sukhov, O. 2020a. 'Journalists Expose Contacts Between Kolomoisky, Zelensky's Chief of Staff'. *Kyiv Post*. 3 April. www.kyivpost.com/ukraine-politics/journalists-expose-contacts-between-kolomoisky-zelenskys-chief-of-staff.html.

Sukhov, O. 2020b. 'New Secret Police Unit Prompts Fears of Pressure on Activists, Businesses'. *Kyiv Post*. 10 June. www.kyivpost.com/ukraine-politics/new-secret-police-unit-prompts-fears-of-pressure-on-activists-businesses.html.

Sukhov, O. 2021. 'Ukrainian President Seeks Total Control Over the Media'. New Europe. 19 November. www.neweurope.eu/article/ukrainian-president-seeks-total-control-over-media/.

Sukhov, O. 2022. 'Court Extends Medvedchuk's House Arrest in Treason Case'. Kyiv Independent. 10 January. https://kyivindependent.com/natio nal/court-extends-medvedchuks-house-arrest-in-treason-case/.

Sukhov, O., Grytsenko, O., & Zhuk, A. 2016. 'All in the Family: The Sequel'. *Kyiv Post*. 7 October. www.kyivpost.com/ukraine-politics/5406 26.html.

Sumskoi, V. 2010. 'Trening po bor'be s oppozitsiei'. *Gazeta*. 25 August. www.gazeta.ru/politics/2010/08/25_a_3411250.shtml.

Svitrov, I. 2019. 'Itogi dnya: o tom, kak ACUM reshil poupravlyat' stranoi kakie dorogi postroyat v Moldove kitaitsy, i gde prodolzhit lechenie Sergei Syrbu'. NewsMaker. 26 March. https://newsmaker.md/rus/novosti/itogi-

dnya-o-tom-kak-acum-reshil-poupravlyat-stranoy-kakie-dorogi-postroyat-
v-mold-42593/.

Synovitz, R. 2016. 'Volodymyr Groysman: Loyal Poroshenko Ally'. *The
Ukranian Weekly*. 15 April. www.ukrweekly.com/uwwp/volodymyr-
groysman-loyal-poroshenko-ally/.

Talant, B. 2019. 'After Laying Low, on Pro-Russian Party Flies High'. *Kyiv
Post*. 12 July. www.kyivpost.com/ukraine-politics/after-laying-low-one-
pro-russian-party-flies-high.html.

Tamkin, E. 2017. '"Russian Laundromat"'. Foreign Policy. 24 March.
http://foreignpolicy.com/2017/03/24/russia-isnt-responding-to-the-
russian-laundromat/.

Tansey, O. 2016. 'The Problem with Autocracy Promotion'. *Democratization*.
23(1): 141–63.

Tansey, O., Koehler, K., & Schmotz, A. 2017. 'Ties to the Rest: Autocratic
Linkages and Regime Survival'. *Comparative Political Studies*: 50(9):
1221–54.

Tarasov, S. 2000. 'Kislovodskiy otpusknik. Petr Luchinskiy gotovit novuyu
strategiyu'. *Vek*. 4 August (no. 31): 4.

The Moscow Times. 2016a. 'Putin's Personal Army: Analysts on Russia's
National Guard'. *The Moscow Times*. 7 April. https://themoscowtimes
.com/articles/putins-personal-army-analysts-on-russias-national-guard-
52445.

The Moscow Times. 2016b. 'Russian National Guard Reaches 340,000
Men'. *The Moscow Times*. 25 November. www.themoscowtimes.com/2
016/11/25/russian-national-guard-reaches-340000-personnel-a56308.

The Moscow Times. 2017. 'Russian Activist Navalny Given 5-Year Suspended
Sentence in Kirovles Retrial'. *The Moscow Times*. 8 February. https://themos
cowtimes.com/news/russian-activist-navalny-sentenced-in-kirovles-case-
57038.

Tikhonenko, I. 2011. 'Ukhod Lukashenko po-arabski'. Voice of America.
11 July. www.golos-ameriki.ru/a/lukashenko-arabic-spring-2011-07-12-
125388398/238596.html.

Timofti, N. 2013. 'Pozdravitel'noe poslanie prezidentu Respubliki Singapur
Toni Tan Ken Yamu'. 9 August. https://presedinte.md/rus/presa/mesajul-
de-felicitare-transmis-de-presedintele-nicolae-timofti-presedintelui-
republicii-singapore-tony-tan-keng-yam.

Tkachuk, D. 2014. 'Opyt bor'by s korruptsei. Singapur'. *Ukrainskaya
Pravda*. 5 December. www.pravda.com.ua/rus/columns/2014/12/5/7046
467/.

Toal, G. 2017. *Near Abroad: Putin, the West, and the Contest over Ukraine
and the Caucasus*. New York: Oxford University Press.

Tolkacheva, E. 2018. 'Surikov: Byla popytka razobshchit' nashe bratstvo, i oni prodolzhayutsya, no nasha zadacha – ne dopustit' etogo'. Tut.by. 30 August. https://news.tut.by/economics/606195.html.

Tolstrup, J. 2014. *Russia vs. the EU: External Actors in Competition for Influence in Post-Soviet States*. Boulder: Lynne Rienner Publishers.

Tosun, J. 2013. *Environmental Policy Change in Emerging Market Democracies: Central and Eastern Europe and Latin America Compared*. Toronto: University of Toronto Press.

Trampusch, C., & Palier, B. 2016. 'Between X and Y: How Process Tracing Contributes to Opening the Black Box of Causality'. *New Political Economy*. 21(5): 437–54.

Trenin, D. 2011. *Post-Imperium*. Washington, DC: Carnegie Endowment for International Peace.

Treisman, D. 2020. 'Democracy by Mistake: How the Errors of Autocrats Trigger Transitions to Freer Government'. *American Political Science Review*. 114(3): 792–810.

Tristan, A. 2014. 'Glavnyi spets po Ukraine'. *Nezavisimaya Moldova*. 5 March (no. 7).

Trofimova, N. 2006. 'Mykola Azarov: 'Ya schitayu vozmozhnym sozdanie koalitsii na baze zdorovykh sil iz vsekh fraktsiy'.' *Den*. 5 June (no. 91).

Troitsky, A. 2017. 'Russia in the 90s: Try at Your Own Peril'. *The Moscow Times*. 17 October. www.themoscowtimes.com/2017/10/17/try-at-your-own-peril-a59191.

Truex, R. 2016. *Making Autocracy Work: Representation and Responsiveness in Modern China*. Cambridge: Cambridge University Press.

Truex, R. 2017. 'Consultative Authoritarianism and its Limits'. *Comparative Political Science*. 50(3): 329–61.

Tsepliaev, V. 2010. 'Fenomen Singapura: kak na pomoike vyrosli neboskrey'. *Argumenty i Fakty*. 24 February. www.aif.ru/money/business/16458.

TSN.ua. 2016a. 'Roskoshnyi osobnyak v Krymu i korolevstvo na zakarpat'e. SMI sobrali kollektsiyu domov Medvedchuka'. 30 June. https://ru.tsn.ua/politika/roskoshnyy-osobnyak-v-krymu-i-korolevstvo-na-zakarpate-smi-sobrali-kollekciyu-domov-medvedchuka-658775.html.

TSN.ua. 2016b. 'Zamestitel' nachal'nika shtaba ATO okazalsya rossiyskim shpionom – SBU'. 16 June. https://ru.tsn.ua/ato/zamestitel-nachalnika-shtaba-ato-okazalsya-rossiyskim-shpionom-sbu-650051.html?_ga=2.115510273.622993251.1515857792-1272113597.1513523705.

TSN.ua. 2017. 'Syna ukrainskogo voennogo kapellana v Belarusi pokhitila FSB – devushka, s kotoroi vstretilsya paren''. 29 August. https://ru.tsn.ua/svit/syna-ukrainskogo-voennogo-kapellana-v-belarusi-pohitila-fsb-devushka-s-kotoroy-vstretilsya-paren-920633.html.

TSN.ua. 2018. 'Ofshori firmi Poroshenka, abo na chomu zaroblyae Prezident'. 27 February. https://tsn.ua/video/video-novini/ofshorni-firmi-poroshenka-abo-na-chomu-zaroblyaye-prezident.html.

Tul'ev, M. 2020. 'V Moldova i Pridnestrov'e zhdut, chto Kozak zaimetsya rabotoi po region'. EurAsia Daily. 30 January. https://eadaily.com/ru/ne ws/2020/01/30/v-moldavii-i-pridnestrove-zhdut-chto-kozak-zaymetsya-rabotoy-po-regionu.

TUT.by. 2009. 'Lukashenko naznachil general-maiora militsii Anatoliya Kuleshova ministrom vnutrennikh del'. 2 June. https://news.tut.by/polit ics/138850.html.

TUT.by. 2015. 'Prezident provel soveshchanie s silovikami: situatsiya s Ukrainoi sama ne rassosetsya'. 15 December. https://news.tut.by/polit ics/477235.html.

TUT.by. 2018. 'Putin naznachil novogo posla i svoego spetspredstavitelya v Belarusi'. 24 August. https://news.tut.by/economics/605602.html.

TV7.md. 2014. 'Moldavane ne znayut navernyaka, kak situatsiya na Ukraine skazhetsya na Moldove'. 18 May. https://point.md/ru/novosti/politika/molda vane-ne-znayut-navernyaka-kak-situaciya-na-ukraine-skazhetsya-na-moldove.

UDF.by. 2014. 'Belorusskiy posol v Kieve presleduet Vitaliya Klichko'. 26 February. http://udf.by/news/main_news/96648-belorusskiy-posol-v-k ieve-presleduet-vitaliya-klichko.html.

UDF.by. 2017. 'Prezidentu Moldovy ne razreshili posledovat' sovetu Lukashenko'. 28 July. http://udf.by/news/politic/160069-prezidentu-moldovy-ne-razreshili-posledovat-sovetu-lukashenko.html.

UDF.by. 2018. '"Lukashenko budut menyat'": rossiyskiy politik raskryl plany Putina po Belarusi'. 26 November. https://udf.by/news/main_news/ 183813-lukashenko-budut-menyat-rossiyskiy-politik-raskryl-plany-putina-po-belarusi.html.

Ukrainskaya Pravda. 2001a. 'Kuchma i Chubais ne dogovorilis' o sovmestnoi rabote energosistem'. *Ukrainskaya Pravda*. 8 August. www .pravda.com.ua/rus/news/2001/08/8/4362327/.

Ukrainskaya Pravda. 2001b. 'Marchuk priznal: "Peregovorov net, est' tol'ko 'consul'tatsii'": A missiyu samogo Marchuka Moroz vidit v raskol'nichestve'. 30 March. www.pravda.com.ua/rus/news/2001/03/30/4361454/.

Ukrainskaya Pravda. 2003a. 'Ivanov i Zlenko "vyshli za ramki diplomaticheskikh obmenov"'. *Ukrainskaya Pravda*. 19 May. www .pravda.com.ua/rus/news/2003/05/19/4372783/.

Ukrainskaya Pravda. 2003b. 'Kravchuk: Posle politreformy Kuchma mozhet stat' i prem'erom, i spikerom'. *Ukrainskaya Pravda*. 26 August. www .pravda.com.ua/rus/news/2003/08/26/4374018/.

Ukrainskaya Pravda. 2004. 'Medvedchuk taino letal k Putinu v Peterburg, a Kushnarev v Moskve'. *Ukrainskaya Pravda*. 16 December. www .pravda.com.ua/rus/news/2004/12/16/4384020/.

Ukrainskaya Pravda. 2006. 'Kinakh reshil, chto emu nravitsya byt' sekretarem'. *Ukrainskaya Pravda*. 7 April. www.pravda.com.ua/rus/new s/2006/04/7/4398664/.

Ukrainskaya Pravda. 2008a. 'Yushchenko sdelal Bogatyrevu glavnoi no kontaktam s Moskvoi'. *Ukrainskaya Pravda*. 2 December. www .pravda.com.ua/rus/news/2008/12/2/4456393/.

Ukrainskaya Pravda. 2008b. 'Yushchenko trebuet ot Timoshenko izbavit'sya ot lyudei Medvedchuka'. *Ukrainskaya Pravda*. 3 April. www .pravda.com.ua/rus/news/2008/04/3/4436871/.

Ukrainskaya Pravda. 2010a. 'Chornovil: Khoroshkovskiy poluchaet ukazaniya iz Moskvy'. *Ukrainskaya Pravda*. 14 December. www .pravda.com.ua/rus/news/2010/12/14/5670396/.

Ukrainskaya Pravda. 2010b. 'Grishchenko i Lavrov napisal sebe plan'. *Ukrainskaya Pravda*. 16 March. www.pravda.com.ua/rus/news/2010/03/16 /4867527/.

Ukrainskaya Pravda. 2010c. 'Grishchenko poletel v Moskvu dogovarivat'sya o Medvedeve'. *Ukrainskaya Pravda*. 16 March. www.pravda.com.ua/rus/ news/2010/03/16/4866324/.

Ukrainskaya Pravda. 2010d. 'Khoroshkovskiy govorit', chto poluchal polozhitel'nye otsenki ot Timoshenko'. Ukrainskaya Pravda. 9 November. www.pravda.com.ua/rus/news/2010/11/9/5554573/.

Ukrainskaya Pravda. 2010e. 'Khoroshkovskiy priznal, chto SBU pokhozha na FSB i KGB'. 29 September. www.pravda.com.ua/rus/news/2010/09/29/542 7148/.

Ukrainskaya Pravda. 2010f. 'Kuchma eshche nemnogo "rulit" – Chornovil'. *Ukrainskaya Pravda*. 24 December. www.pravda.com.ua/rus/news/2010/ 12/24/5709647/.

Ukrainskaya Pravda. 2010g. 'Levochkin lichno 'ekzameniroval' potentsial'nykh podchinennykh Popova'. *Ukrainskaya Pravda*. 26 November. www .pravda.com.ua/rus/news/2010/11/26/5614596/.

Ukrainskaya Pravda. 2010h. 'Novomu poslu nravitsya "dvizhnyakh" v Moskve'. *Ukrainskaya Pravda*. 21 July. www.pravda.com.ua/rus/news/ 2010/07/21/5236319/.

Ukrainskaya Pravda. 2010i. 'V Partii regionov podozrevayut, chto Levochkin predast Yanukovicha'. *Ukrainskaya Pravda*. 28 February. www.pravda.com.ua/rus/news/2010/02/28/4819887/.

Ukrainskaya Pravda. 2011. 'Politilog: Yanukovich idet v Singapur, a Yushchenko ne otoshel ot klanov'. *Ukrainskaya Pravda*. www .pravda.com.ua/rus/news/2011/04/30/6155407/.

Ukrainskaya Pravda. 2012a. 'Klyuev priekhal v Radu lomat' deputatov'. *Ukrainskaya Pravda*. 24 May. www.pravda.com.ua/rus/news/2012/05/2 4/6965229/.

Ukrainskaya Pravda. 2012b. 'Klyuev: Yanukovich khochet usilit' rol' SNBO'. *Ukrainskaya Pravda*. 24 March. www.pravda.com.ua/rus/news/ 2012/03/24/6961373/.

Ukrainskaya Pravda. 2012c. 'Vizity Klyueva v administratsiyu prezidenta nazvali konfidentsial'nymi'. *Ukrainskaya Pravda*. 12 October. www .pravda.com.ua/rus/news/2012/10/12/6974504/.

Ukrainskaya Pravda. 2012d. 'Yanukovich, pod pokhvalu posla Belarusi, obshchal usovershenstvovat' izbiratel'nye pravila'. *Ukrainskaya Pravda*. 14 December. www.pravda.com.ua/rus/news/2012/12/14/6979778/.

Ukrainskaya Pravda. 2012e. 'Yanukovich uvolil Klyueva, potomu chto koe-chto o nem uznal?' *Ukrainskaya Pravda*. 16 February. www .pravda.com.ua/rus/news/2012/02/16/6958864/.

Ukrainskaya Pravda. 2013a. 'Novyi glava SBU sluzhil v rossiyskoi armii i ne lyubit SMI'. *Ukrainskaya Pravda*. 10 January. www.pravda.com.ua/rus/ news/2013/01/10/6981198/.

Ukrainskaya Pravda. 2013b. 'Putin ustroil Yanukovichu neformal'nuyu vstrechu'. *Ukrainskaya Pravda*. 27 October. www.pravda.com.ua/rus/ne ws/2013/10/27/7000815/.

Ukrainskaya Pravda. 2013c. 'U Yanukovicha poyavilsya eshche odin sovetnik'. *Ukrainskaya Pravda*. 5 February. www.pravda.com.ua/rus/ne ws/2013/02/5/6982893/.

Ukrainskaya Pravda. 2014a. '6 Fevralya: ONLAIN'. *Ukrainskaya Pravda*. 6 February. www.pravda.com.ua/rus/articles/2014/02/6/7012 969/.

Ukrainskaya Pravda. 2014b. 'Noch' i den' 21 yanvarya: Titushko-safari'. *Ukrainskaya Pravda*. 21 January. www.pravda.com.ua/rus/articles/2014/ 01/21/7010201/.

Ukrainskaya Pravda. 2014c. 'Ot Yanukovicha begut ego sovetniki?' *Ukrainskaya Pravda*. 21 February. www.pravda.com.ua/rus/news/2014/ 02/21/7015609/.

Ukrainskaya Pravda. 2014d. 'Poroshenko otpravit ukrainskikh bortsov s korruptsiei uchit'sya v Singapur'. *Ukrainskaya Pravda*. 9 December. www.pravda.com.ua/rus/news/2014/12/9/7046911/.

Ukrainskaya Pravda. 2014e. 'S Maidana bessledno ischezli 36 aktivistov'. *Ukrainskaya Pravda*. 2 February. www.pravda.com.ua/rus/news/2014/0 2/2/7012396/.

Ukrainskaya Pravda. 2015a. 'Gritsak: Zamnachal'nika kontrrazvedki Kieva rabotal na RF'. *Ukrainskaya Pravda*. 10 October. www.pravda.com.ua/r us/news/2015/10/10/7084405/.

Ukrainskaya Pravda. 2015b. 'Nalyvaychenko rasskazal, kak FSBshniki khozyainichali v SBU'. *Ukrainskaya Pravda.* 1 April. www.pravda.com.ua /rus/news/2015/04/1/7063368/.

Ukrainskaya Pravda. 2015c. 'SBU rassekretila dokumenty po Evromaidanu'. *Ukrainskaya Pravda.* 31 March. www.pravda.com.ua/rus/news/2015/03/ 31/7063253/.

Ukrayins'ka Pravda. 2016. 'ZMI: y BPP 22% chleniv oblrad i 12% parlamentariv – eks "regionali"'. *Ukrainskaya Pravda.* 7 February. www .pravda.com.ua/news/2016/02/7/7098140/.

Ukrainskaya Pravda. 2018a. 'Medvedchuk vozit v Rossiyu postoronnikh lits – "Skhemy"'. *Ukrainskaya Pravda.* 23 November. www.pravda.com.ua/rus/ news/2018/11/23/7199095/.

Ukrainskaya Pravda. 2018b. '"Skhemy" rasskazali o tainykh vstrechakh Medvedchuka s Poroshenko'. *Ukrainskaya Pravda.* 22 November. www .pravda.com.ua/rus/news/2018/11/22/7199039/.

Ukrayins'ka Pravda. 2018c. '2 roki bez Pavala'. *Ukrainskaya Pravda.* 20 July. www.pravda.com.ua/articles/2018/07/20/7186847/.

Ukrainskaya Pravda. 2020. 'Avakov sozdal tainyi department politsii – TsPK'. *Ukrainskaya Pravda.* 25 May. www.pravda.com.ua/rus/news/20 20/05/25/7253056/.

Umland, A. 2011. 'Chetyre izmereniya ukrainskoi integratsii v Evropu. Vnutri – i vneshnepoliticheskie vygody sblizheniya mezhdu Ukrainoi i ES'. *Zerkalo Nedeli.* 13 May (no. 17).

Unian.info. 2011. 'Posol Ukrainy schitaet, chto Belarusy zhivut v rayu'. LB. 10 October. https://lb.ua/news/2011/10/10/118574_posol_ukraini_schi taet_chto_belar.html.

Usov, P. 2020. 'The Price of Power'. *New Eastern Europe.* 3: 70–5.

Van de Velde, J. 2017. 'The "Foreign Agent Problem": An International Legal Solution To Domestic Restrictions On Non-Governmental Organizations'. *Cardozo Law Review.* 40(2): 687–747.

Vanderhill, R. 2013. *Promoting Authoritarianism Abroad.* Boulder: Lynne Rienner Publishers.

Vanderhill, R. 2014. 'Promoting Democracy and Promoting Authoritarianism: Comparing the Cases of Belarus and Slovakia'. *Europe-Asia Studies.* 66(2): 255–83.

Vedomosti. 2010. 'Ot redaktsii: Model' Nazarbaeva'. *Vedomosti.* 7 July (no. 123): 4.

Veretennikova, K. 2005. 'Podotchetnye revolyutsionery'. Vremya. 29 June. www.vremya.ru/2005/114/4/128508.html.

Vesti.md. 2011. 'Oppozitsiya protiv obsuzhdeniya 7 aprelya za zakrytymi dveryami'. Point.md. 14 April. https://point.md/ru/novosti/politika/oppo ziciya-protiv-obsuzhdeniya-7-aprelya-za-zakritimi-dveryami.

Vinogradov, M. 2004. 'Gosduma rasstalas' s monetizatsiei l'got'. *Izvestiya*. 6 August (no. 142m): 1.

Vinokurov, A. 2016a. 'Chetvertomu sroku nuzhen novyi Putin'. *Gazeta*. 11 July. www.gazeta.ru/politics/2016/11/06_a_10311137.shtml.

Vinokurov, A. 2016b. 'Kirienko prismatrivaetsya k gubernatoram'. *Gazeta*. 2 December. www.gazeta.ru/politics/2016/12/02_a_10395611 .shtml.

Vishnev'skyy, Y., & Pivnev, E. 2014. '15 golovnikh radnkiv Poroshenka'. Espreso. 14 June. https://espreso.tv/article/2014/06/10/15_holovnykh_ radnykiv_poroshenka.

Vlas, C. 2017. 'Moldova Socialists to Sign Cooperation Agreement with "United Russia" Party'. 13 February. www.moldova.org/en/moldova-socialists-sign-cooperation-agreement-united-russia-party/.

Vodchyts, A. 2014. '5 faktov o Sergee Teterine'. Gazetaby. 22 August. https:// gazetaby.com/cont/art.php?sn_nid=80344.

Volanin, V. 2000. 'Konets Komandy'. *BelGazeta*. 2 October (no. 38).

von Soest, C. 2015. 'Democracy Prevention: The International Collaboration of Authoritarian Regimes'. *European Journal of Political Research*. 54(4): 623–38.

Vyachorka, F. 2004. 'Padpol'ny litsei, snoubord, autastop, piratstva, piva u parku dy inshyya metady uzvyshen'nya uzrounyu adrenalinu'. Radio Free Europe/Radio Liberty. 4 September. www.svaboda.org/a/785803 .html.

Vygovsky, N. 2017. 'Pochemu gosudarstvennymi sekretaryami stali lyudi staroi sistemy?' *Zerkalo Nedeli*. 21 January (no. 2): 3.

Wade, S. 2016. 'Chinese Cyberchiefs Preach Net Sovereignty in Moscow'. China Digital Times. 27 April. http://chinadigitaltimes.net/2016/04/chin ese-cyberchiefs-preach-internet-sovereignty-moscow/.

Way, L. A. 2012. 'Deer in Headlights: Incompetence and Weak Authoritarianism after the Cold War'. *Slavic Review*. 71(3): 619–46.

Way, L. A. 2015. 'The Limits of Autocracy Promotion: The Case of Russia in the "Near Abroad"'. *European Journal of Political Research*. 54(4): 691–706.

Wenger, E. 1998. *Communities of Practice: Learning, Meaning, and Identity*. New York: Cambridge University Press.

Wenger, E., McDermott, R., & Snyder, W. M. 2002. *Cultivating Communities of Practice*. Boston, MA: Harvard Business School Press.

Wilson, A. 2005. *Ukraine's Orange Revolution*. New Haven: Yale University Press.

Wilson, A. 2009. 'Europe's Next Revolution?' *New York Times*. 8 April. www.nytimes.com/2009/04/09/opinion/09iht-edwilson.html?hpw.

Wilson, A. 2012. 'Putin Returns, but Will Russia Revert to "Virtual Vemocracy"?' Open Democracy. 7 May. www.opendemocracy.net/od-russia/andrew-wilson/putin-returns-but-will-russia-revert-to-%E2%80%98virtual-democracy%E2%80%99.

Wilson, A. 2014a. 'Another Black Thursday in Ukraine'. European Council on Foreign Relations. 16 January. www.ecfr.eu/blog/entry/another_black_thursday_in_ukraine.

Wilson, A. 2014b. 'Supporting the Ukrainian Revolution'. European Council on Foreign Relations. 15 February. www.ecfr.eu/page/-/ECFR96_UKRAINE_MEMO.pdf.

Wilson, A. 2014c. *Ukraine Crisis: What It Means for the West.* New Haven: Yale University Press.

Wilson, A. 2018. 'Softly, Softly Belarus'. *New Eastern Europe.* 5: 7–13.

Wilson, A. 2021a. *Belarus: The Last European Dictatorship* (2nd ed.), New Haven: Yale University Press.

Wilson, A. 2021b. 'Faltering Fightback: Zelensky's Piecemeal Campaign Against Ukraine's Oligarchs'. European Council on Foreign Relations. 6 July. https://ecfr.eu/publication/faltering-fightback-zelenskys-piecemeal-campaign-against-ukraines-oligarchs/.

Yablokov, I. 2018. *Fortress Russia: Conspiracy Theories in Post-Soviet Russia.* Cambridge: Polity Press.

Yakouchyk, K. 2016. 'The Good, the Bad, and the Ambitious: Democracy and Autocracy Promoters Competing in Belarus'. *European Political Science Review.* 8(2): 195–224.

Yang, Y. 2019. 'The Great Firewall of China – Web of Control'. *Financial Times.* 12 March. www.ft.com/content/e19b3022-40eb-11e9-9bee-efab61506f44.

Yanushevskaya, S. 2012. 'Glava MID Shvetsii: Belorusskie gosmedia zapustili kampaniyu klevety na Shevtsiyu i nashego posla'. Tut.by. 6 August. https://news.tut.by/politics/303463.html.

Zaets, I. 2003. 'Roli raspredeleny: Viktor Yanukovych konsolidiruetsya pered stratom'. *Delovaya Ukraina.* 21 November (no. 73): 2.

Zelensky, M. 2016. 'Rossiya gotovitsya zablokirovat' LinkedIn: Zachem?' *Republic (Slon).* 26 October (no. 10-26).

Zerkalo Nedeli. 2004. 'Vsem ostavat'sya po domam. Sovetuet ministr vnutrennikh del'. *Zerkalo Nedeli.* 30 October (no. 44).

Zerkalo Nedeli. 2017. 'Vitse-spiker prizvala Poroshenko otpravit' v ostsavku'. ZN.ua. 6 December. https://zn.ua/POLITICS/vice-spiker-prizvala-poroshenko-otpravit-lucenko-v-otstavku-268467_.html.

Zerkalo Nedeli. 2019. 'Rukovodit' izbiratel'nym shtabom partii Poroshenko budet Berezenko'. ZN.ua. 30 May. https://zn.ua/POLITICS/rukovodit-

izbiratelnym-shtabom-partii-poroshenko-budet-berezenko-smi-319181_
.html.

Zhao, S. 2010. 'The China Model: Can It Replace the Western Model of Modernization?' *Journal of Contemporary China*. 19(65): 419–36.

Zito, A. R., & Schout, A. 2009. 'Learning Theory Reconsidered: EU Integration Theories and Learning'. *Journal of European Public Policy*. 16(8): 1103–23.

Zygar, M. 2016. *All the Kremlin's Men: Inside the Court of Vladimir Putin*. New York: PublicAffairs.

# Index

Printed in the USA
CPSIA information can be obtained
at www.ICGtesting.com
LVHW082159221123
764744LV00006B/33